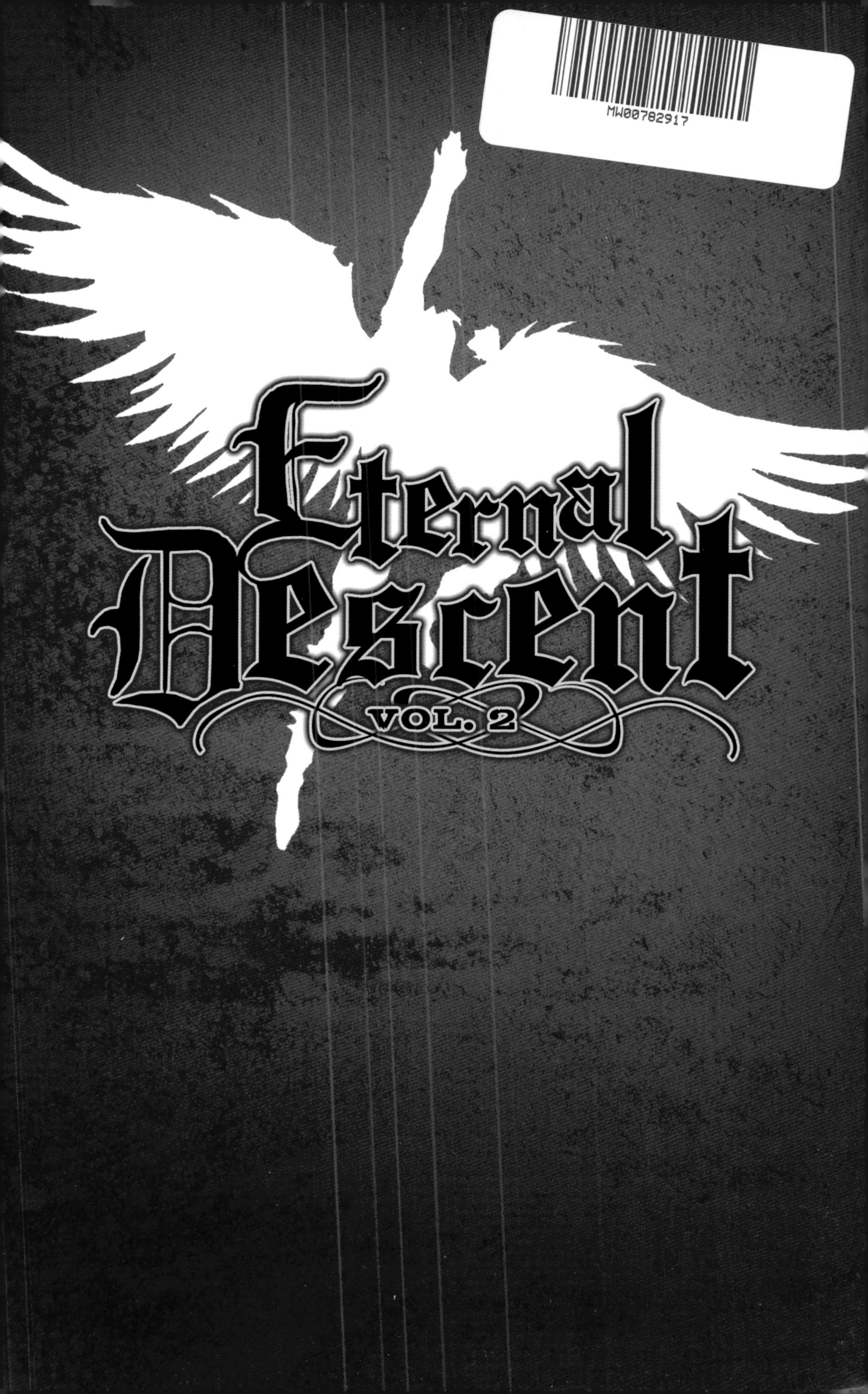
Eternal
Descent
VOL. 2

WRITTEN BY
LLEXI LEON,
SHAUN McLAUGHLIN,
AND JUSTIN PENISTON

COLLECTION COVER BY
IVAN FERNANDEZ,
JASON GORDER, AND
JAVIER TARTAGLIA

Original Series Edited by Kris Oprisko and Denton J. Tipton

Collection Edited by Justin Eisinger and Alonzo Simon

Collection Design by Shawn Lee

IDW founded by Ted Adams, Alex Garner, Kris Oprisko, and Robbie Robbins

ISBN: 978-1-61377-510-3

16 15 14 13 1 2 3 4

IDW

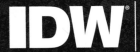

Ted Adams, CEO & Publisher
Greg Goldstein, President & COO
Robbie Robbins, EVP/Sr. Graphic Artist
Chris Ryall, Chief Creative Officer/Editor-in-Chief
Matthew Ruzicka, CPA, Chief Financial Officer
Alan Payne, VP of Sales
Dirk Wood, VP of Marketing
Lorelei Bunjes, VP of Digital Services

Become our fan on Facebook facebook.com/idwpublishing
Follow us on Twitter @idwpublishing
Check us out on YouTube youtube.com/idwpublishing
www.IDWPUBLISHING.com

Originally published as ETERNAL DESCENT VOL. 2 Issues #1–6.

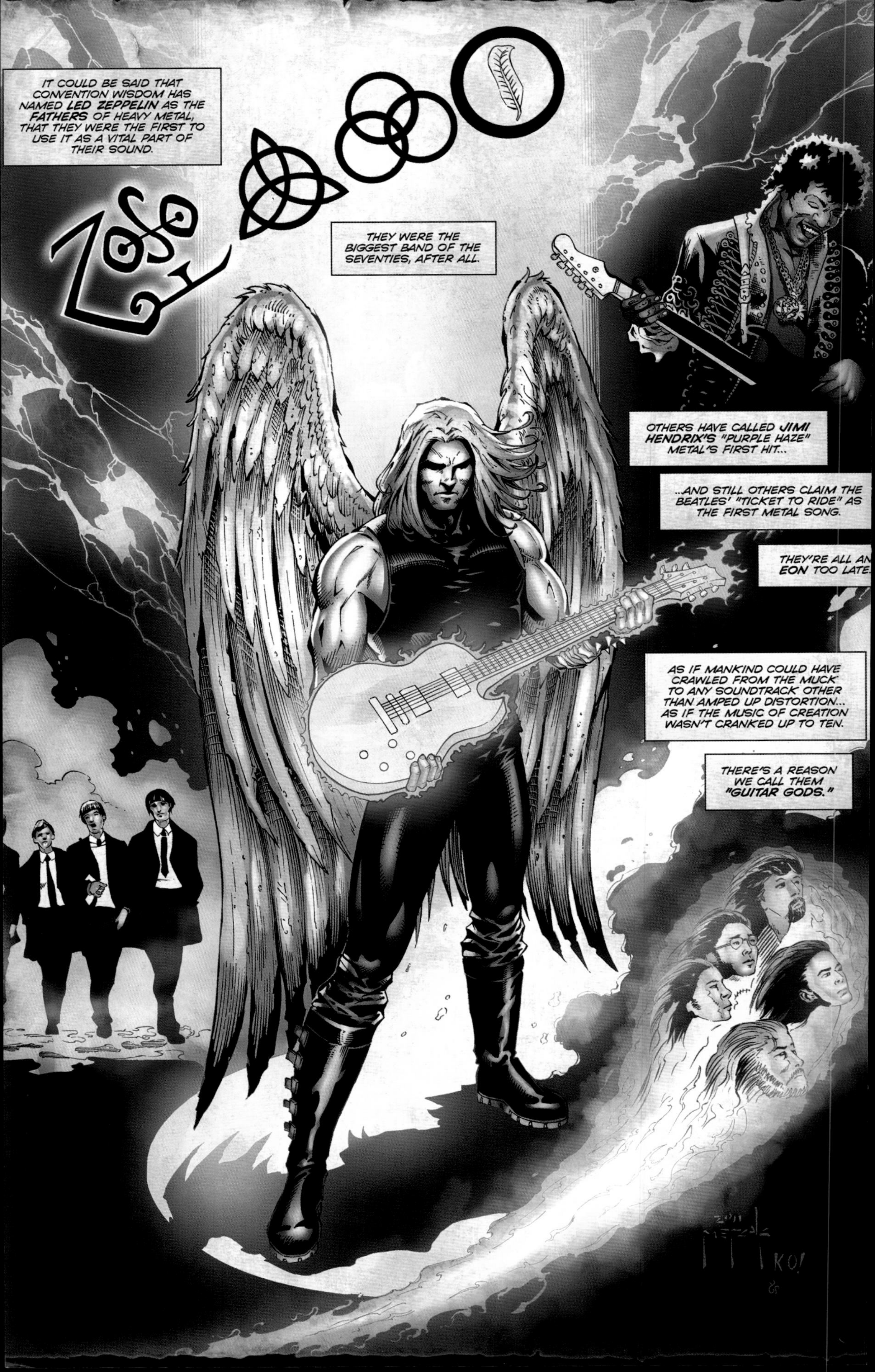

IT COULD BE SAID THAT CONVENTION WISDOM HAS NAMED LED ZEPPELIN AS THE FATHERS OF HEAVY METAL, THAT THEY WERE THE FIRST TO USE IT AS A VITAL PART OF THEIR SOUND.
ZOSO
THEY WERE THE BIGGEST BAND OF THE SEVENTIES, AFTER ALL.
OTHERS HAVE CALLED JIMI HENDRIX'S "PURPLE HAZE" METAL'S FIRST HIT...
...AND STILL OTHERS CLAIM THE BEATLES' "TICKET TO RIDE" AS THE FIRST METAL SONG.
THEY'RE ALL AN EON TOO LATE.
AS IF MANKIND COULD HAVE CRAWLED FROM THE MUCK TO ANY SOUNDTRACK OTHER THAN AMPED UP DISTORTION... AS IF THE MUSIC OF CREATION WASN'T CRANKED UP TO TEN.
THERE'S A REASON WE CALL THEM "GUITAR GODS."

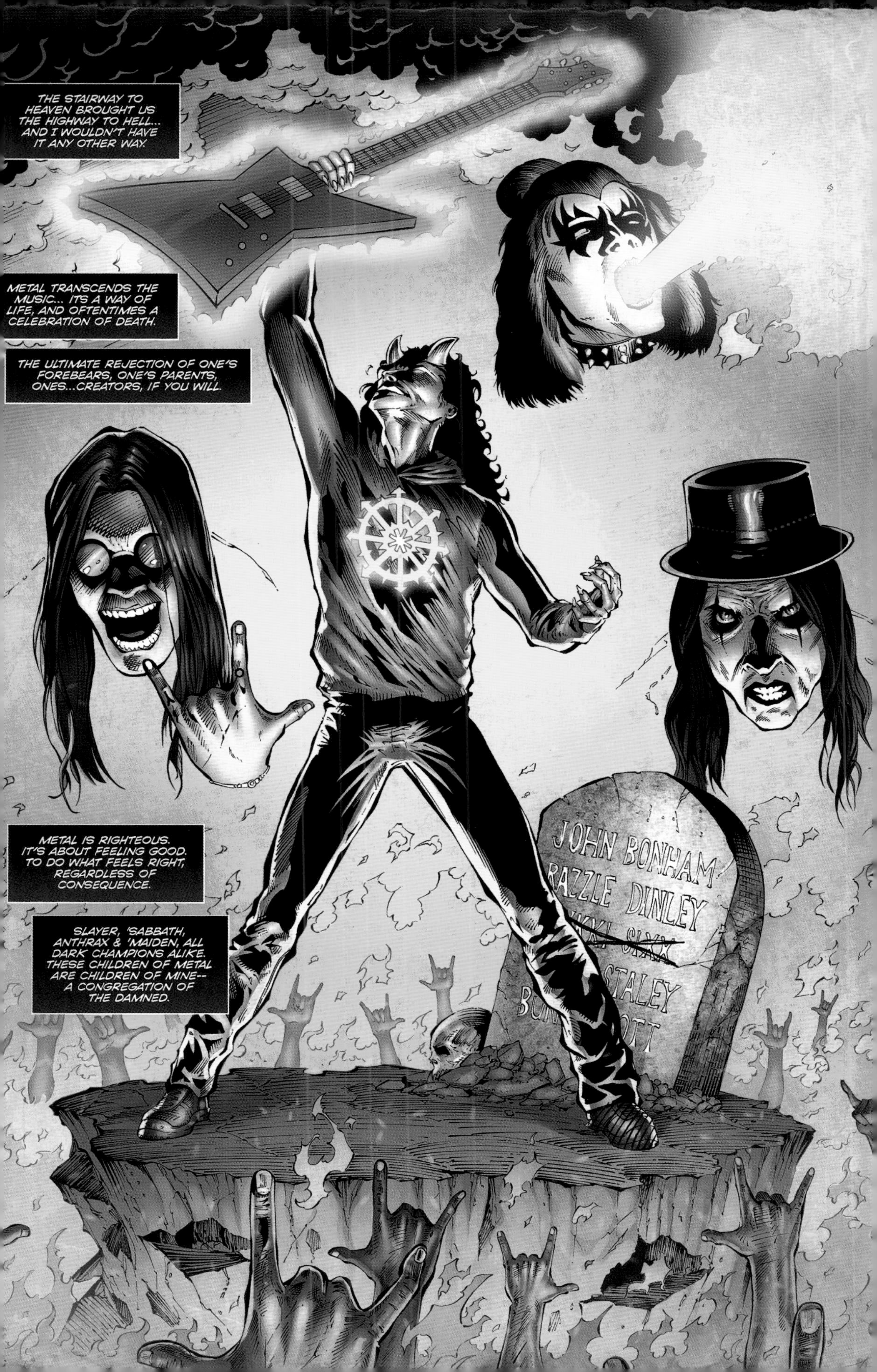
THE STAIRWAY TO HEAVEN BROUGHT US THE HIGHWAY TO HELL... AND I WOULDN'T HAVE IT ANY OTHER WAY.
METAL TRANSCENDS THE MUSIC... ITS A WAY OF LIFE, AND OFTENTIMES A CELEBRATION OF DEATH.
THE ULTIMATE REJECTION OF ONE'S FOREBEARS, ONE'S PARENTS, ONES...CREATORS, IF YOU WILL.
METAL IS RIGHTEOUS. IT'S ABOUT FEELING GOOD. TO DO WHAT FEELS RIGHT, REGARDLESS OF CONSEQUENCE.
SLAYER, 'SABBATH, ANTHRAX & 'MAIDEN, ALL DARK CHAMPIONS ALIKE. THESE CHILDREN OF METAL ARE CHILDREN OF MINE-- A CONGREGATION OF THE DAMNED.
JOHN BONHAM
RAZZLE DINLEY
STALEY

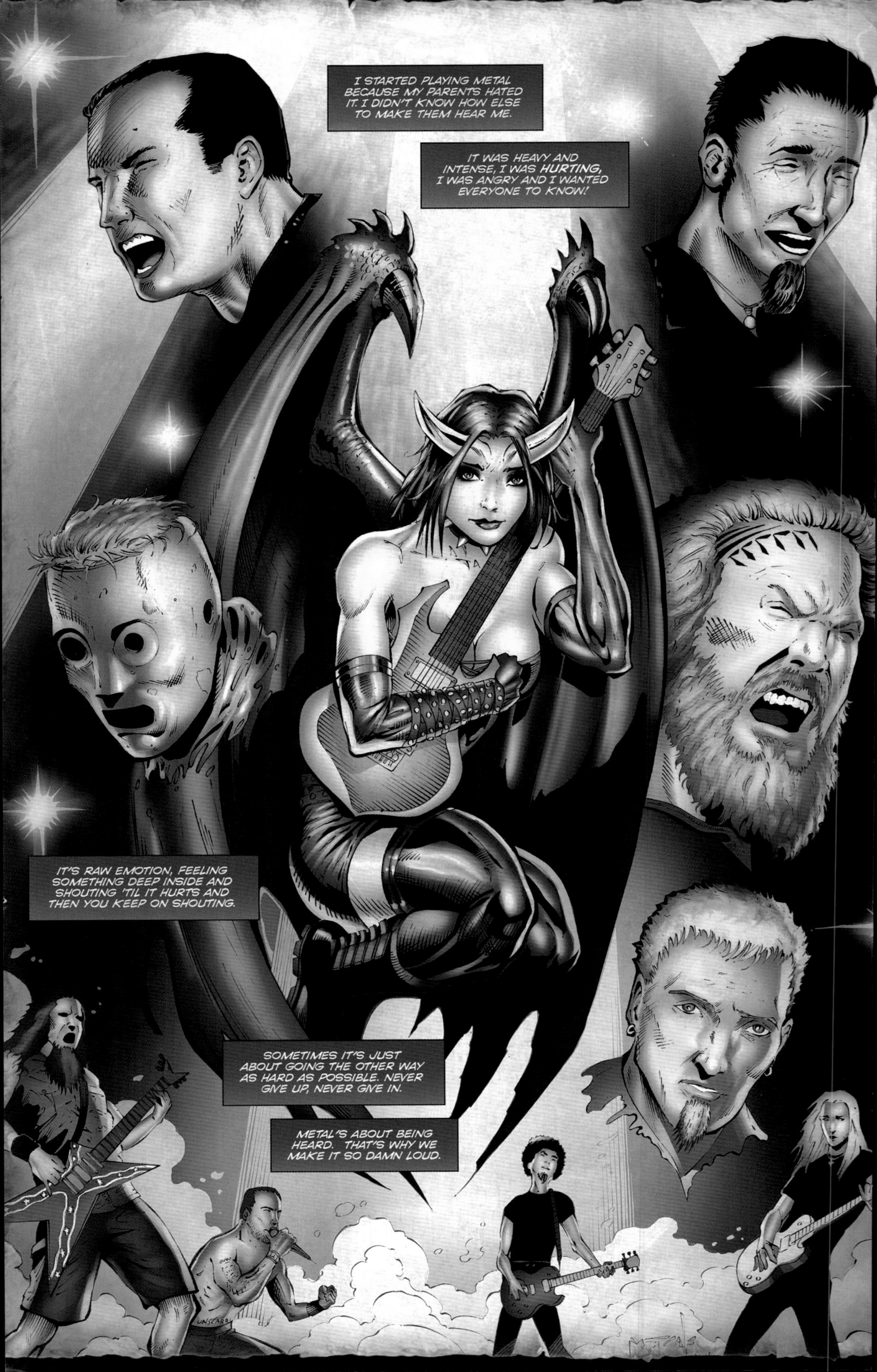
I STARTED PLAYING METAL BECAUSE MY PARENTS HATED IT. I DIDN'T KNOW HOW ELSE TO MAKE THEM HEAR ME.
IT WAS HEAVY AND INTENSE, I WAS HURTING, I WAS ANGRY AND I WANTED EVERYONE TO KNOW!
IT'S RAW EMOTION, FEELING SOMETHING DEEP INSIDE AND SHOUTING 'TIL IT HURTS AND THEN YOU KEEP ON SHOUTING.
SOMETIMES IT'S JUST ABOUT GOING THE OTHER WAY AS HARD AS POSSIBLE. NEVER GIVE UP, NEVER GIVE IN.
METAL'S ABOUT BEING HEARD. THAT'S WHY WE MAKE IT SO DAMN LOUD.

Eternal Descent

CHAPTER ONE:
INTO THE FIRE

Written by
Llexi Leon and **Shaun McLaughlin**
Pencils by
Ivan Fernandez and **Sergio Fernandez**
Inks by
Tony Kordos, Juan Castro,
and **Sergio Abad**
Colors by
Chris Summers and **Garry Henderson**
Lettering by
Charles Pritchett

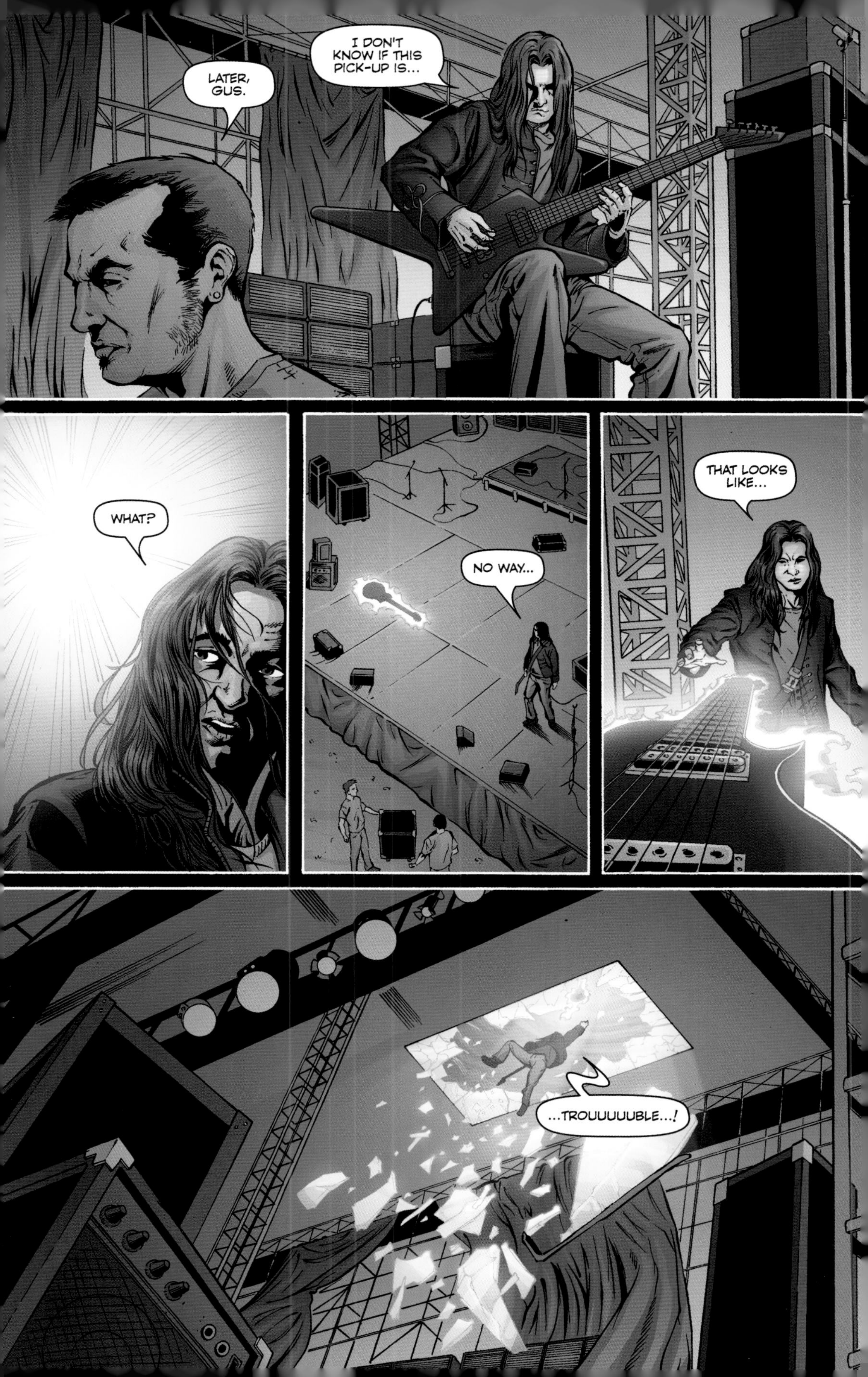
LATER, GUS.
I DON'T KNOW IF THIS PICK-UP IS...
WHAT?
NO WAY...
THAT LOOKS LIKE...
...TROUUUUUBLE...!

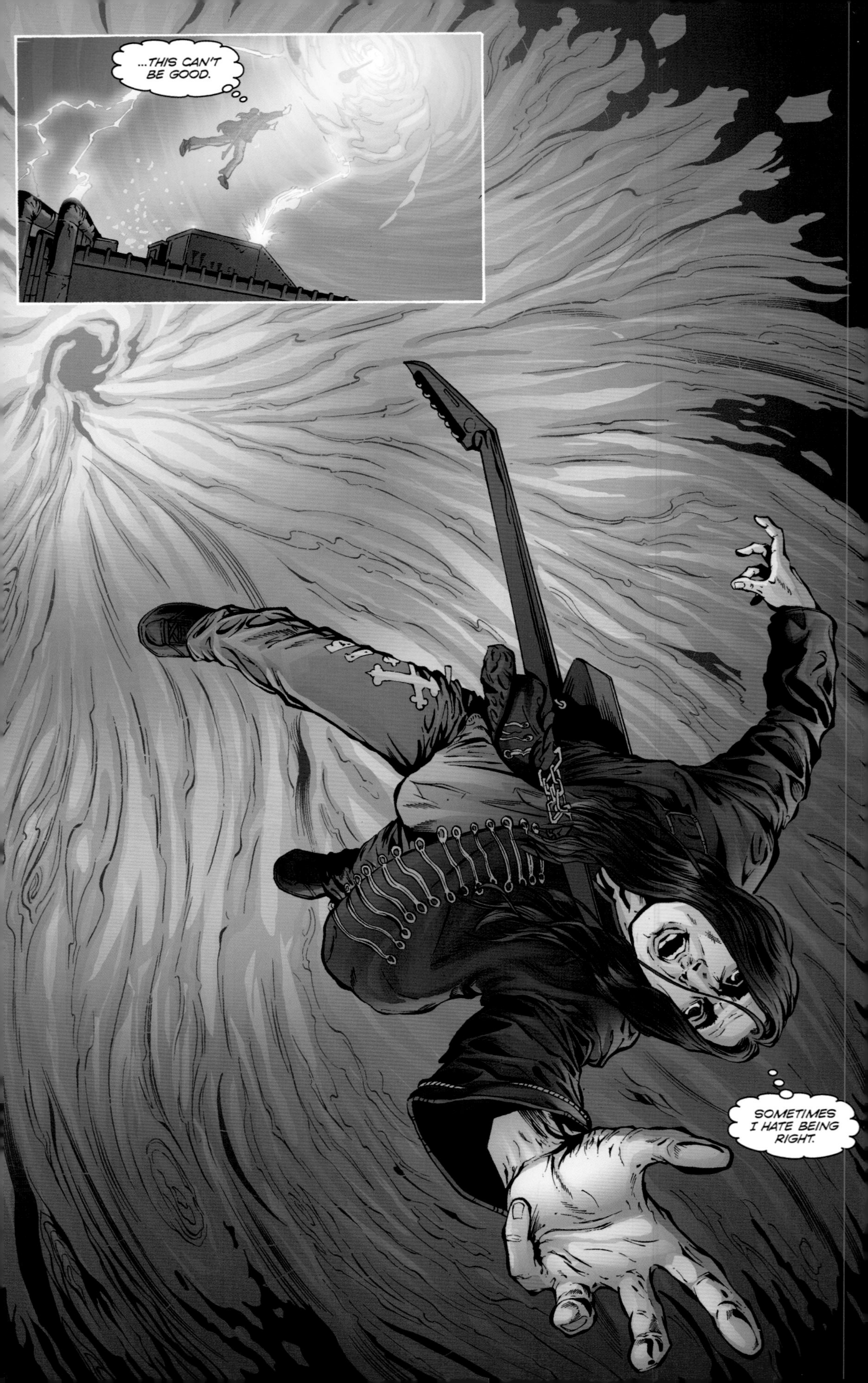
...THIS CAN'T BE GOOD.
SOMETIMES I HATE BEING RIGHT.

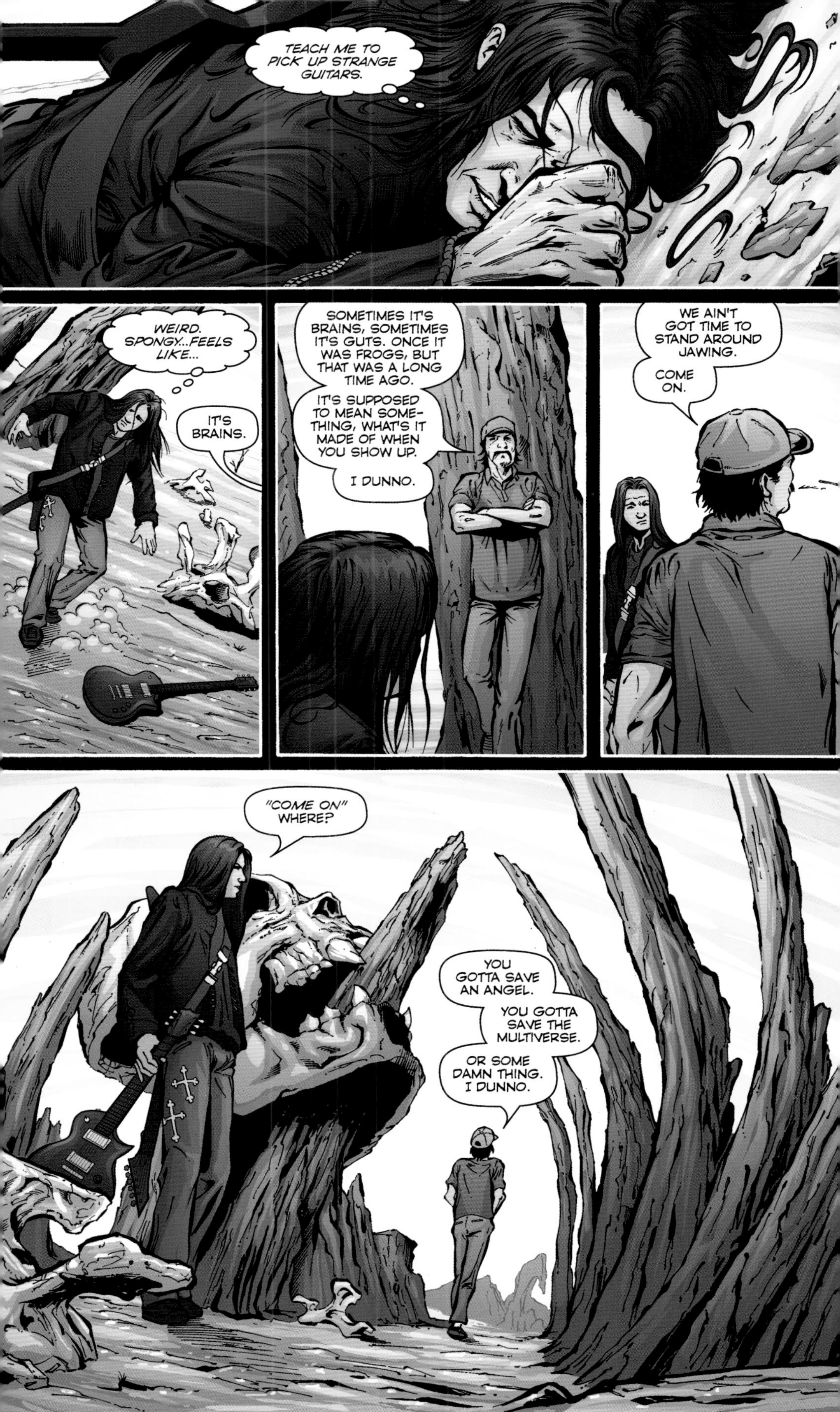
TEACH ME TO PICK UP STRANGE GUITARS.
WEIRD. SPONGY...FEELS LIKE...
IT'S BRAINS.
SOMETIMES IT'S BRAINS, SOMETIMES IT'S GUTS. ONCE IT WAS FROGS, BUT THAT WAS A LONG TIME AGO.
IT'S SUPPOSED TO MEAN SOME-THING, WHAT'S IT MADE OF WHEN YOU SHOW UP.
I DUNNO.
WE AIN'T GOT TIME TO STAND AROUND JAWING.
COME ON.
"COME ON" WHERE?
YOU GOTTA SAVE AN ANGEL.
YOU GOTTA SAVE THE MULTIVERSE.
OR SOME DAMN THING. I DUNNO.

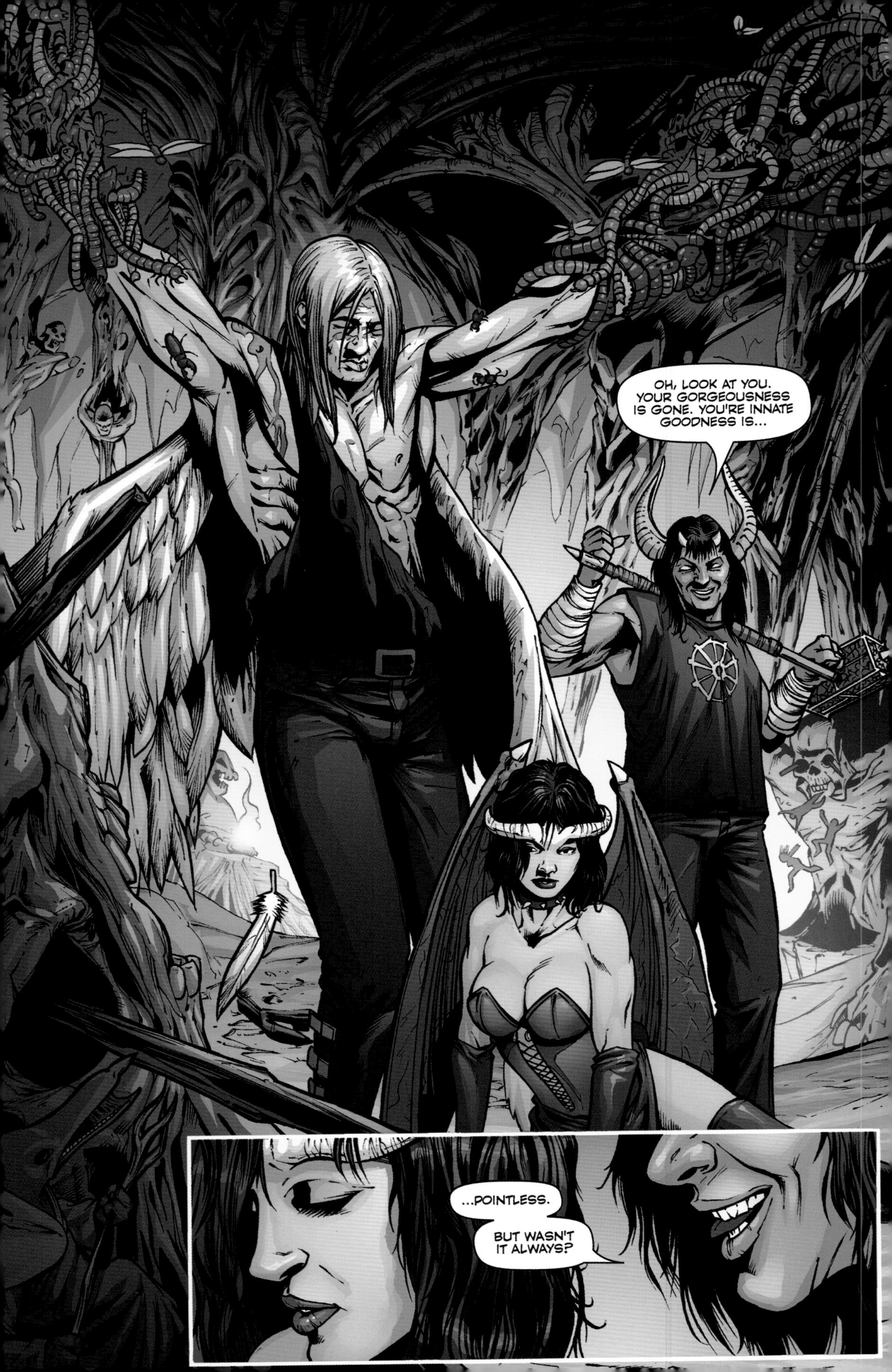
OH, LOOK AT YOU. YOUR GORGEOUSNESS IS GONE. YOU'RE INNATE GOODNESS IS...
...POINTLESS.
BUT WASN'T IT ALWAYS?

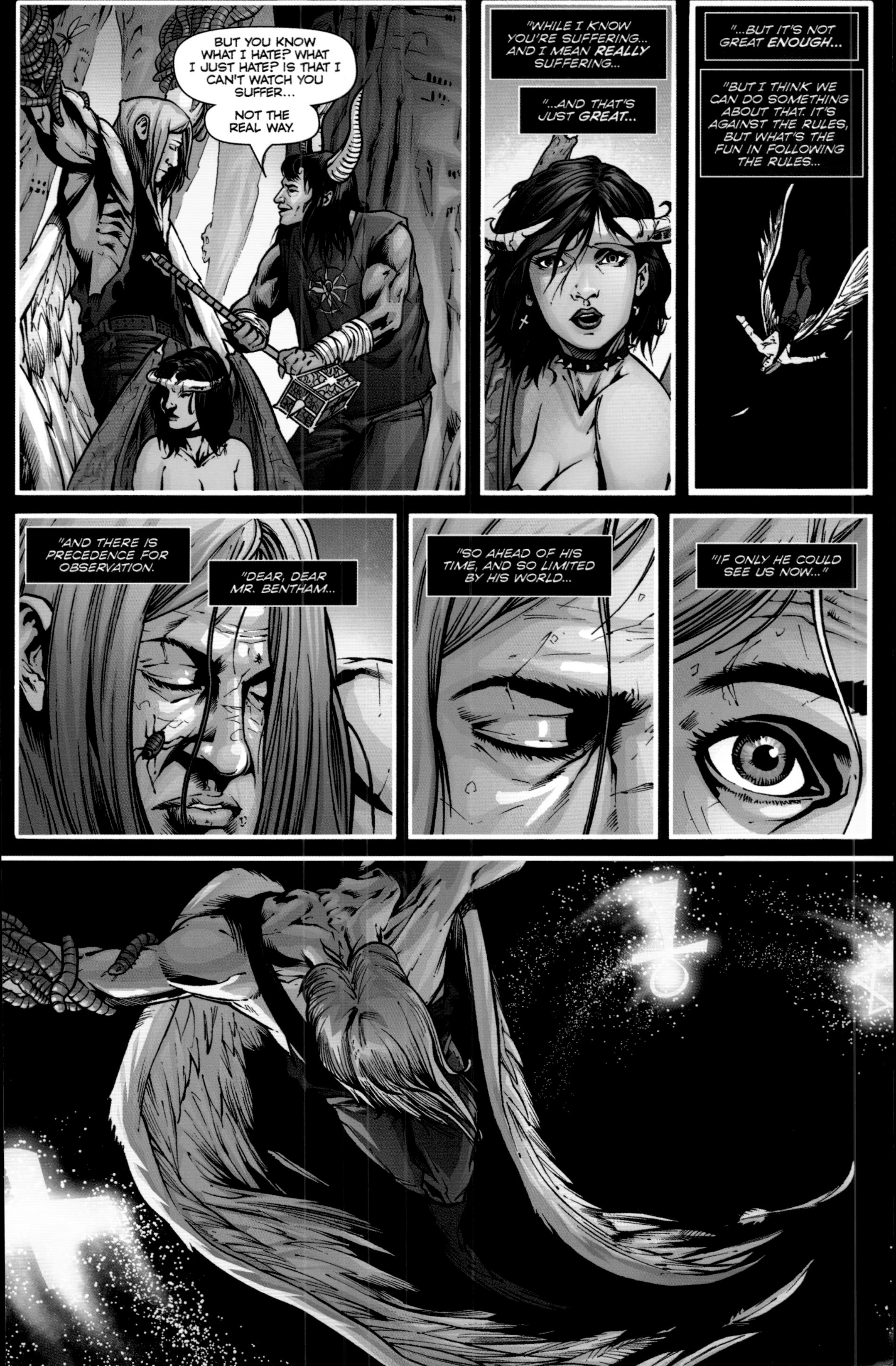
BUT YOU KNOW WHAT I HATE? WHAT I JUST HATE? IS THAT I CAN'T WATCH YOU SUFFER...
NOT THE REAL WAY.
"WHILE I KNOW YOU'RE SUFFERING... AND I MEAN REALLY SUFFERING...
"...AND THAT'S JUST GREAT...
"...BUT IT'S NOT GREAT ENOUGH...
"BUT I THINK WE CAN DO SOMETHING ABOUT THAT. IT'S AGAINST THE RULES, BUT WHAT'S THE FUN IN FOLLOWING THE RULES...
"AND THERE IS PRECEDENCE FOR OBSERVATION.
"DEAR, DEAR MR. BENTHAM...
"SO AHEAD OF HIS TIME, AND SO LIMITED BY HIS WORLD...
"IF ONLY HE COULD SEE US NOW..."

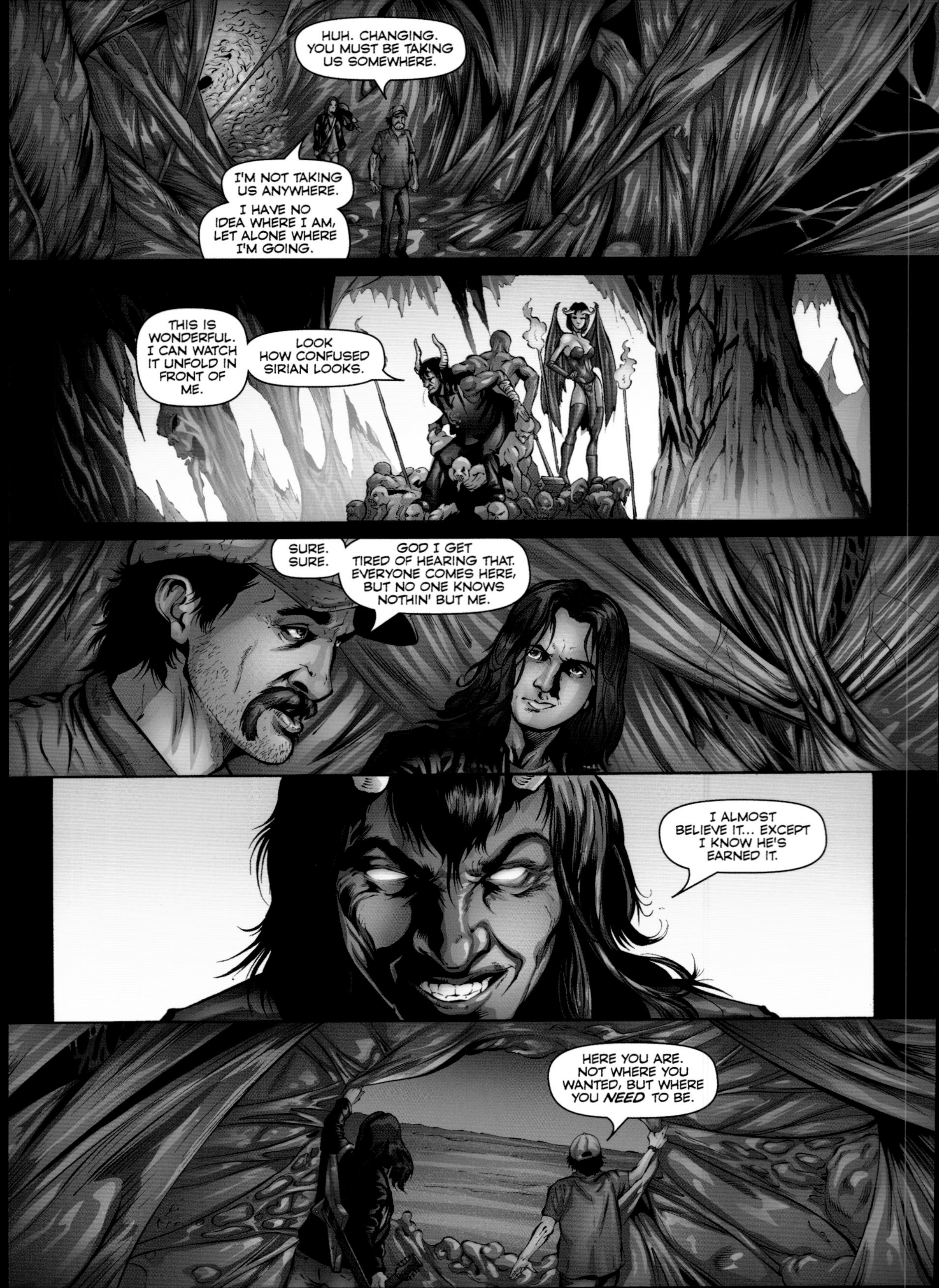
HUH. CHANGING. YOU MUST BE TAKING US SOMEWHERE.
I'M NOT TAKING US ANYWHERE.
I HAVE NO IDEA WHERE I AM, LET ALONE WHERE I'M GOING.
THIS IS WONDERFUL. I CAN WATCH IT UNFOLD IN FRONT OF ME.
LOOK HOW CONFUSED SIRIAN LOOKS.
SURE. SURE.
GOD I GET TIRED OF HEARING THAT. EVERYONE COMES HERE, BUT NO ONE KNOWS NOTHIN' BUT ME.
I ALMOST BELIEVE IT... EXCEPT I KNOW HE'S EARNED IT.
HERE YOU ARE. NOT WHERE YOU WANTED, BUT WHERE YOU *NEED* TO BE.

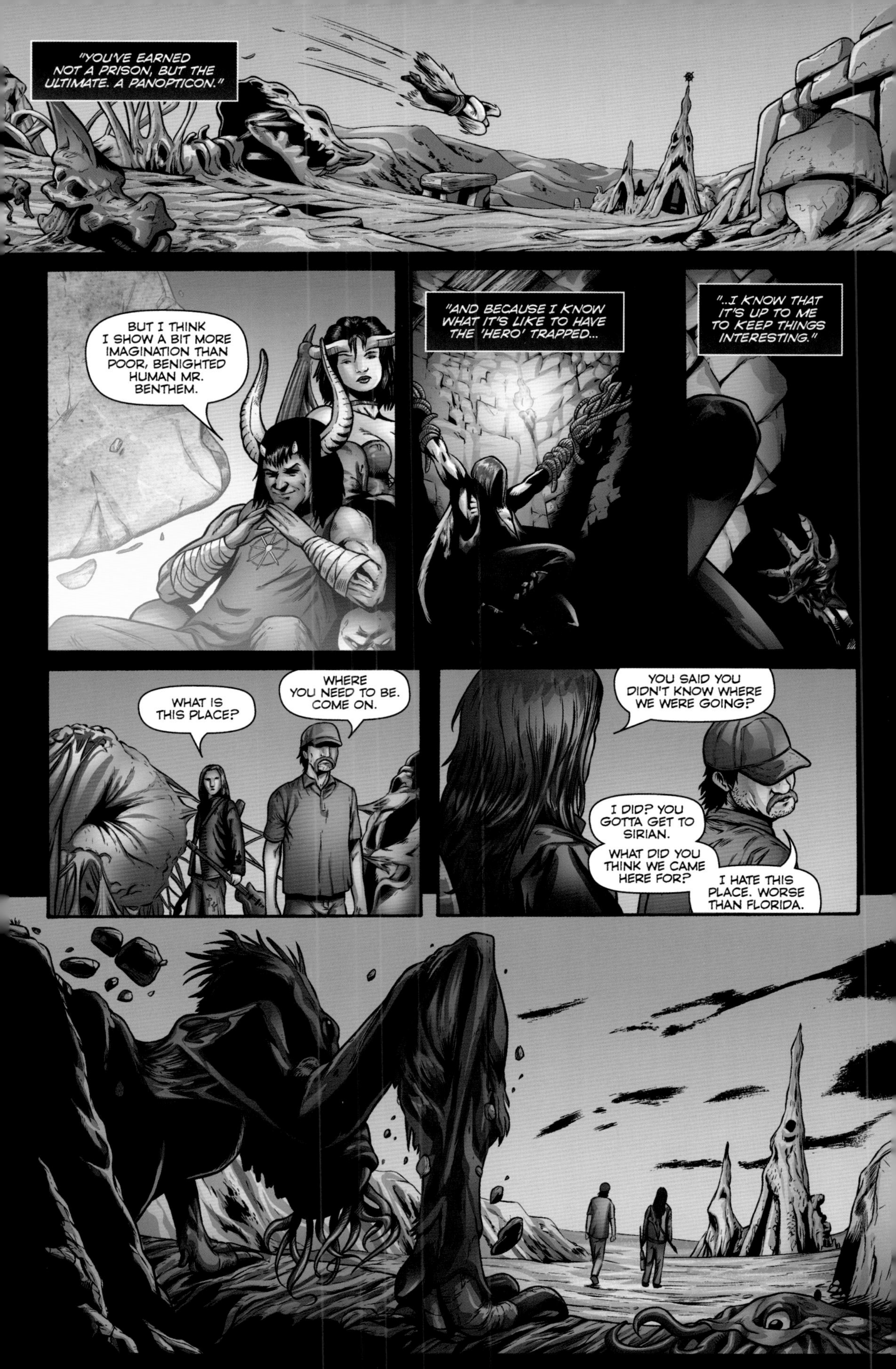
"YOU'VE EARNED NOT A PRISON, BUT THE ULTIMATE. A PANOPTICON."
BUT I THINK I SHOW A BIT MORE IMAGINATION THAN POOR, BENIGHTED HUMAN MR. BENTHEM.
"AND BECAUSE I KNOW WHAT IT'S LIKE TO HAVE THE 'HERO' TRAPPED...
"...I KNOW THAT IT'S UP TO ME TO KEEP THINGS INTERESTING."
WHAT IS THIS PLACE?
WHERE YOU NEED TO BE. COME ON.
YOU SAID YOU DIDN'T KNOW WHERE WE WERE GOING?
I DID? YOU GOTTA GET TO SIRIAN.
WHAT DID YOU THINK WE CAME HERE FOR?
I HATE THIS PLACE. WORSE THAN FLORIDA.

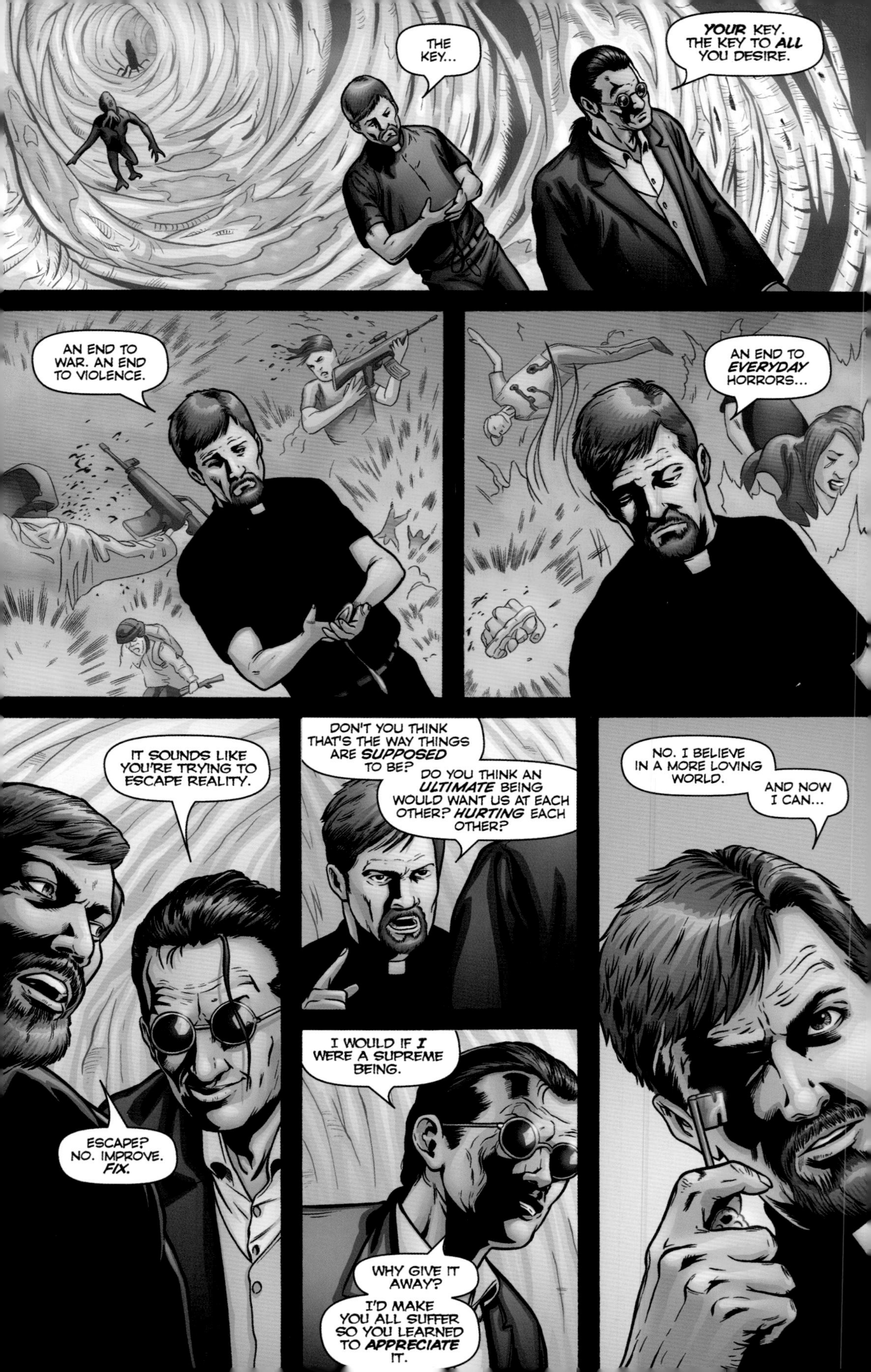
THE KEY...
YOUR KEY. THE KEY TO ALL YOU DESIRE.
AN END TO WAR. AN END TO VIOLENCE.
AN END TO EVERYDAY HORRORS...
IT SOUNDS LIKE YOU'RE TRYING TO ESCAPE REALITY.
ESCAPE? NO. IMPROVE. FIX.
DON'T YOU THINK THAT'S THE WAY THINGS ARE SUPPOSED TO BE?
DO YOU THINK AN ULTIMATE BEING WOULD WANT US AT EACH OTHER? HURTING EACH OTHER?
I WOULD IF I WERE A SUPREME BEING.
WHY GIVE IT AWAY?
I'D MAKE YOU ALL SUFFER SO YOU LEARNED TO APPRECIATE IT.
NO. I BELIEVE IN A MORE LOVING WORLD.
AND NOW I CAN...

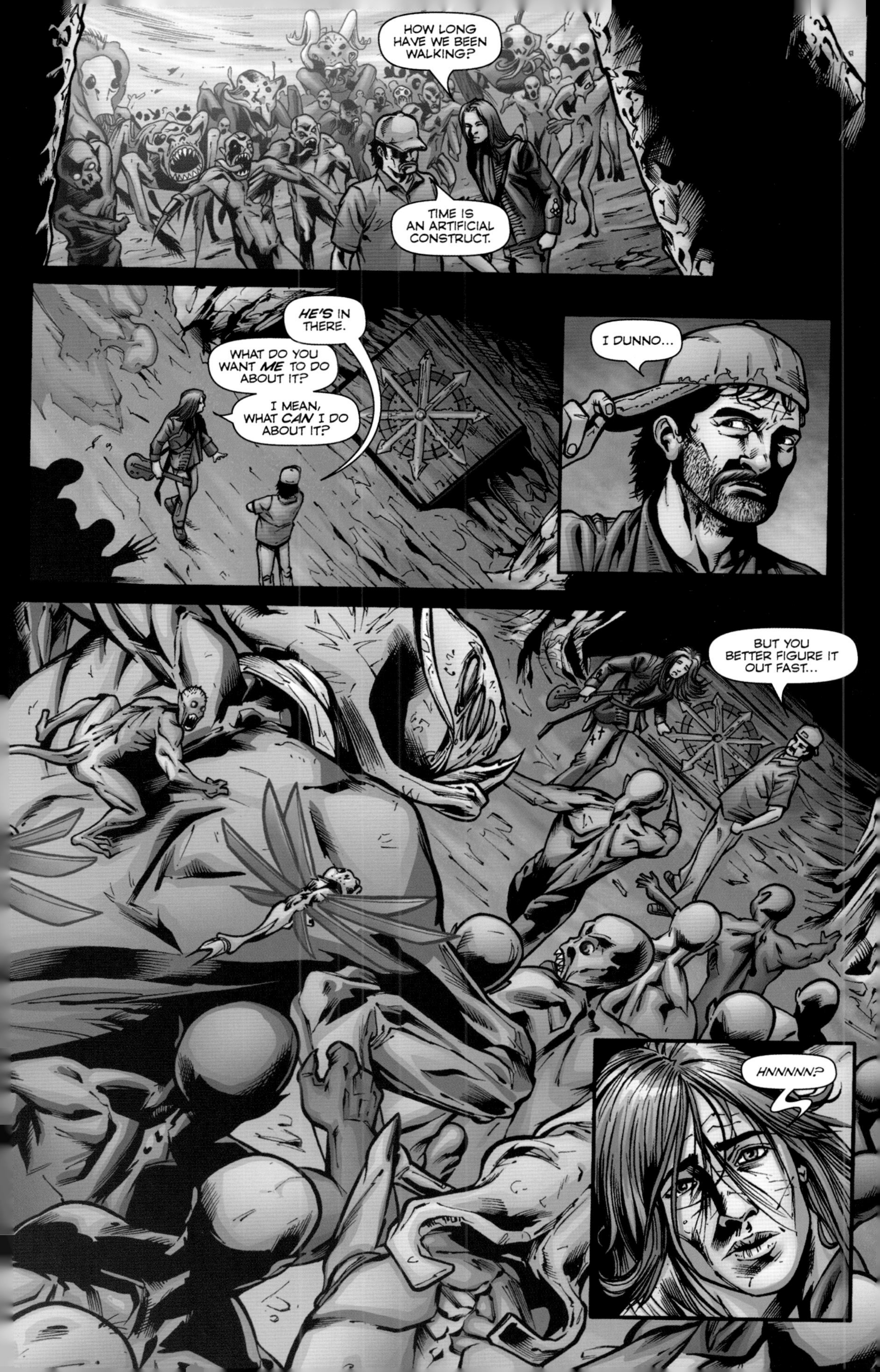
HOW LONG HAVE WE BEEN WALKING?
TIME IS AN ARTIFICIAL CONSTRUCT.
HE'S IN THERE.
WHAT DO YOU WANT ME TO DO ABOUT IT?
I MEAN, WHAT CAN I DO ABOUT IT?
I DUNNO...
BUT YOU BETTER FIGURE IT OUT FAST...
HNNNNN?

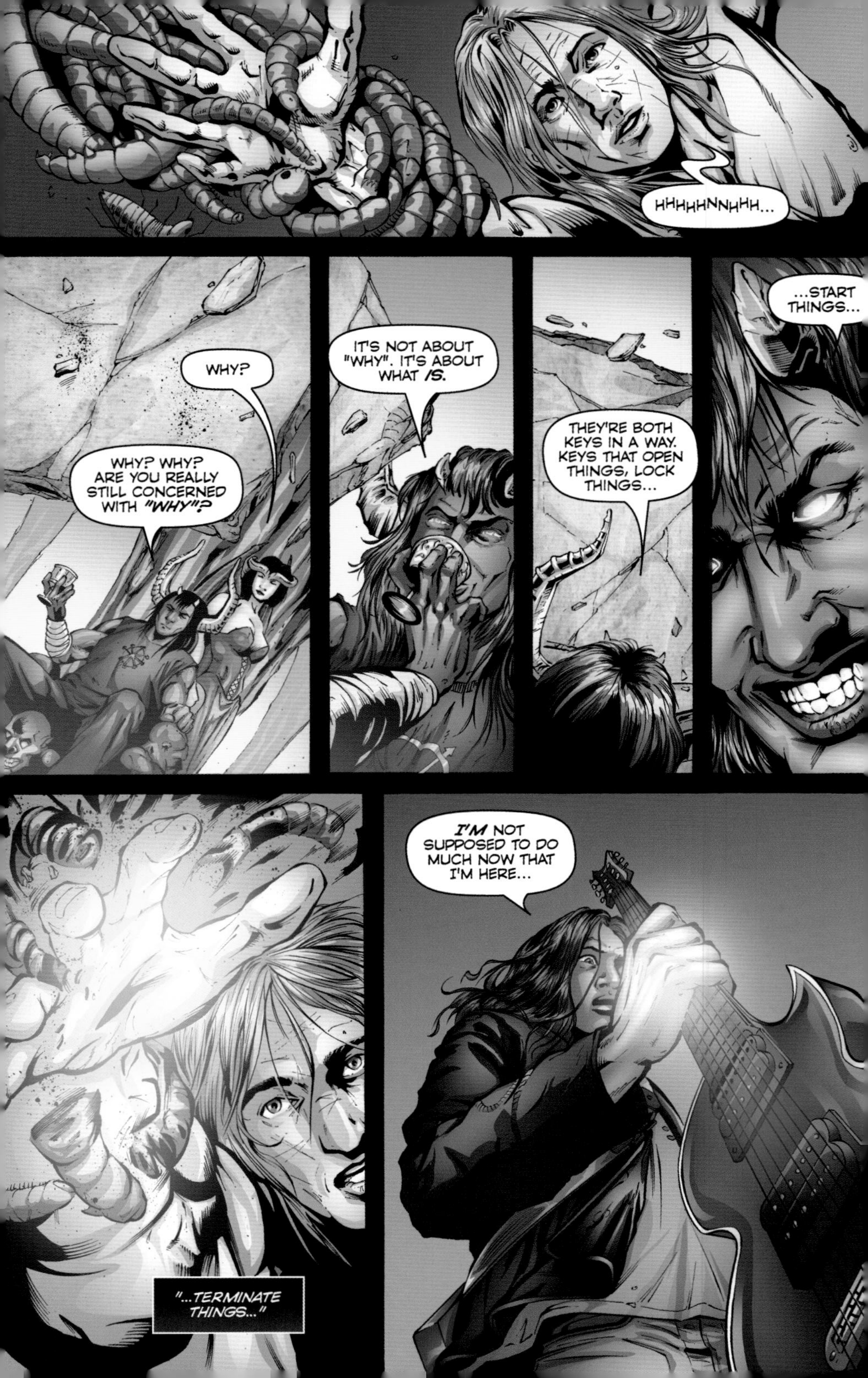
HHHHHNNHHH...
WHY?
WHY? WHY? ARE YOU REALLY STILL CONCERNED WITH "WHY"?
IT'S NOT ABOUT "WHY". IT'S ABOUT WHAT IS.
THEY'RE BOTH KEYS IN A WAY. KEYS THAT OPEN THINGS, LOCK THINGS...
...START THINGS...
"...TERMINATE THINGS..."
I'M NOT SUPPOSED TO DO MUCH NOW THAT I'M HERE...

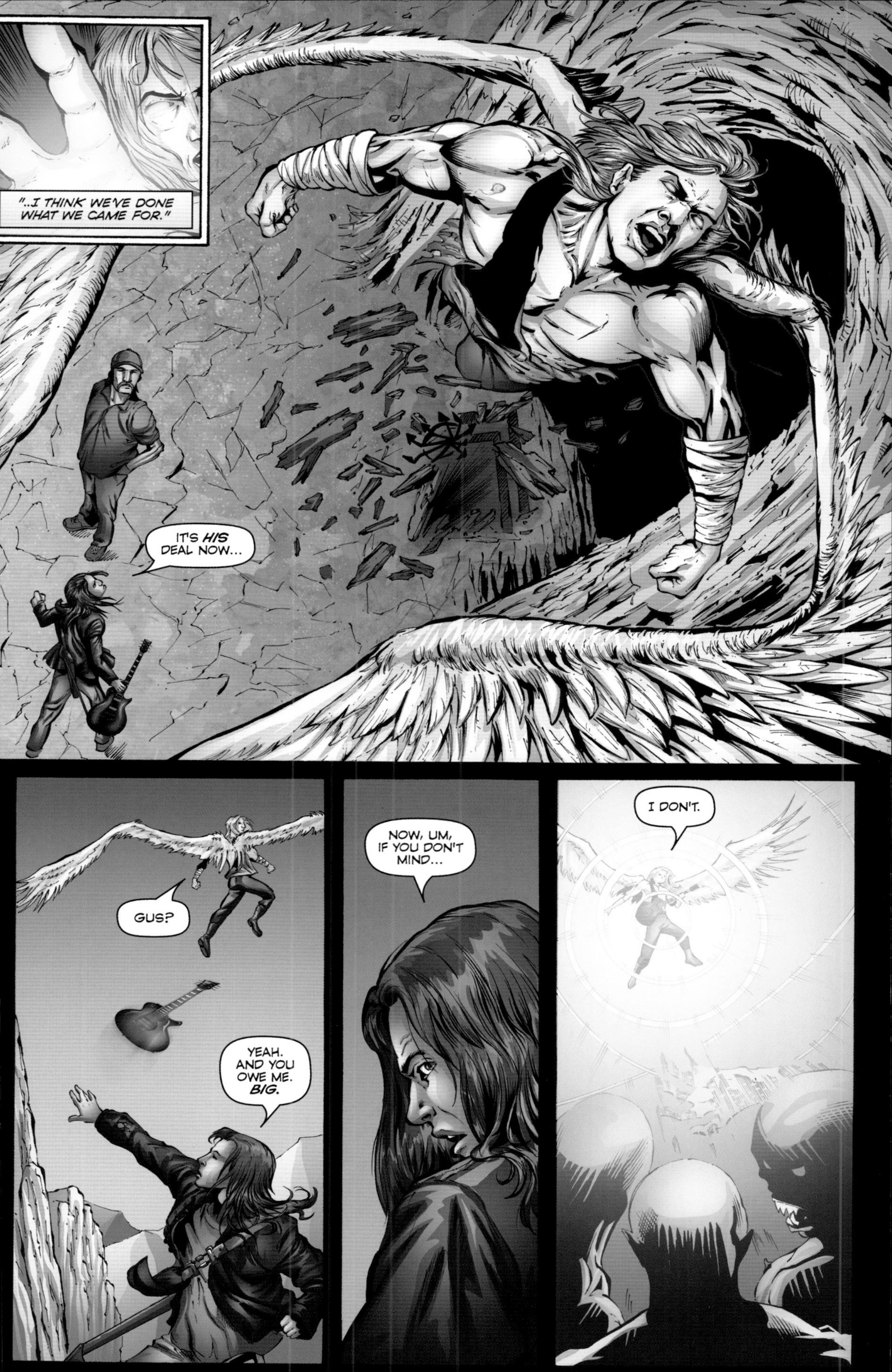
"...I THINK WE'VE DONE WHAT WE CAME FOR."
IT'S *HIS* DEAL NOW...
GUS?
YEAH. AND YOU OWE ME. *BIG.*
NOW, UM, IF YOU DON'T MIND...
I DON'T.

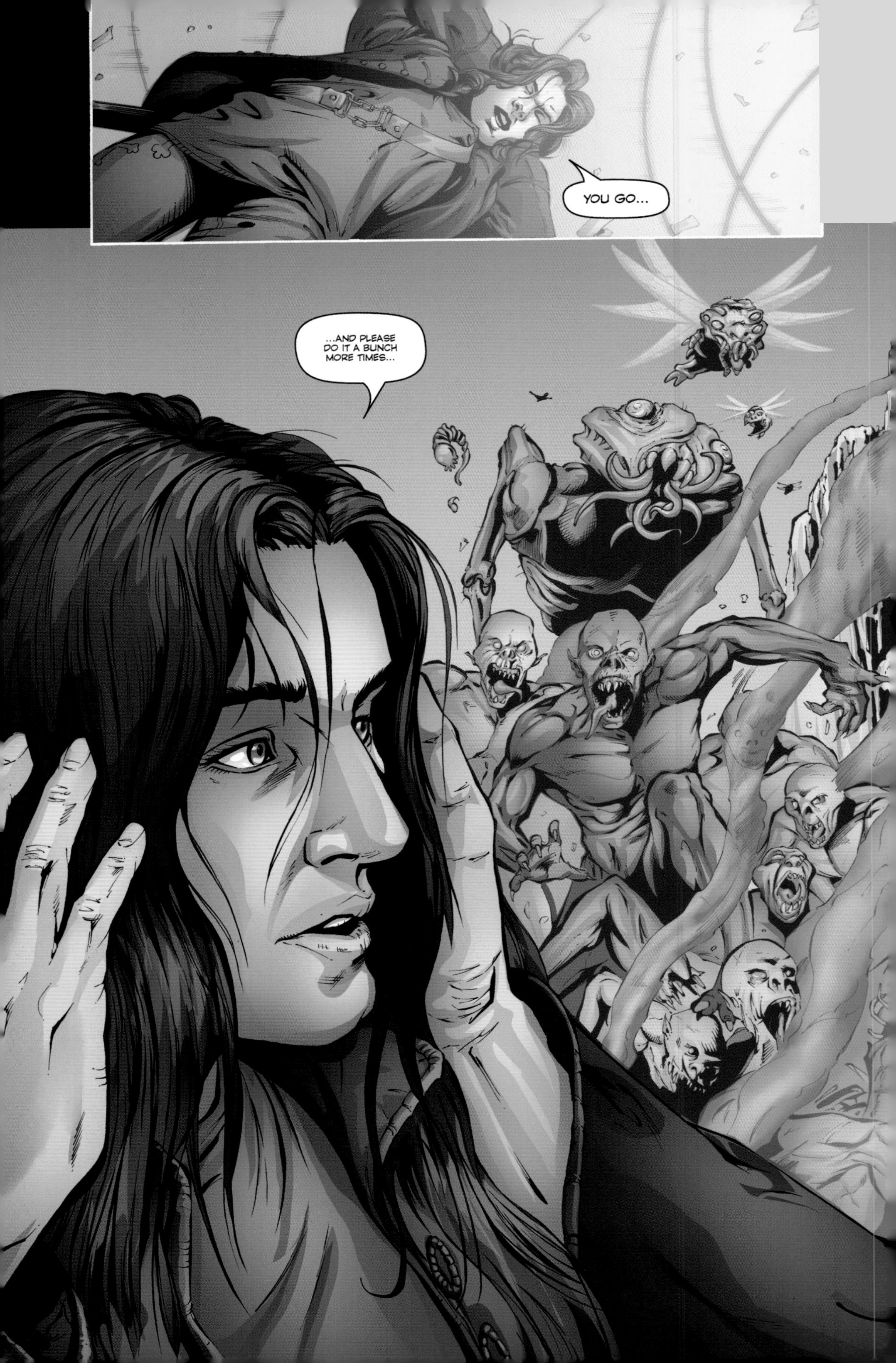
YOU GO...
...AND PLEASE DO IT A BUNCH MORE TIMES...

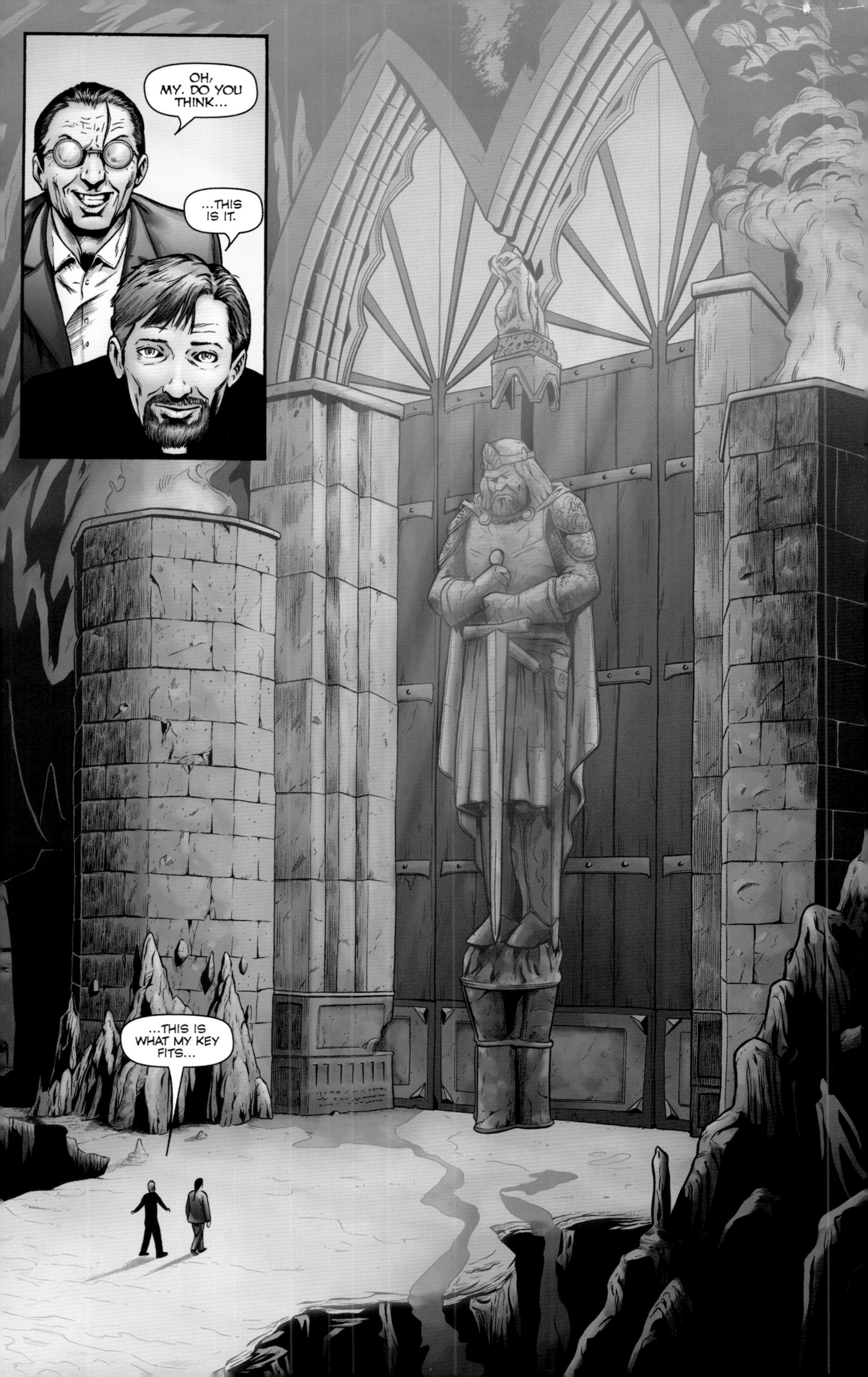
OH, MY. DO YOU THINK...
...THIS IS IT.
...THIS IS WHAT MY KEY FITS...

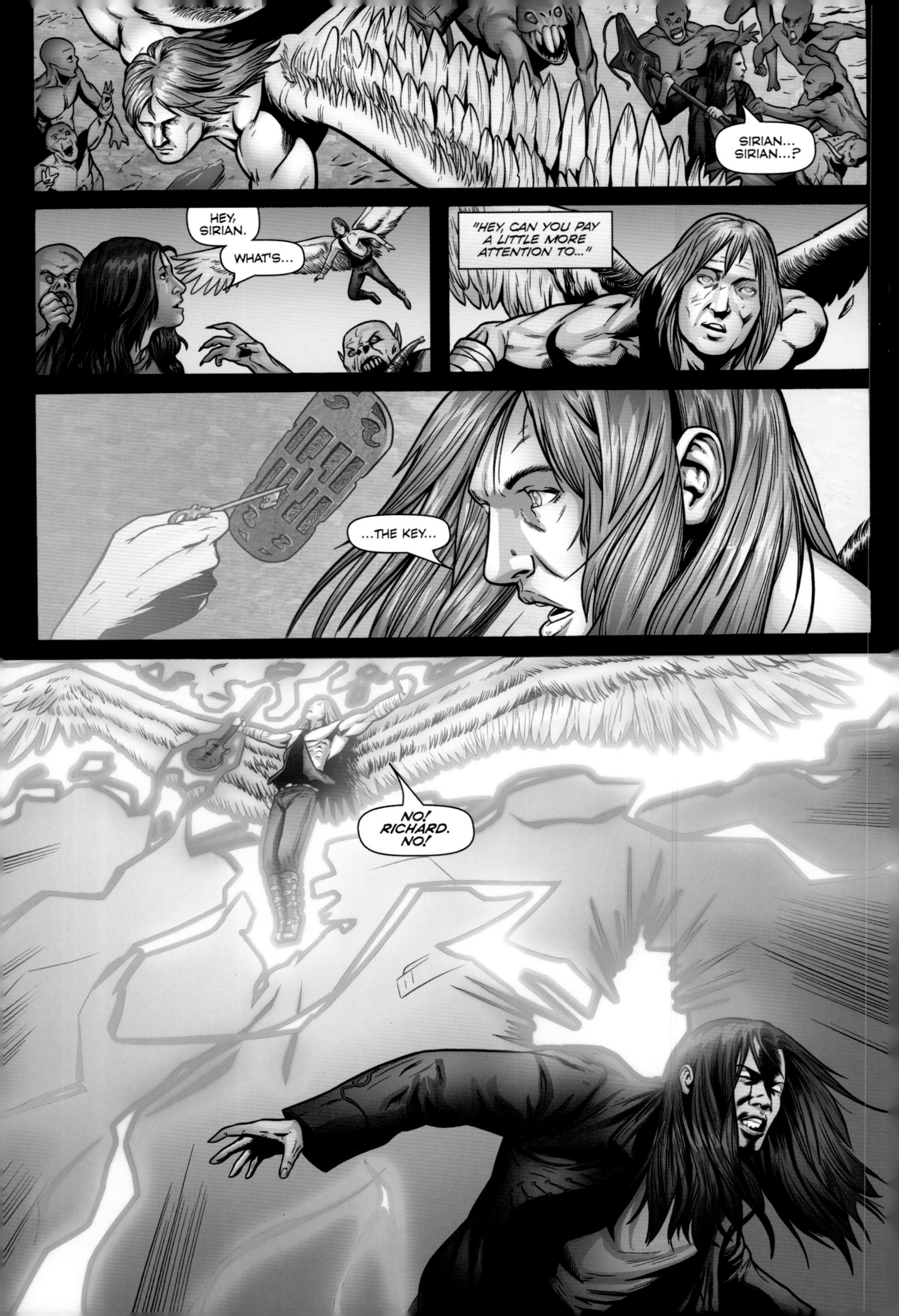
SIRIAN... SIRIAN...?
HEY, SIRIAN.
WHAT'S...
"HEY, CAN YOU PAY A LITTLE MORE ATTENTION TO..."
...THE KEY...
NO! RICHARD. NO!

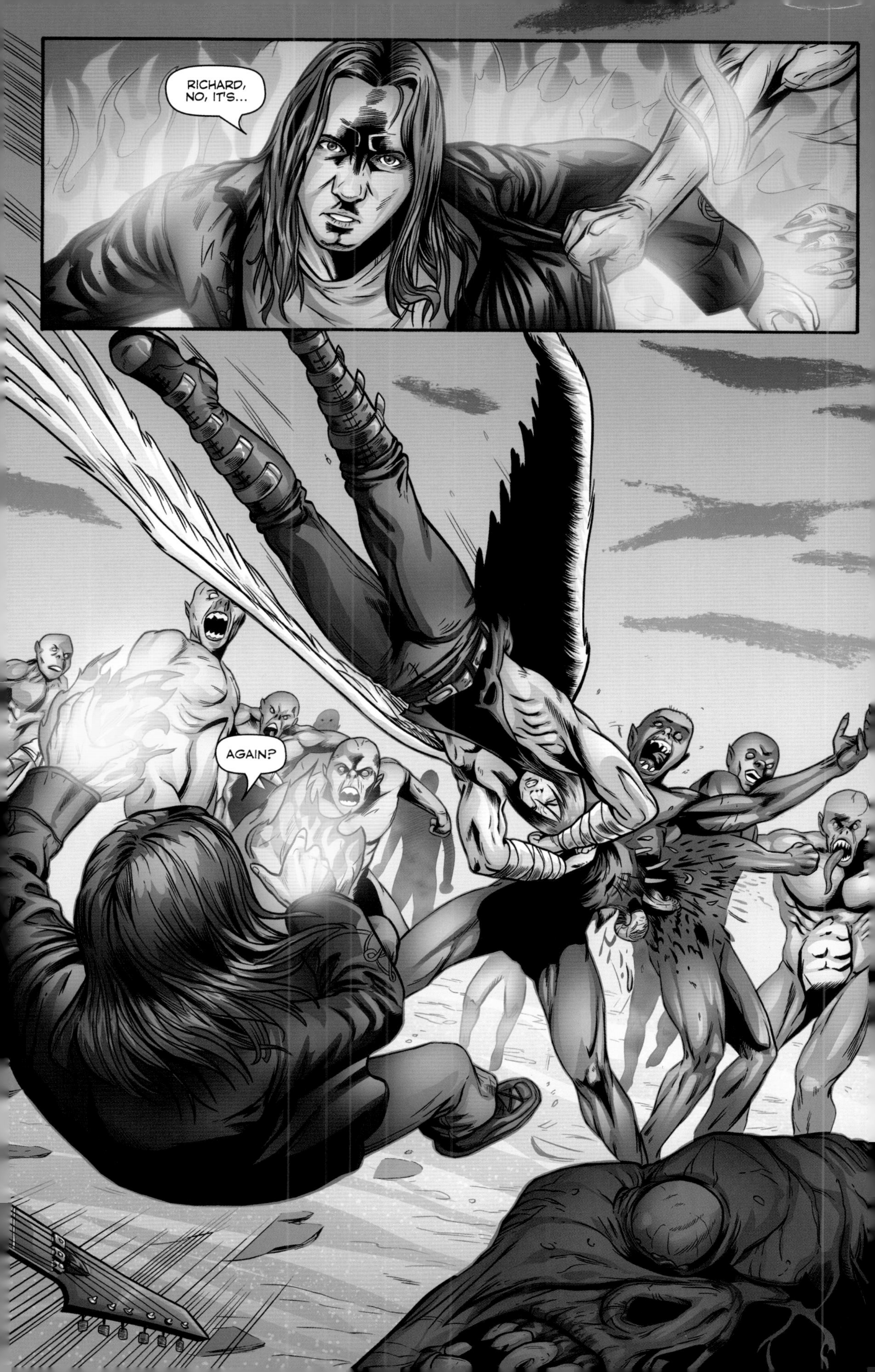
RICHARD, NO, IT'S...
AGAIN?

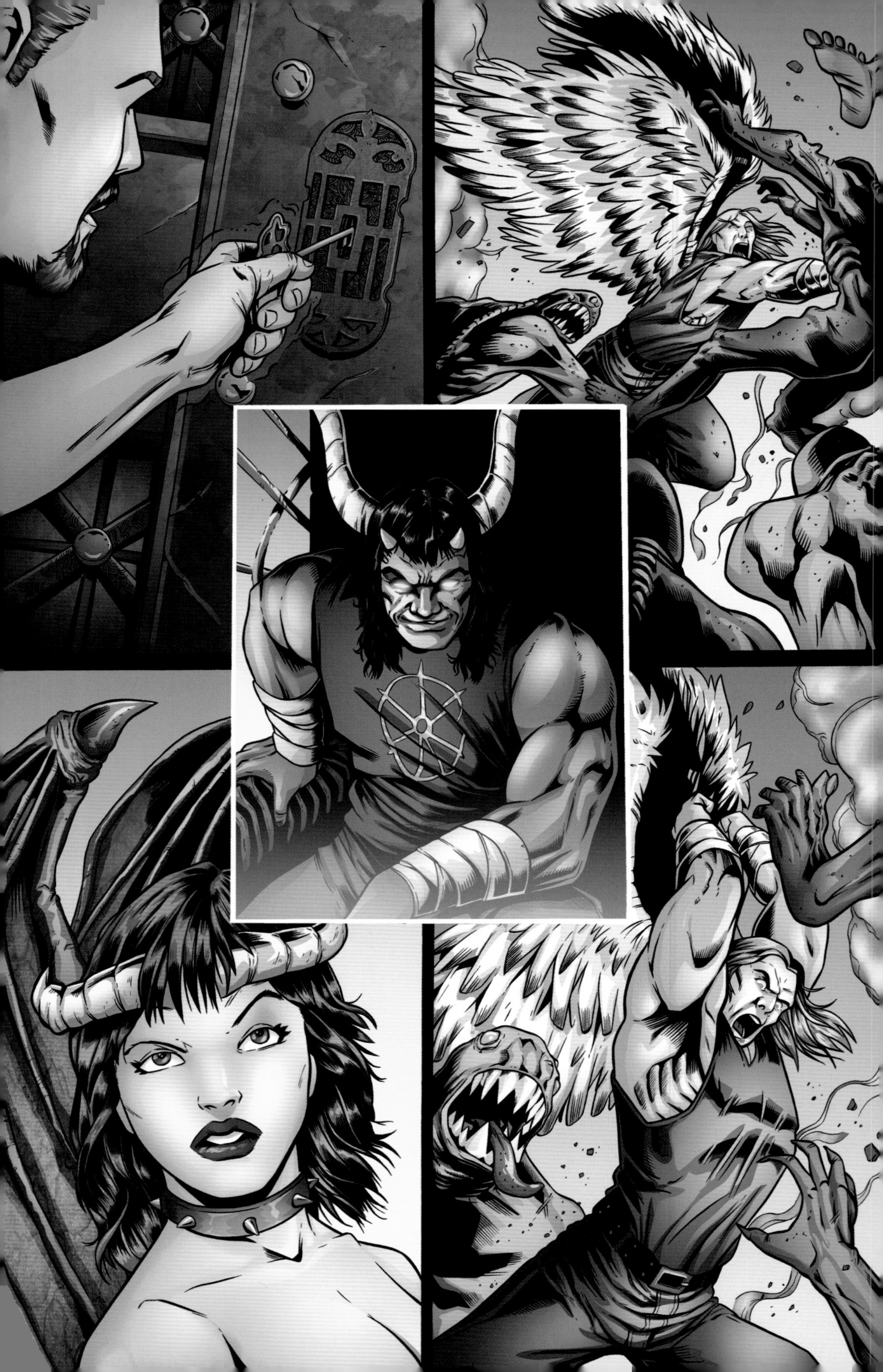

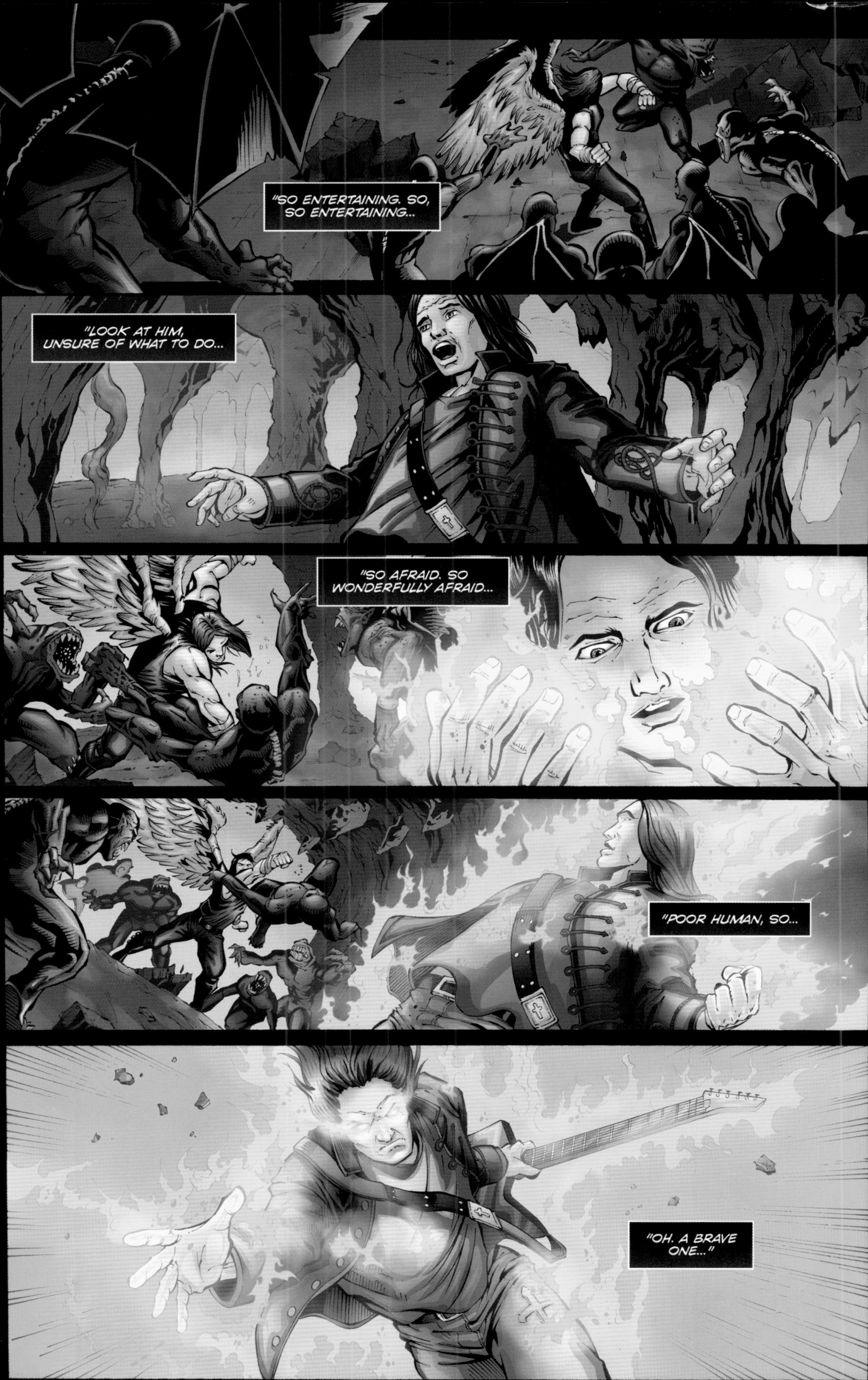
"SO ENTERTAINING. SO, SO ENTERTAINING...
"LOOK AT HIM, UNSURE OF WHAT TO DO...
"SO AFRAID. SO WONDERFULLY AFRAID...
"POOR HUMAN, SO...
"OH. A BRAVE ONE..."

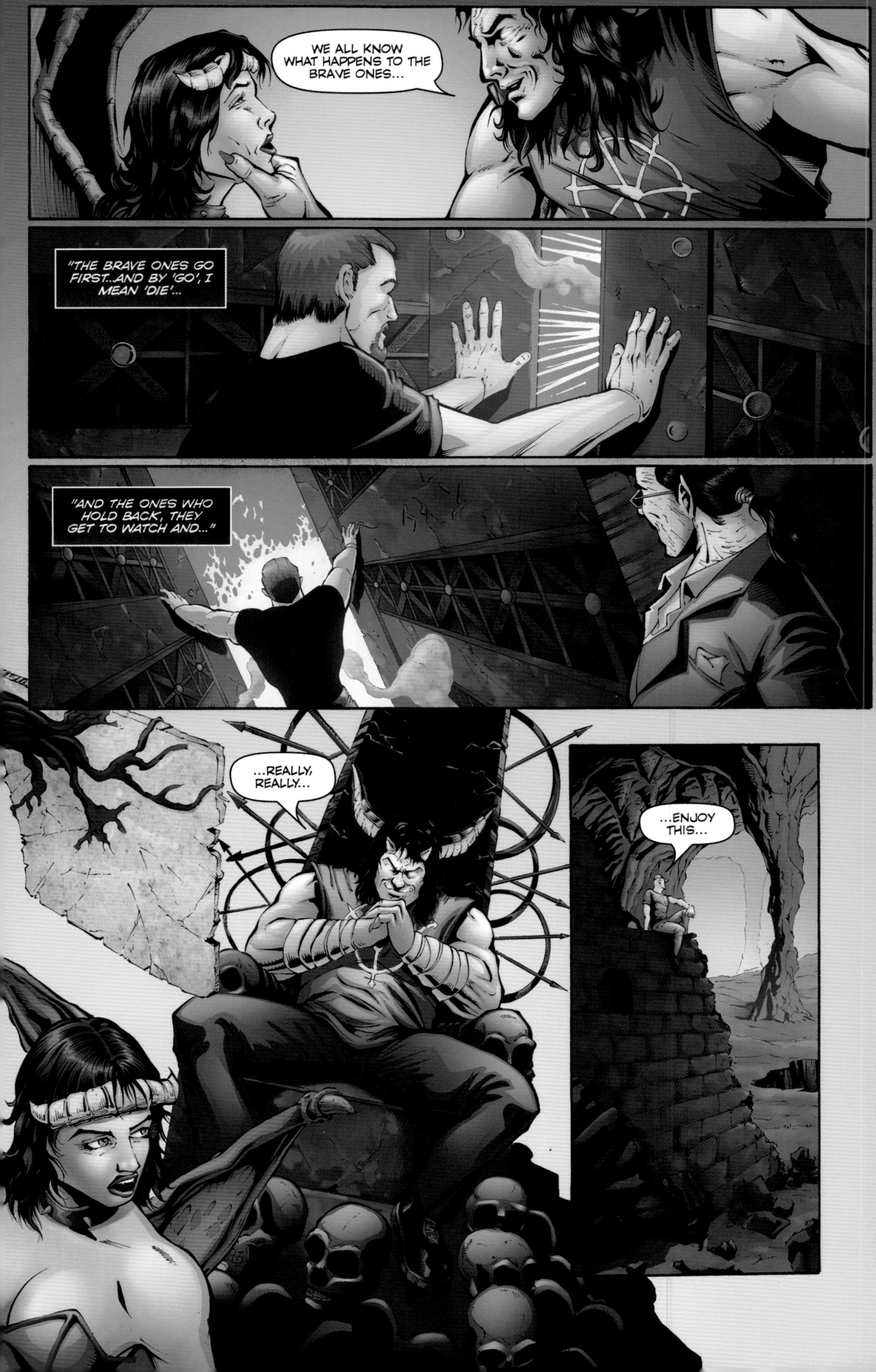
WE ALL KNOW WHAT HAPPENS TO THE BRAVE ONES...
"THE BRAVE ONES GO FIRST...AND BY 'GO', I MEAN 'DIE'...
"AND THE ONES WHO HOLD BACK, THEY GET TO WATCH AND..."
...REALLY, REALLY...
...ENJOY THIS...

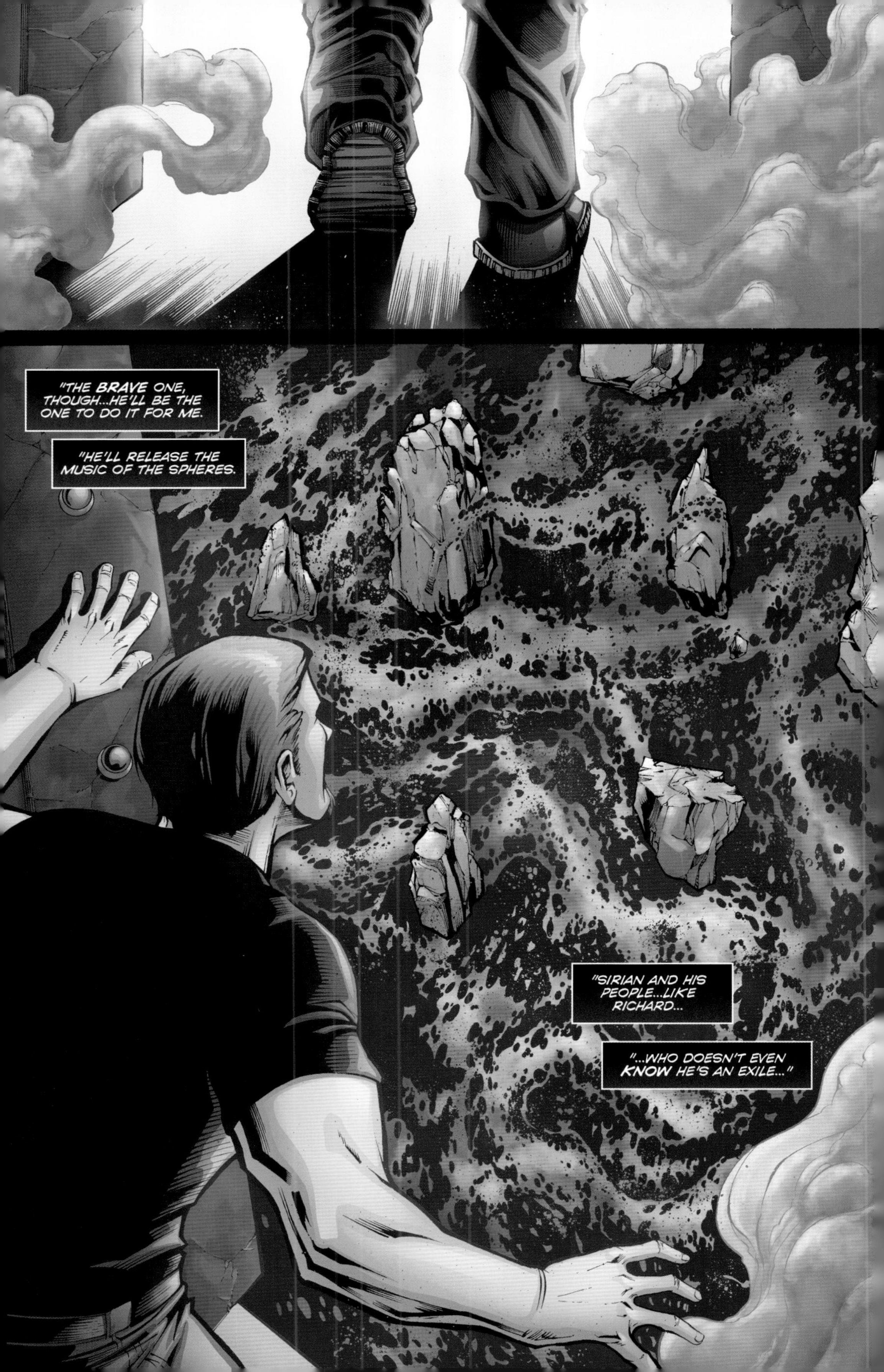
"THE BRAVE ONE, THOUGH...HE'LL BE THE ONE TO DO IT FOR ME.
"HE'LL RELEASE THE MUSIC OF THE SPHERES.
"SIRIAN AND HIS PEOPLE...LIKE RICHARD...
"...WHO DOESN'T EVEN KNOW HE'S AN EXILE..."

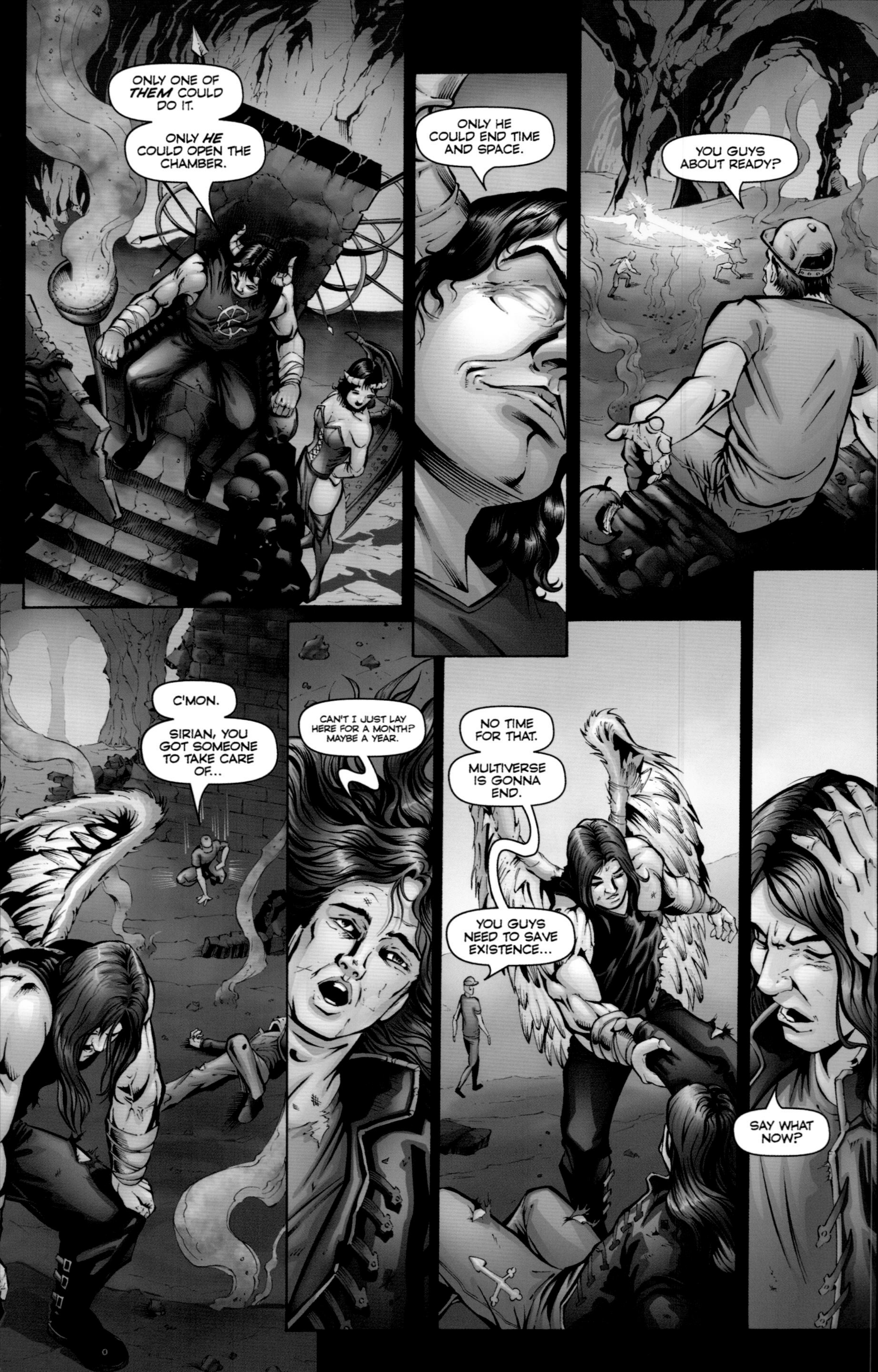
ONLY ONE OF THEM COULD DO IT.
ONLY HE COULD OPEN THE CHAMBER.
ONLY HE COULD END TIME AND SPACE.
YOU GUYS ABOUT READY?
C'MON.
SIRIAN, YOU GOT SOMEONE TO TAKE CARE OF...
CAN'T I JUST LAY HERE FOR A MONTH? MAYBE A YEAR.
NO TIME FOR THAT.
MULTIVERSE IS GONNA END.
YOU GUYS NEED TO SAVE EXISTENCE...
SAY WHAT NOW?

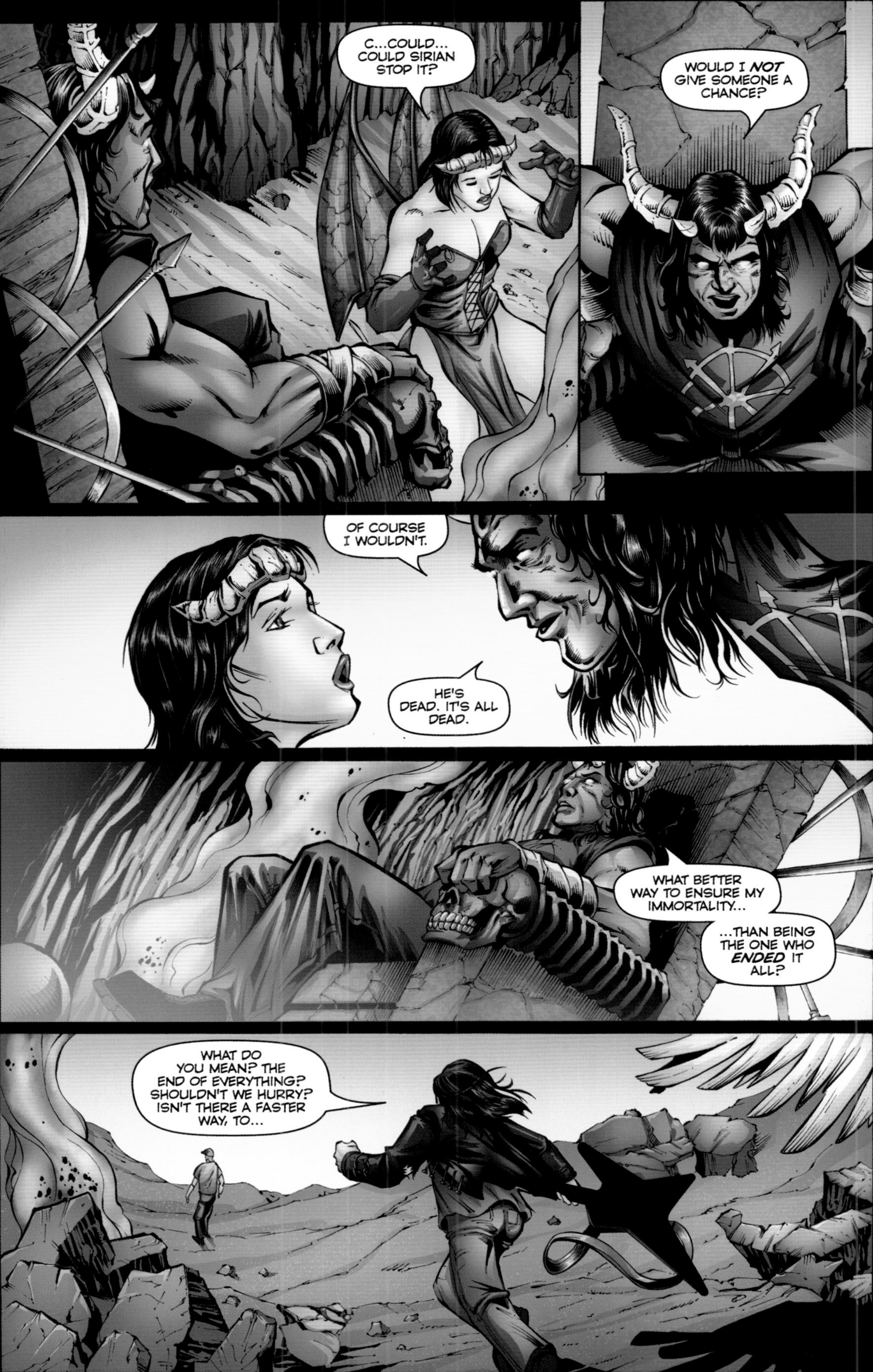
C...COULD... COULD SIRIAN STOP IT?
WOULD I NOT GIVE SOMEONE A CHANCE?
OF COURSE I WOULDN'T.
HE'S DEAD. IT'S ALL DEAD.
WHAT BETTER WAY TO ENSURE MY IMMORTALITY...
...THAN BEING THE ONE WHO ENDED IT ALL?
WHAT DO YOU MEAN? THE END OF EVERYTHING? SHOULDN'T WE HURRY? ISN'T THERE A FASTER WAY, TO...

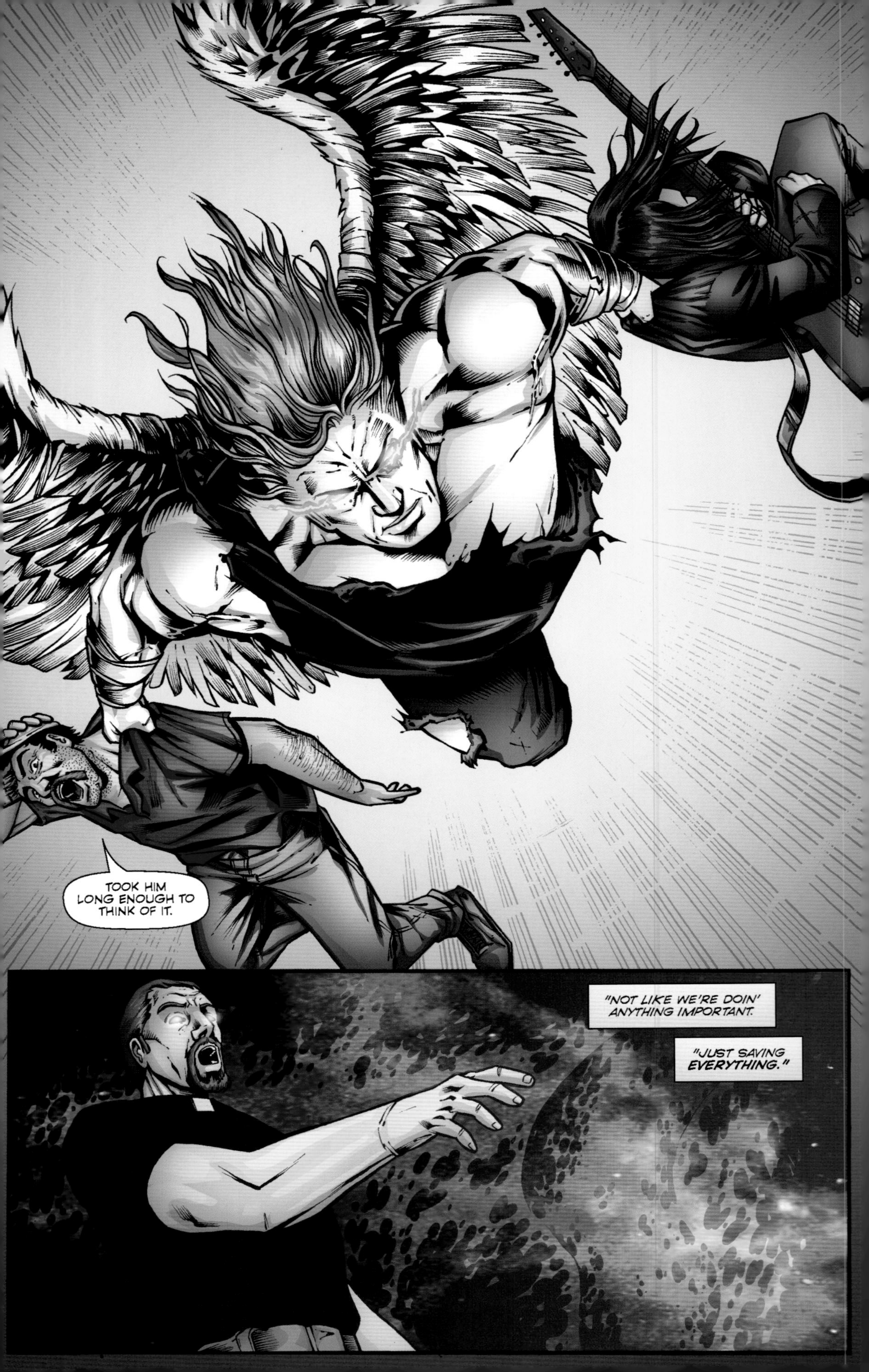
TOOK HIM LONG ENOUGH TO THINK OF IT.
"NOT LIKE WE'RE DOIN' ANYTHING IMPORTANT.
"JUST SAVING *EVERYTHING*."

Eternal Descent

Chapter Two:
Falling to Pieces

Written by
Llexi Leon and **Shaun McLaughlin**
Pencils by
Ivan Fernandez
Inks by
Tony Kordos
Colors by
Javier Tartaglia
Lettering by
Charles Pritchett

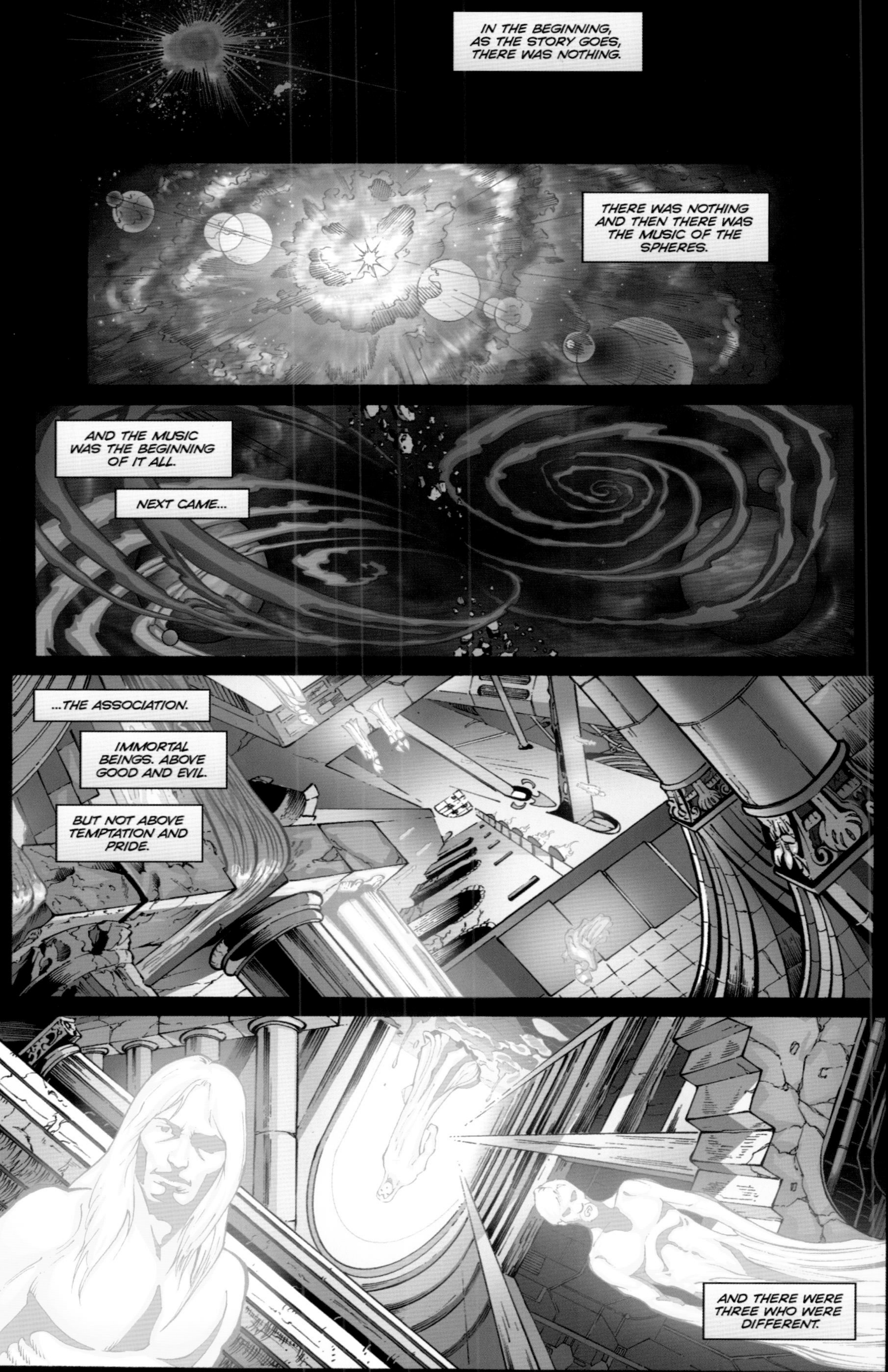
IN THE BEGINNING, AS THE STORY GOES, THERE WAS NOTHING.
THERE WAS NOTHING AND THEN THERE WAS THE MUSIC OF THE SPHERES.
AND THE MUSIC WAS THE BEGINNING OF IT ALL.
NEXT CAME...
...THE ASSOCIATION.
IMMORTAL BEINGS. ABOVE GOOD AND EVIL.
BUT NOT ABOVE TEMPTATION AND PRIDE.
AND THERE WERE THREE WHO WERE DIFFERENT.

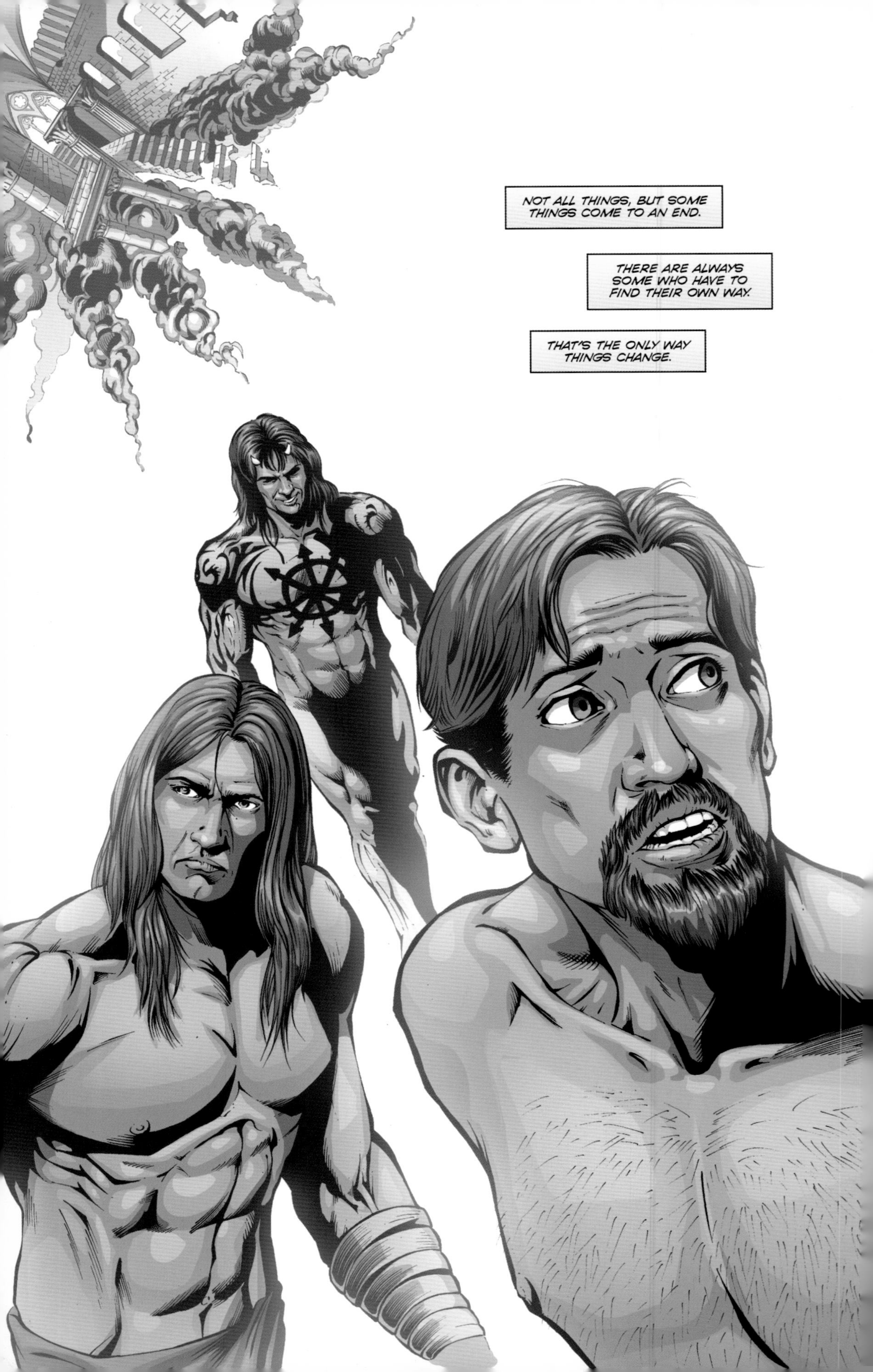
NOT ALL THINGS, BUT SOME THINGS COME TO AN END.
THERE ARE ALWAYS SOME WHO HAVE TO FIND THEIR OWN WAY.
THAT'S THE ONLY WAY THINGS CHANGE.

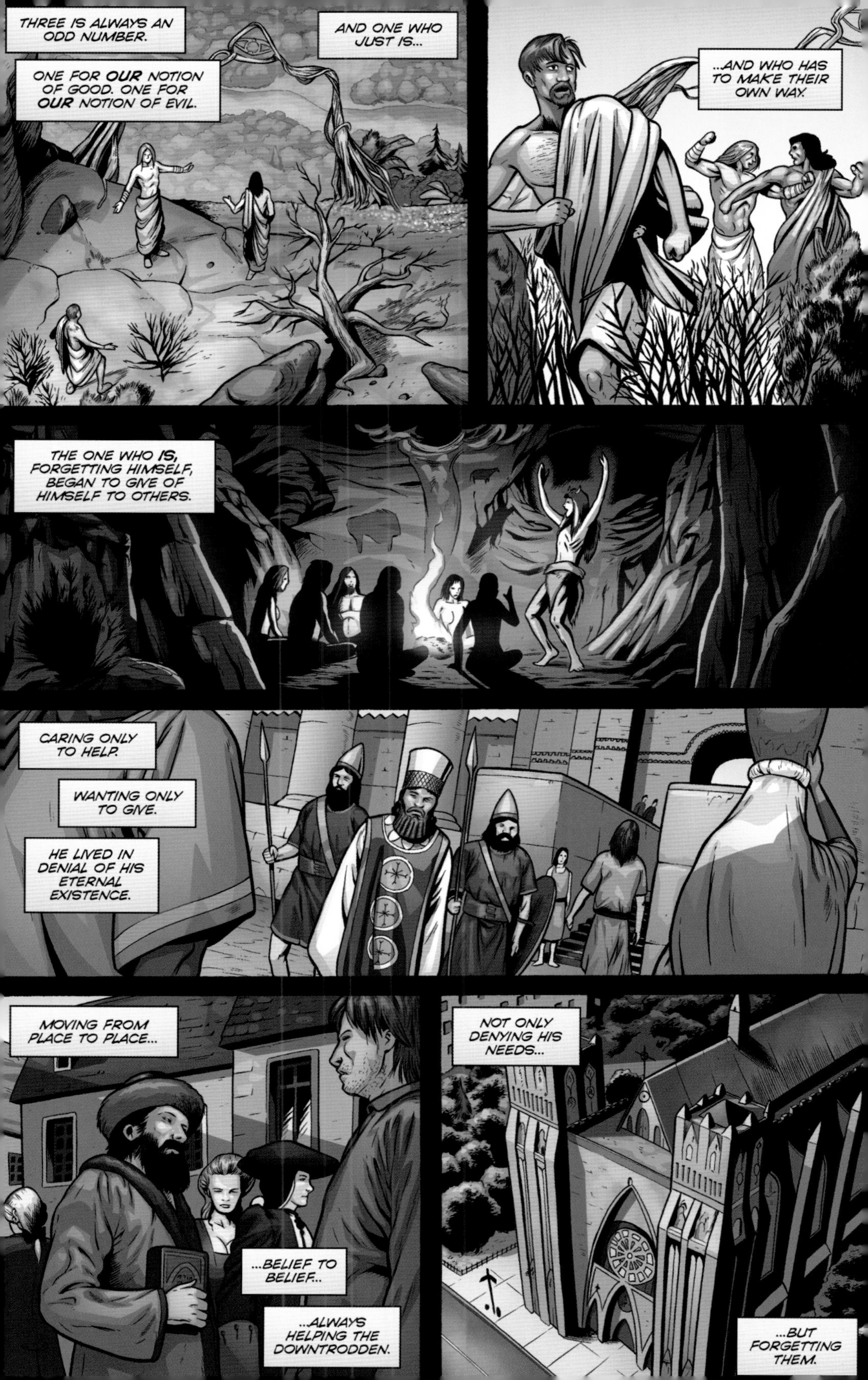
THREE IS ALWAYS AN ODD NUMBER.
ONE FOR **OUR** NOTION OF GOOD. ONE FOR **OUR** NOTION OF EVIL.
AND ONE WHO JUST IS...
...AND WHO HAS TO MAKE THEIR OWN WAY.
THE ONE WHO **IS**, FORGETTING HIMSELF, BEGAN TO GIVE OF HIMSELF TO OTHERS.
CARING ONLY TO HELP.
WANTING ONLY TO GIVE.
HE LIVED IN DENIAL OF HIS ETERNAL EXISTENCE.
MOVING FROM PLACE TO PLACE...
...BELIEF TO BELIEF...
...ALWAYS HELPING THE DOWNTRODDEN.
NOT ONLY DENYING HIS NEEDS...
...BUT FORGETTING THEM.

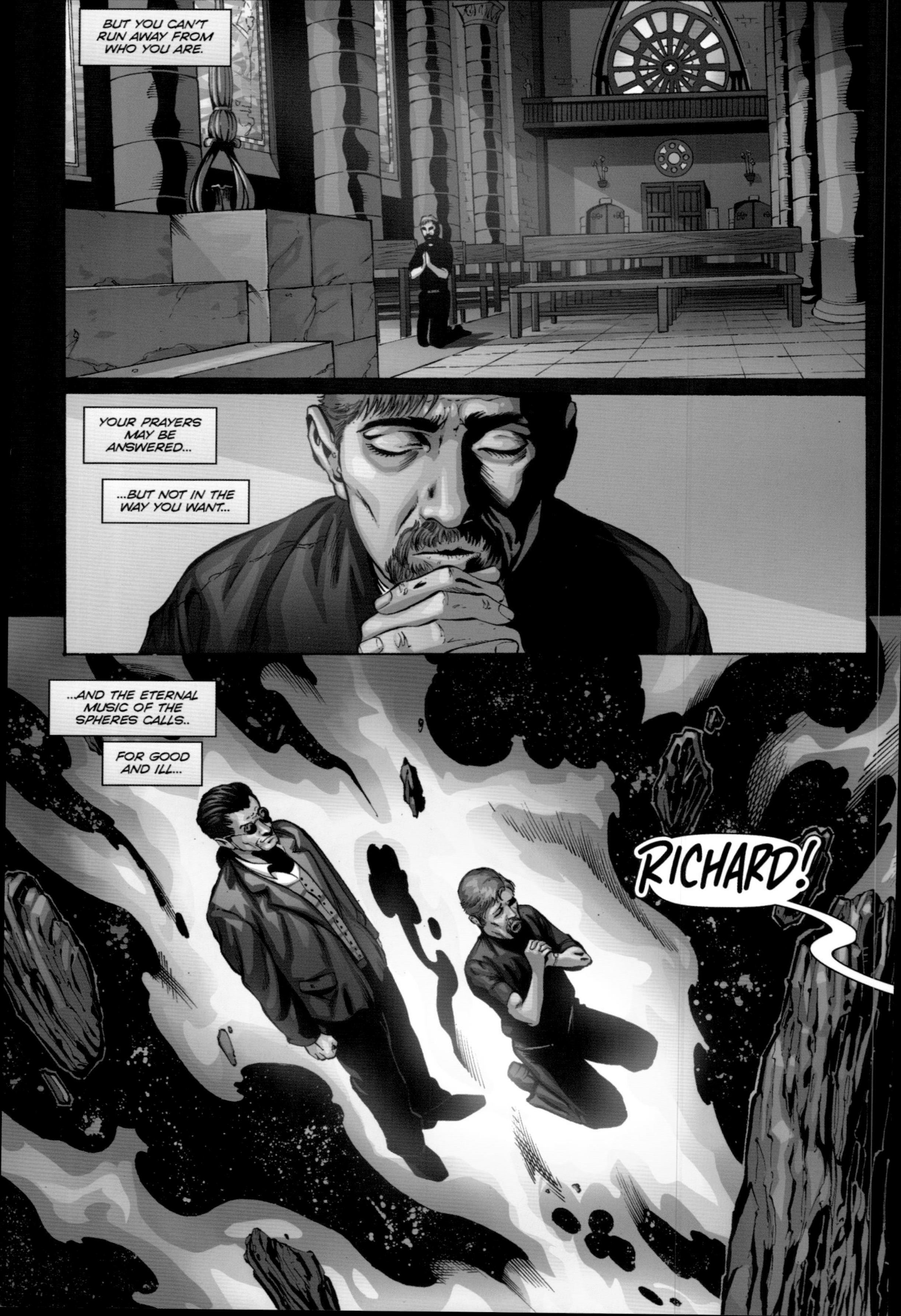
BUT YOU CAN'T RUN AWAY FROM WHO YOU ARE.
YOUR PRAYERS MAY BE ANSWERED...
...BUT NOT IN THE WAY YOU WANT...
...AND THE ETERNAL MUSIC OF THE SPHERES CALLS..
FOR GOOD AND ILL...
RICHARD!

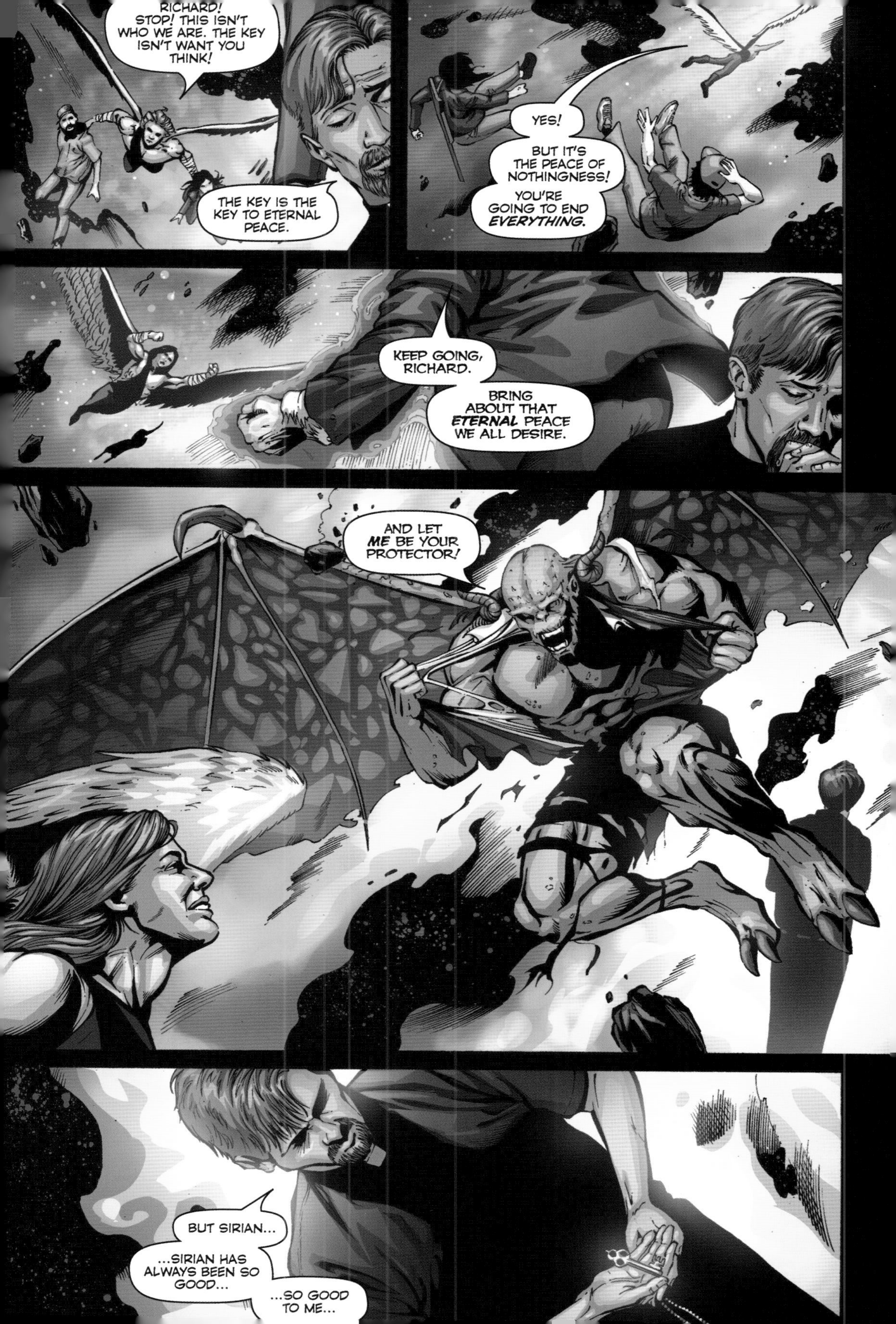

RICHARD! STOP! THIS ISN'T WHO WE ARE. THE KEY ISN'T WANT YOU THINK!
THE KEY IS THE KEY TO ETERNAL PEACE.
YES!
BUT IT'S THE PEACE OF NOTHINGNESS!
YOU'RE GOING TO END EVERYTHING.
KEEP GOING, RICHARD.
BRING ABOUT THAT ETERNAL PEACE WE ALL DESIRE.
AND LET ME BE YOUR PROTECTOR!
BUT SIRIAN...
...SIRIAN HAS ALWAYS BEEN SO GOOD...
...SO GOOD TO ME...

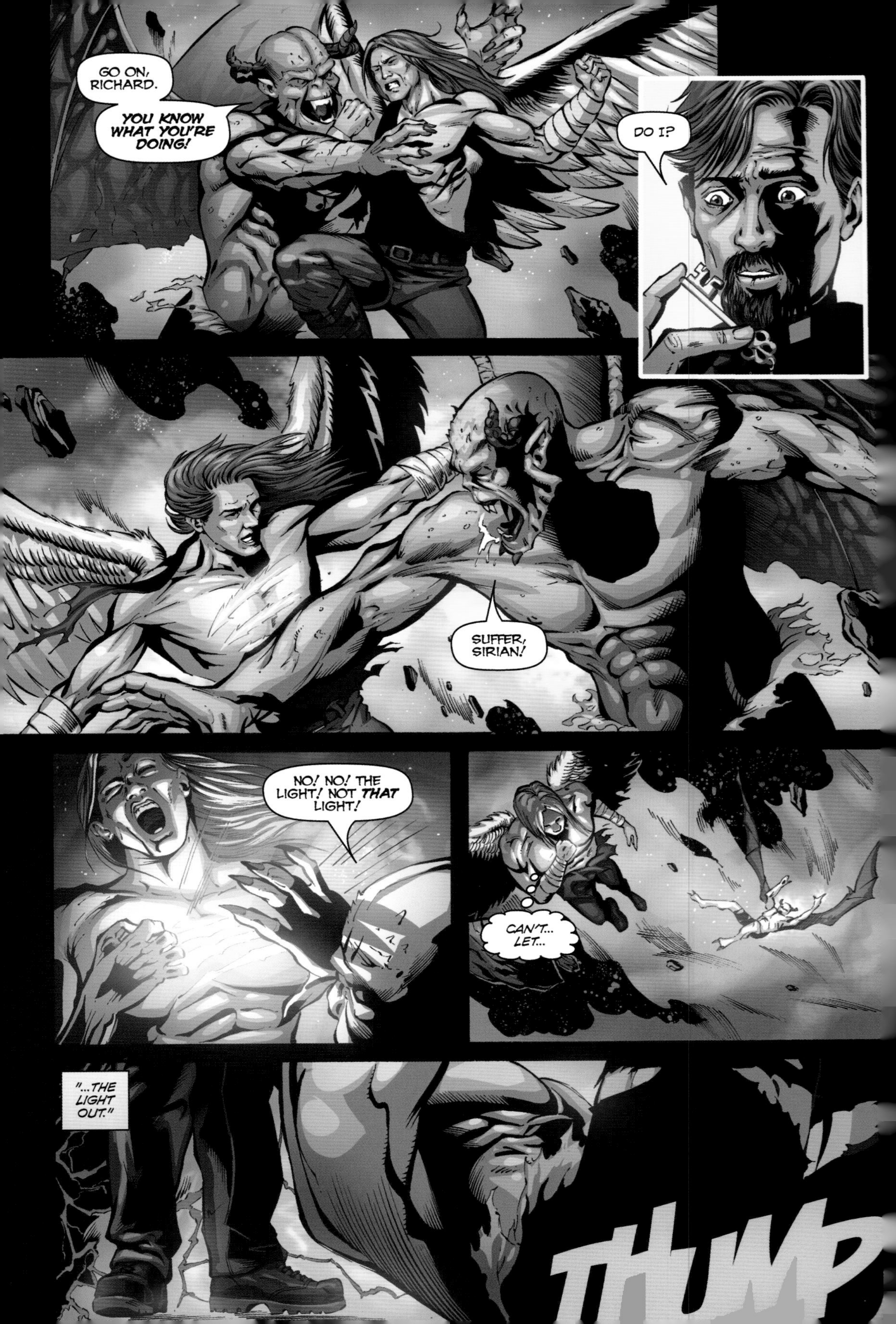
GO ON, RICHARD.
YOU KNOW WHAT YOU'RE DOING!
DO I?
SUFFER, SIRIAN!
NO! NO! THE LIGHT! NOT THAT LIGHT!
CAN'T... LET...
"...THE LIGHT OUT."
THUMP

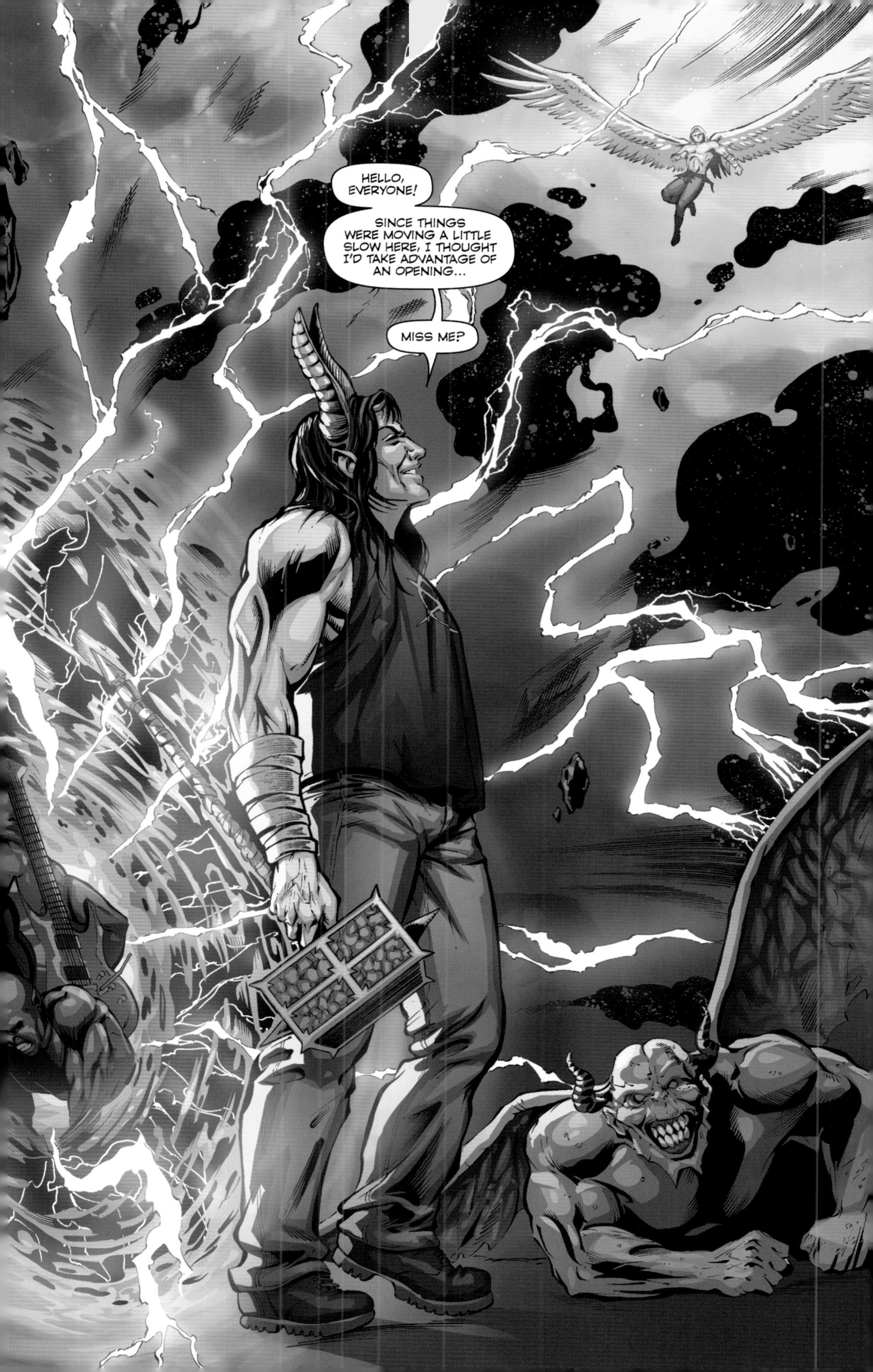
HELLO, EVERYONE!
SINCE THINGS WERE MOVING A LITTLE SLOW HERE, I THOUGHT I'D TAKE ADVANTAGE OF AN OPENING...
MISS ME?

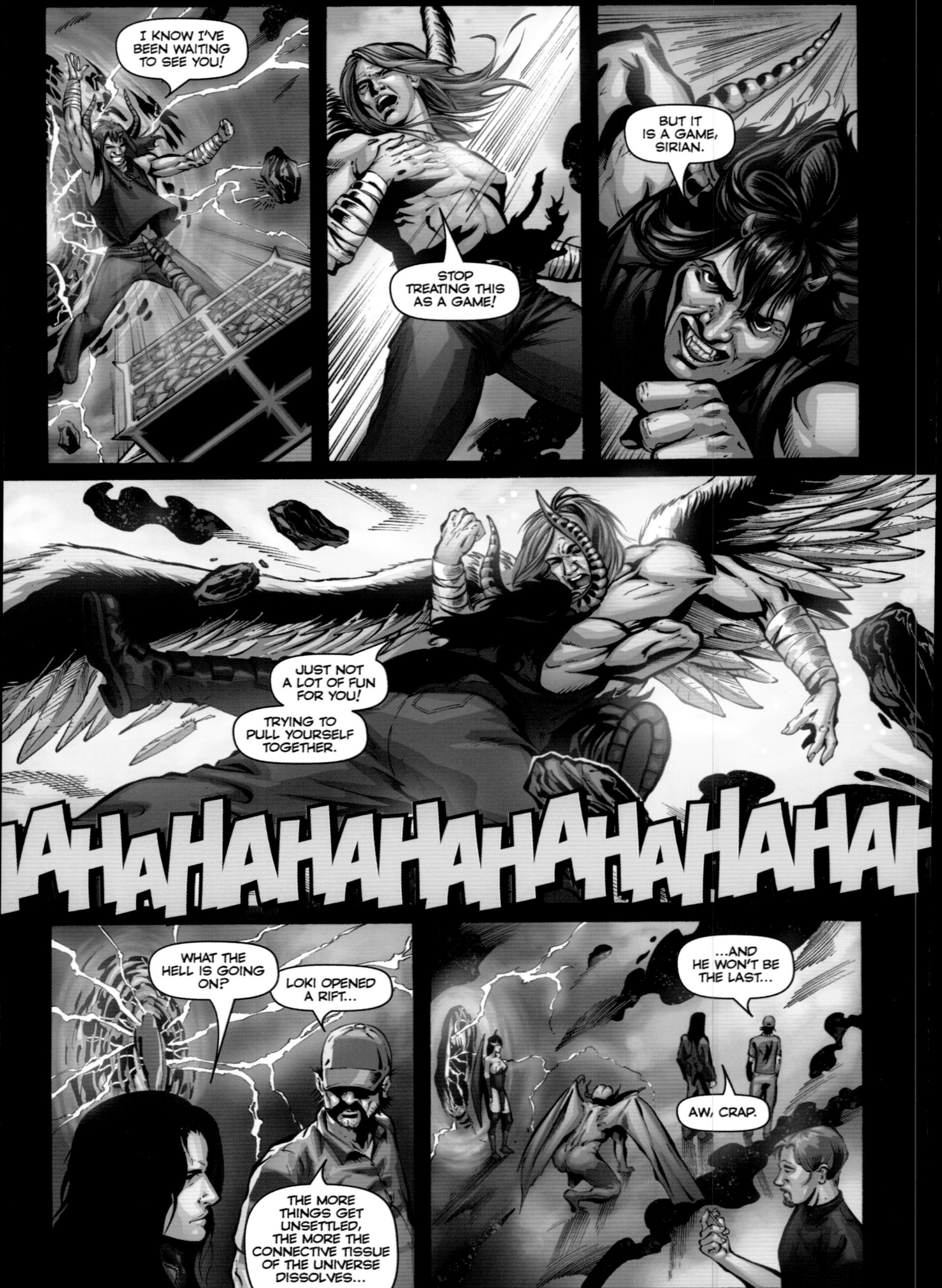
I KNOW I'VE BEEN WAITING TO SEE YOU!
STOP TREATING THIS AS A GAME!
BUT IT IS A GAME, SIRIAN.
JUST NOT A LOT OF FUN FOR YOU!
TRYING TO PULL YOURSELF TOGETHER.
HAHAHAHAHAHAHAHAHAHAH
WHAT THE HELL IS GOING ON?
LOKI OPENED A RIFT...
THE MORE THINGS GET UNSETTLED, THE MORE THE CONNECTIVE TISSUE OF THE UNIVERSE DISSOLVES...
...AND HE WON'T BE THE LAST...
AW, CRAP.

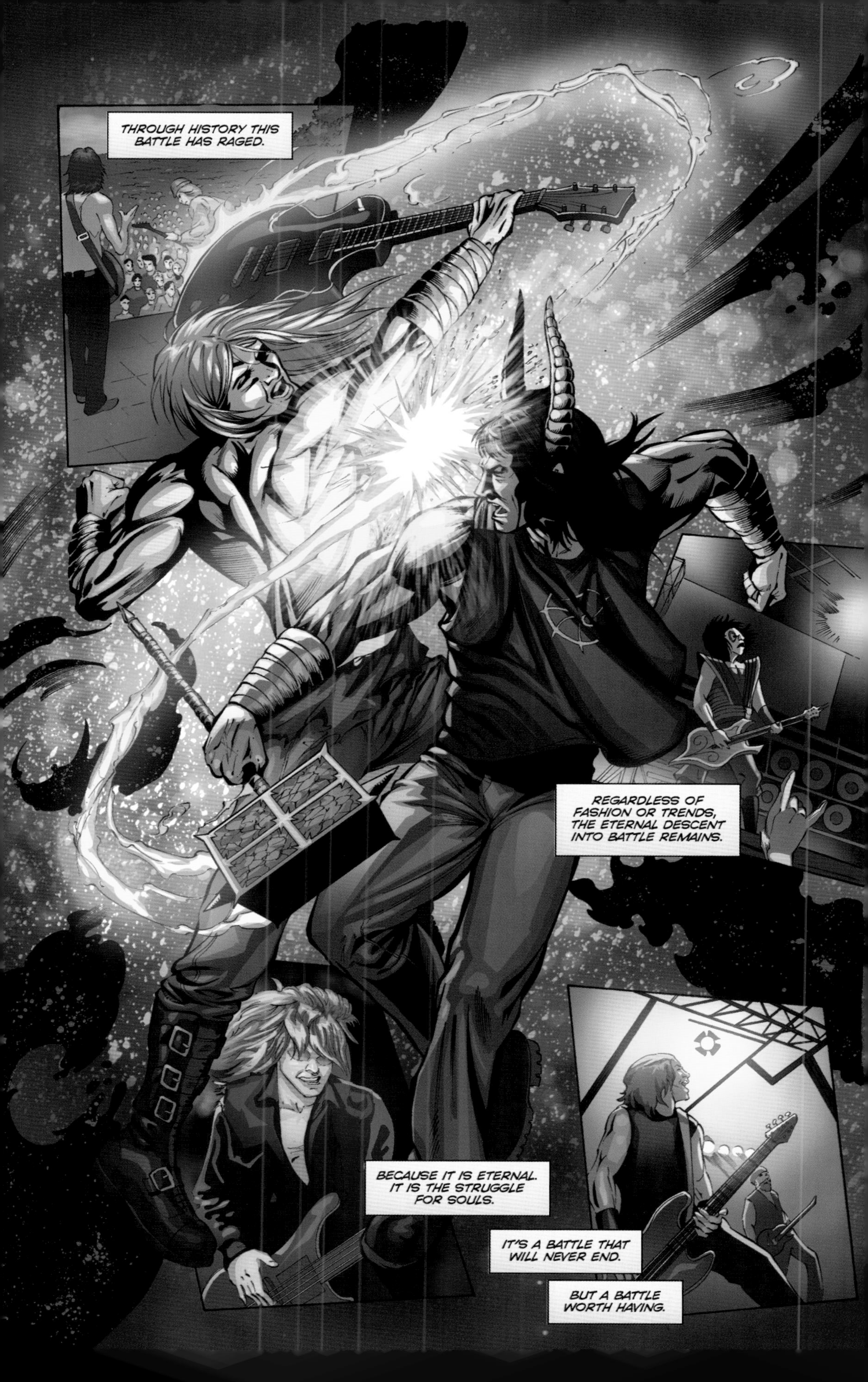
THROUGH HISTORY THIS BATTLE HAS RAGED.
REGARDLESS OF FASHION OR TRENDS, THE ETERNAL DESCENT INTO BATTLE REMAINS.
BECAUSE IT IS ETERNAL. IT IS THE STRUGGLE FOR SOULS.
IT'S A BATTLE THAT WILL NEVER END.
BUT A BATTLE WORTH HAVING.

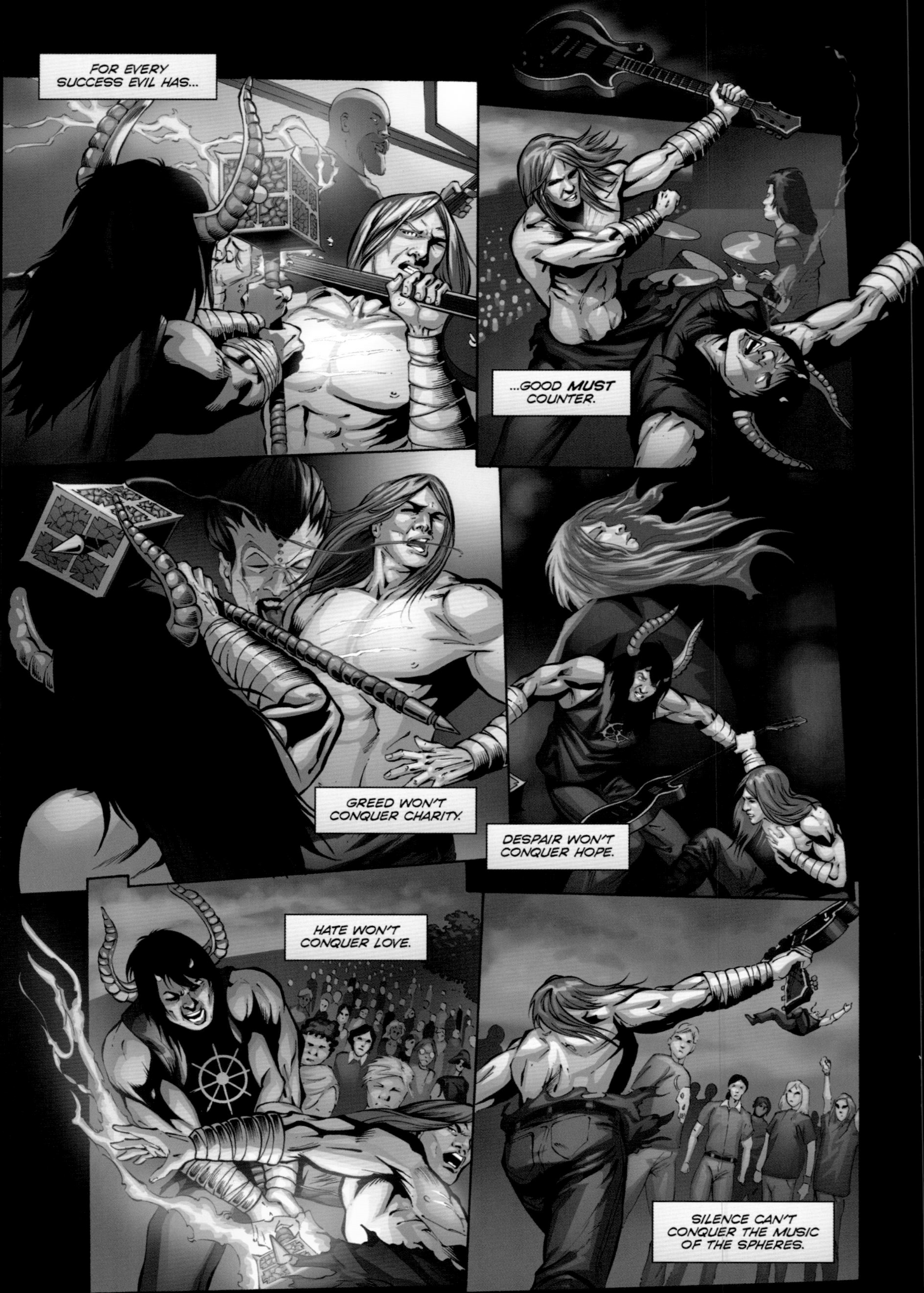
FOR EVERY SUCCESS EVIL HAS...
...GOOD **MUST** COUNTER.
GREED WON'T CONQUER CHARITY.
DESPAIR WON'T CONQUER HOPE.
HATE WON'T CONQUER LOVE.
SILENCE CAN'T CONQUER THE MUSIC OF THE SPHERES.

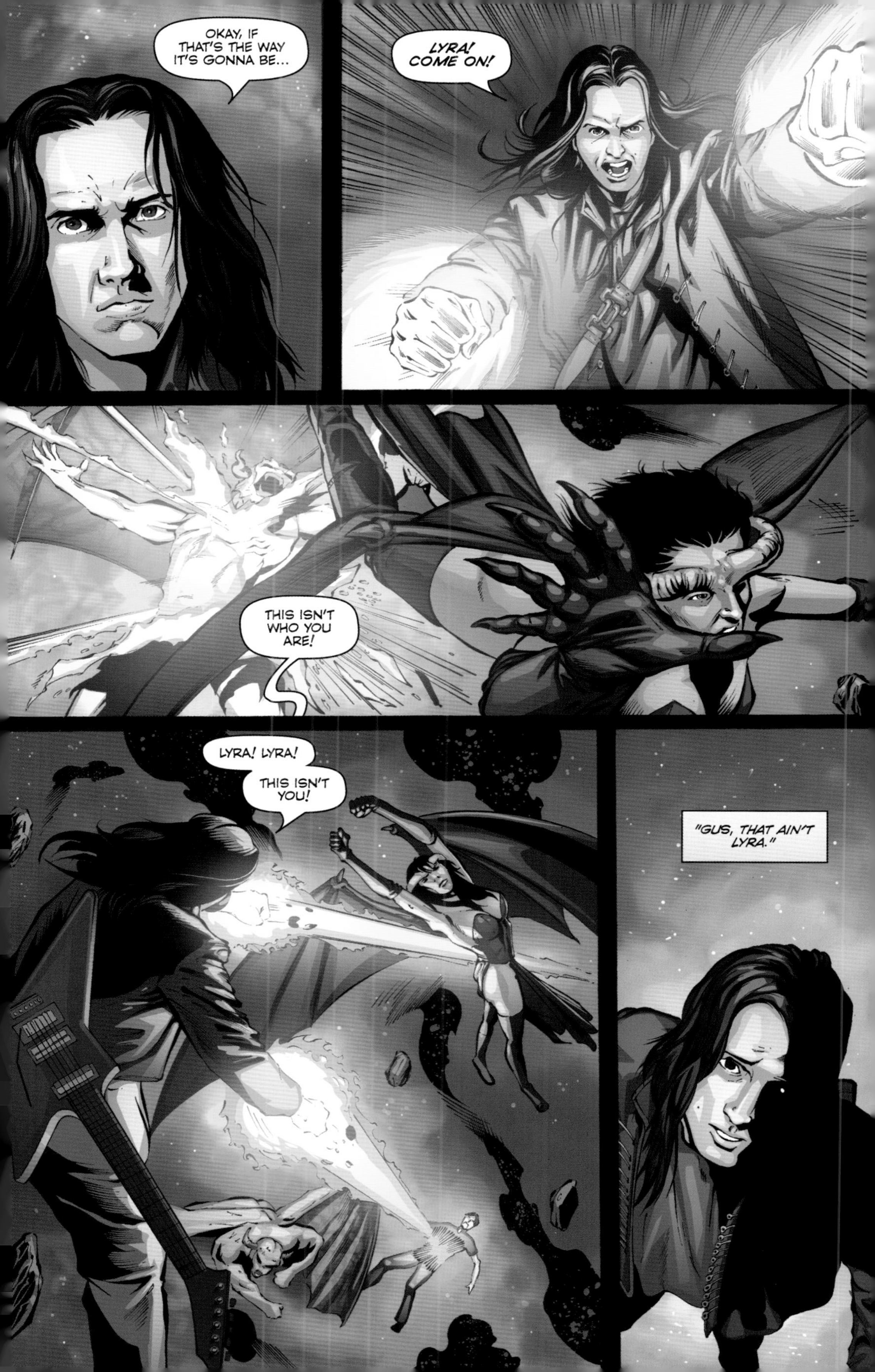
OKAY, IF THAT'S THE WAY IT'S GONNA BE...
LYRA! COME ON!
THIS ISN'T WHO YOU ARE!
LYRA! LYRA!
THIS ISN'T YOU!
"GUS, THAT AIN'T LYRA."

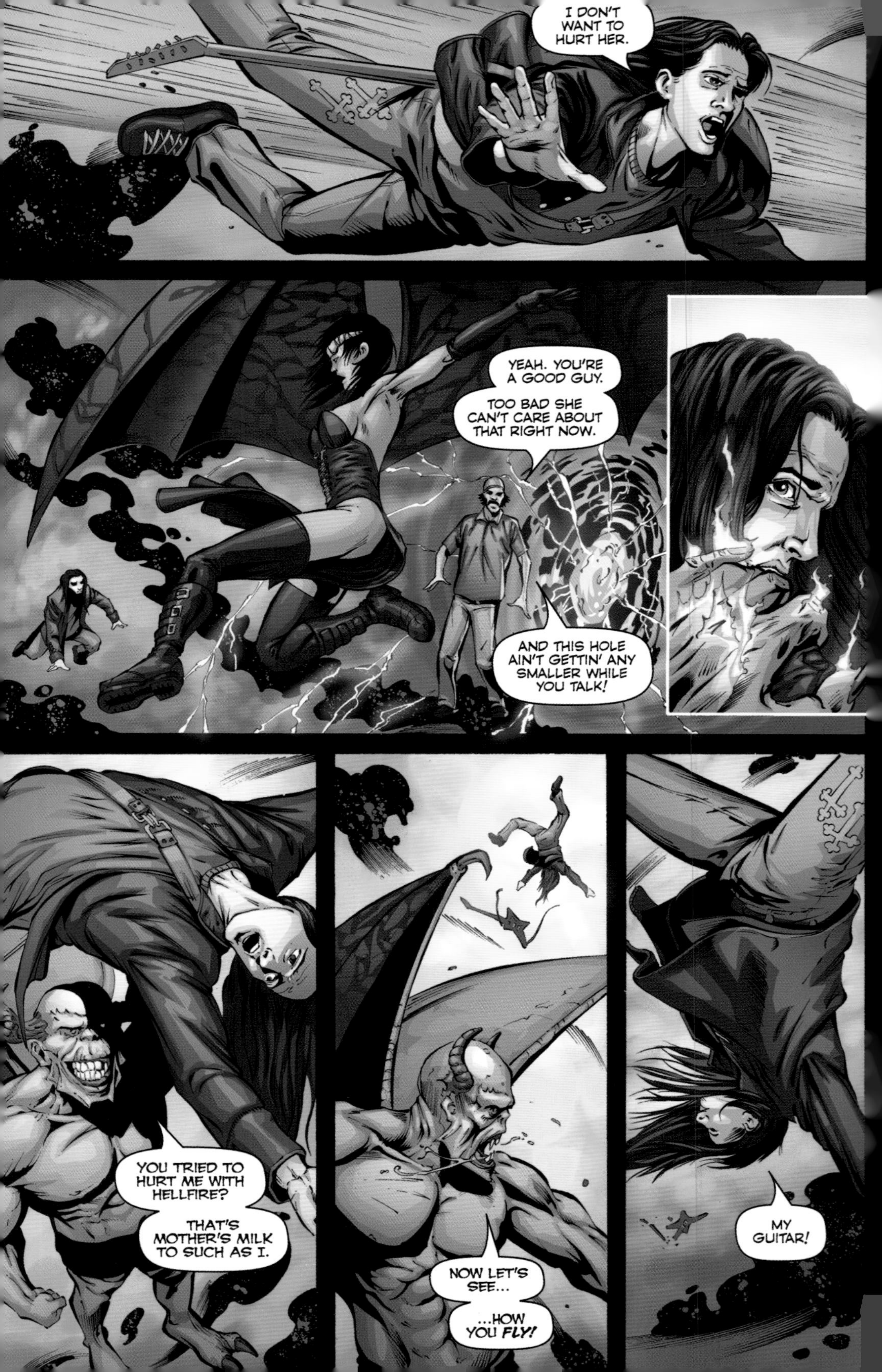

I DON'T WANT TO HURT HER.
YEAH. YOU'RE A GOOD GUY.
TOO BAD SHE CAN'T CARE ABOUT THAT RIGHT NOW.
AND THIS HOLE AIN'T GETTIN' ANY SMALLER WHILE YOU TALK!
YOU TRIED TO HURT ME WITH HELLFIRE?
THAT'S MOTHER'S MILK TO SUCH AS I.
NOW LET'S SEE...
...HOW YOU *FLY!*
MY GUITAR!

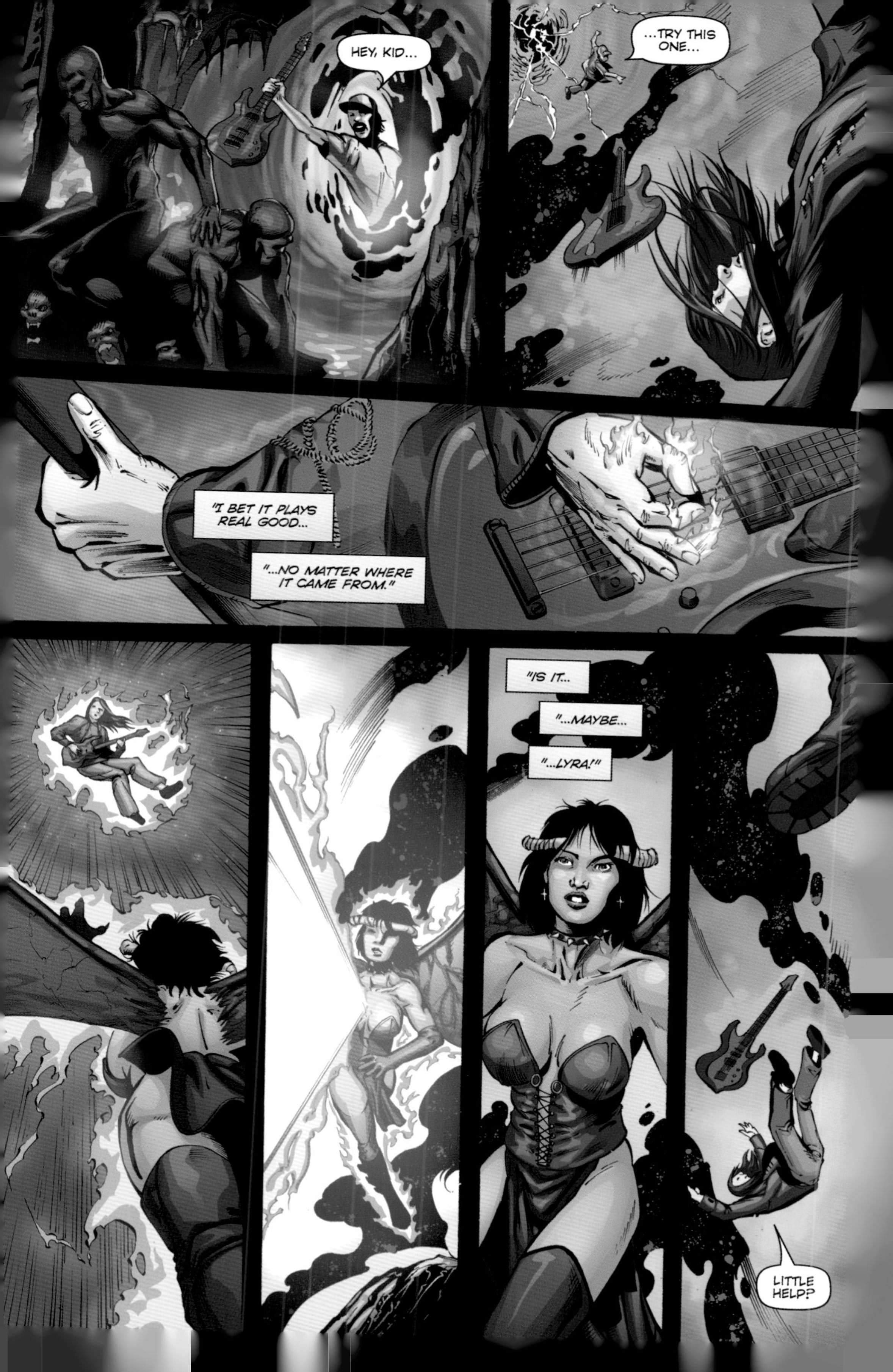
HEY, KID...
...TRY THIS ONE...
"I BET IT PLAYS REAL GOOD...
"...NO MATTER WHERE IT CAME FROM."
"IS IT...
"...MAYBE...
"...LYRA!"
LITTLE HELP?

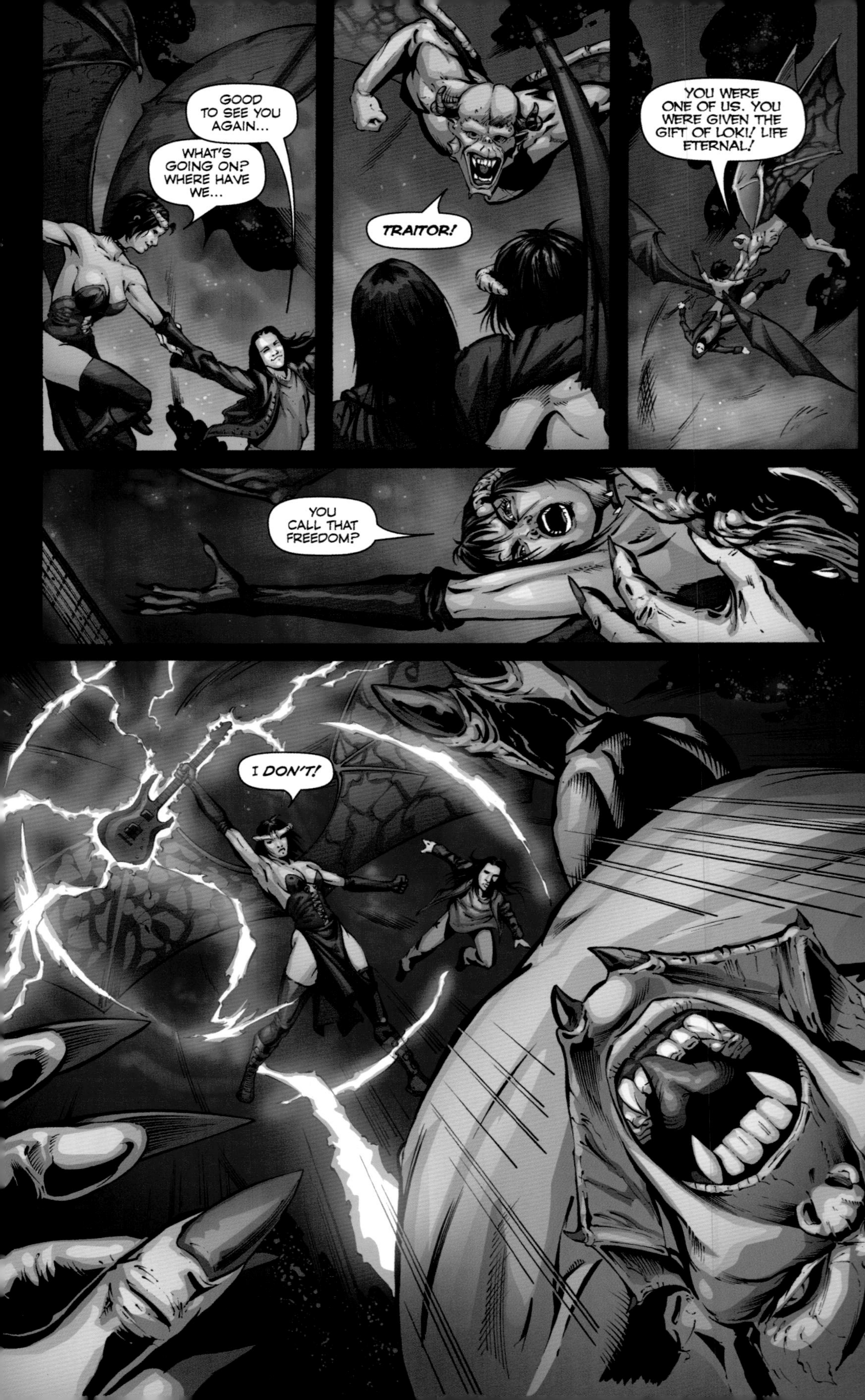
GOOD TO SEE YOU AGAIN...
WHAT'S GOING ON? WHERE HAVE WE...
TRAITOR!
YOU WERE ONE OF US. YOU WERE GIVEN THE GIFT OF LOKI! LIFE ETERNAL!
YOU CALL THAT FREEDOM?
I DON'T!

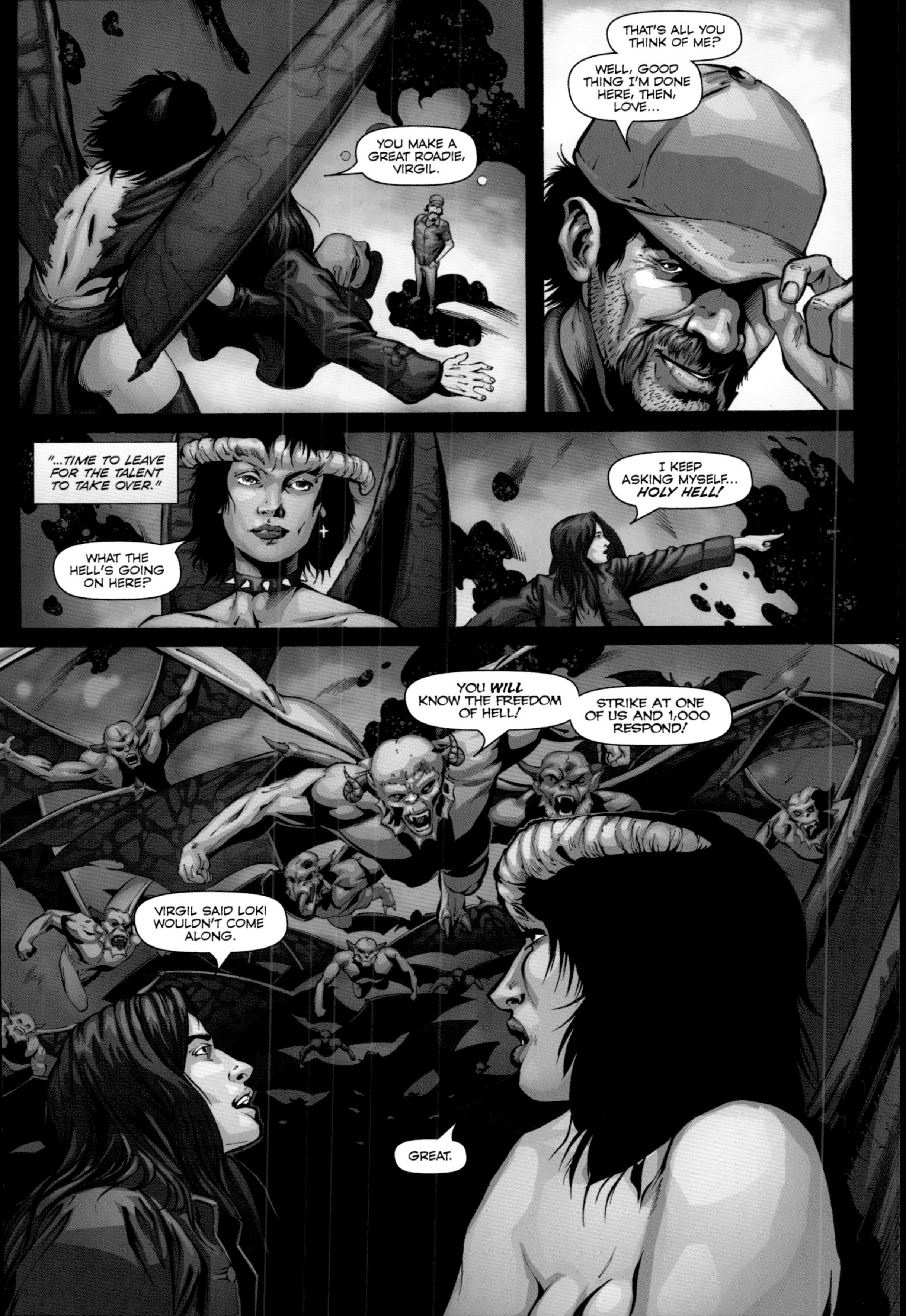
YOU MAKE A GREAT ROADIE, VIRGIL.
THAT'S ALL YOU THINK OF ME?
WELL, GOOD THING I'M DONE HERE, THEN, LOVE...
"...TIME TO LEAVE FOR THE TALENT TO TAKE OVER."
WHAT THE HELL'S GOING ON HERE?
I KEEP ASKING MYSELF... HOLY HELL!
YOU WILL KNOW THE FREEDOM OF HELL!
STRIKE AT ONE OF US AND 1,000 RESPOND!
VIRGIL SAID LOKI WOULDN'T COME ALONG.
GREAT.

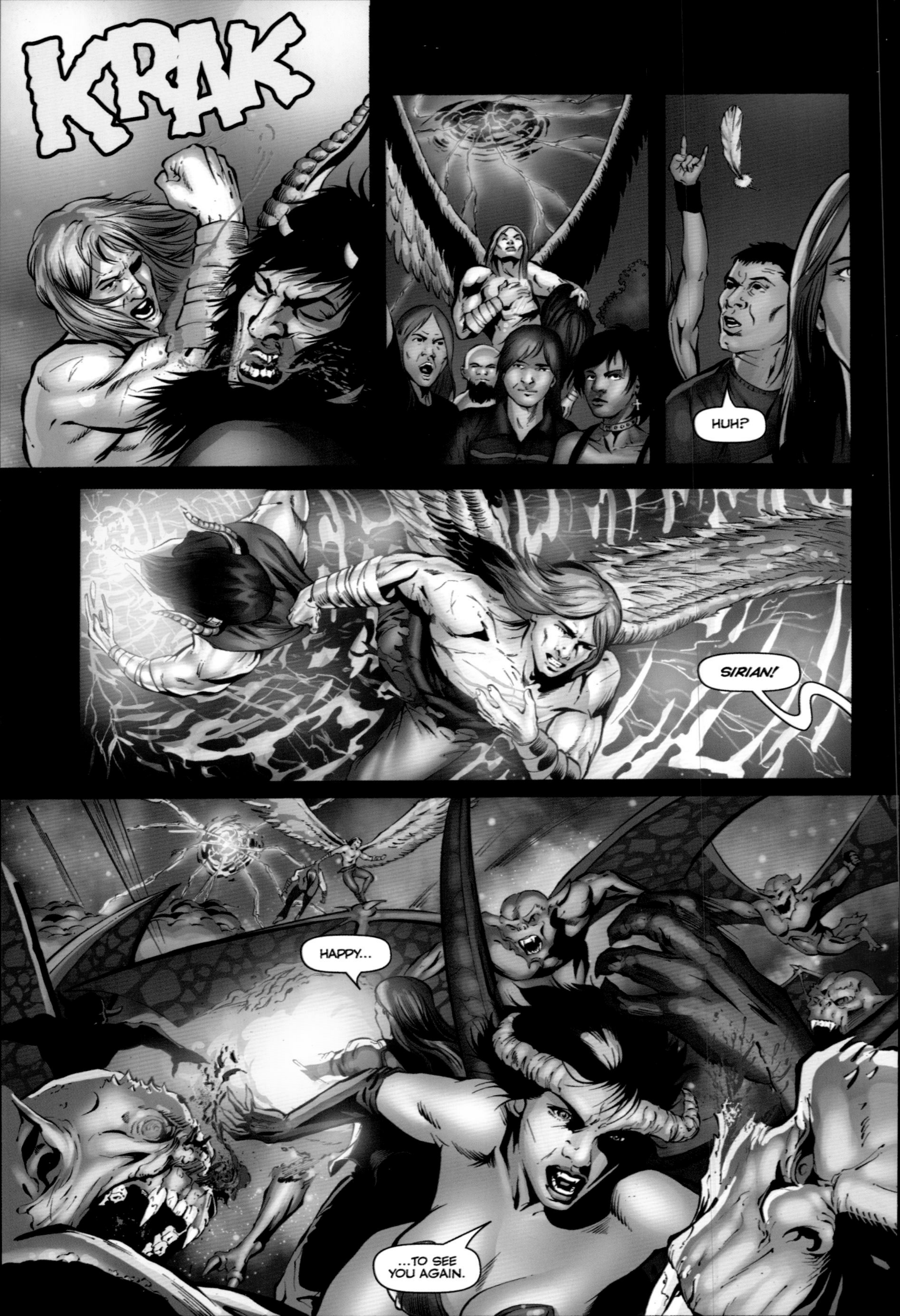
KRAK
HUH?
SIRIAN!
HAPPY...
...TO SEE YOU AGAIN.

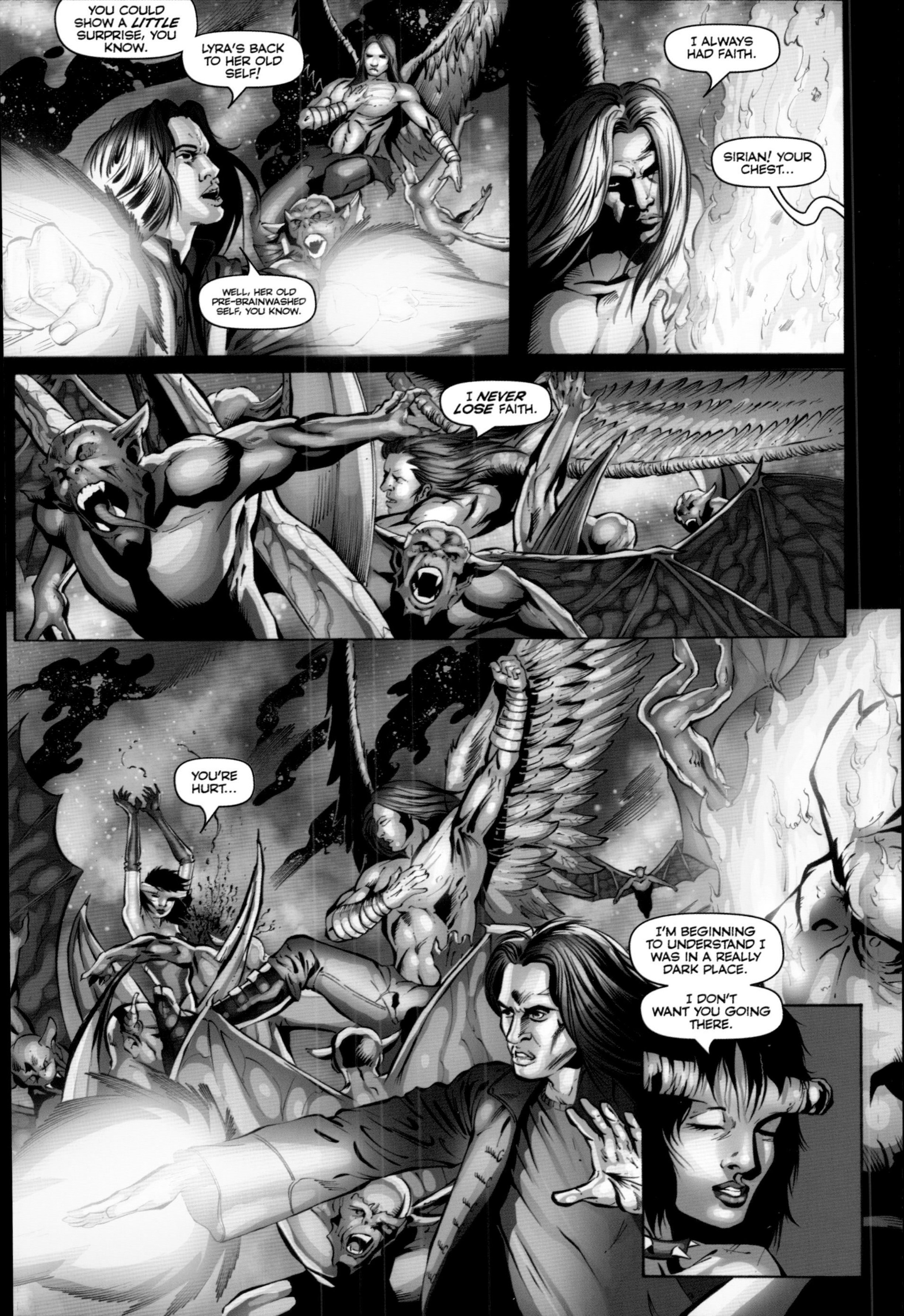
YOU COULD SHOW A LITTLE SURPRISE, YOU KNOW.
LYRA'S BACK TO HER OLD SELF!
WELL, HER OLD PRE-BRAINWASHED SELF, YOU KNOW.
I ALWAYS HAD FAITH.
SIRIAN! YOUR CHEST...
I NEVER LOSE FAITH.
YOU'RE HURT...
I'M BEGINNING TO UNDERSTAND I WAS IN A REALLY DARK PLACE.
I DON'T WANT YOU GOING THERE.

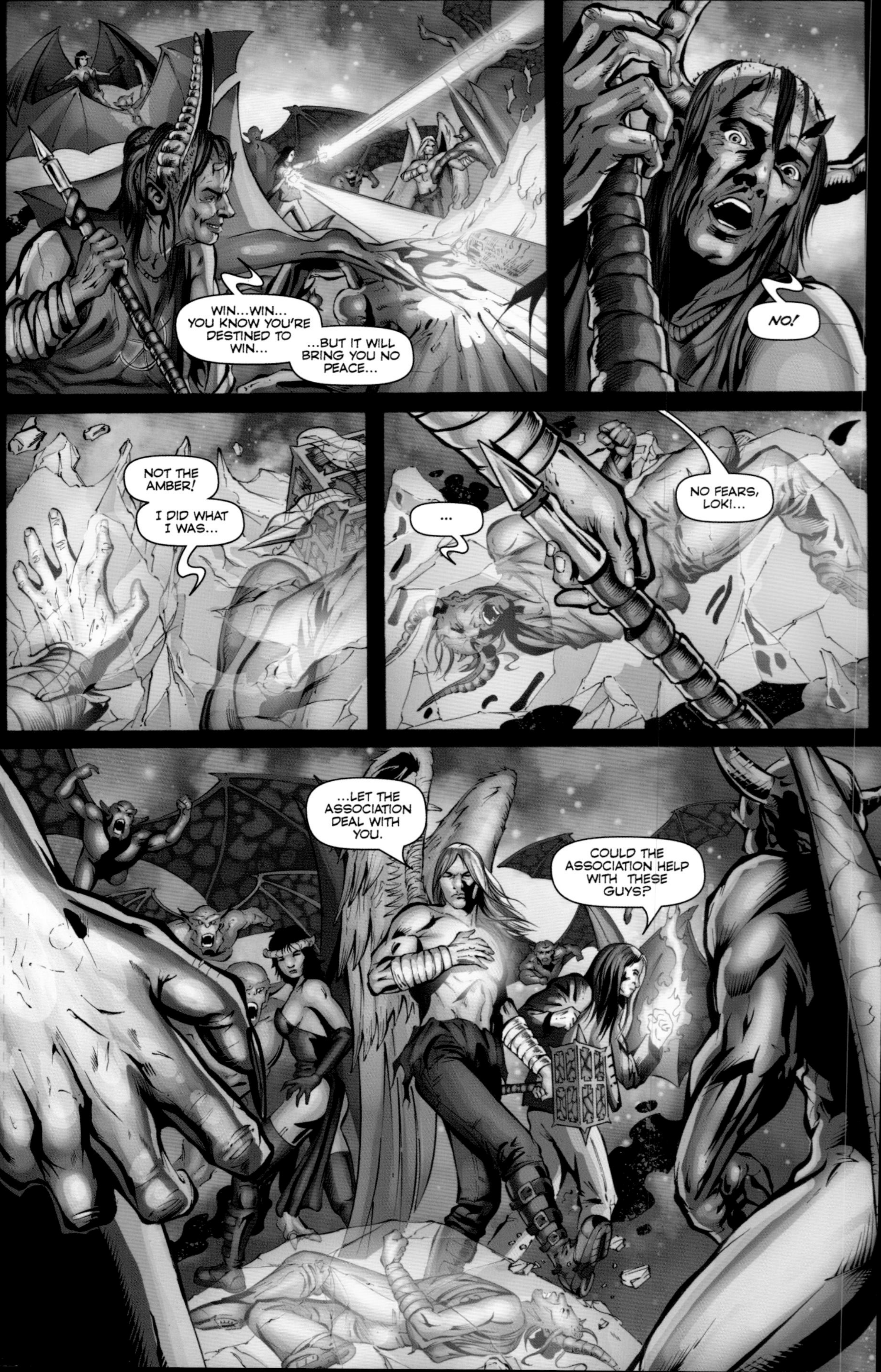

WIN...WIN... YOU KNOW YOU'RE DESTINED TO WIN...
...BUT IT WILL BRING YOU NO PEACE...
NO!
NOT THE AMBER!
I DID WHAT I WAS...
...
NO FEARS, LOKI...
...LET THE ASSOCIATION DEAL WITH YOU.
COULD THE ASSOCIATION HELP WITH THESE GUYS?

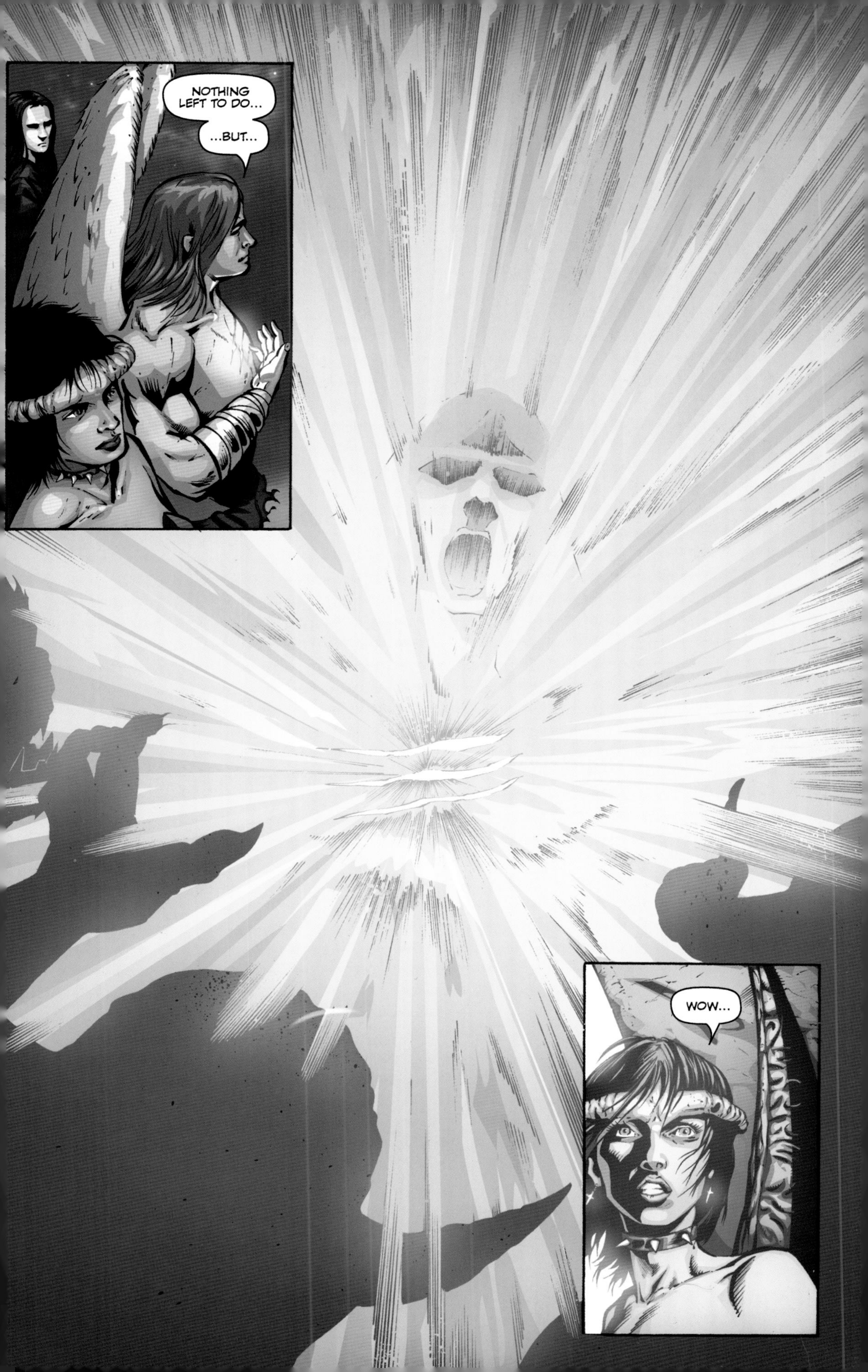
NOTHING LEFT TO DO...
...BUT...
WOW...

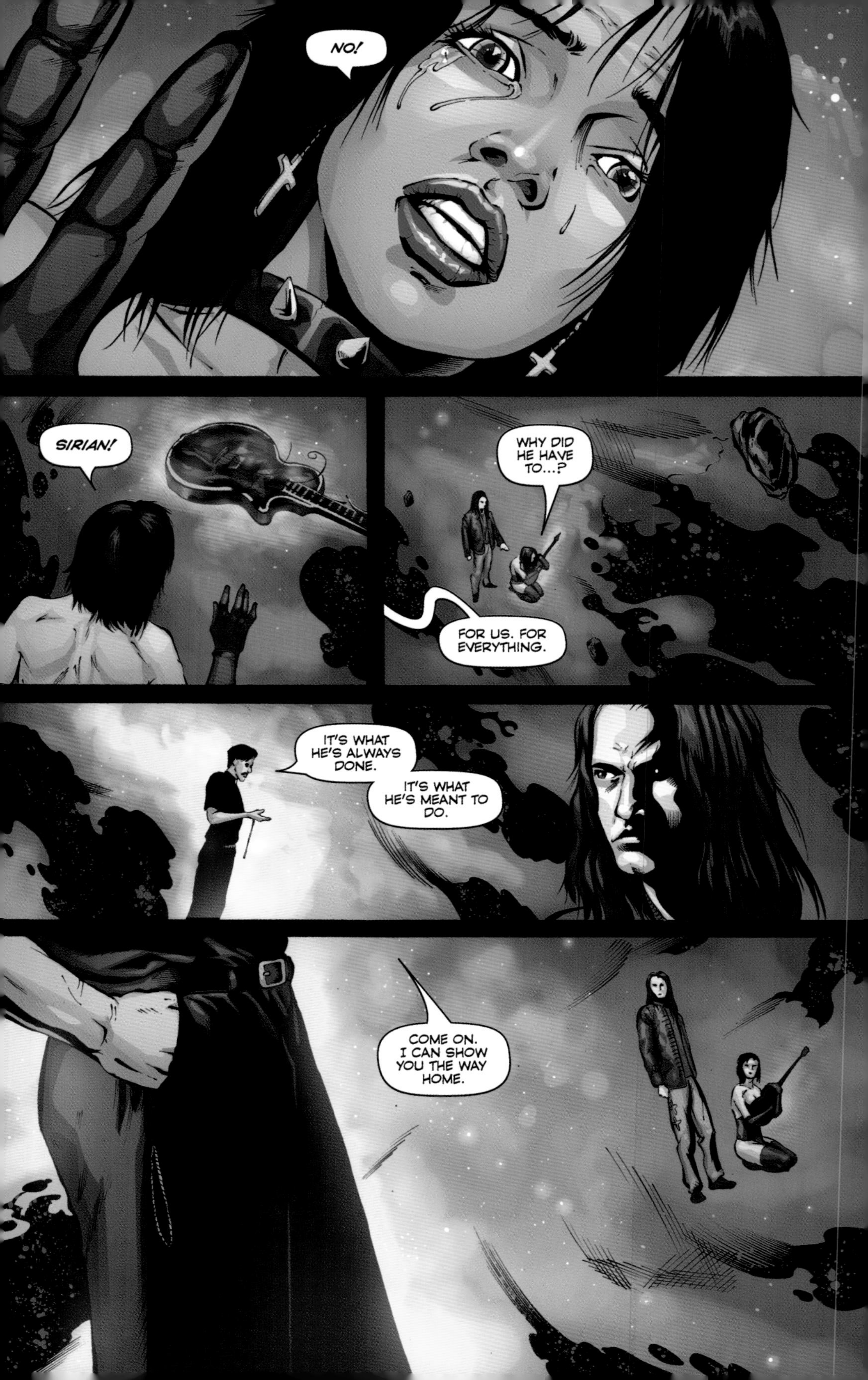
NO!
SIRIAN!
WHY DID HE HAVE TO...?
FOR US. FOR EVERYTHING.
IT'S WHAT HE'S ALWAYS DONE.
IT'S WHAT HE'S MEANT TO DO.
COME ON. I CAN SHOW YOU THE WAY HOME.

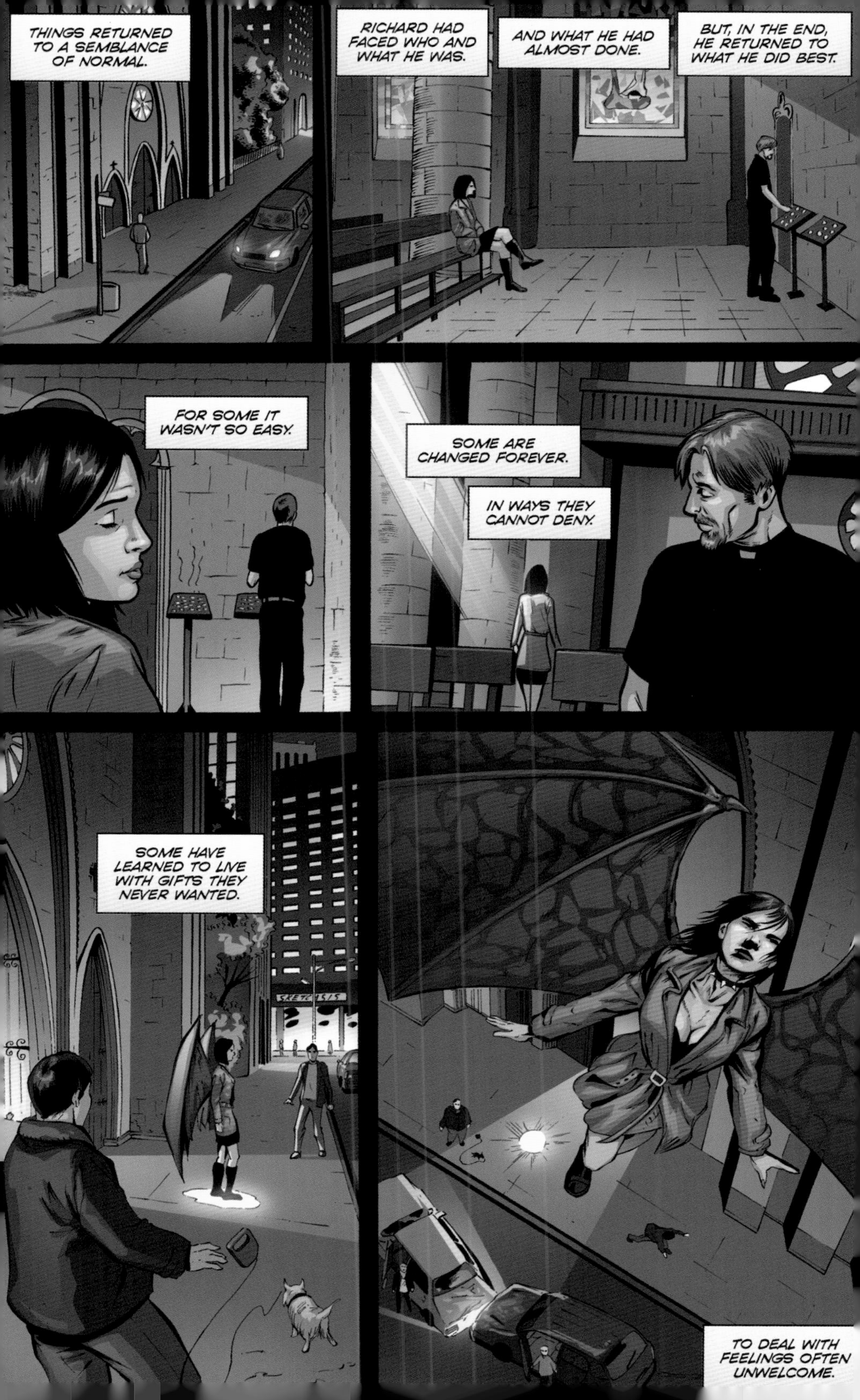
THINGS RETURNED TO A SEMBLANCE OF NORMAL.
RICHARD HAD FACED WHO AND WHAT HE WAS.
AND WHAT HE HAD ALMOST DONE.
BUT, IN THE END, HE RETURNED TO WHAT HE DID BEST.
FOR SOME IT WASN'T SO EASY.
SOME ARE CHANGED FOREVER.
IN WAYS THEY CANNOT DENY.
SOME HAVE LEARNED TO LIVE WITH GIFTS THEY NEVER WANTED.
TO DEAL WITH FEELINGS OFTEN UNWELCOME.

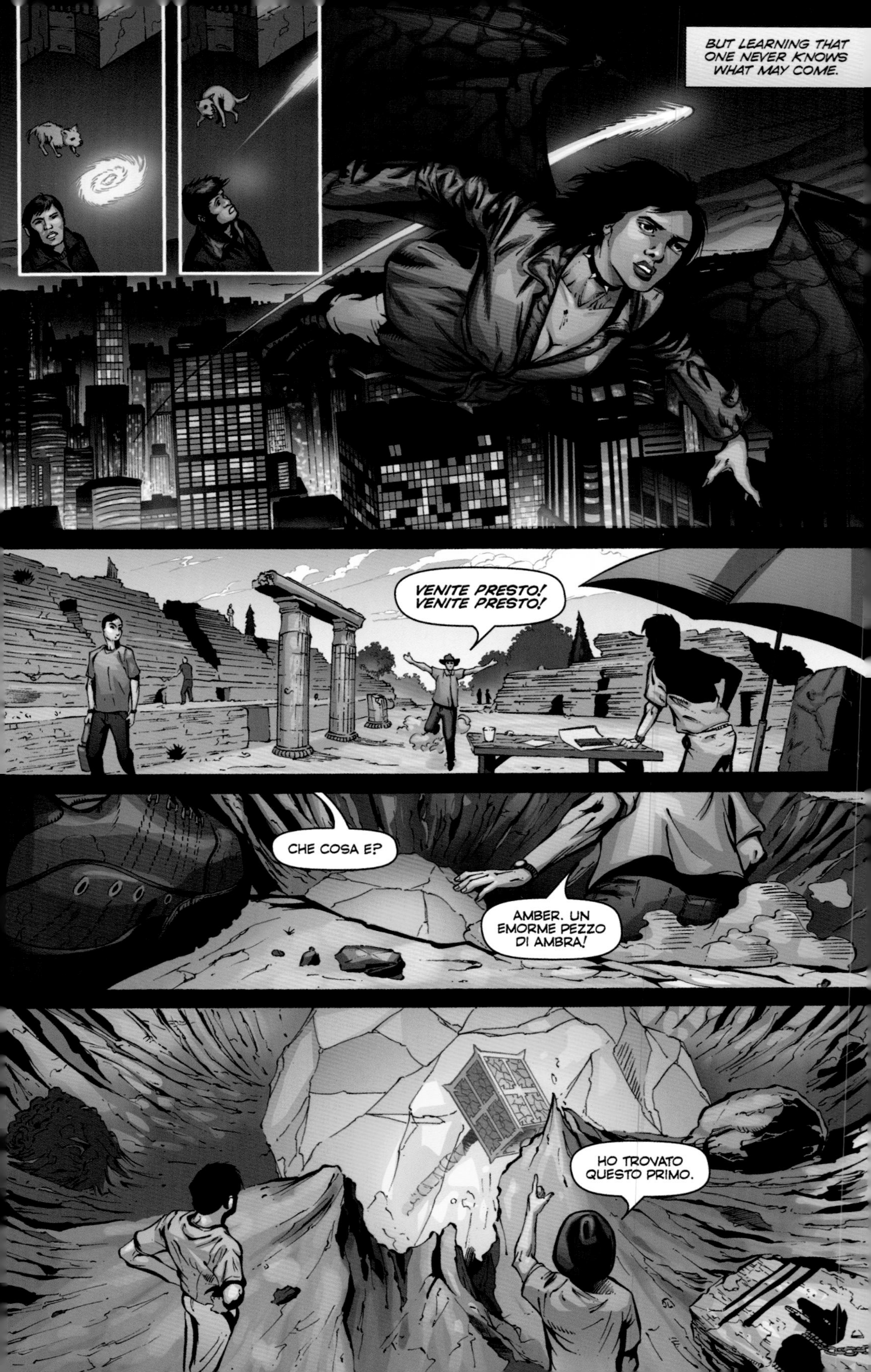
BUT LEARNING THAT ONE NEVER KNOWS WHAT MAY COME.
VENITE PRESTO! VENITE PRESTO!
CHE COSA E?
AMBER. UN EMORME PEZZO DI AMBRA!
HO TROVATO QUESTO PRIMO.

Eternal Descent

CHAPTER THREE:
NOT OF THIS EARTH

Written by
Llexi Leon and **Justin Peniston**
Pencils by
Ivan Fernandez
Inks by
Tony Kordos
Colors by
Javier Tartaglia
Lettering by
Charles Pritchett

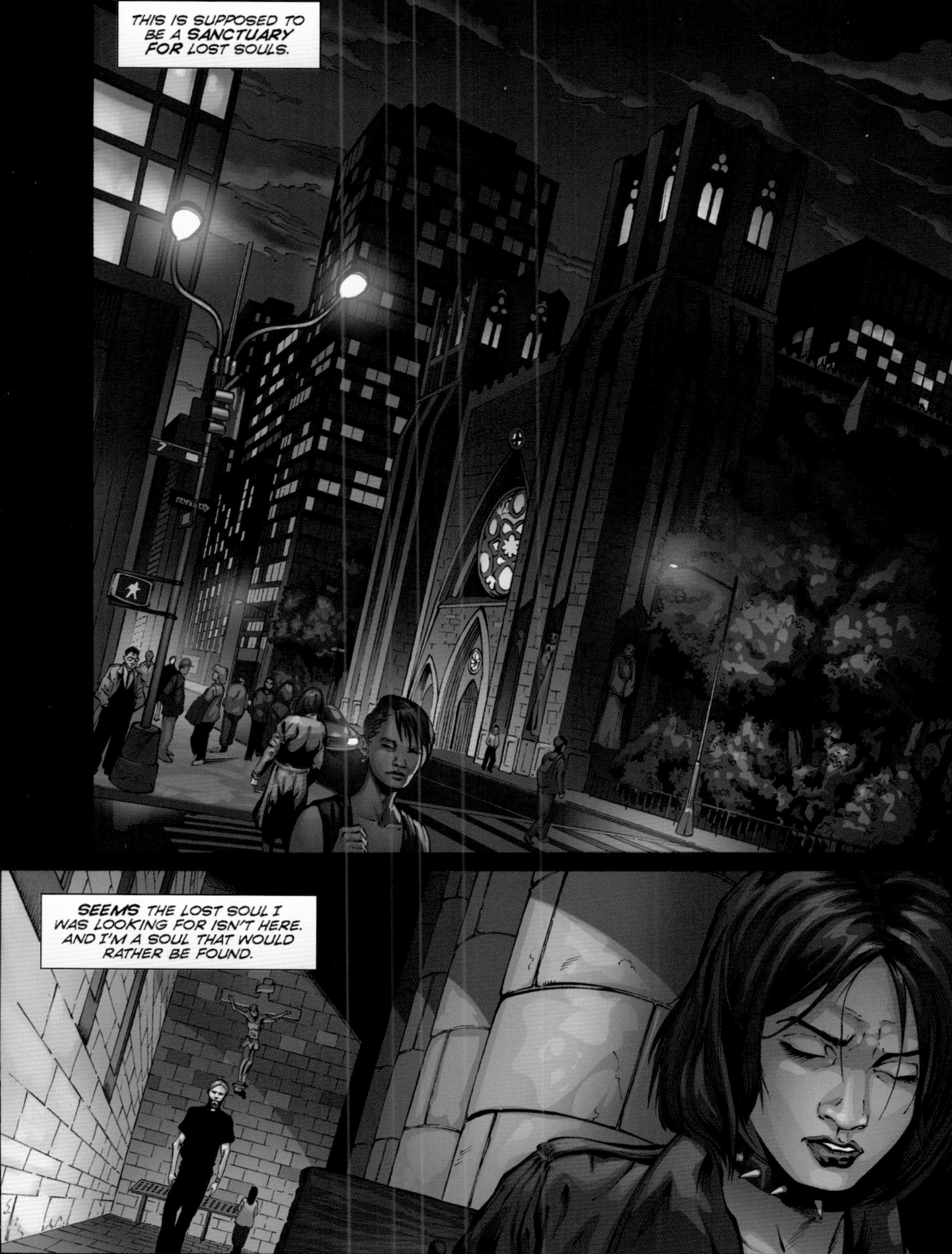
THIS IS SUPPOSED TO BE A SANCTUARY FOR LOST SOULS.
SEEMS THE LOST SOUL I WAS LOOKING FOR ISN'T HERE. AND I'M A SOUL THAT WOULD RATHER BE FOUND.

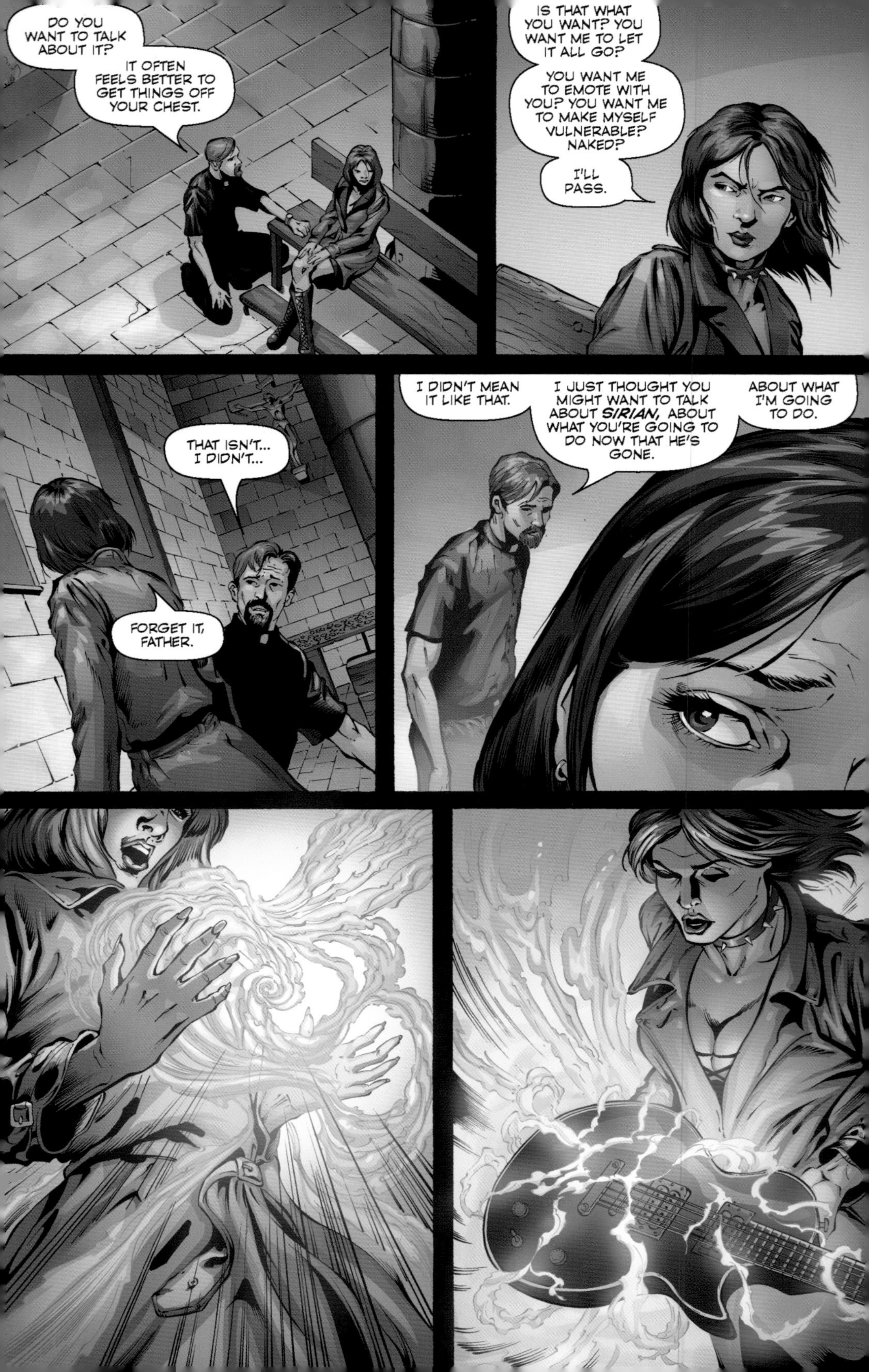
DO YOU WANT TO TALK ABOUT IT?
IT OFTEN FEELS BETTER TO GET THINGS OFF YOUR CHEST.
IS THAT WHAT YOU WANT? YOU WANT ME TO LET IT ALL GO?
YOU WANT ME TO EMOTE WITH YOU? YOU WANT ME TO MAKE MYSELF VULNERABLE? NAKED?
I'LL PASS.
THAT ISN'T... I DIDN'T...
FORGET IT, FATHER.
I DIDN'T MEAN IT LIKE THAT.
I JUST THOUGHT YOU MIGHT WANT TO TALK ABOUT SIRIAN, ABOUT WHAT YOU'RE GOING TO DO NOW THAT HE'S GONE.
ABOUT WHAT I'M GOING TO DO.

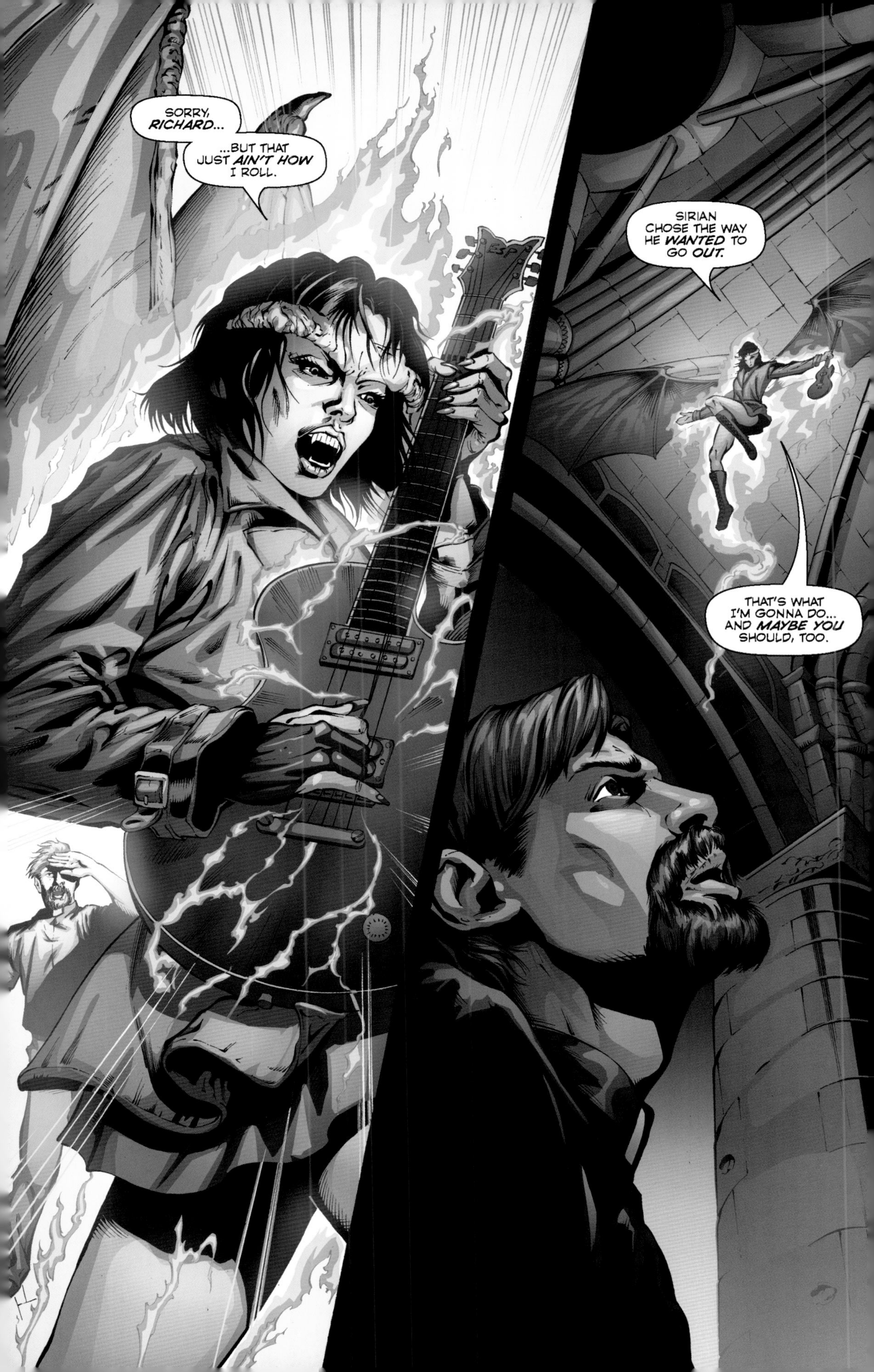
SORRY, RICHARD...
...BUT THAT JUST AIN'T HOW I ROLL.
SIRIAN CHOSE THE WAY HE WANTED TO GO OUT.
THAT'S WHAT I'M GONNA DO... AND MAYBE YOU SHOULD, TOO.

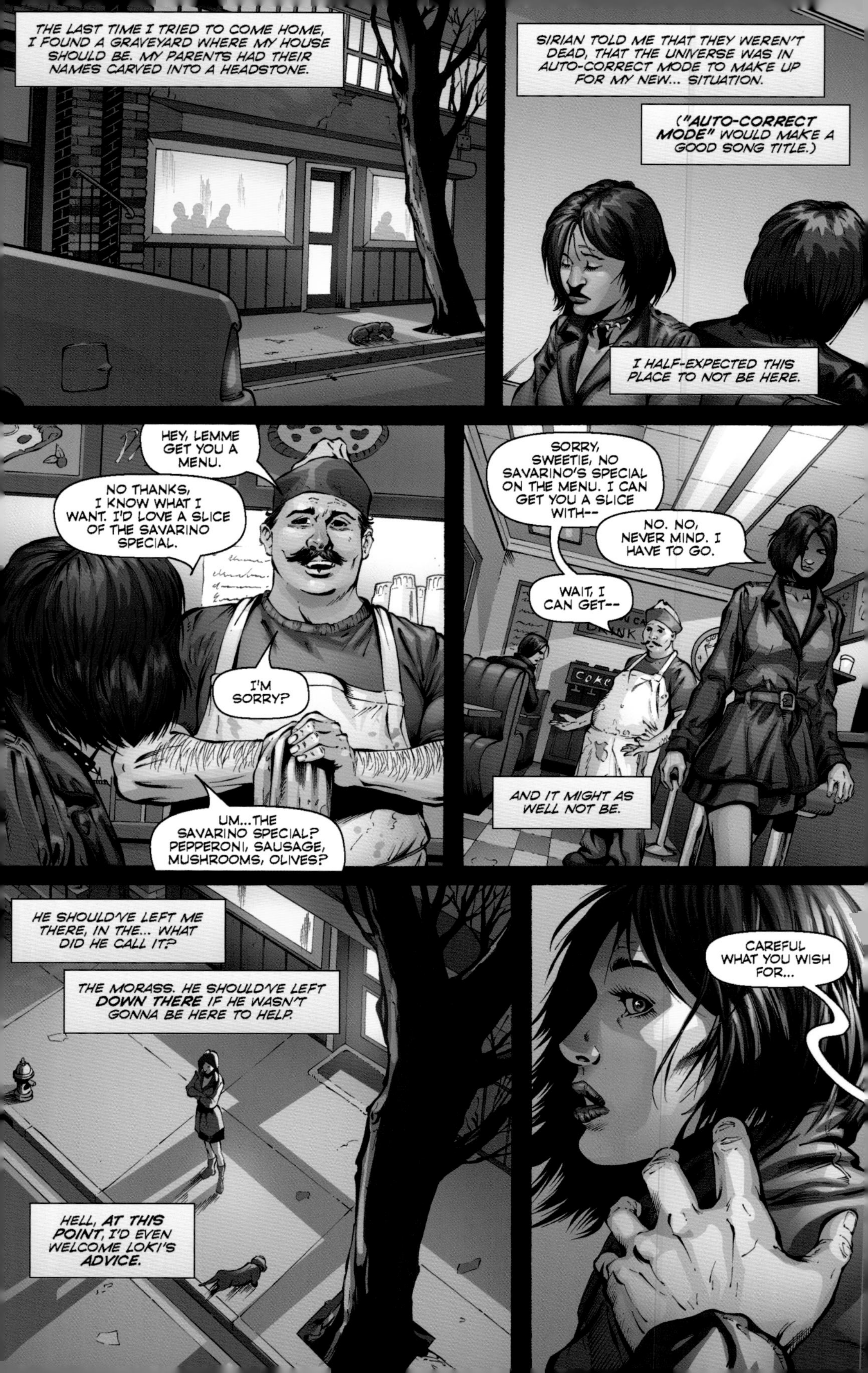
THE LAST TIME I TRIED TO COME HOME, I FOUND A GRAVEYARD WHERE MY HOUSE SHOULD BE. MY PARENTS HAD THEIR NAMES CARVED INTO A HEADSTONE.
SIRIAN TOLD ME THAT THEY WEREN'T DEAD, THAT THE UNIVERSE WAS IN AUTO-CORRECT MODE TO MAKE UP FOR MY NEW... SITUATION.
("AUTO-CORRECT MODE" WOULD MAKE A GOOD SONG TITLE.)
I HALF-EXPECTED THIS PLACE TO NOT BE HERE.
HEY, LEMME GET YOU A MENU.
NO THANKS, I KNOW WHAT I WANT. I'D LOVE A SLICE OF THE SAVARINO SPECIAL.
I'M SORRY?
UM...THE SAVARINO SPECIAL? PEPPERONI, SAUSAGE, MUSHROOMS, OLIVES?
SORRY, SWEETIE, NO SAVARINO'S SPECIAL ON THE MENU. I CAN GET YOU A SLICE WITH--
NO. NO, NEVER MIND. I HAVE TO GO.
WAIT, I CAN GET--
AND IT MIGHT AS WELL NOT BE.
HE SHOULD'VE LEFT ME THERE, IN THE... WHAT DID HE CALL IT?
THE MORASS. HE SHOULD'VE LEFT DOWN THERE IF HE WASN'T GONNA BE HERE TO HELP.
HELL, AT THIS POINT, I'D EVEN WELCOME LOKI'S ADVICE.
CAREFUL WHAT YOU WISH FOR...

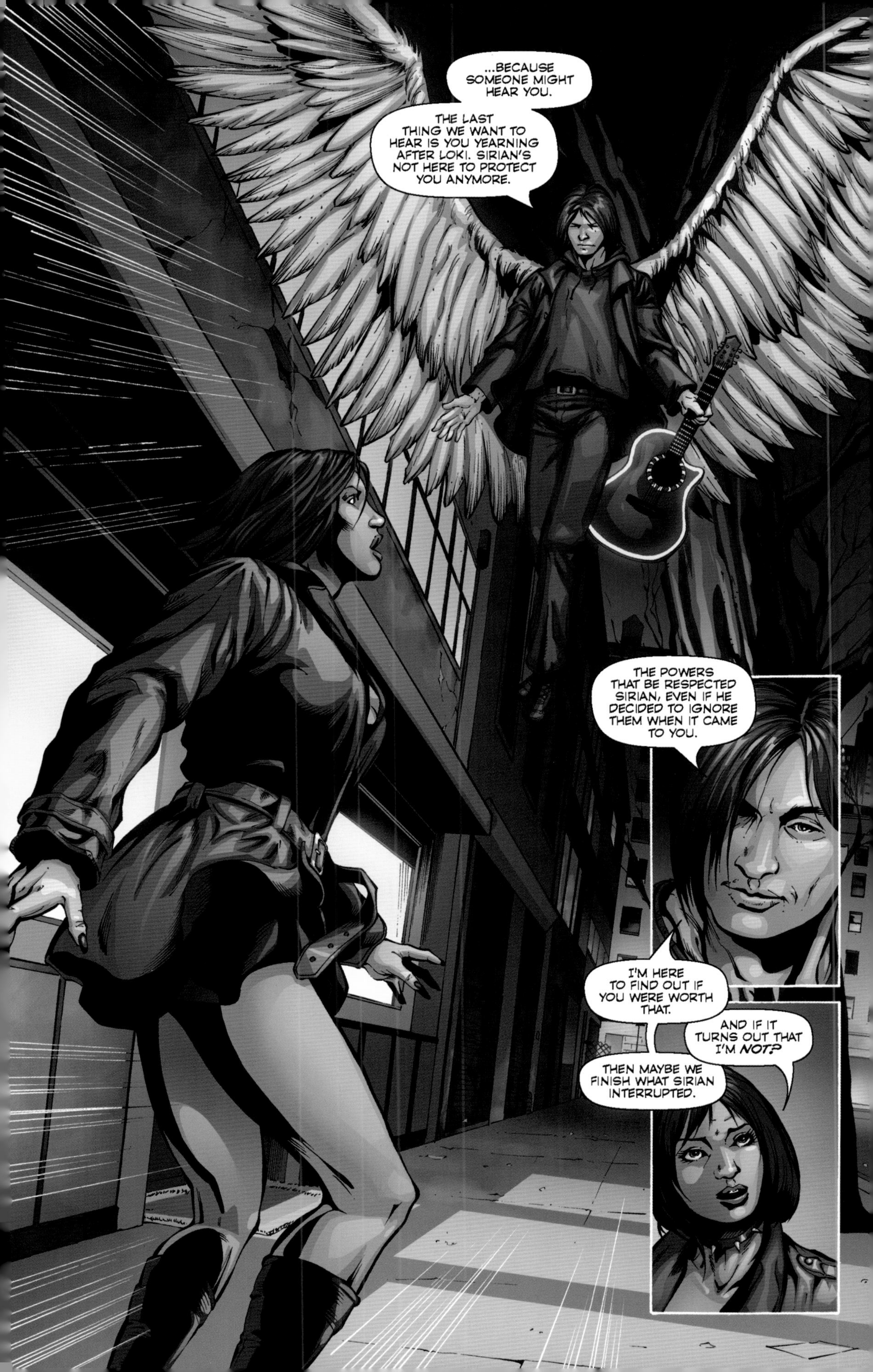
...BECAUSE SOMEONE MIGHT HEAR YOU.
THE LAST THING WE WANT TO HEAR IS YOU YEARNING AFTER LOKI. SIRIAN'S NOT HERE TO PROTECT YOU ANYMORE.
THE POWERS THAT BE RESPECTED SIRIAN, EVEN IF HE DECIDED TO IGNORE THEM WHEN IT CAME TO YOU.
I'M HERE TO FIND OUT IF YOU WERE WORTH THAT.
AND IF IT TURNS OUT THAT I'M *NOT?*
THEN MAYBE WE FINISH WHAT SIRIAN INTERRUPTED.

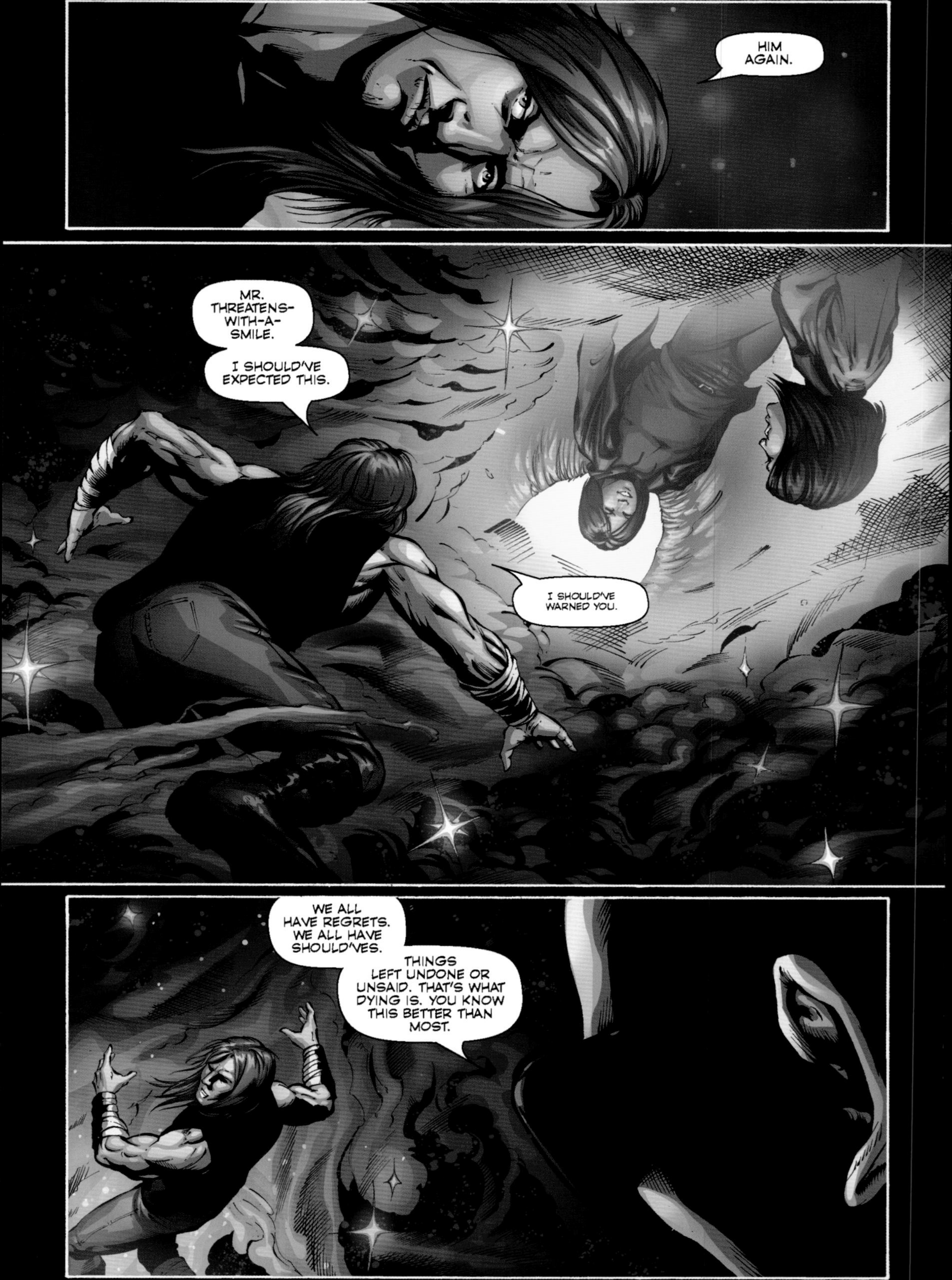
HIM AGAIN.
MR. THREATENS-WITH-A-SMILE.
I SHOULD'VE EXPECTED THIS.
I SHOULD'VE WARNED YOU.
WE ALL HAVE REGRETS. WE ALL HAVE SHOULD'VES.
THINGS LEFT UNDONE OR UNSAID. THAT'S WHAT DYING IS. YOU KNOW THIS BETTER THAN MOST.

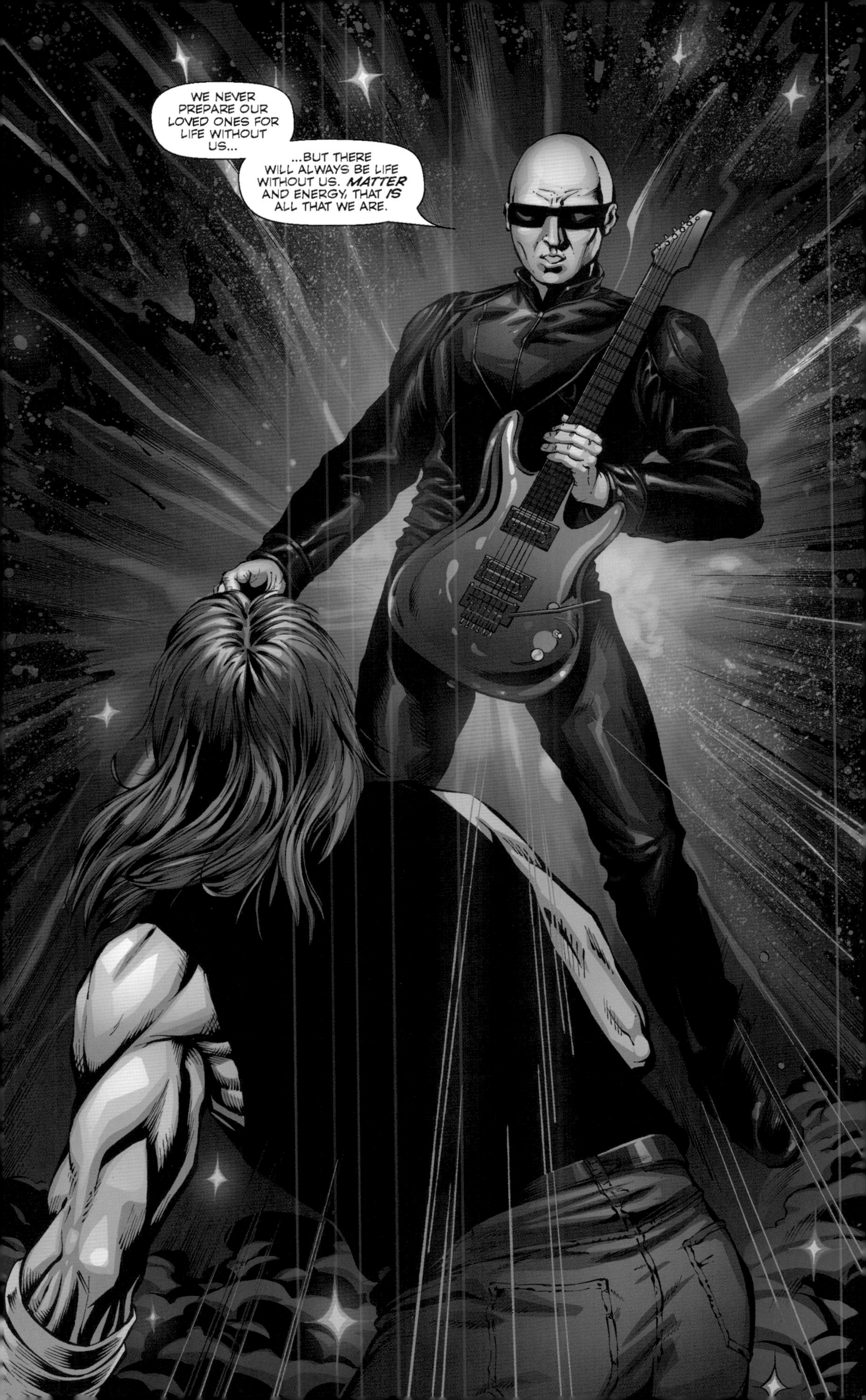
WE NEVER PREPARE OUR LOVED ONES FOR LIFE WITHOUT US...
...BUT THERE WILL ALWAYS BE LIFE WITHOUT US. MATTER AND ENERGY, THAT IS ALL THAT WE ARE.

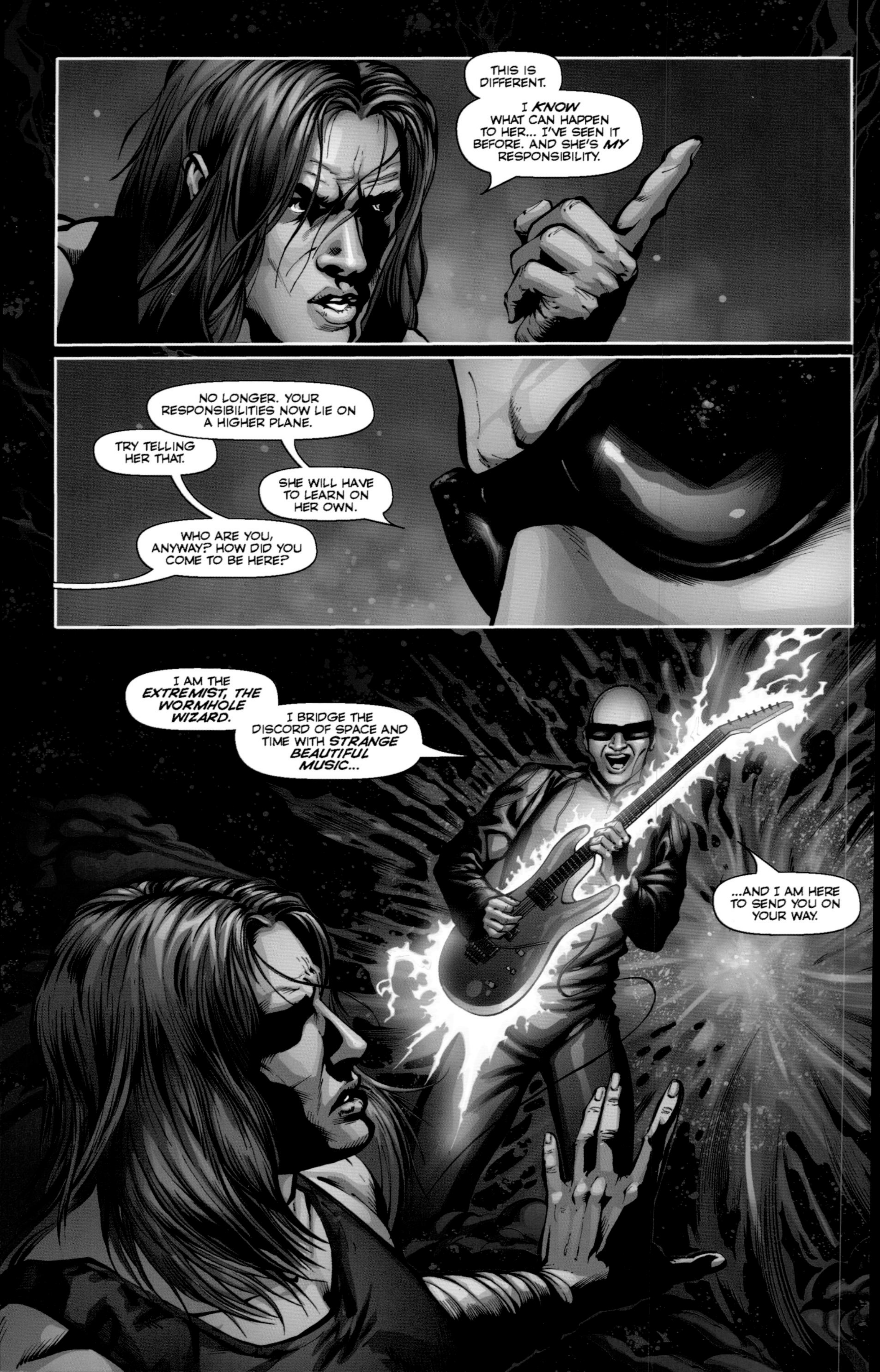
THIS IS DIFFERENT.
I KNOW WHAT CAN HAPPEN TO HER... I'VE SEEN IT BEFORE. AND SHE'S MY RESPONSIBILITY.
NO LONGER. YOUR RESPONSIBILITIES NOW LIE ON A HIGHER PLANE.
TRY TELLING HER THAT.
SHE WILL HAVE TO LEARN ON HER OWN.
WHO ARE YOU, ANYWAY? HOW DID YOU COME TO BE HERE?
I AM THE EXTREMIST, THE WORMHOLE WIZARD.
I BRIDGE THE DISCORD OF SPACE AND TIME WITH STRANGE BEAUTIFUL MUSIC...
...AND I AM HERE TO SEND YOU ON YOUR WAY.

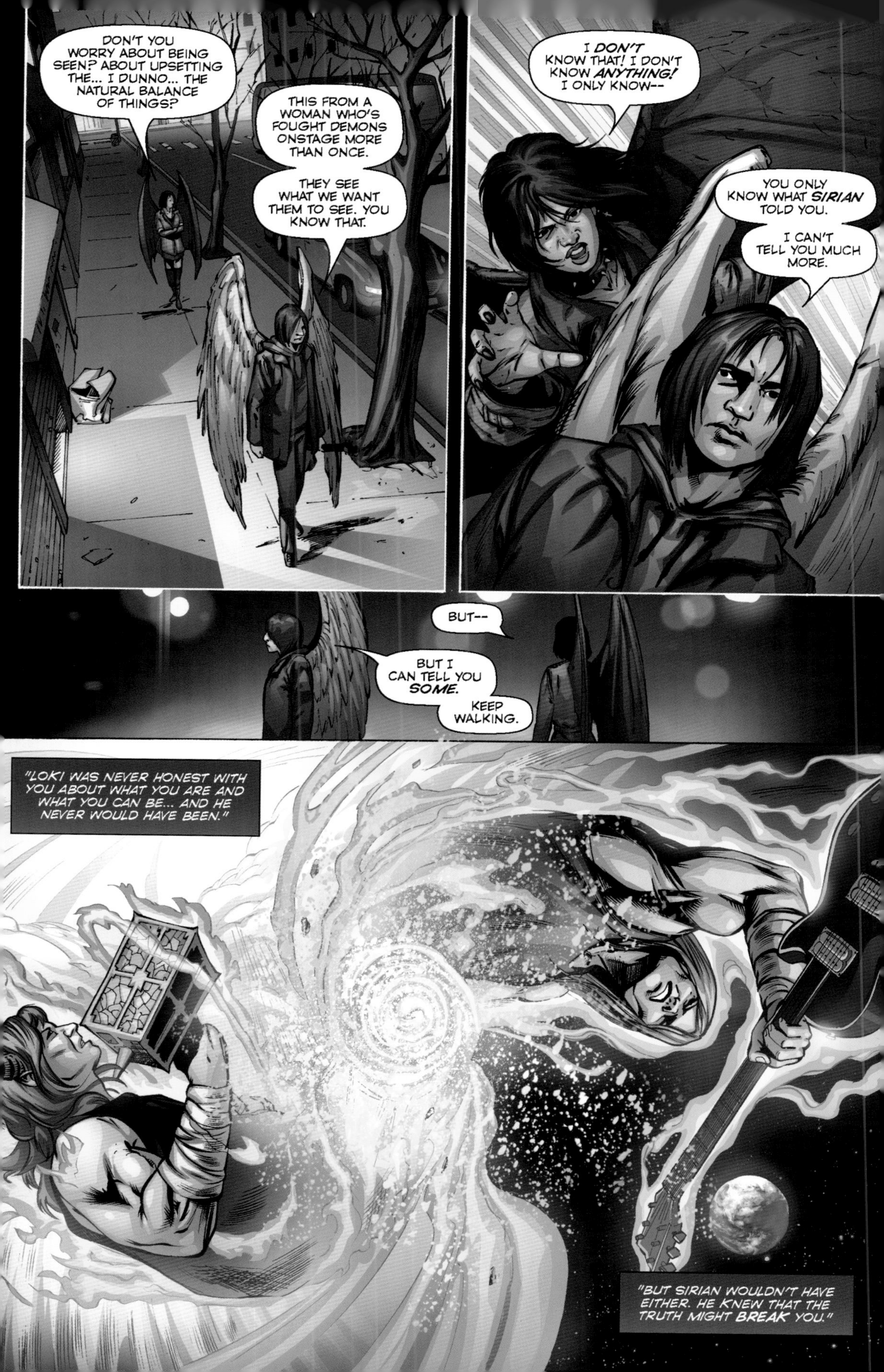
DON'T YOU WORRY ABOUT BEING SEEN? ABOUT UPSETTING THE... I DUNNO... THE NATURAL BALANCE OF THINGS?
THIS FROM A WOMAN WHO'S FOUGHT DEMONS ONSTAGE MORE THAN ONCE.
THEY SEE WHAT WE WANT THEM TO SEE. YOU KNOW THAT.
I DON'T KNOW THAT! I DON'T KNOW ANYTHING! I ONLY KNOW--
YOU ONLY KNOW WHAT SIRIAN TOLD YOU.
I CAN'T TELL YOU MUCH MORE.
BUT--
BUT I CAN TELL YOU SOME.
KEEP WALKING.
"LOKI WAS NEVER HONEST WITH YOU ABOUT WHAT YOU ARE AND WHAT YOU CAN BE... AND HE NEVER WOULD HAVE BEEN."
"BUT SIRIAN WOULDN'T HAVE EITHER. HE KNEW THAT THE TRUTH MIGHT BREAK YOU."

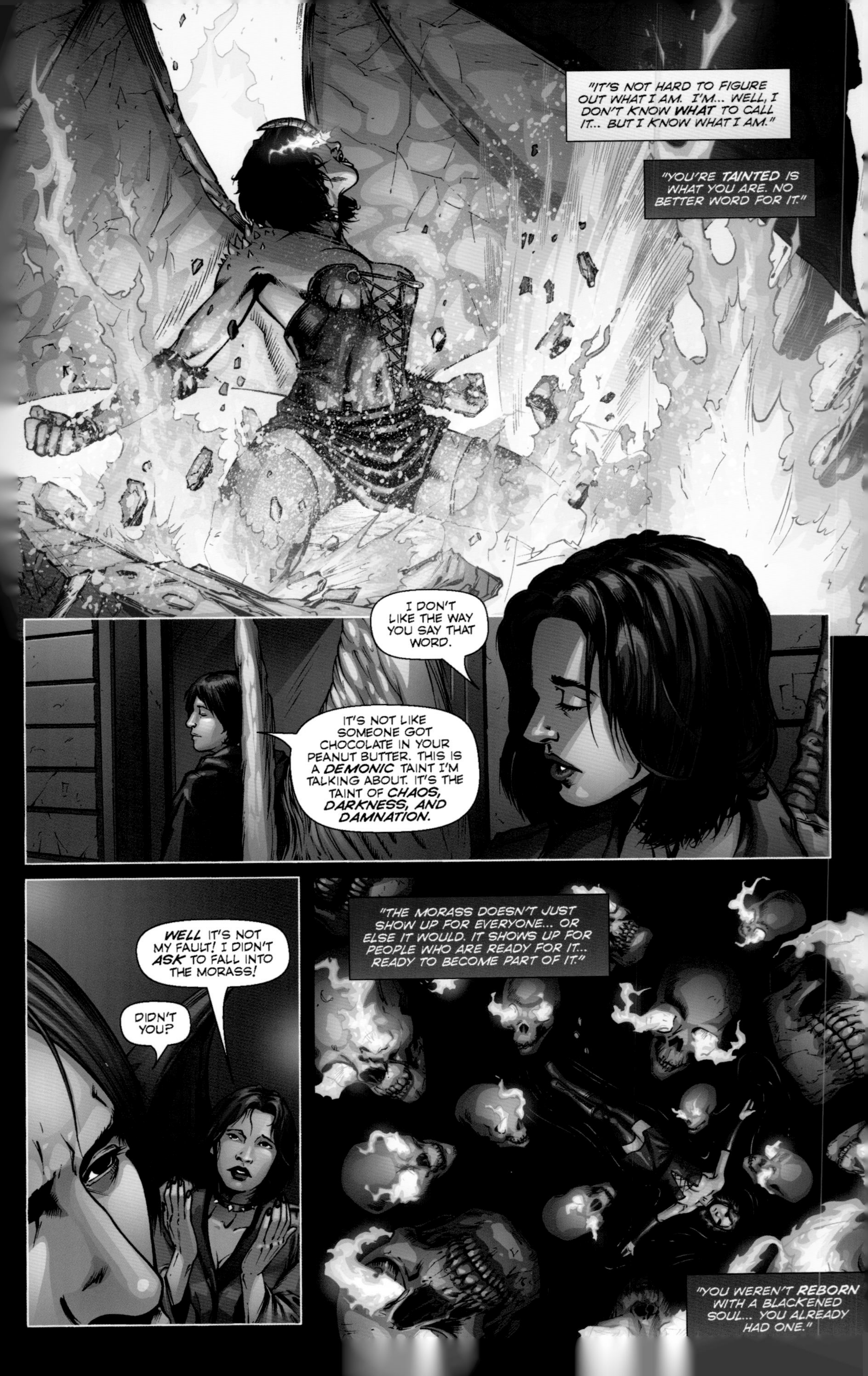
"IT'S NOT HARD TO FIGURE OUT WHAT I AM. I'M... WELL, I DON'T KNOW WHAT TO CALL IT... BUT I KNOW WHAT I AM."
"YOU'RE TAINTED IS WHAT YOU ARE. NO BETTER WORD FOR IT."
I DON'T LIKE THE WAY YOU SAY THAT WORD.
IT'S NOT LIKE SOMEONE GOT CHOCOLATE IN YOUR PEANUT BUTTER. THIS IS A DEMONIC TAINT I'M TALKING ABOUT. IT'S THE TAINT OF CHAOS, DARKNESS, AND DAMNATION.
WELL IT'S NOT MY FAULT! I DIDN'T ASK TO FALL INTO THE MORASS!
DIDN'T YOU?
"THE MORASS DOESN'T JUST SHOW UP FOR EVERYONE... OR ELSE IT WOULD. IT SHOWS UP FOR PEOPLE WHO ARE READY FOR IT... READY TO BECOME PART OF IT."
"YOU WEREN'T REBORN WITH A BLACKENED SOUL... YOU ALREADY HAD ONE."

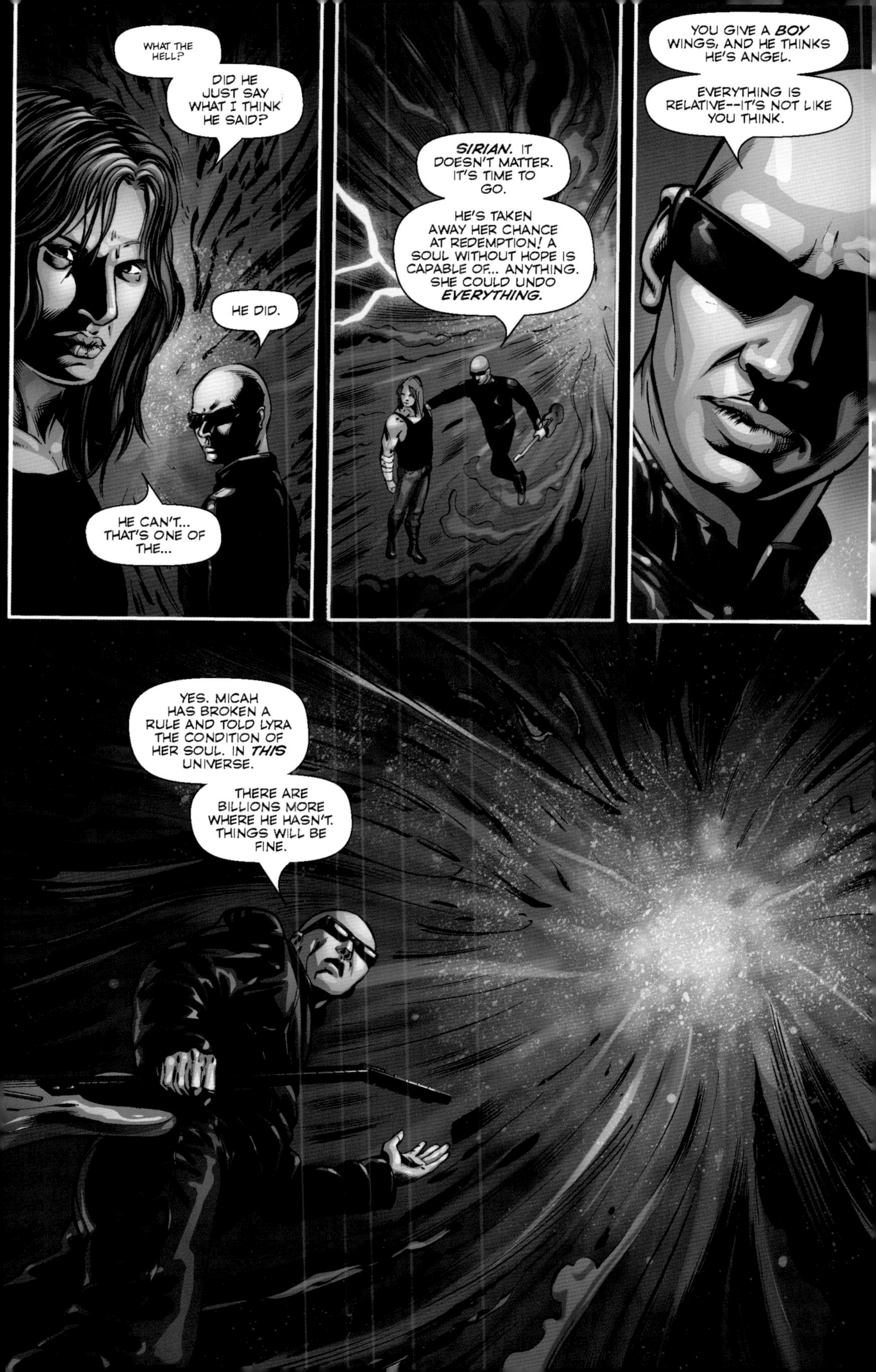

WHAT THE HELL?
DID HE JUST SAY WHAT I THINK HE SAID?
HE DID.
HE CAN'T... THAT'S ONE OF THE...
SIRIAN. IT DOESN'T MATTER. IT'S TIME TO GO.
HE'S TAKEN AWAY HER CHANCE AT REDEMPTION! A SOUL WITHOUT HOPE IS CAPABLE OF... ANYTHING. SHE COULD UNDO EVERYTHING.
YOU GIVE A BOY WINGS, AND HE THINKS HE'S ANGEL.
EVERYTHING IS RELATIVE--IT'S NOT LIKE YOU THINK.
YES. MICAH HAS BROKEN A RULE AND TOLD LYRA THE CONDITION OF HER SOUL. IN THIS UNIVERSE.
THERE ARE BILLIONS MORE WHERE HE HASN'T. THINGS WILL BE FINE.

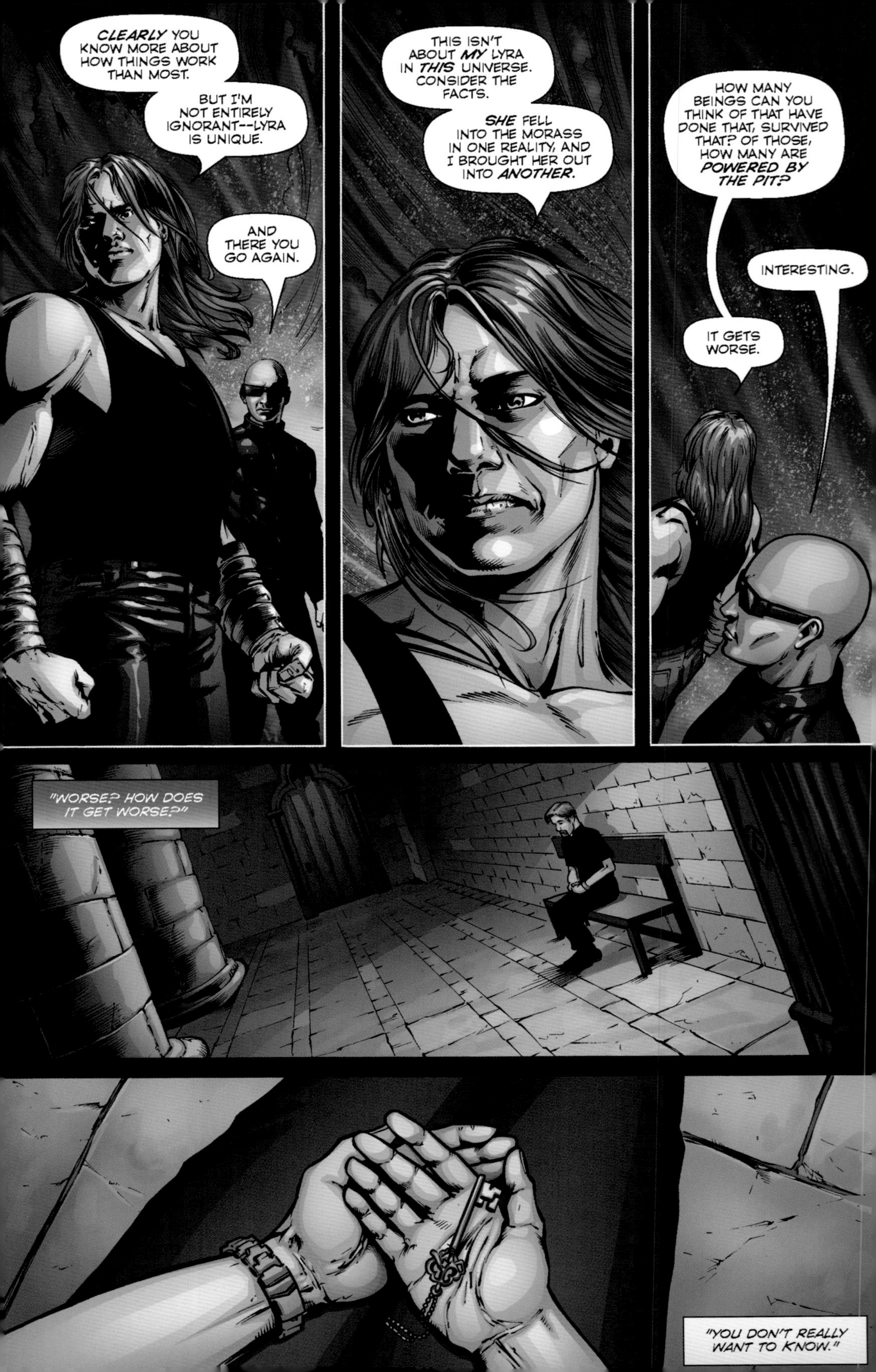
CLEARLY YOU KNOW MORE ABOUT HOW THINGS WORK THAN MOST.
BUT I'M NOT ENTIRELY IGNORANT--LYRA IS UNIQUE.
AND THERE YOU GO AGAIN.
THIS ISN'T ABOUT MY LYRA IN THIS UNIVERSE. CONSIDER THE FACTS.
SHE FELL INTO THE MORASS IN ONE REALITY, AND I BROUGHT HER OUT INTO ANOTHER.
HOW MANY BEINGS CAN YOU THINK OF THAT HAVE DONE THAT, SURVIVED THAT? OF THOSE, HOW MANY ARE POWERED BY THE PIT?
INTERESTING.
IT GETS WORSE.
"WORSE? HOW DOES IT GET WORSE?"
"YOU DON'T REALLY WANT TO KNOW."

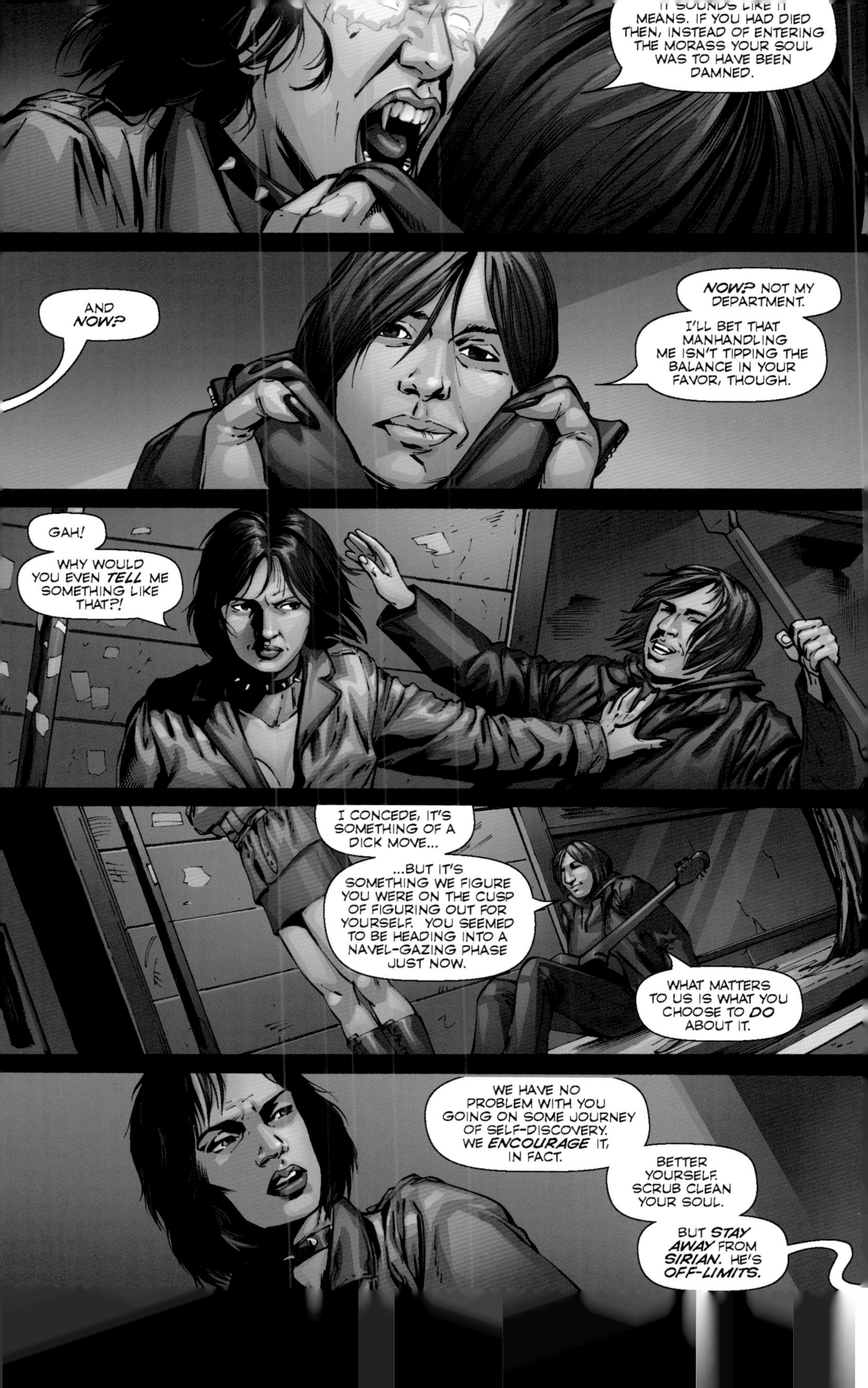
IT SOUNDS LIKE IT MEANS. IF YOU HAD DIED THEN, INSTEAD OF ENTERING THE MORASS YOUR SOUL WAS TO HAVE BEEN DAMNED.
AND *NOW?*
NOW? NOT MY DEPARTMENT.
I'LL BET THAT MANHANDLING ME ISN'T TIPPING THE BALANCE IN YOUR FAVOR, THOUGH.
GAH!
WHY WOULD YOU EVEN *TELL* ME SOMETHING LIKE THAT?!
I CONCEDE, IT'S SOMETHING OF A DICK MOVE...
...BUT IT'S SOMETHING WE FIGURE YOU WERE ON THE CUSP OF FIGURING OUT FOR YOURSELF. YOU SEEMED TO BE HEADING INTO A NAVEL-GAZING PHASE JUST NOW.
WHAT MATTERS TO US IS WHAT YOU CHOOSE TO *DO* ABOUT IT.
WE HAVE NO PROBLEM WITH YOU GOING ON SOME JOURNEY OF SELF-DISCOVERY. WE *ENCOURAGE* IT, IN FACT.
BETTER YOURSELF. SCRUB CLEAN YOUR SOUL.
BUT *STAY AWAY* FROM *SIRIAN*. HE'S *OFF-LIMITS*.

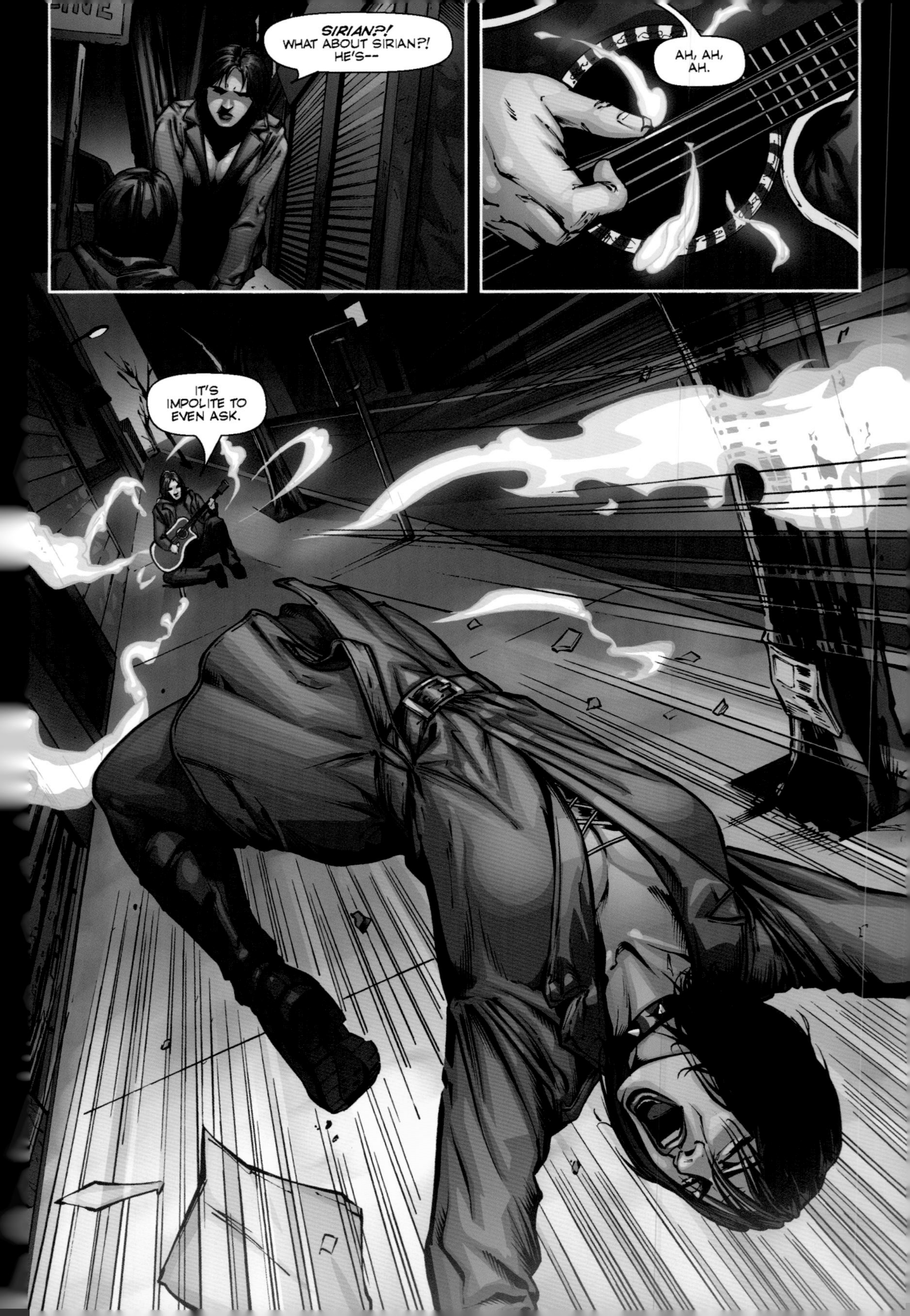
SIRIAN?! WHAT ABOUT SIRIAN?! HE'S--
AH, AH, AH.
IT'S IMPOLITE TO EVEN ASK.

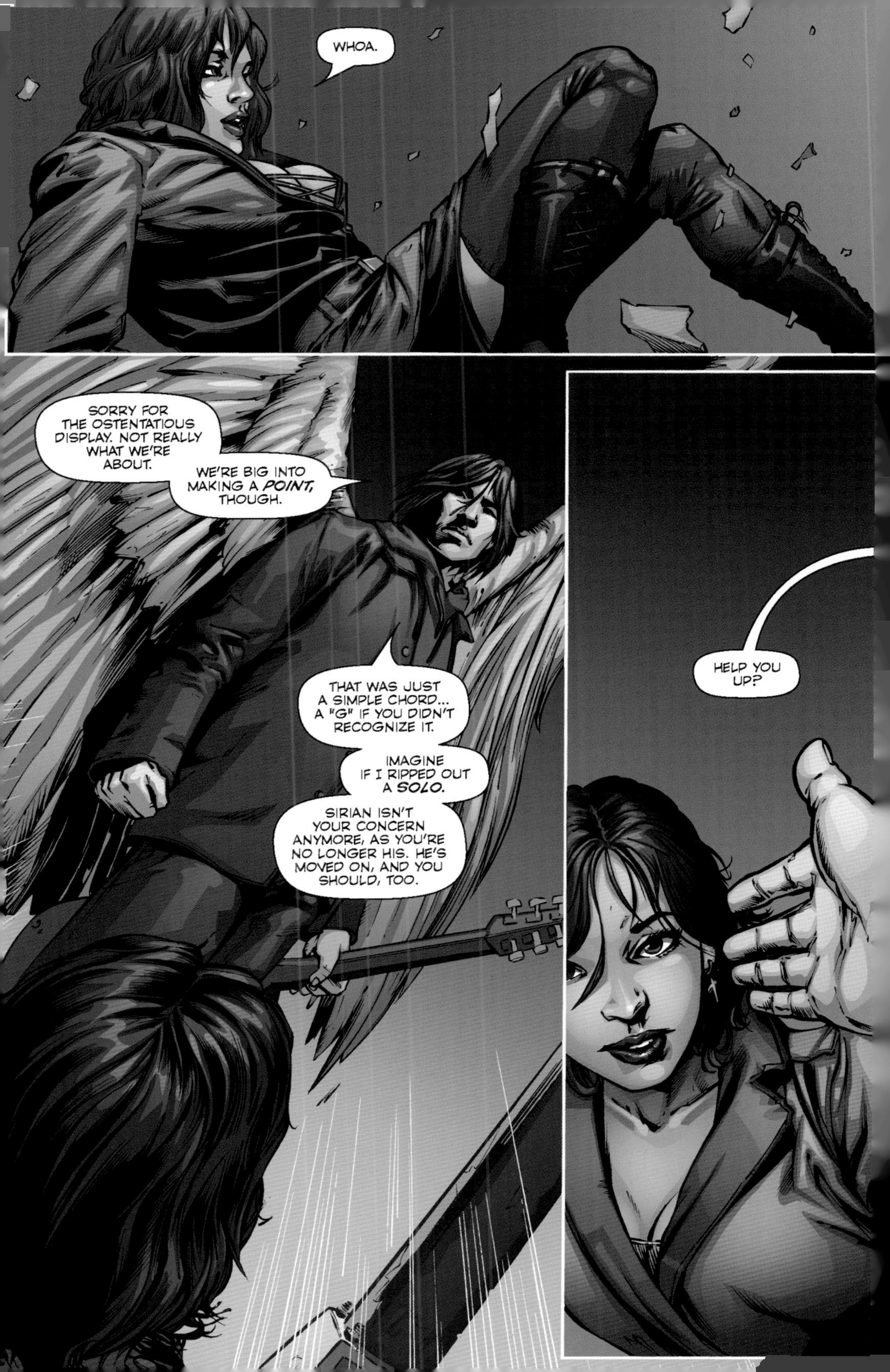
WHOA.
SORRY FOR THE OSTENTATIOUS DISPLAY. NOT REALLY WHAT WE'RE ABOUT.
WE'RE BIG INTO MAKING A *POINT,* THOUGH.
THAT WAS JUST A SIMPLE CHORD... A "G" IF YOU DIDN'T RECOGNIZE IT.
IMAGINE IF I RIPPED OUT A *SOLO.*
SIRIAN ISN'T YOUR CONCERN ANYMORE, AS YOU'RE NO LONGER HIS. HE'S MOVED ON, AND YOU SHOULD, TOO.
HELP YOU UP?

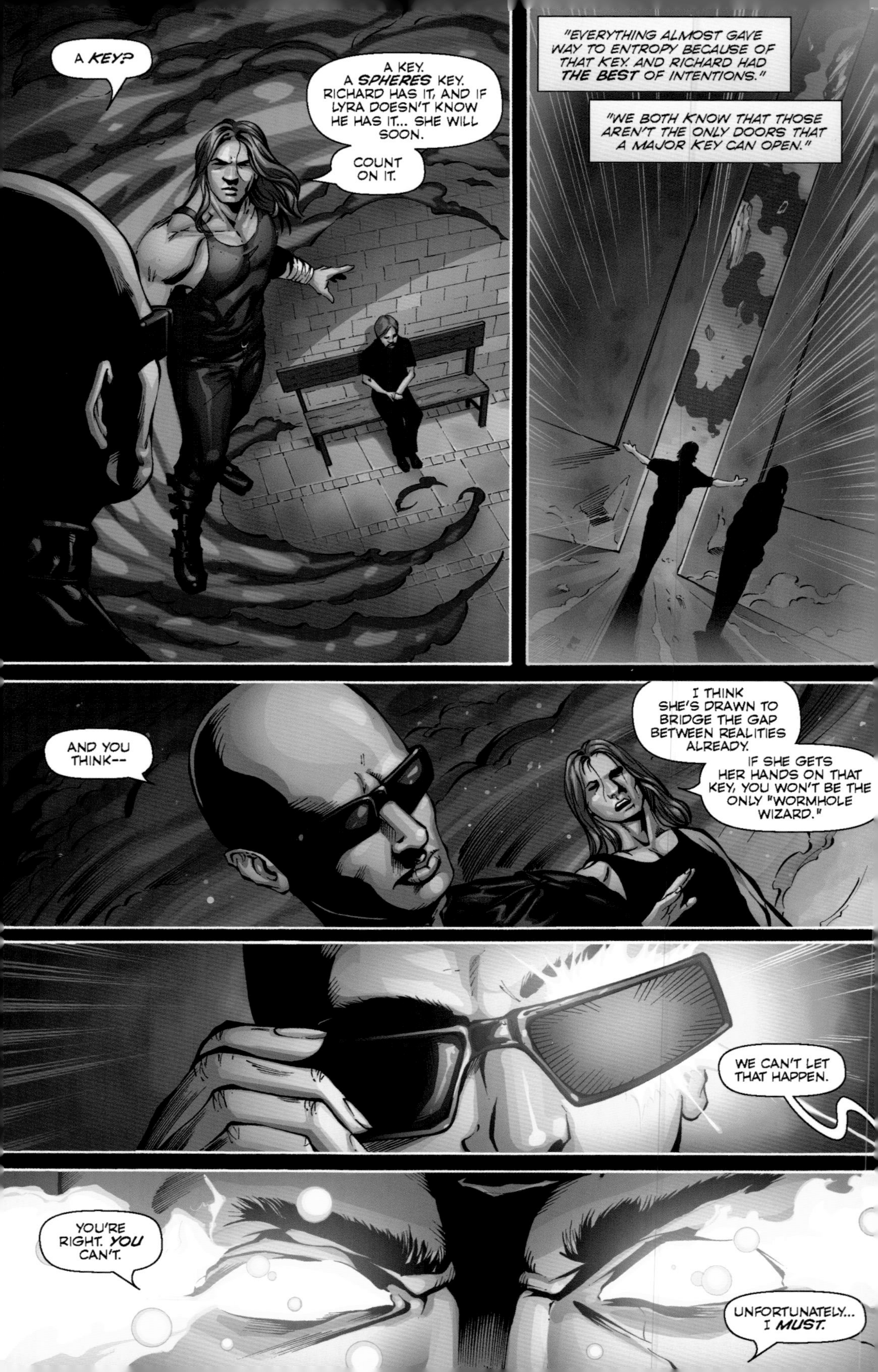
A KEY?
A KEY.
A SPHERES KEY.
RICHARD HAS IT, AND IF LYRA DOESN'T KNOW HE HAS IT... SHE WILL SOON.
COUNT ON IT.
"EVERYTHING ALMOST GAVE WAY TO ENTROPY BECAUSE OF THAT KEY. AND RICHARD HAD THE BEST OF INTENTIONS."
"WE BOTH KNOW THAT THOSE AREN'T THE ONLY DOORS THAT A MAJOR KEY CAN OPEN."
AND YOU THINK--
I THINK SHE'S DRAWN TO BRIDGE THE GAP BETWEEN REALITIES ALREADY.
IF SHE GETS HER HANDS ON THAT KEY, YOU WON'T BE THE ONLY "WORMHOLE WIZARD."
WE CAN'T LET THAT HAPPEN.
YOU'RE RIGHT. YOU CAN'T.
UNFORTUNATELY... I MUST.

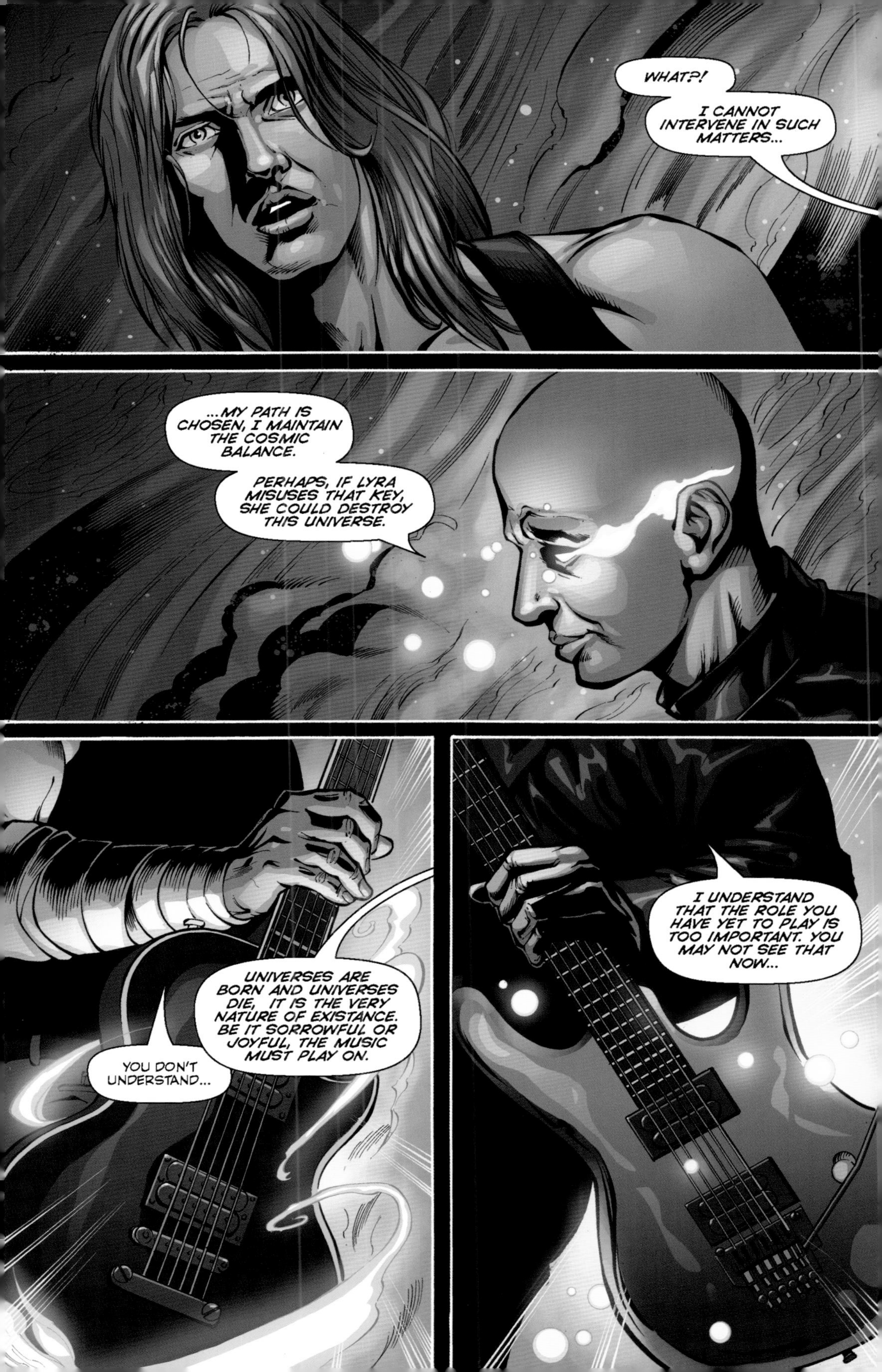
WHAT?!
I CANNOT INTERVENE IN SUCH MATTERS...
...MY PATH IS CHOSEN, I MAINTAIN THE COSMIC BALANCE.
PERHAPS, IF LYRA MISUSES THAT KEY, SHE COULD DESTROY THIS UNIVERSE.
YOU DON'T UNDERSTAND...
UNIVERSES ARE BORN AND UNIVERSES DIE, IT IS THE VERY NATURE OF EXISTANCE. BE IT SORROWFUL OR JOYFUL, THE MUSIC MUST PLAY ON.
I UNDERSTAND THAT THE ROLE YOU HAVE YET TO PLAY IS TOO IMPORTANT. YOU MAY NOT SEE THAT NOW...

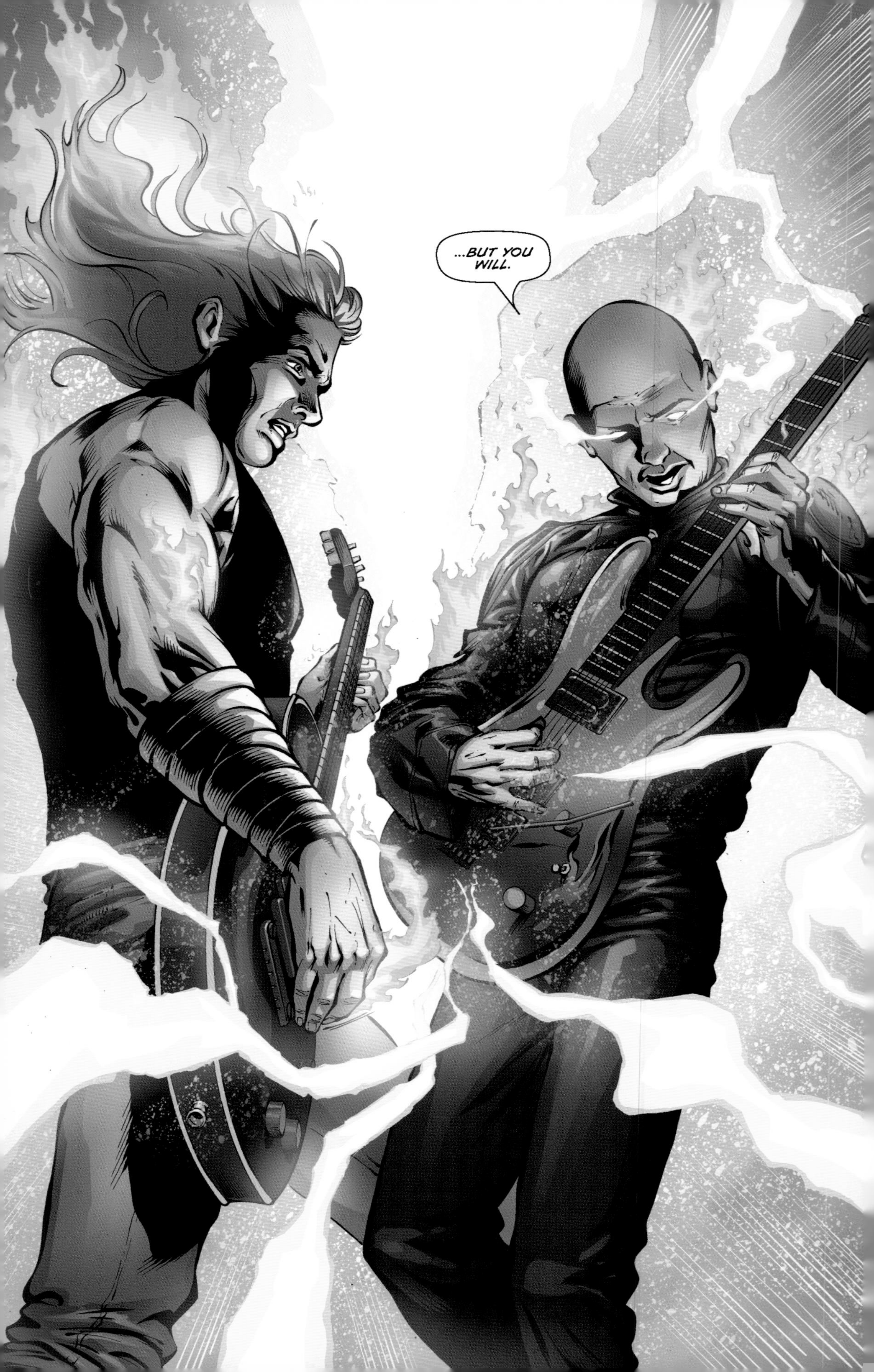
...BUT YOU WILL.

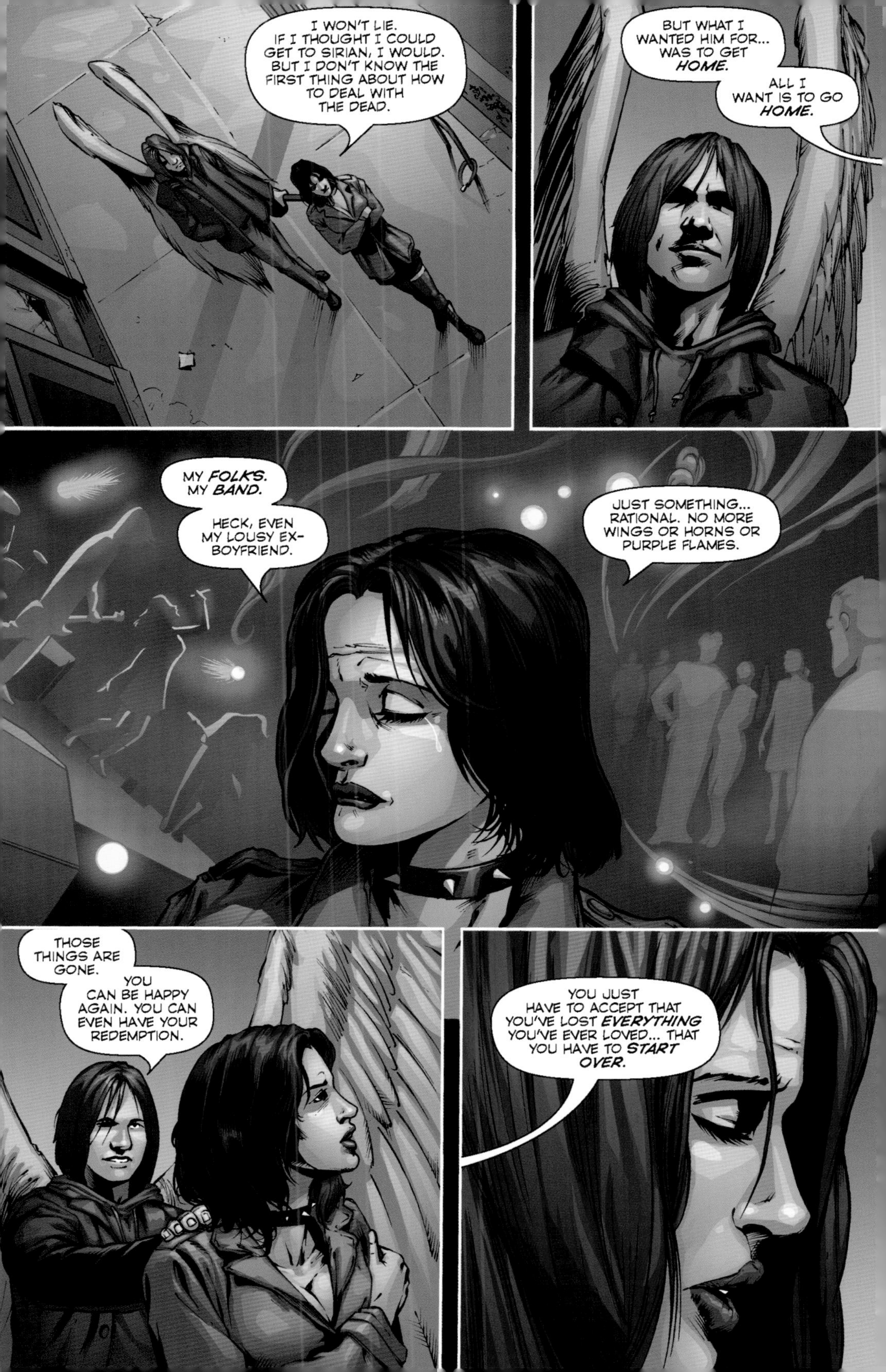
I WON'T LIE. IF I THOUGHT I COULD GET TO SIRIAN, I WOULD. BUT I DON'T KNOW THE FIRST THING ABOUT HOW TO DEAL WITH THE DEAD.
BUT WHAT I WANTED HIM FOR... WAS TO GET HOME.
ALL I WANT IS TO GO HOME.
MY FOLKS. MY BAND.
HECK, EVEN MY LOUSY EX-BOYFRIEND.
JUST SOMETHING... RATIONAL. NO MORE WINGS OR HORNS OR PURPLE FLAMES.
THOSE THINGS ARE GONE.
YOU CAN BE HAPPY AGAIN. YOU CAN EVEN HAVE YOUR REDEMPTION.
YOU JUST HAVE TO ACCEPT THAT YOU'VE LOST EVERYTHING YOU'VE EVER LOVED... THAT YOU HAVE TO START OVER.

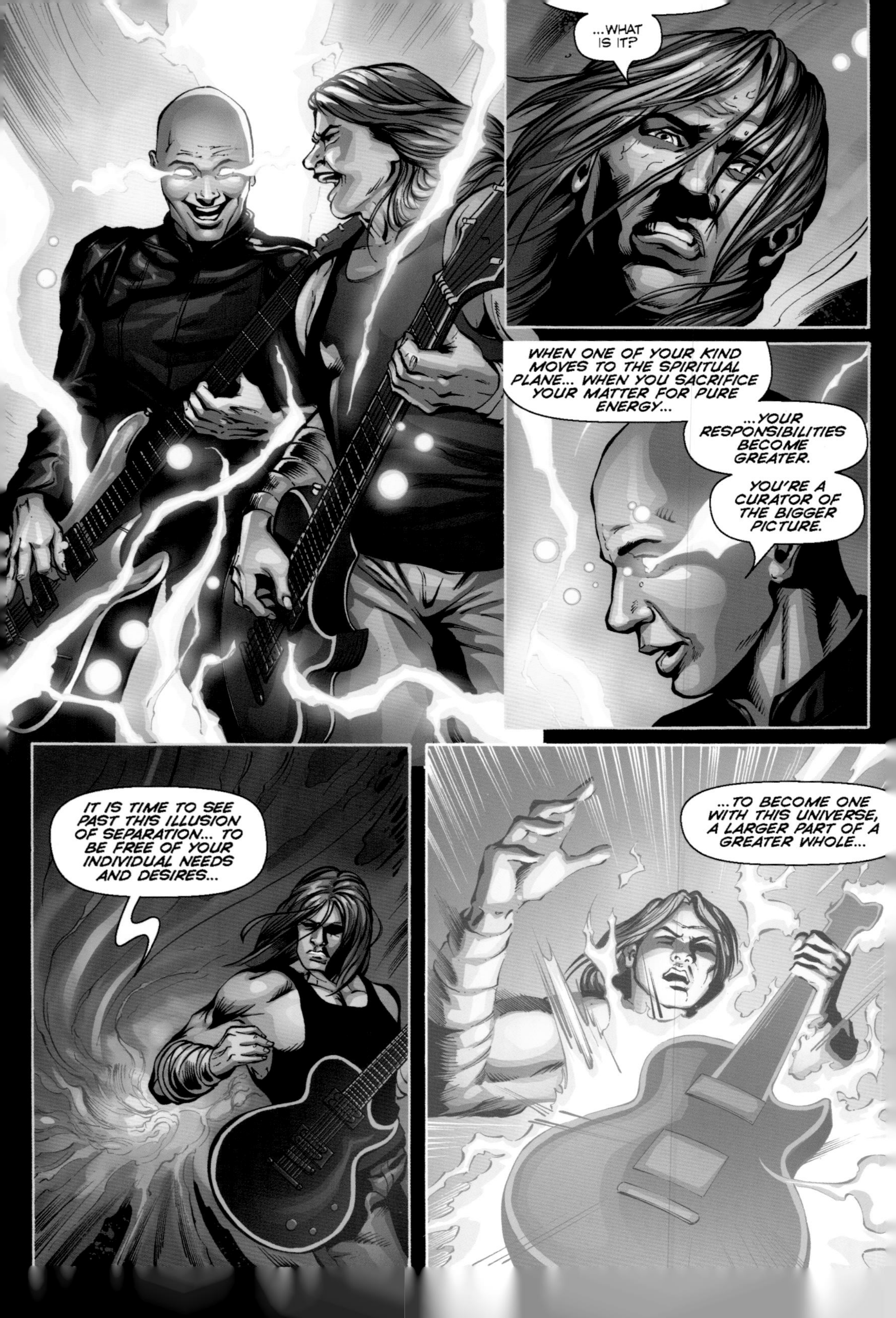
...WHAT IS IT?
WHEN ONE OF YOUR KIND MOVES TO THE SPIRITUAL PLANE... WHEN YOU SACRIFICE YOUR MATTER FOR PURE ENERGY...
...YOUR RESPONSIBILITIES BECOME GREATER.
YOU'RE A CURATOR OF THE BIGGER PICTURE.
IT IS TIME TO SEE PAST THIS ILLUSION OF SEPARATION... TO BE FREE OF YOUR INDIVIDUAL NEEDS AND DESIRES...
...TO BECOME ONE WITH THIS UNIVERSE, A LARGER PART OF A GREATER WHOLE...

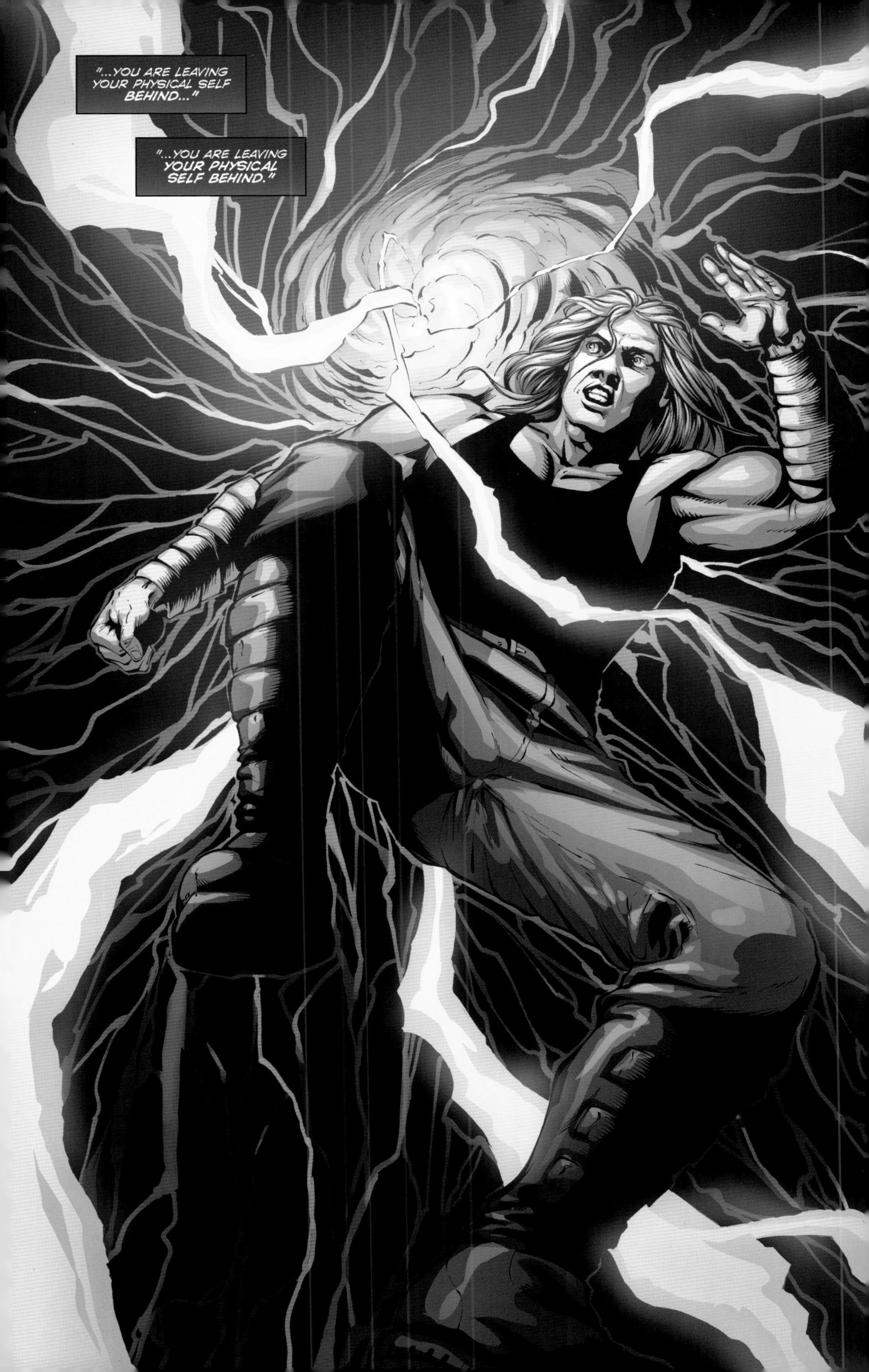
"...YOU ARE LEAVING YOUR PHYSICAL SELF BEHIND..."
"...YOU ARE LEAVING YOUR PHYSICAL SELF BEHIND."

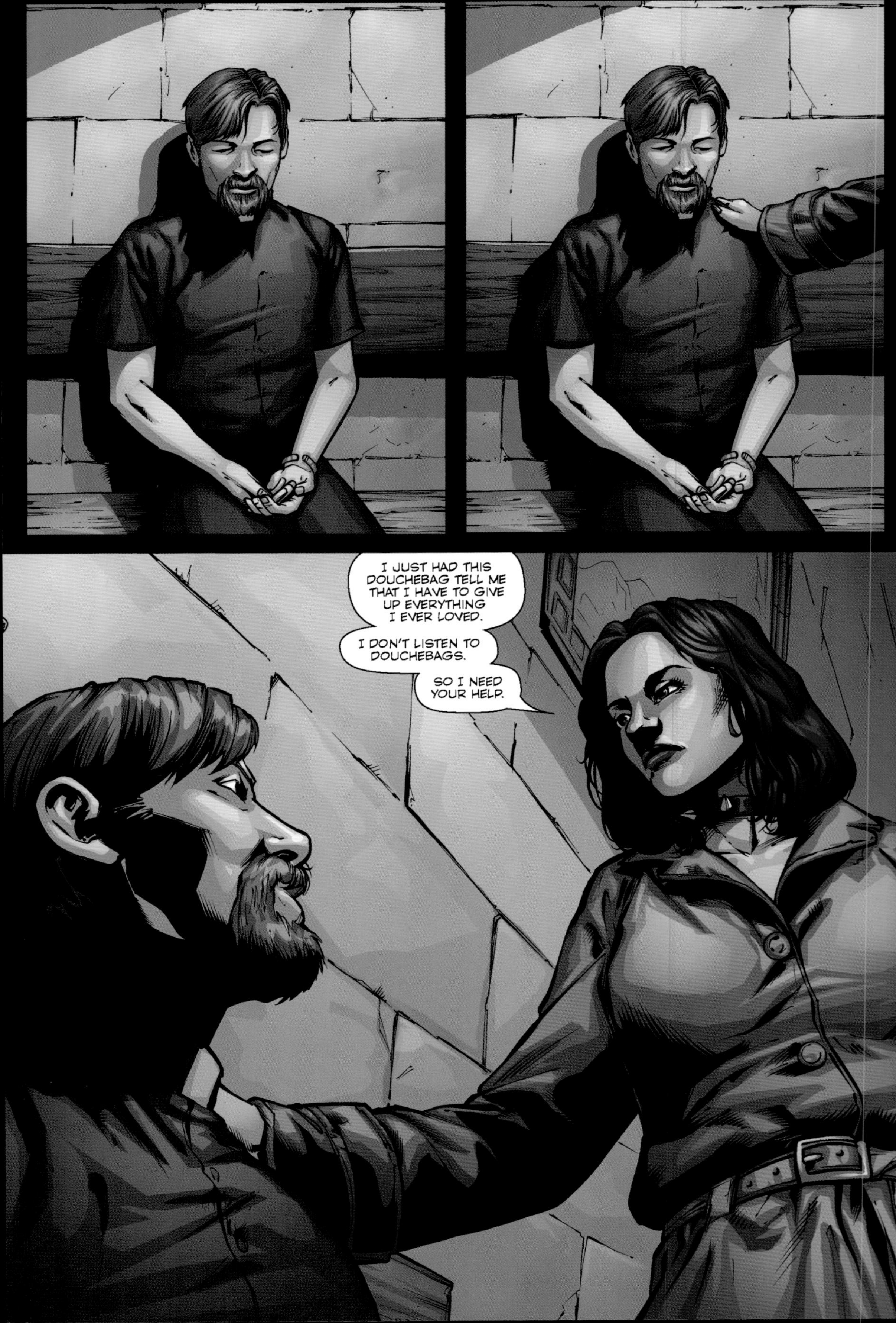
I JUST HAD THIS DOUCHEBAG TELL ME THAT I HAVE TO GIVE UP EVERYTHING I EVER LOVED.
I DON'T LISTEN TO DOUCHEBAGS.
SO I NEED YOUR HELP.

Eternal Descent

CHAPTER FOUR:
LUCK AS A CONSTANT

Written by
Llexi Leon and **Justin Peniston**
Pencils by
Ivan Fernandez
Inks by
Juan Castro
Colors by
Javier Tartaglia
Lettering by
Charles Pritchett

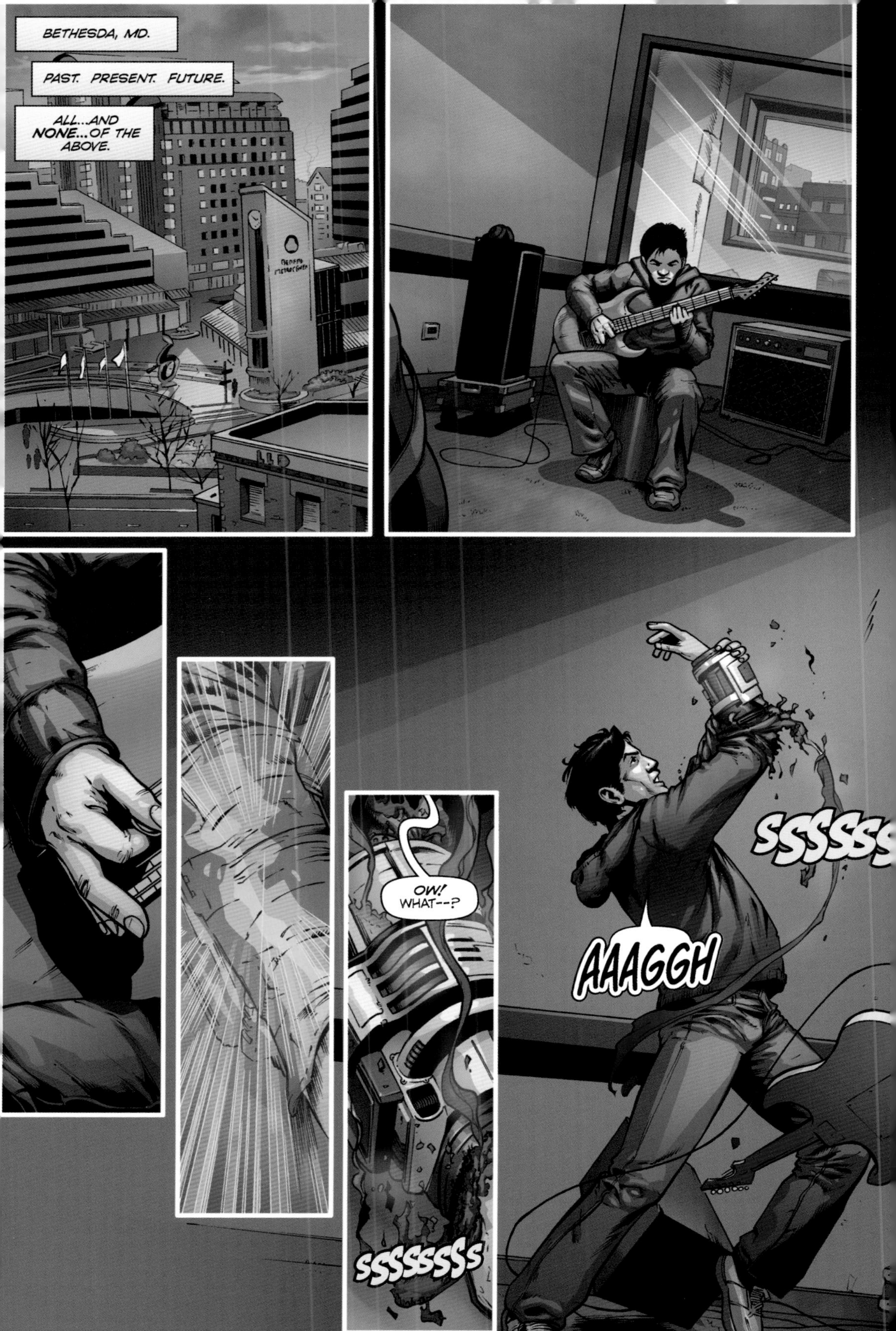
BETHESDA, MD.
PAST. PRESENT. FUTURE.
ALL...AND NONE...OF THE ABOVE.
OW! WHAT--?
SSSSSSSs
AAAGGH
SSSSSS

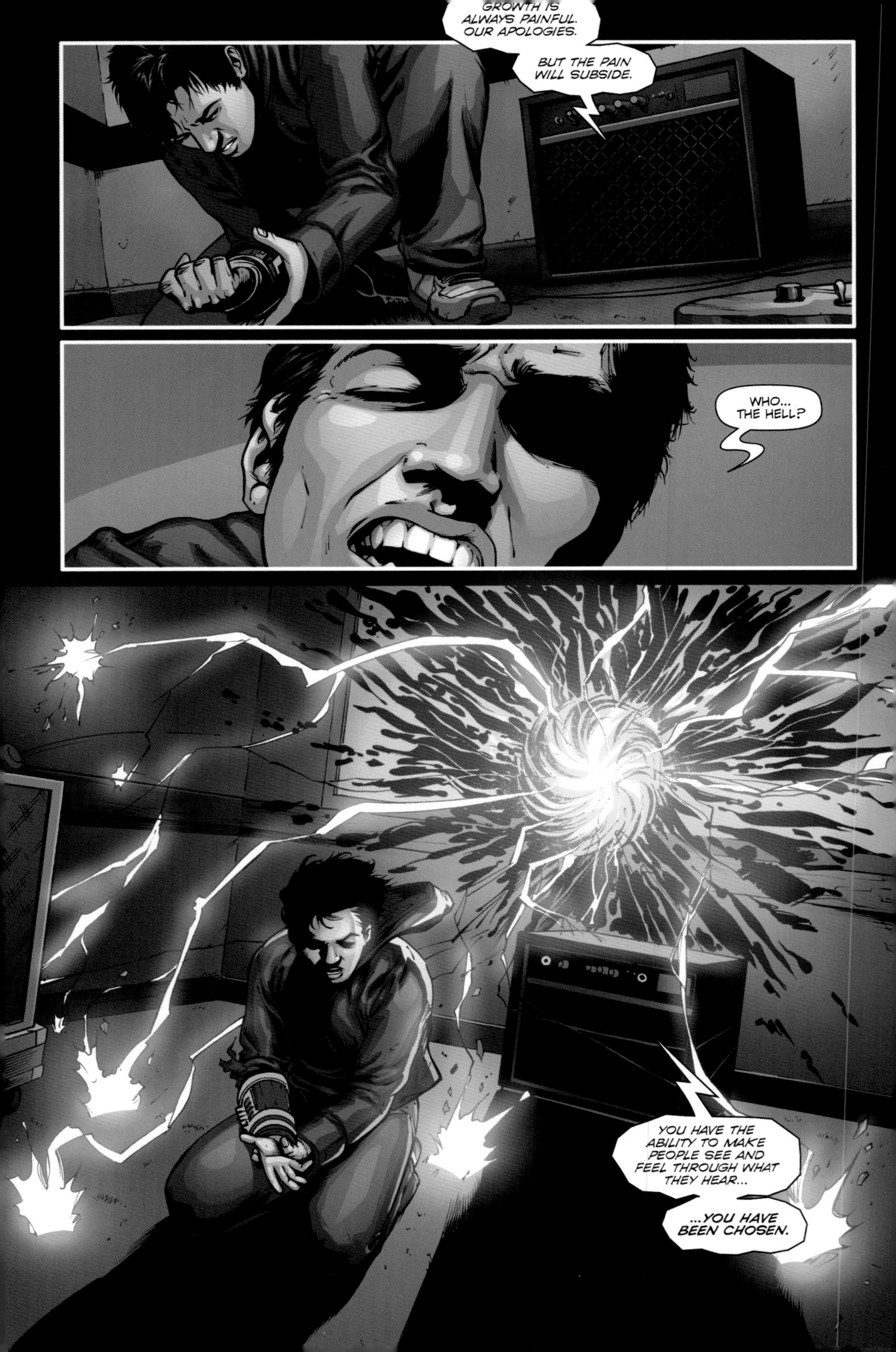
GROWTH IS ALWAYS PAINFUL. OUR APOLOGIES.
BUT THE PAIN WILL SUBSIDE.
WHO... THE HELL?
YOU HAVE THE ABILITY TO MAKE PEOPLE SEE AND FEEL THROUGH WHAT THEY HEAR...
...YOU HAVE BEEN CHOSEN.

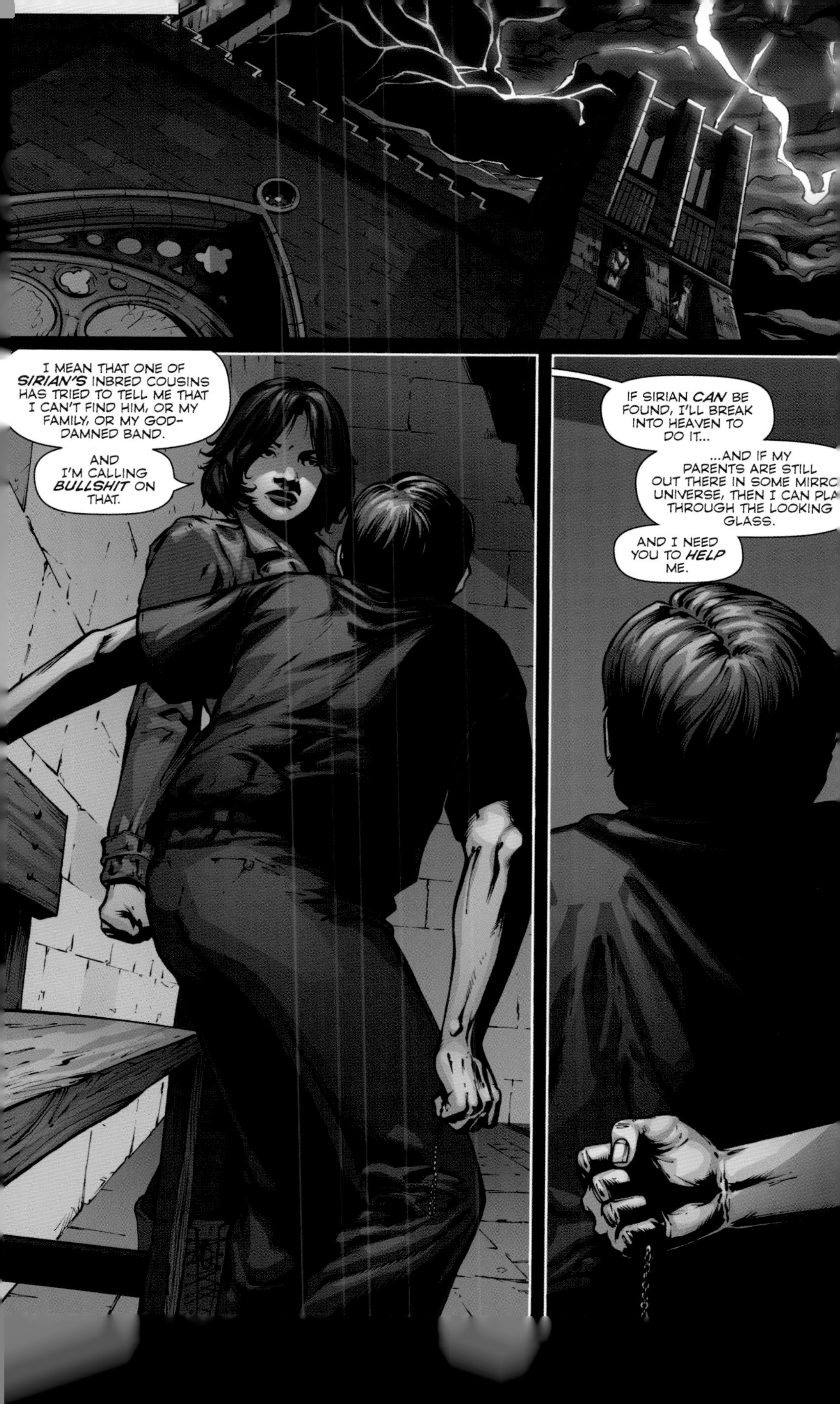
I MEAN THAT ONE OF SIRIAN'S INBRED COUSINS HAS TRIED TO TELL ME THAT I CAN'T FIND HIM, OR MY FAMILY, OR MY GOD-DAMNED BAND.
AND I'M CALLING BULLSHIT ON THAT.
IF SIRIAN CAN BE FOUND, I'LL BREAK INTO HEAVEN TO DO IT...
...AND IF MY PARENTS ARE STILL OUT THERE IN SOME MIRRO UNIVERSE, THEN I CAN PLA THROUGH THE LOOKING GLASS.
AND I NEED YOU TO HELP ME.

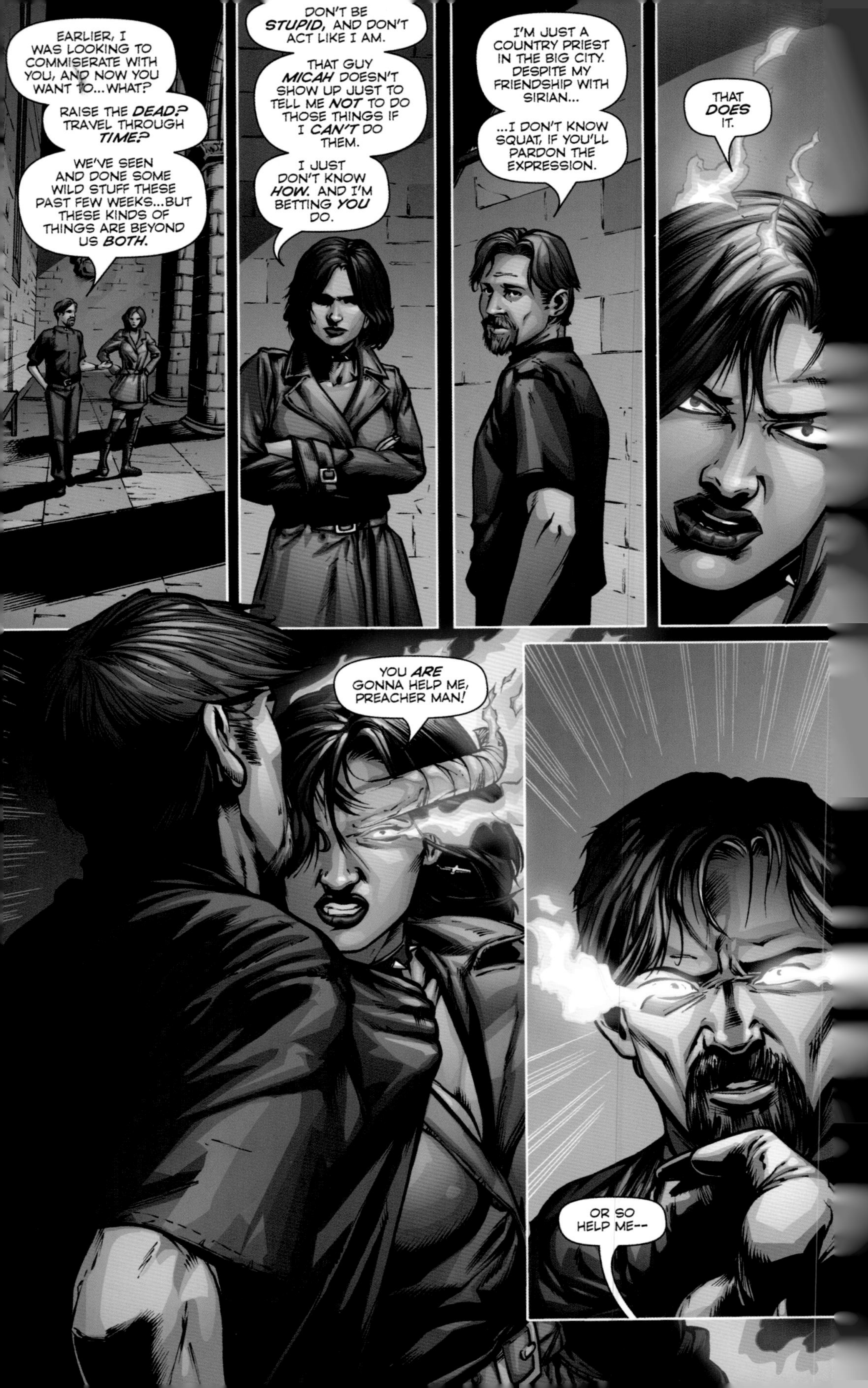
EARLIER, I WAS LOOKING TO COMMISERATE WITH YOU, AND NOW YOU WANT TO...WHAT?
RAISE THE *DEAD?* TRAVEL THROUGH *TIME?*
WE'VE SEEN AND DONE SOME WILD STUFF THESE PAST FEW WEEKS...BUT THESE KINDS OF THINGS ARE BEYOND US *BOTH*.
DON'T BE *STUPID,* AND DON'T ACT LIKE I AM.
THAT GUY *MICAH* DOESN'T SHOW UP JUST TO TELL ME *NOT* TO DO THOSE THINGS IF I *CAN'T* DO THEM.
I JUST DON'T KNOW *HOW.* AND I'M BETTING *YOU* DO.
I'M JUST A COUNTRY PRIEST IN THE BIG CITY. DESPITE MY FRIENDSHIP WITH SIRIAN...
...I DON'T KNOW SQUAT, IF YOU'LL PARDON THE EXPRESSION.
THAT *DOES* IT.
YOU *ARE* GONNA HELP ME, PREACHER MAN!
OR SO HELP ME--

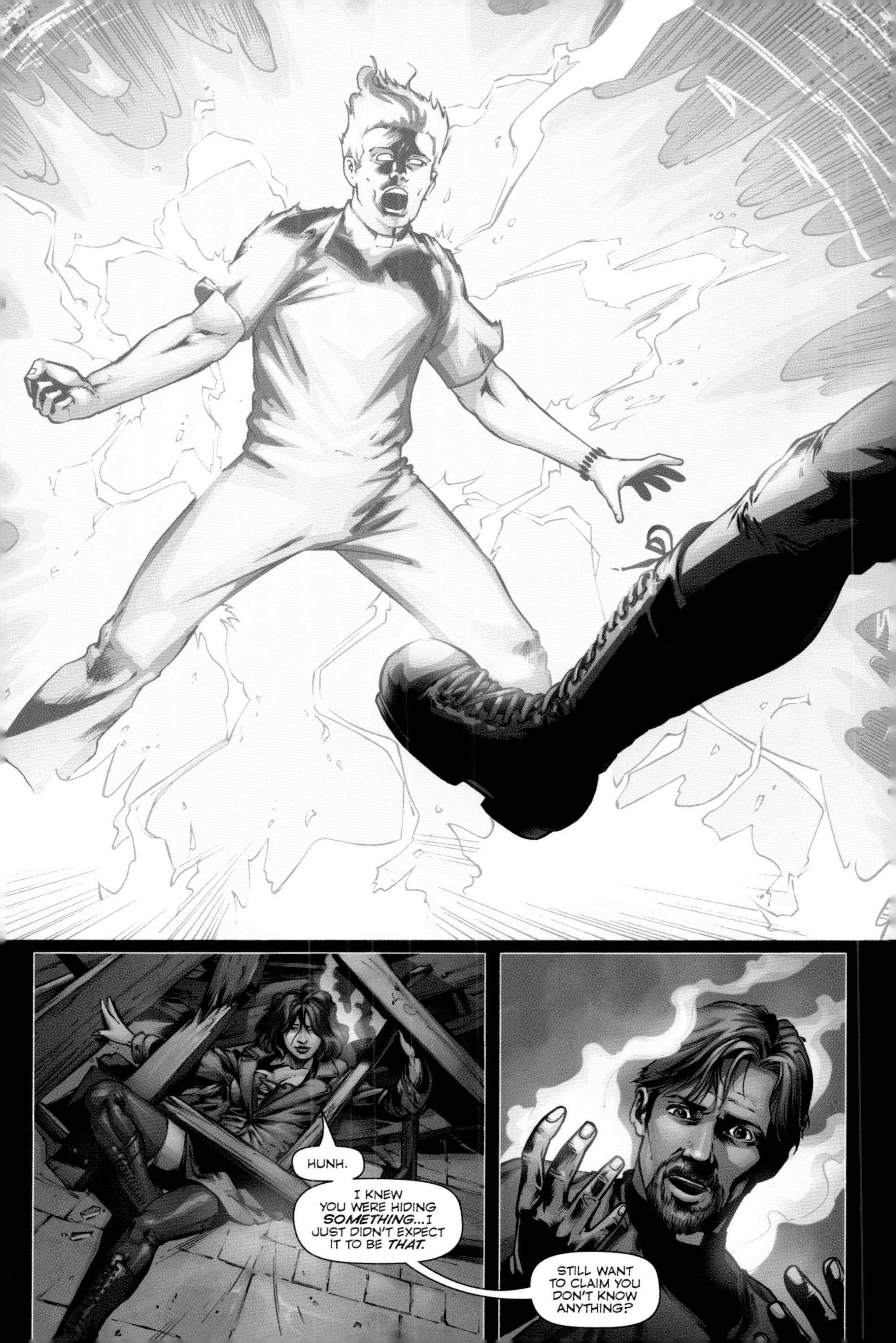
HUNH.
I KNEW YOU WERE HIDING SOMETHING...I JUST DIDN'T EXPECT IT TO BE THAT.
STILL WANT TO CLAIM YOU DON'T KNOW ANYTHING?

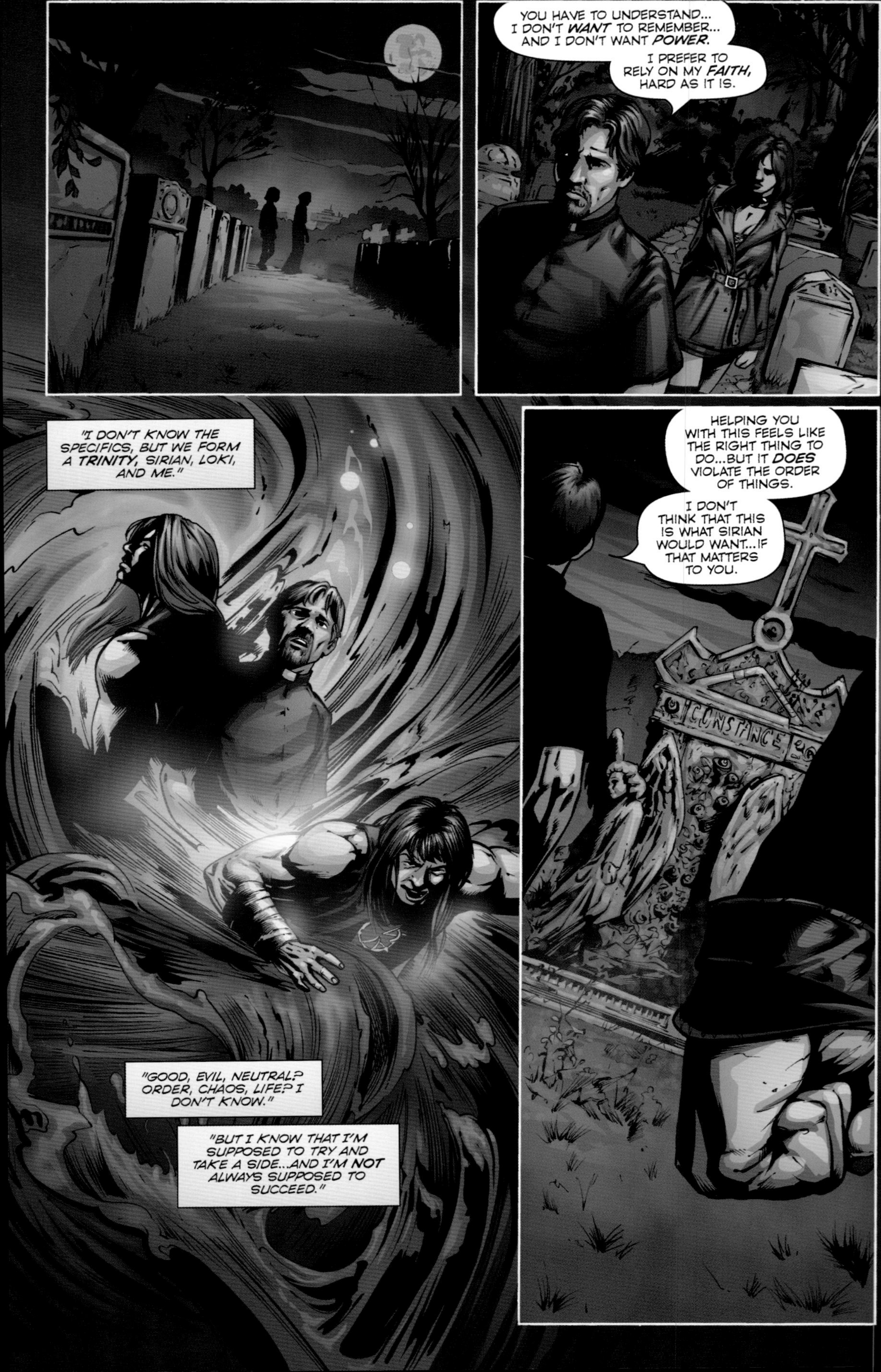
YOU HAVE TO UNDERSTAND... I DON'T **WANT** TO REMEMBER... AND I DON'T WANT **POWER**.
I PREFER TO RELY ON MY **FAITH**, HARD AS IT IS.
"I DON'T KNOW THE SPECIFICS, BUT WE FORM A **TRINITY**, SIRIAN, LOKI, AND ME."
"GOOD, EVIL, NEUTRAL? ORDER, CHAOS, LIFE? I DON'T KNOW."
"BUT I KNOW THAT I'M SUPPOSED TO TRY AND TAKE A SIDE...AND I'M **NOT** ALWAYS SUPPOSED TO SUCCEED."
HELPING YOU WITH THIS FEELS LIKE THE RIGHT THING TO DO...BUT IT **DOES** VIOLATE THE ORDER OF THINGS.
I DON'T THINK THAT THIS IS WHAT SIRIAN WOULD WANT...IF THAT MATTERS TO YOU.
CONSTANCE

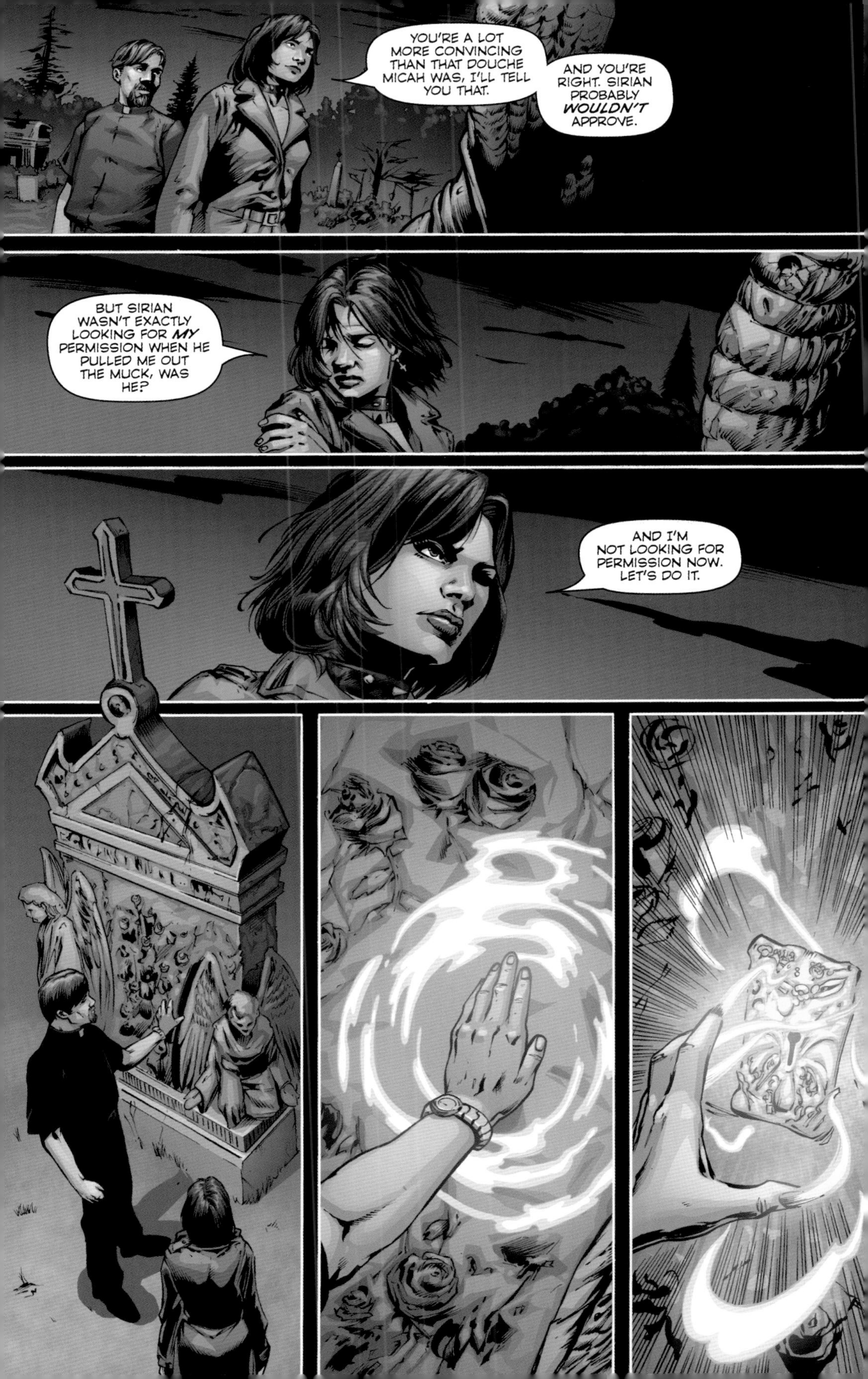
YOU'RE A LOT MORE CONVINCING THAN THAT DOUCHE MICAH WAS, I'LL TELL YOU THAT.
AND YOU'RE RIGHT. SIRIAN PROBABLY *WOULDN'T* APPROVE.
BUT SIRIAN WASN'T EXACTLY LOOKING FOR *MY* PERMISSION WHEN HE PULLED ME OUT THE MUCK, WAS HE?
AND I'M NOT LOOKING FOR PERMISSION NOW. LET'S DO IT.

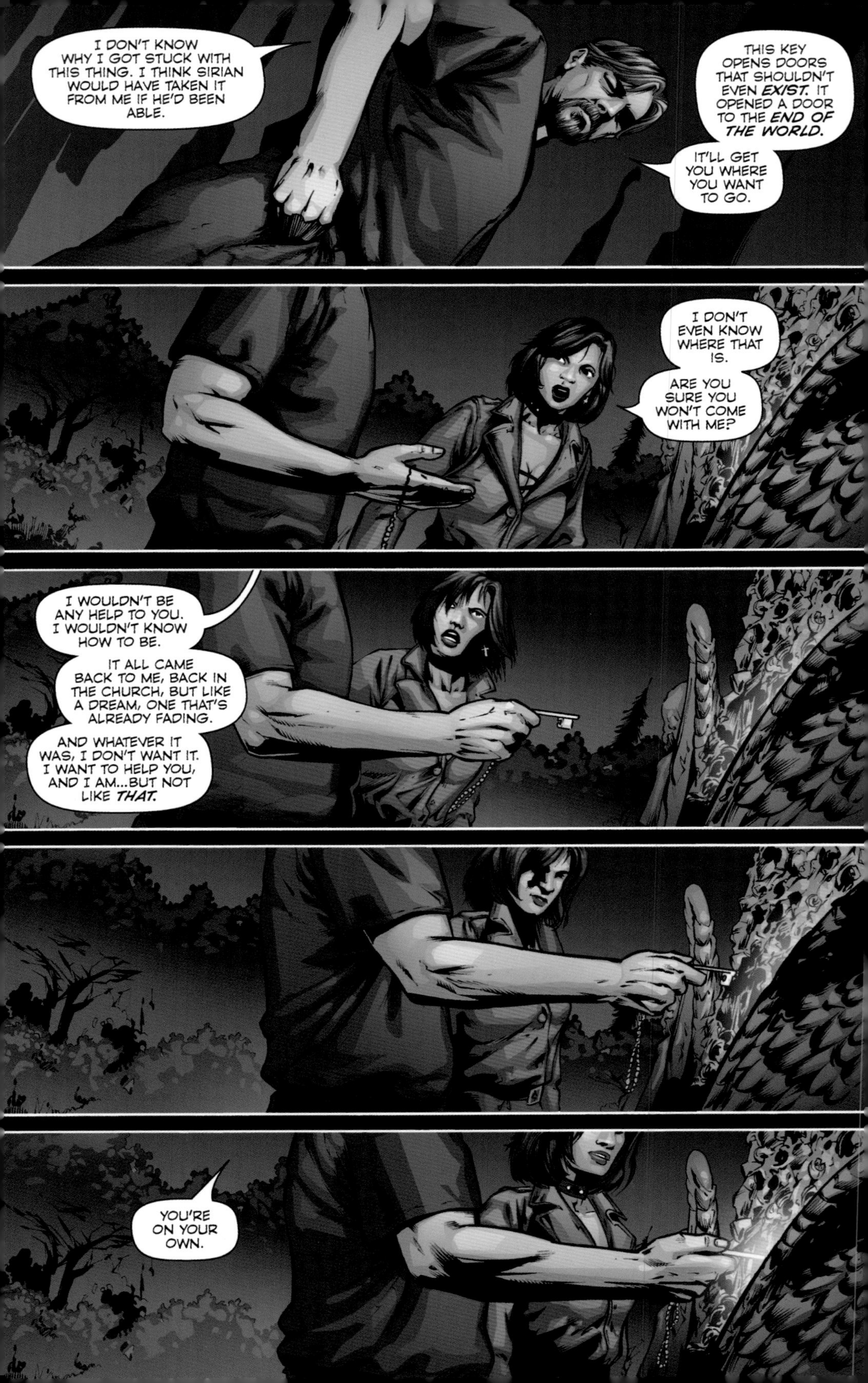

I DON'T KNOW WHY I GOT STUCK WITH THIS THING. I THINK SIRIAN WOULD HAVE TAKEN IT FROM ME IF HE'D BEEN ABLE.
THIS KEY OPENS DOORS THAT SHOULDN'T EVEN ***EXIST.*** IT OPENED A DOOR TO THE ***END OF THE WORLD.***
IT'LL GET YOU WHERE YOU WANT TO GO.
I DON'T EVEN KNOW WHERE THAT IS.
ARE YOU SURE YOU WON'T COME WITH ME?
I WOULDN'T BE ANY HELP TO YOU. I WOULDN'T KNOW HOW TO BE.
IT ALL CAME BACK TO ME, BACK IN THE CHURCH, BUT LIKE A DREAM, ONE THAT'S ALREADY FADING.
AND WHATEVER IT WAS, I DON'T WANT IT. I WANT TO HELP YOU, AND I AM...BUT NOT LIKE ***THAT.***
YOU'RE ON YOUR OWN.

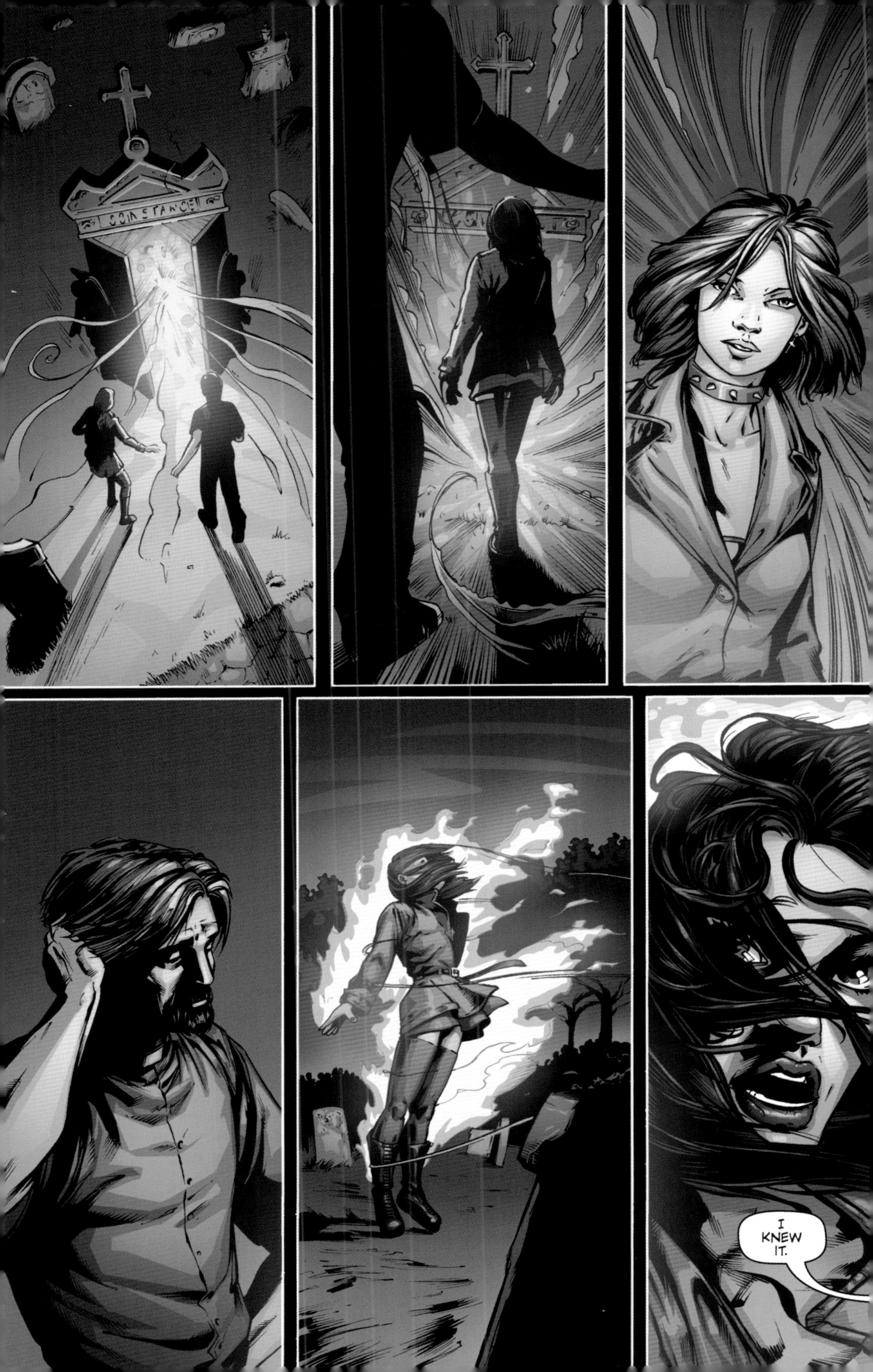
CONSTANCE
I KNEW IT.

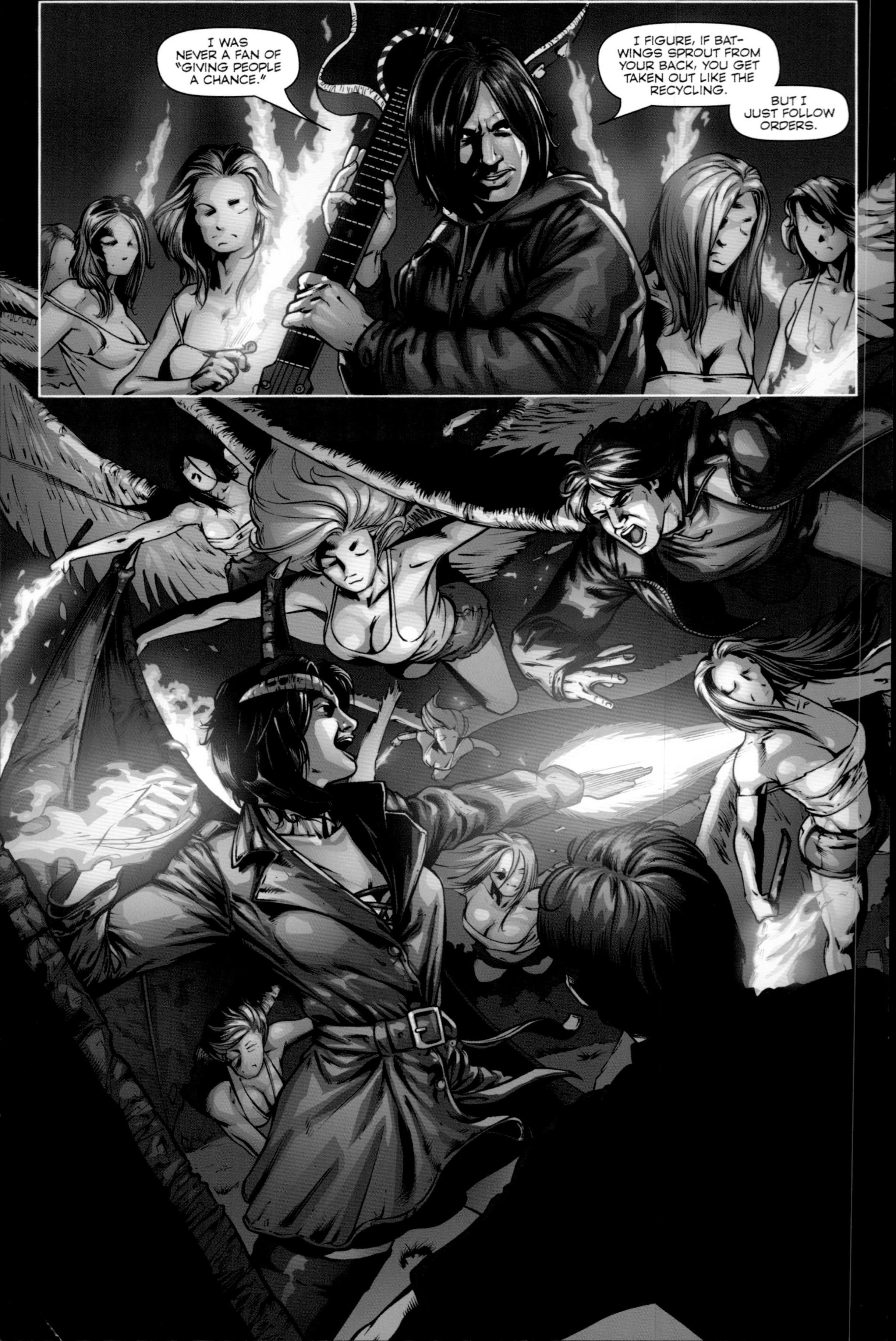
I WAS NEVER A FAN OF "GIVING PEOPLE A CHANCE."
I FIGURE, IF BAT-WINGS SPROUT FROM YOUR BACK, YOU GET TAKEN OUT LIKE THE RECYCLING.
BUT I JUST FOLLOW ORDERS.

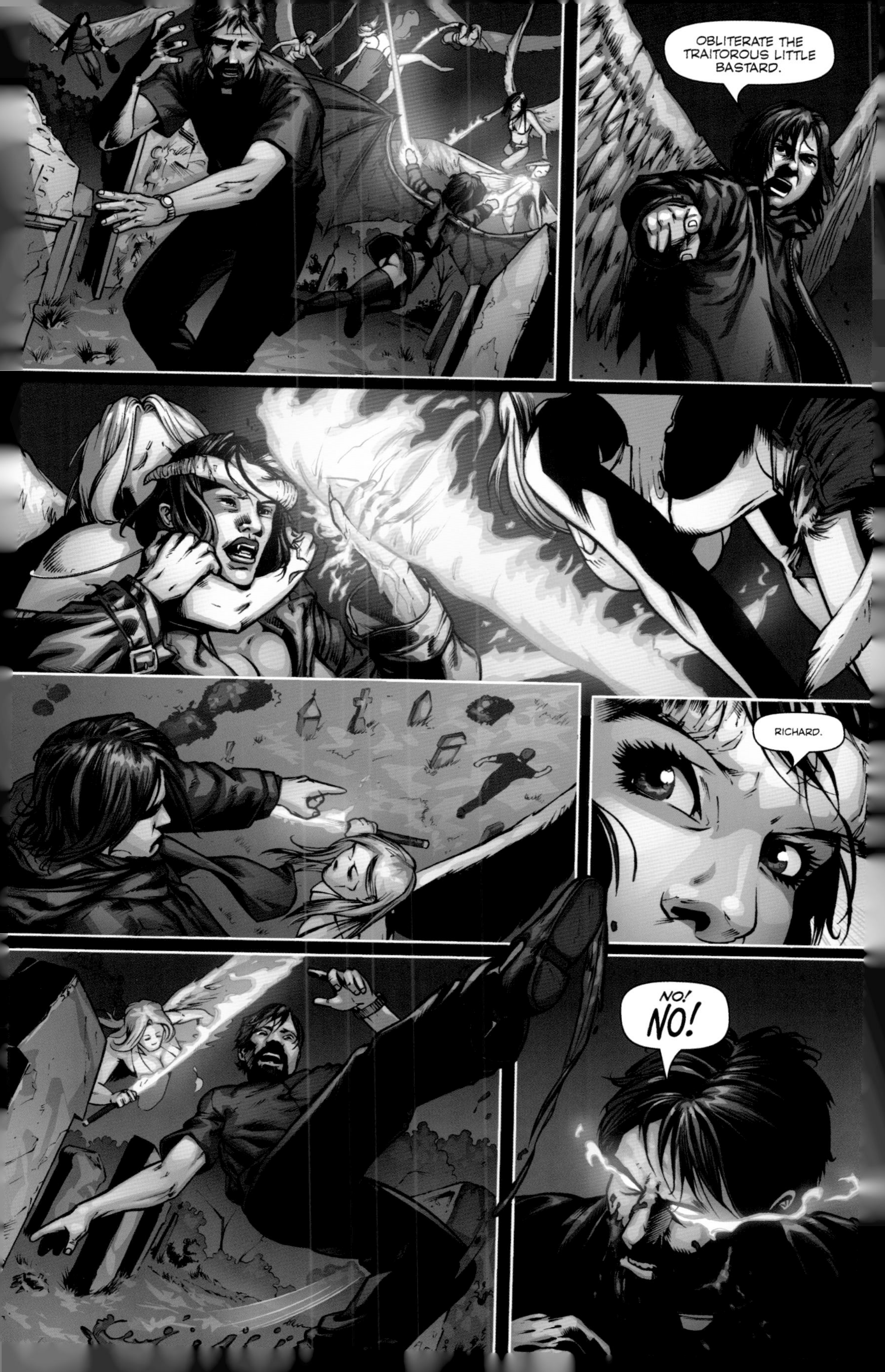
OBLITERATE THE TRAITOROUS LITTLE BASTARD.
RICHARD.
NO! NO!

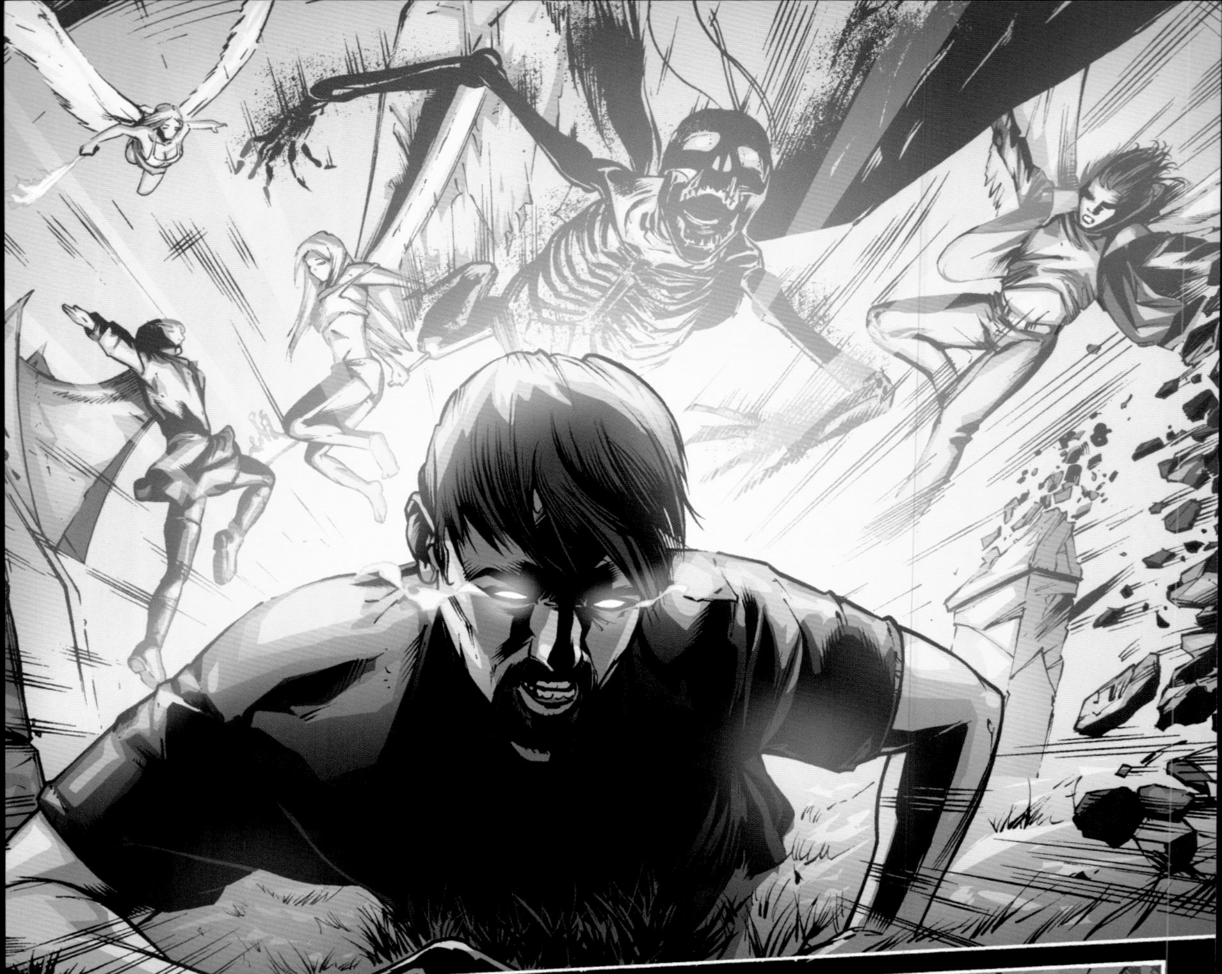

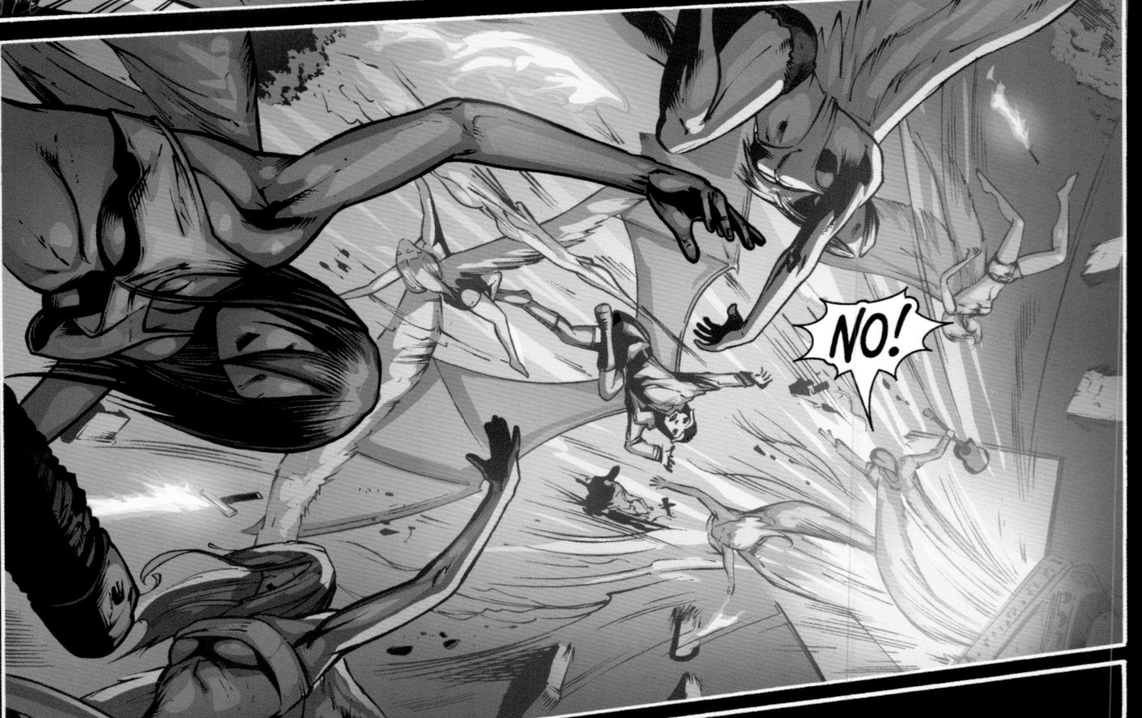
NO!

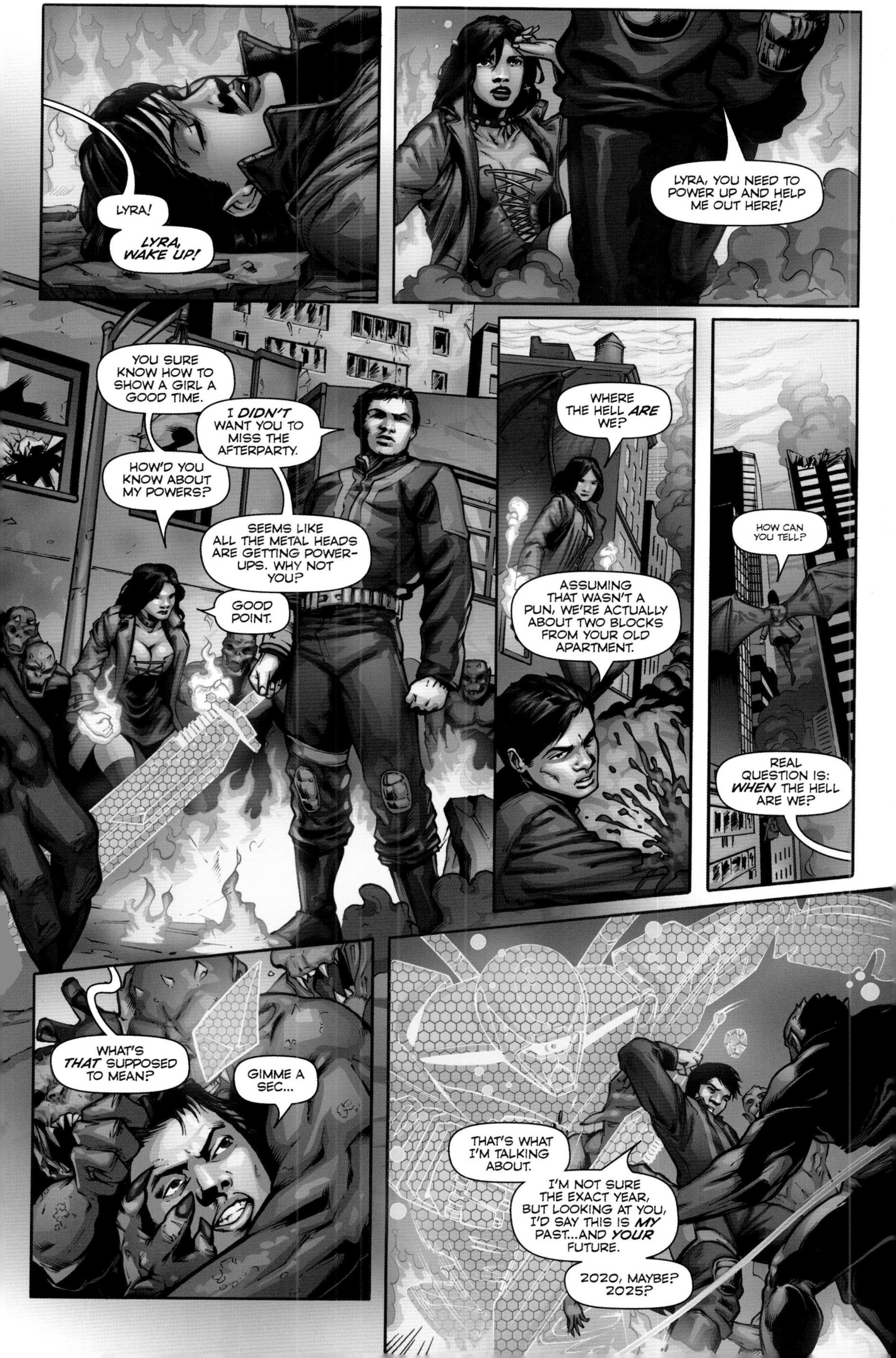
LYRA!
LYRA, WAKE UP!
LYRA, YOU NEED TO POWER UP AND HELP ME OUT HERE!
YOU SURE KNOW HOW TO SHOW A GIRL A GOOD TIME.
I DIDN'T WANT YOU TO MISS THE AFTERPARTY.
HOW'D YOU KNOW ABOUT MY POWERS?
SEEMS LIKE ALL THE METAL HEADS ARE GETTING POWER-UPS. WHY NOT YOU?
GOOD POINT.
WHERE THE HELL ARE WE?
ASSUMING THAT WASN'T A PUN, WE'RE ACTUALLY ABOUT TWO BLOCKS FROM YOUR OLD APARTMENT.
HOW CAN YOU TELL?
REAL QUESTION IS: WHEN THE HELL ARE WE?
WHAT'S THAT SUPPOSED TO MEAN?
GIMME A SEC...
THAT'S WHAT I'M TALKING ABOUT.
I'M NOT SURE THE EXACT YEAR, BUT LOOKING AT YOU, I'D SAY THIS IS MY PAST...AND YOUR FUTURE.
2020, MAYBE? 2025?

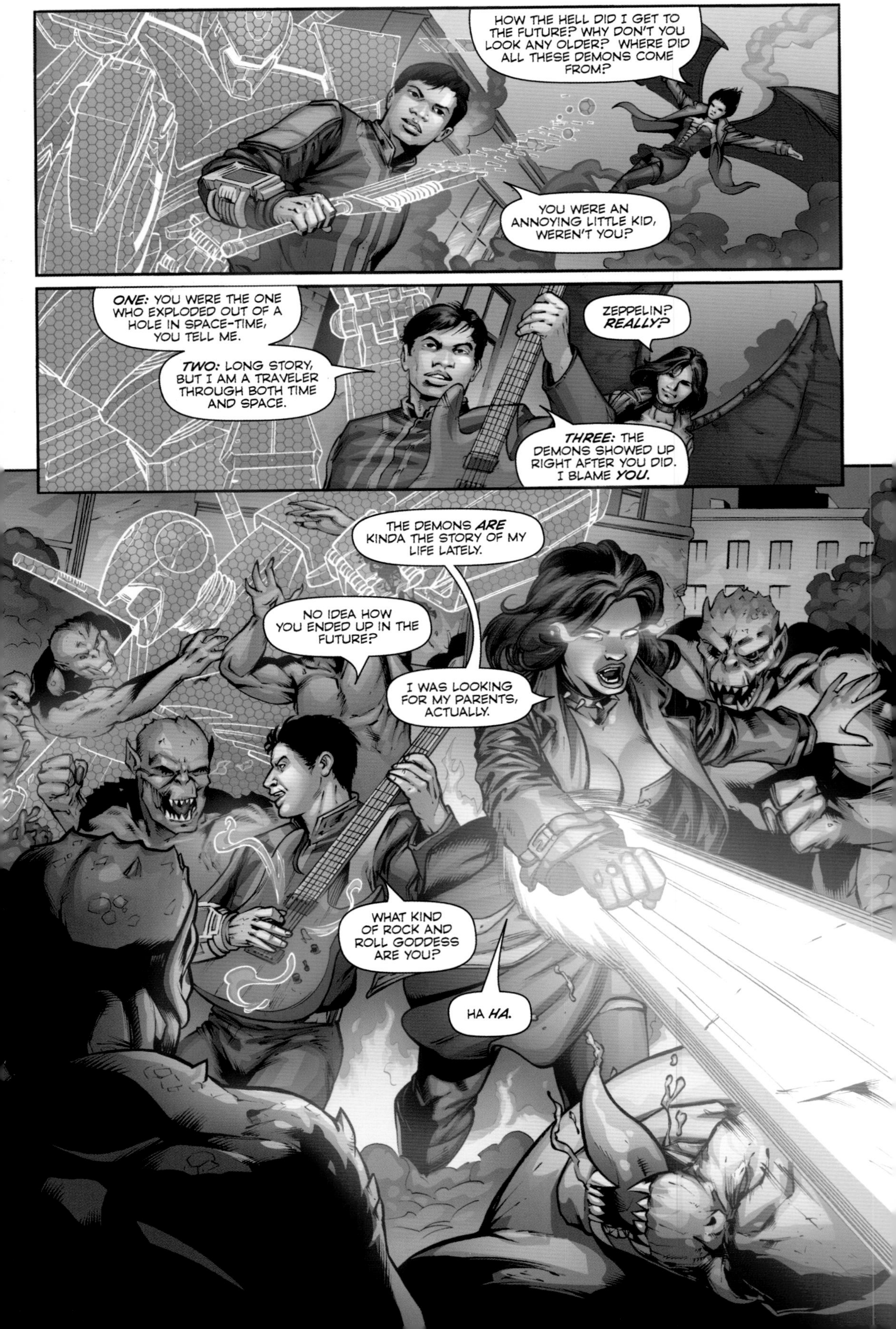
HOW THE HELL DID I GET TO THE FUTURE? WHY DON'T YOU LOOK ANY OLDER? WHERE DID ALL THESE DEMONS COME FROM?
YOU WERE AN ANNOYING LITTLE KID, WEREN'T YOU?
ONE: YOU WERE THE ONE WHO EXPLODED OUT OF A HOLE IN SPACE-TIME, YOU TELL ME.
TWO: LONG STORY, BUT I AM A TRAVELER THROUGH BOTH TIME AND SPACE.
ZEPPELIN? REALLY?
THREE: THE DEMONS SHOWED UP RIGHT AFTER YOU DID. I BLAME YOU.
THE DEMONS ARE KINDA THE STORY OF MY LIFE LATELY.
NO IDEA HOW YOU ENDED UP IN THE FUTURE?
I WAS LOOKING FOR MY PARENTS, ACTUALLY.
WHAT KIND OF ROCK AND ROLL GODDESS ARE YOU?
HA HA.

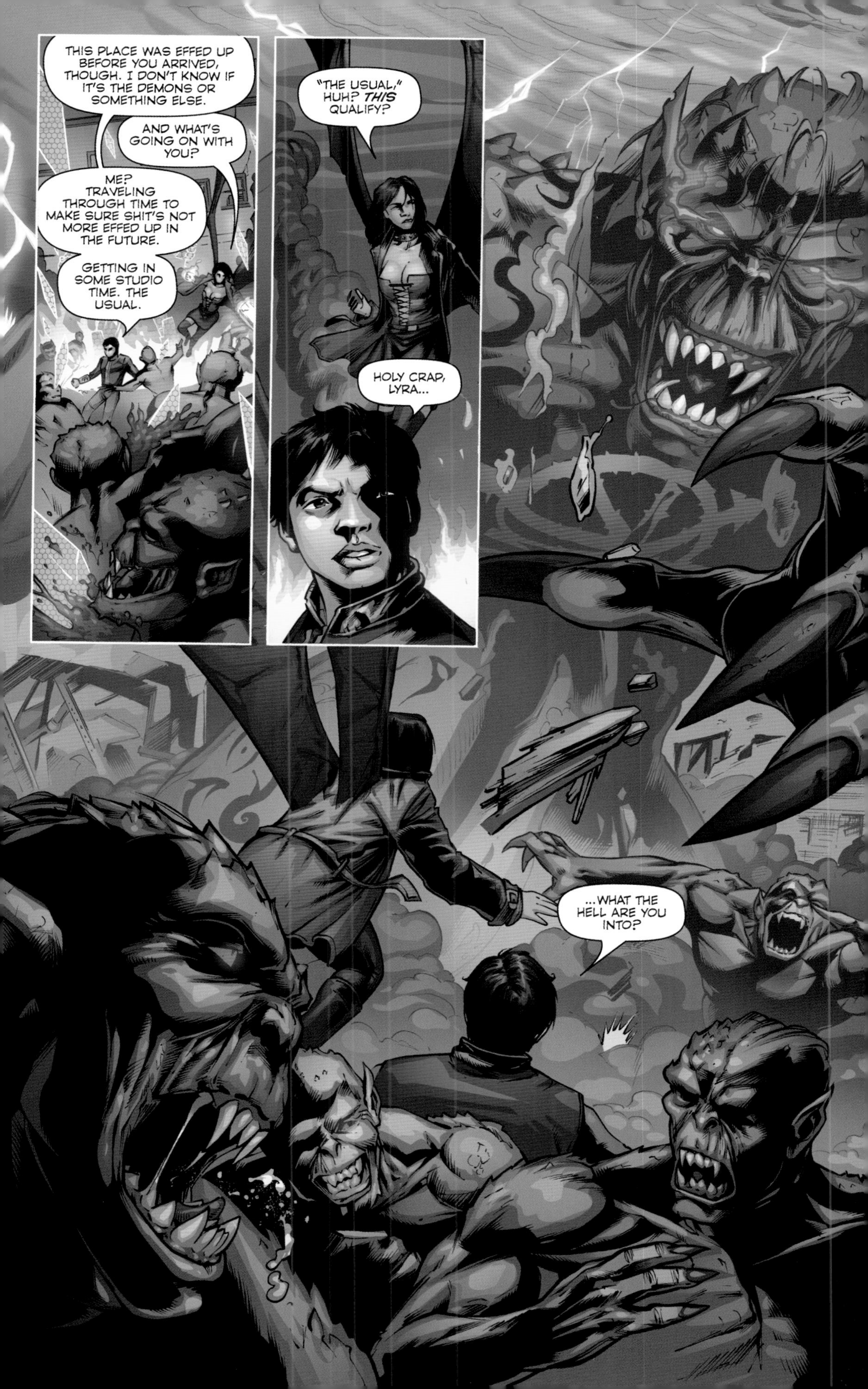
THIS PLACE WAS EFFED UP BEFORE YOU ARRIVED, THOUGH. I DON'T KNOW IF IT'S THE DEMONS OR SOMETHING ELSE.
AND WHAT'S GOING ON WITH YOU?
ME? TRAVELING THROUGH TIME TO MAKE SURE SHIT'S NOT MORE EFFED UP IN THE FUTURE.
GETTING IN SOME STUDIO TIME. THE USUAL.
"THE USUAL," HUH? *THIS* QUALIFY?
HOLY CRAP, LYRA...
...WHAT THE HELL ARE YOU INTO?

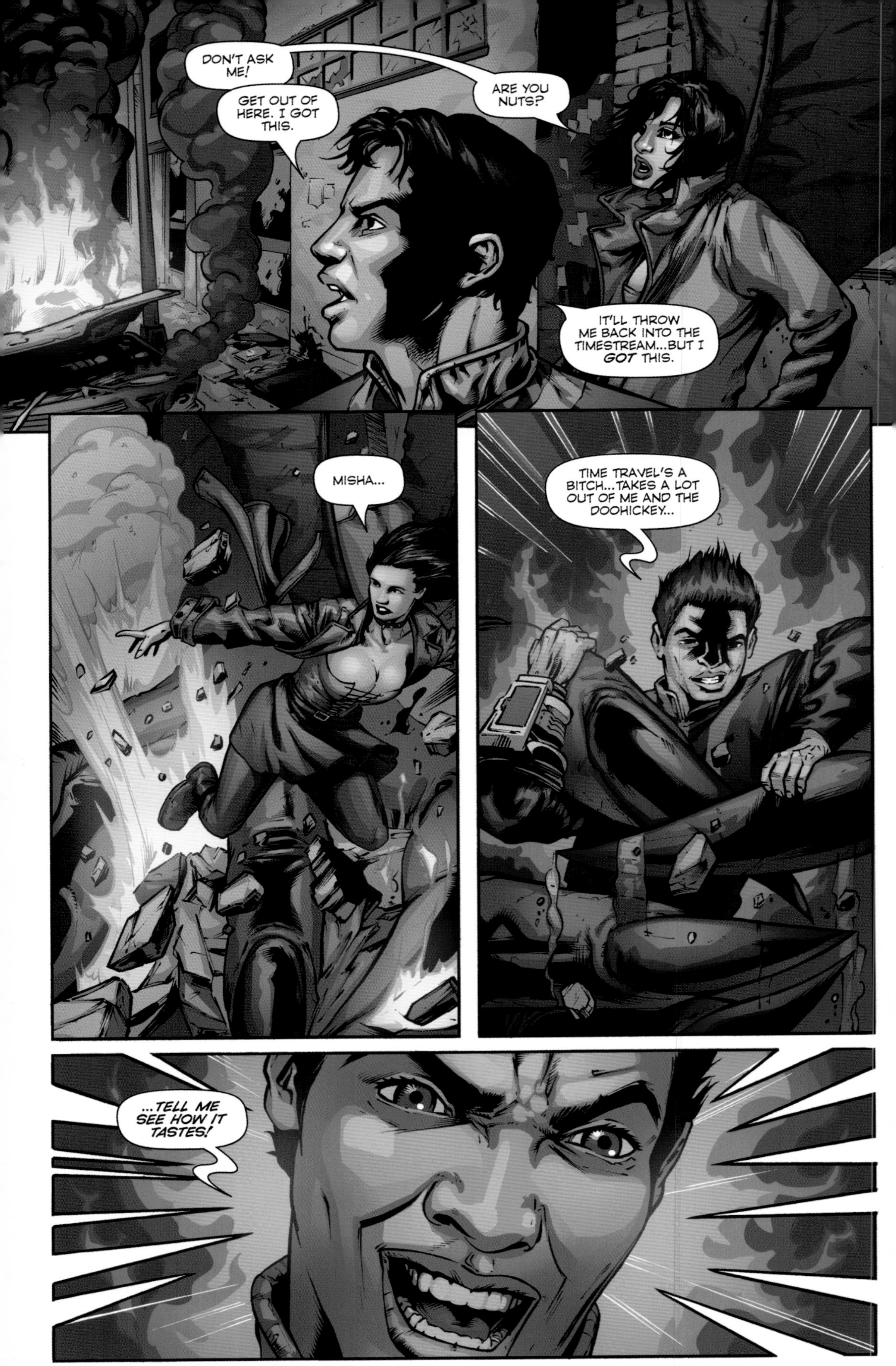
DON'T ASK ME!
ARE YOU NUTS?
GET OUT OF HERE. I GOT THIS.
IT'LL THROW ME BACK INTO THE TIMESTREAM...BUT I *GOT* THIS.
MISHA...
TIME TRAVEL'S A BITCH...TAKES A LOT OUT OF ME AND THE DOOHICKEY...
...TELL ME SEE HOW IT TASTES!

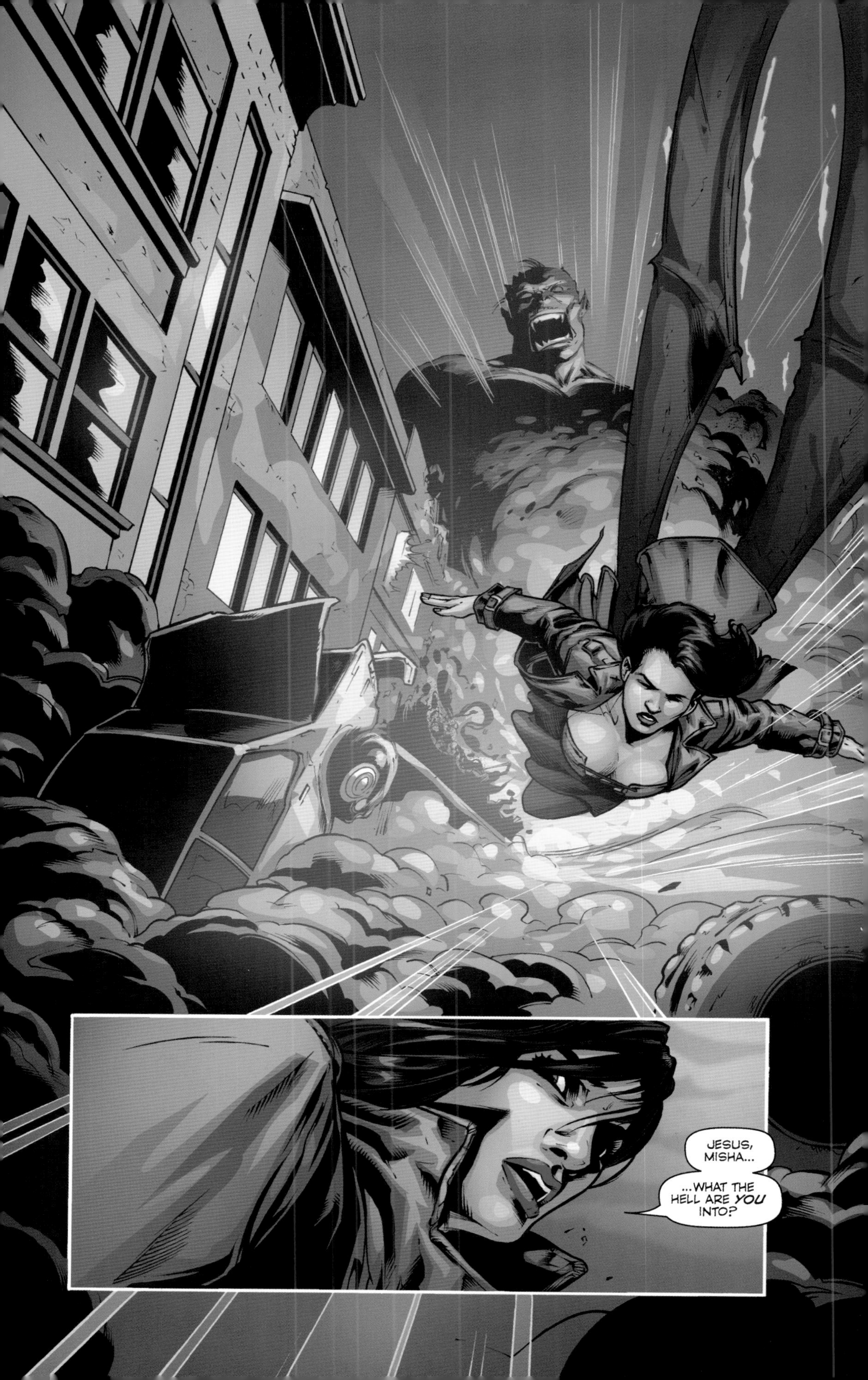
JESUS, MISHA...
...WHAT THE HELL ARE *YOU* INTO?

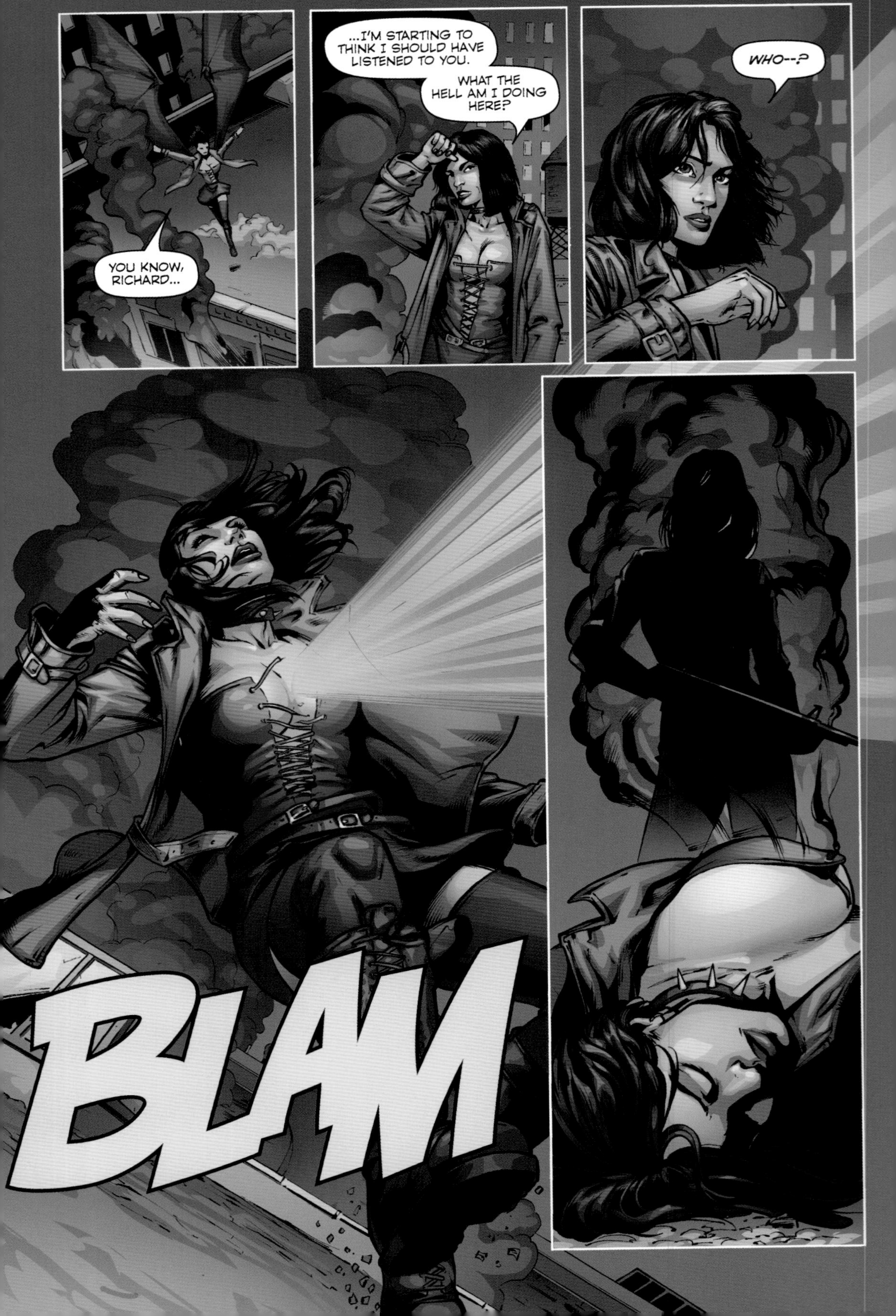
YOU KNOW, RICHARD...
...I'M STARTING TO THINK I SHOULD HAVE LISTENED TO YOU.
WHAT THE HELL AM I DOING HERE?
WHO--?
BLAM

Eternal Descent

CHAPTER FIVE:
RISE OF THE
TYRANT

Written by
Llexi Leon and **Justin Peniston**

Pencils by
Ivan Fernandez

Inks by
Juan Castro

Colors by
Javier Tartaglia

Lettering by
Charles Pritchett

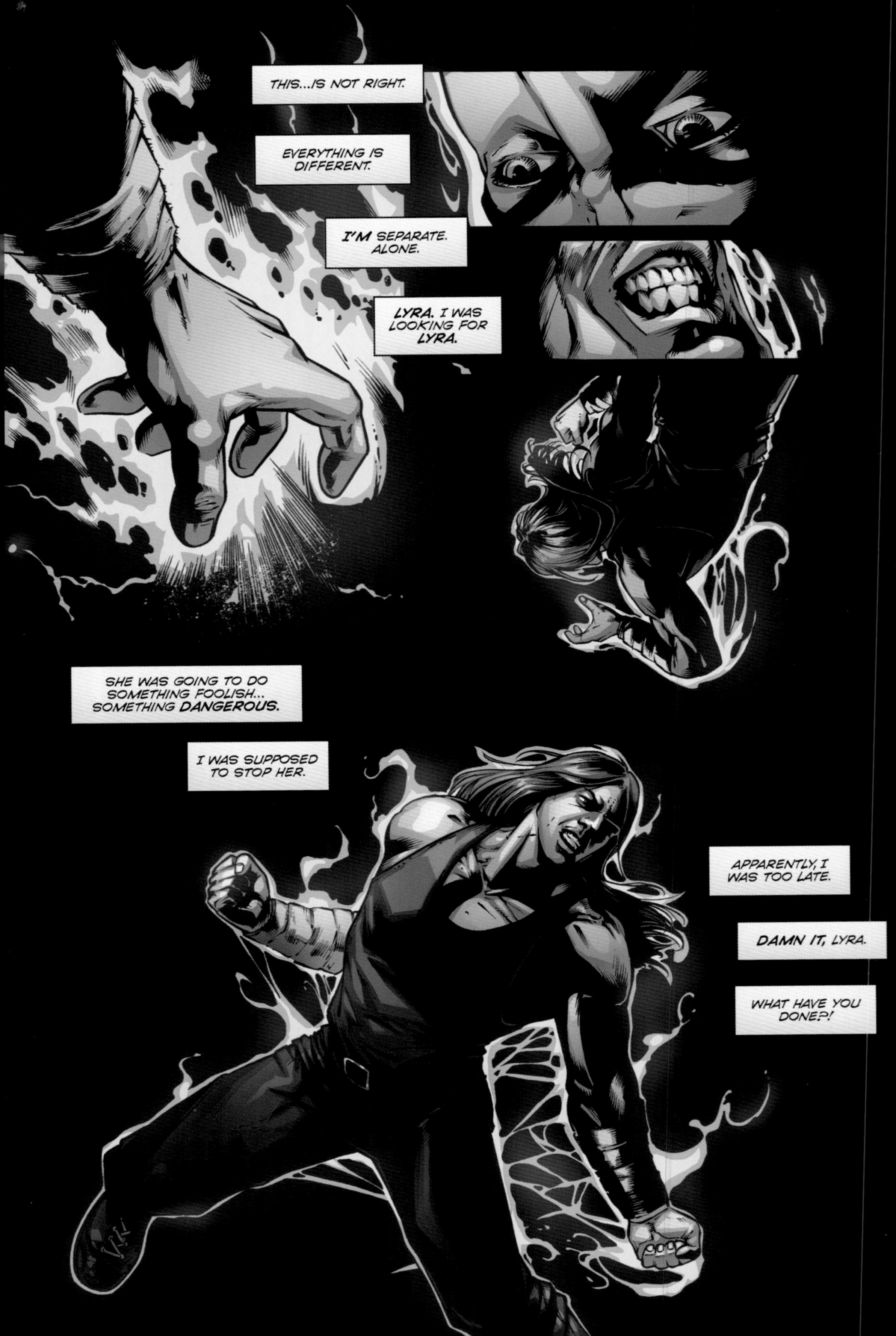
THIS...IS NOT RIGHT.
EVERYTHING IS DIFFERENT.
I'M SEPARATE. ALONE.
LYRA. I WAS LOOKING FOR LYRA.
SHE WAS GOING TO DO SOMETHING FOOLISH... SOMETHING DANGEROUS.
I WAS SUPPOSED TO STOP HER.
APPARENTLY, I WAS TOO LATE.
DAMN IT, LYRA.
WHAT HAVE YOU DONE?!

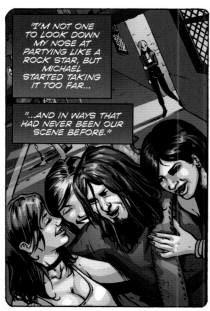

"I'M NOT ONE TO LOOK DOWN MY NOSE AT PARTYING LIKE A ROCK STAR, BUT MICHAEL STARTED TAKING IT TOO FAR..."

"...AND IN WAYS THAT HAD NEVER BEEN OUR SCENE BEFORE."

"AND HE SEEMED TO STOP SLEEPING. HE WAS ALWAYS IN THE STUDIO... ALWAYS PLAYING THAT GUITAR."

"HIS DEDICATION TURNED INTO OBSESSION."

"ALL OF THAT WAS DIFFERENT, DISTURBING EVEN, BUT IT WASN'T... UNNATURAL."

"AND THEN..."

I'M HUNGRY.

ME, TOO. LET'S ORDER SOMETHING.

I'LL TAKE CARE OF IT.

UM...THANKS MICHAEL, BUT WE WERE GONNA ORDER--

NOK NOK

WE, UH, TOTALLY SCREWED THE POOCH ON THIS ORDER...WRONG SIDE OF TOWN. ANYBODY HERE INTERESTED IN SOME CHINESE? ON THE HOUSE?

"NO ONE WANTED TO SAY THAT HE HAD CAUSED IT TO HAPPEN...BY PLAYING HIS FREAKY NEW GUITAR..."

"...BUT WE WERE ALL THINKING IT."

"WE STILL ATE THE CHINESE, THOUGH."

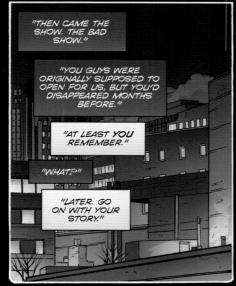

"THEN CAME THE SHOW. THE BAD SHOW."

"YOU GUYS WERE ORIGINALLY SUPPOSED TO OPEN FOR US, BUT YOU'D DISAPPEARED MONTHS BEFORE."

"AT LEAST *YOU* REMEMBER."

"WHAT?"

"LATER. GO ON WITH YOUR STORY."

"MICHAEL HAD TAKEN CHARGE OF THE STAGE PREP, WHICH HE SOMETIMES DID. I THOUGHT IT MEANT HE WAS REINVESTING IN THE BAND. I WAS HAPPY ABOUT IT."

"IT TURNS OUT I SHOULDN'T HAVE BEEN."

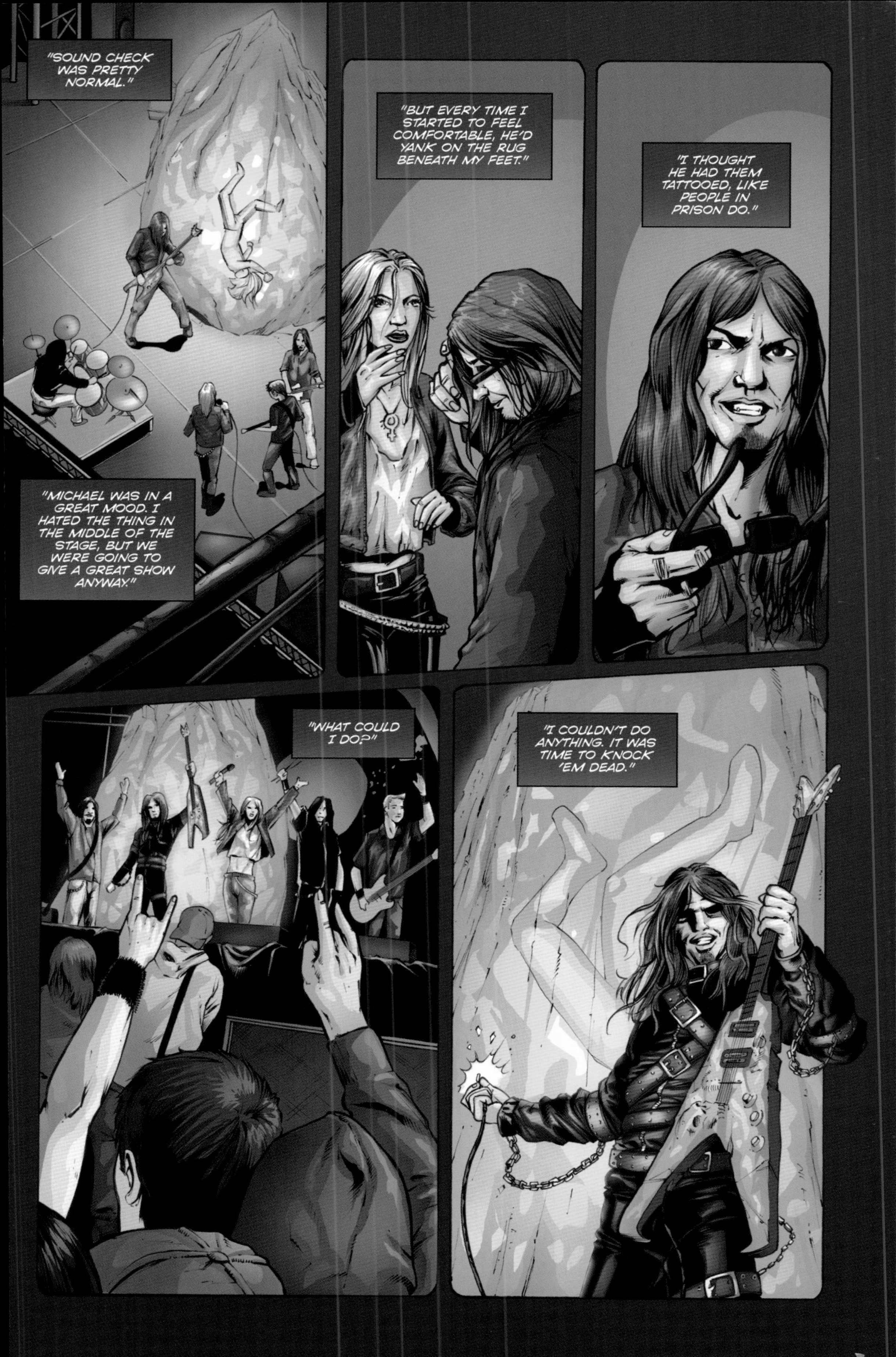
"SOUND CHECK WAS PRETTY NORMAL."
"MICHAEL WAS IN A GREAT MOOD. I HATED THE THING IN THE MIDDLE OF THE STAGE, BUT WE WERE GOING TO GIVE A GREAT SHOW ANYWAY."
"BUT EVERY TIME I STARTED TO FEEL COMFORTABLE, HE'D YANK ON THE RUG BENEATH MY FEET."
"I THOUGHT HE HAD THEM TATTOOED, LIKE PEOPLE IN PRISON DO."
"WHAT COULD I DO?"
"I COULDN'T DO ANYTHING. IT WAS TIME TO KNOCK 'EM DEAD."

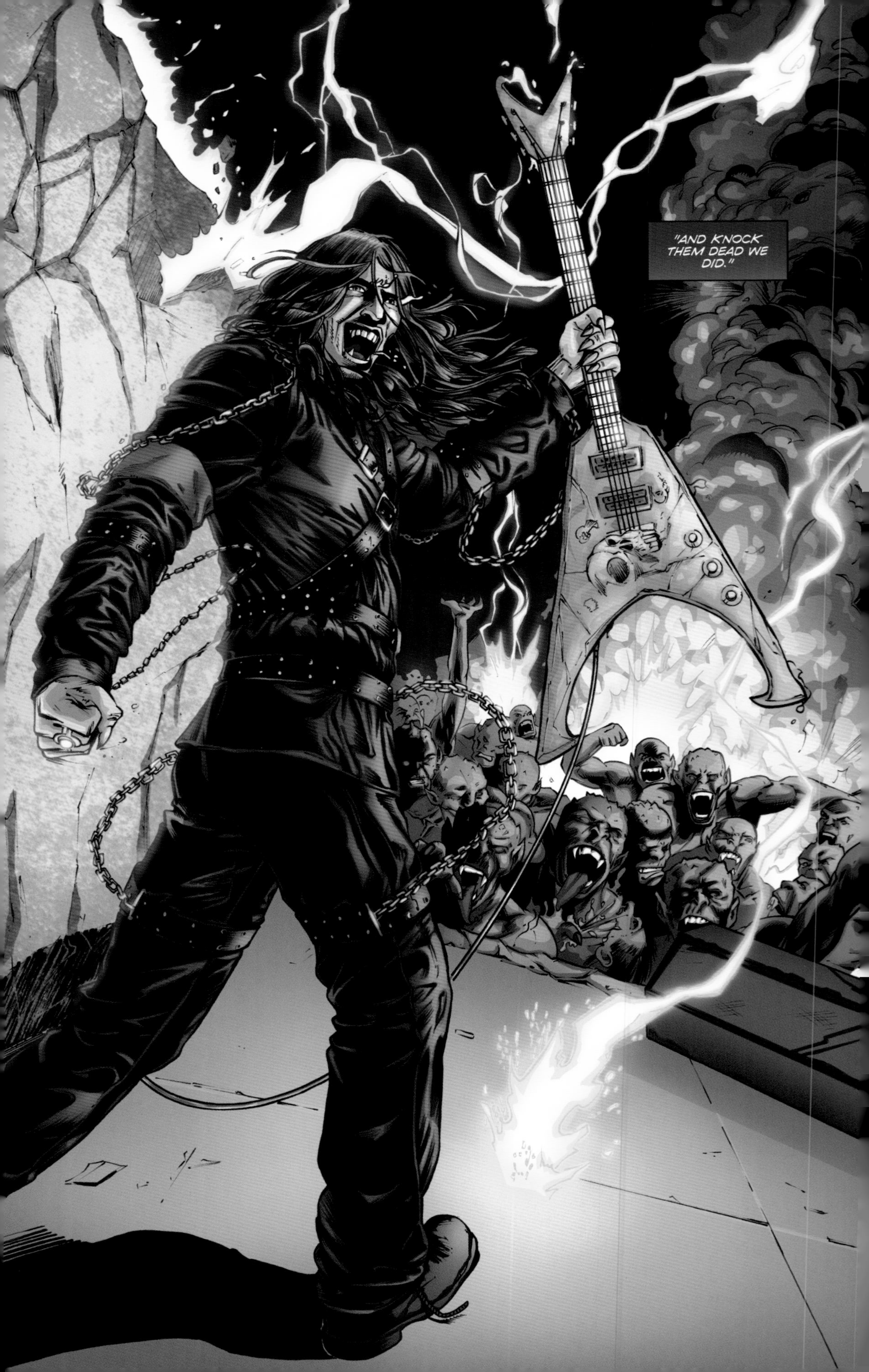
"AND KNOCK THEM DEAD WE DID."

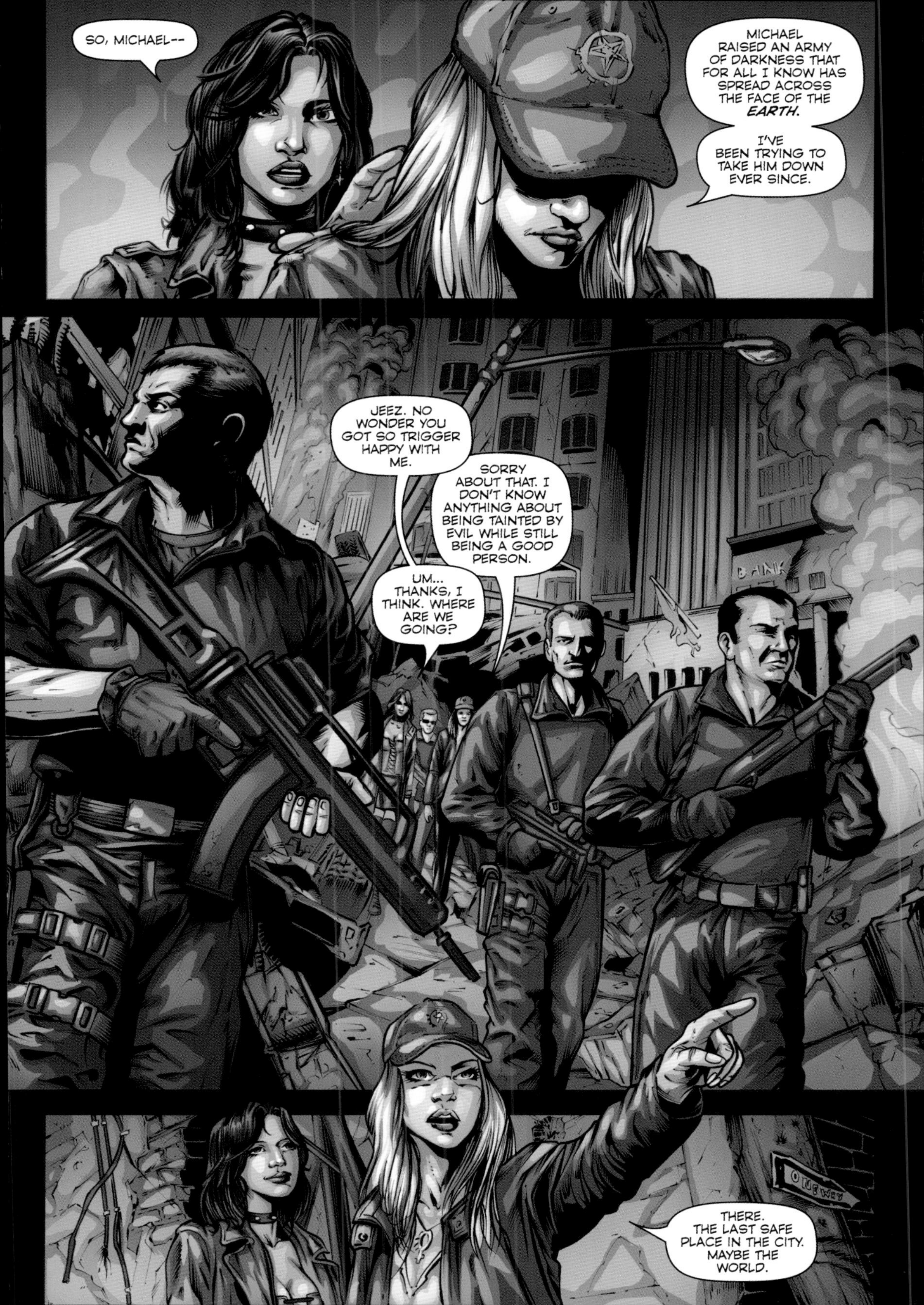
SO, MICHAEL--
MICHAEL RAISED AN ARMY OF DARKNESS THAT FOR ALL I KNOW HAS SPREAD ACROSS THE FACE OF THE EARTH.
I'VE BEEN TRYING TO TAKE HIM DOWN EVER SINCE.
JEEZ. NO WONDER YOU GOT SO TRIGGER HAPPY WITH ME.
SORRY ABOUT THAT. I DON'T KNOW ANYTHING ABOUT BEING TAINTED BY EVIL WHILE STILL BEING A GOOD PERSON.
UM... THANKS, I THINK. WHERE ARE WE GOING?
BANK
ONE WAY
THERE. THE LAST SAFE PLACE IN THE CITY. MAYBE THE WORLD.

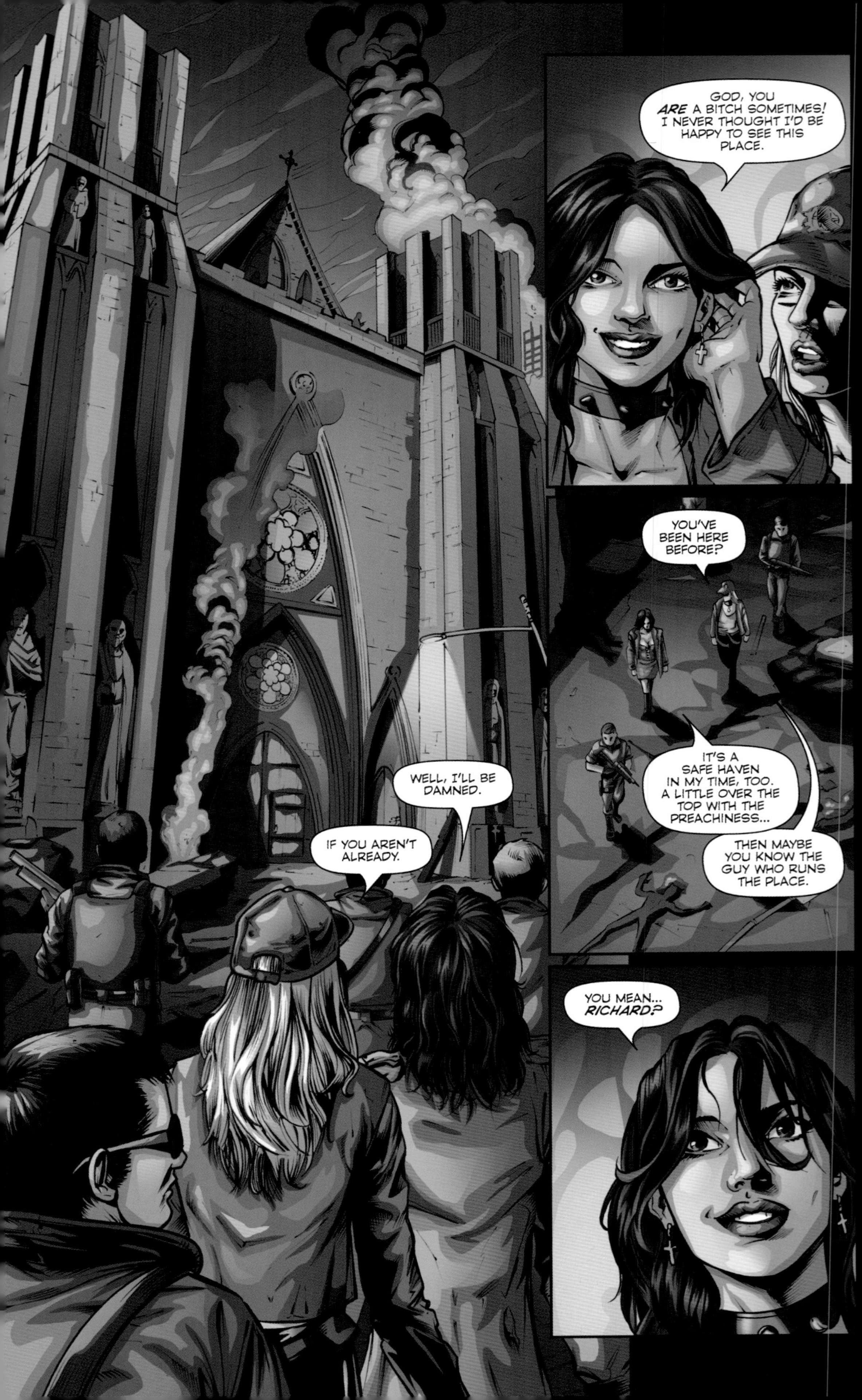
GOD, YOU ARE A BITCH SOMETIMES! I NEVER THOUGHT I'D BE HAPPY TO SEE THIS PLACE.
WELL, I'LL BE DAMNED.
IF YOU AREN'T ALREADY.
YOU'VE BEEN HERE BEFORE?
IT'S A SAFE HAVEN IN MY TIME, TOO. A LITTLE OVER THE TOP WITH THE PREACHINESS...
THEN MAYBE YOU KNOW THE GUY WHO RUNS THE PLACE.
YOU MEAN... RICHARD?

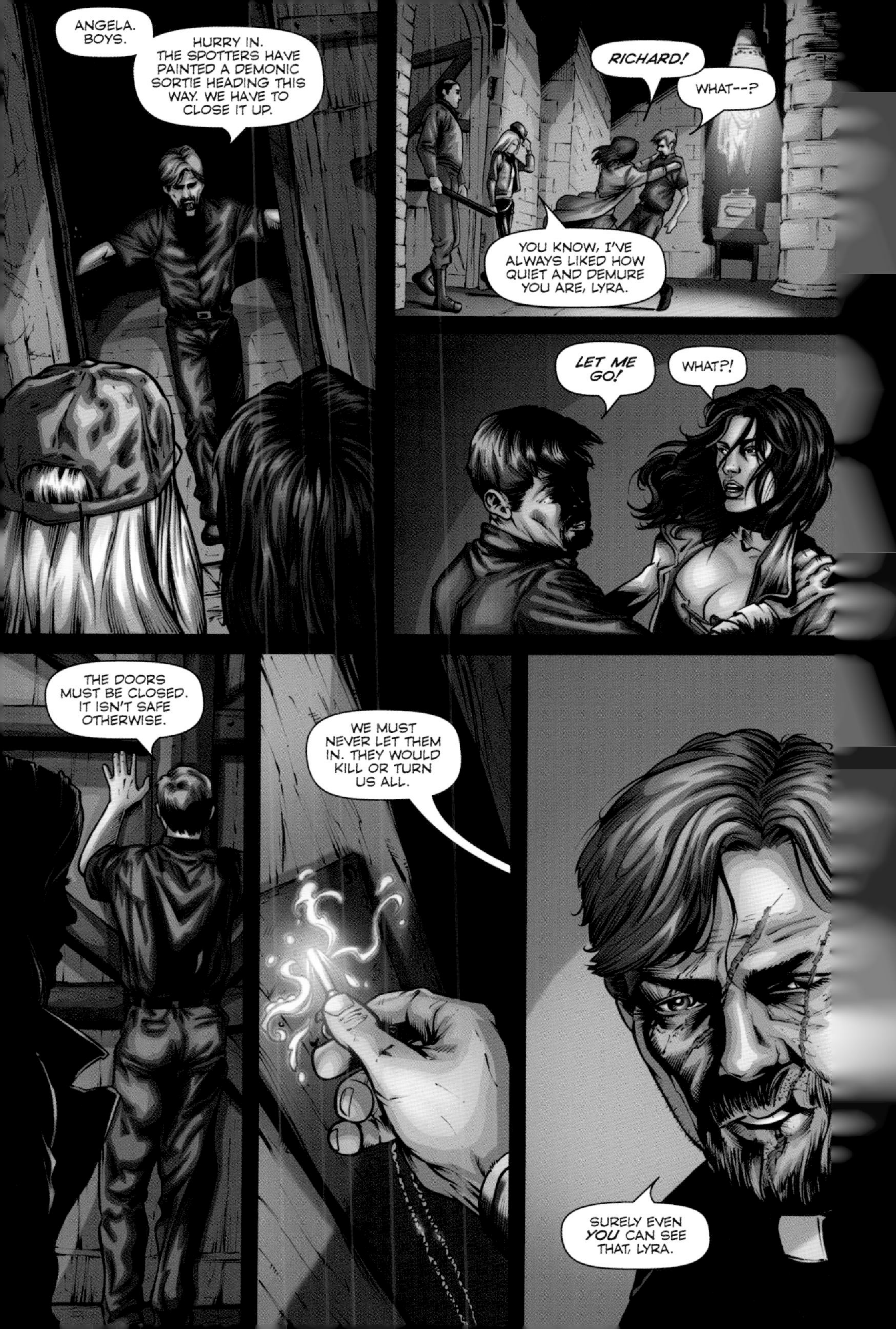
ANGELA. BOYS.
HURRY IN. THE SPOTTERS HAVE PAINTED A DEMONIC SORTIE HEADING THIS WAY. WE HAVE TO CLOSE IT UP.
RICHARD!
WHAT--?
YOU KNOW, I'VE ALWAYS LIKED HOW QUIET AND DEMURE YOU ARE, LYRA.
LET ME GO!
WHAT?!
THE DOORS MUST BE CLOSED. IT ISN'T SAFE OTHERWISE.
WE MUST NEVER LET THEM IN. THEY WOULD KILL OR TURN US ALL.
SURELY EVEN YOU CAN SEE THAT, LYRA.

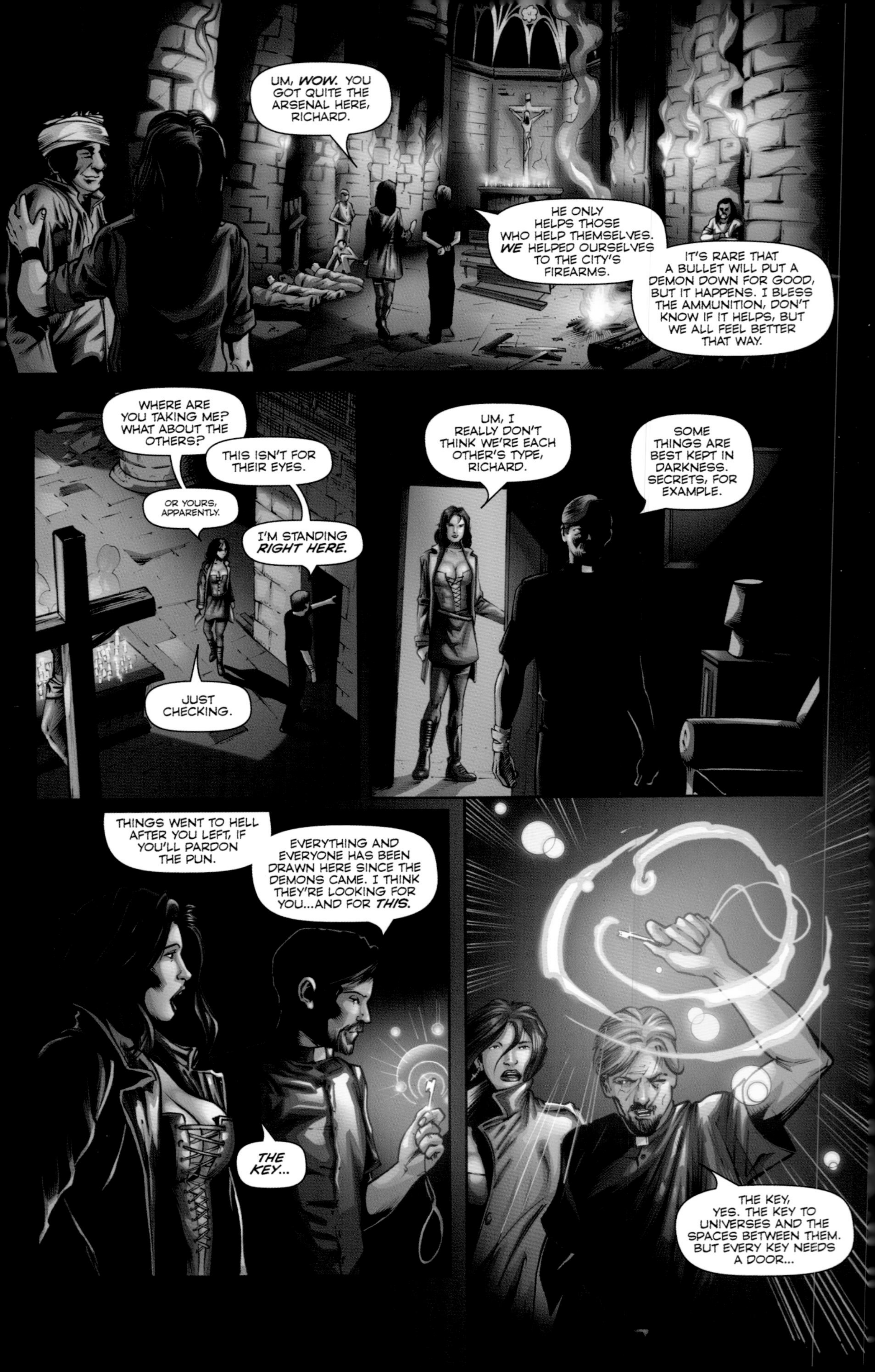
UM, WOW. YOU GOT QUITE THE ARSENAL HERE, RICHARD.
HE ONLY HELPS THOSE WHO HELP THEMSELVES. WE HELPED OURSELVES TO THE CITY'S FIREARMS.
IT'S RARE THAT A BULLET WILL PUT A DEMON DOWN FOR GOOD, BUT IT HAPPENS. I BLESS THE AMMUNITION, DON'T KNOW IF IT HELPS, BUT WE ALL FEEL BETTER THAT WAY.
WHERE ARE YOU TAKING ME? WHAT ABOUT THE OTHERS?
THIS ISN'T FOR THEIR EYES.
OR YOURS, APPARENTLY.
I'M STANDING RIGHT HERE.
JUST CHECKING.
UM, I REALLY DON'T THINK WE'RE EACH OTHER'S TYPE, RICHARD.
SOME THINGS ARE BEST KEPT IN DARKNESS. SECRETS, FOR EXAMPLE.
THINGS WENT TO HELL AFTER YOU LEFT, IF YOU'LL PARDON THE PUN.
EVERYTHING AND EVERYONE HAS BEEN DRAWN HERE SINCE THE DEMONS CAME. I THINK THEY'RE LOOKING FOR YOU...AND FOR THIS.
THE KEY...
THE KEY, YES. THE KEY TO UNIVERSES AND THE SPACES BETWEEN THEM. BUT EVERY KEY NEEDS A DOOR...

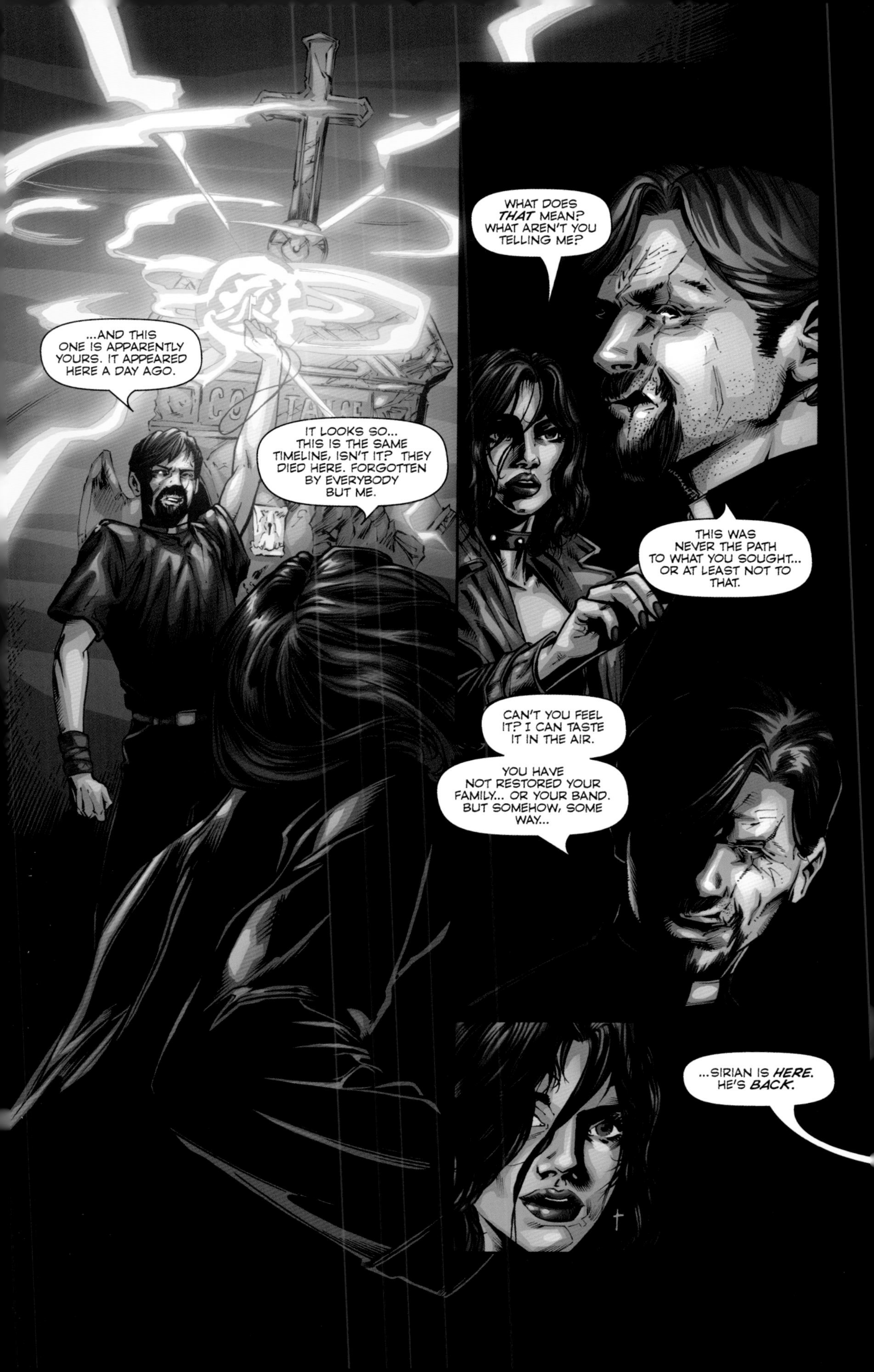
...AND THIS ONE IS APPARENTLY YOURS. IT APPEARED HERE A DAY AGO.
IT LOOKS SO... THIS IS THE SAME TIMELINE, ISN'T IT? THEY DIED HERE. FORGOTTEN BY EVERYBODY BUT ME.
WHAT DOES THAT MEAN? WHAT AREN'T YOU TELLING ME?
THIS WAS NEVER THE PATH TO WHAT YOU SOUGHT... OR AT LEAST NOT TO THAT.
CAN'T YOU FEEL IT? I CAN TASTE IT IN THE AIR.
YOU HAVE NOT RESTORED YOUR FAMILY... OR YOUR BAND. BUT SOMEHOW, SOME WAY...
...SIRIAN IS HERE. HE'S BACK.

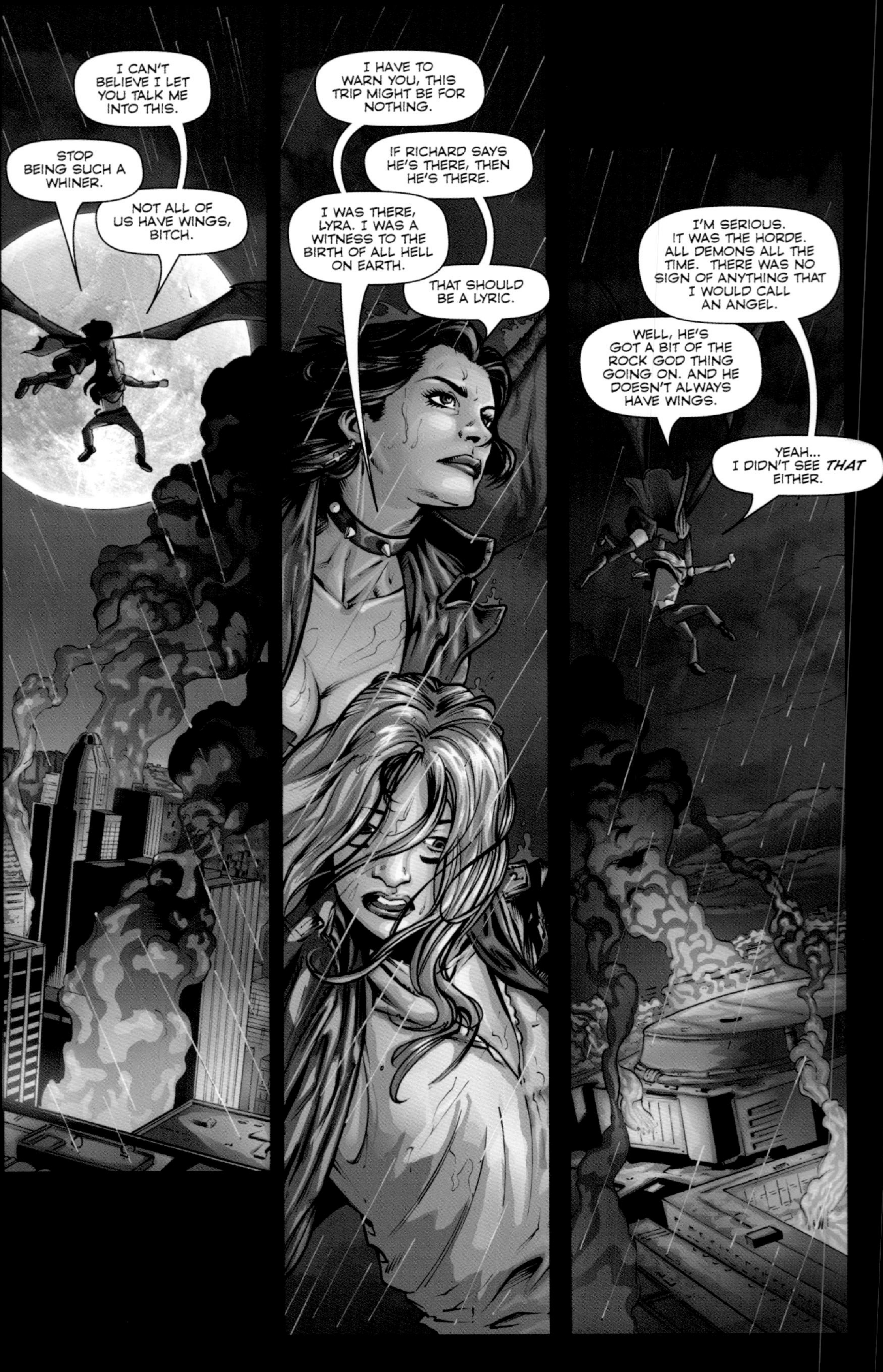
I CAN'T BELIEVE I LET YOU TALK ME INTO THIS.
STOP BEING SUCH A WHINER.
NOT ALL OF US HAVE WINGS, BITCH.
I HAVE TO WARN YOU, THIS TRIP MIGHT BE FOR NOTHING.
IF RICHARD SAYS HE'S THERE, THEN HE'S THERE.
I WAS THERE, LYRA. I WAS A WITNESS TO THE BIRTH OF ALL HELL ON EARTH.
THAT SHOULD BE A LYRIC.
I'M SERIOUS. IT WAS THE HORDE. ALL DEMONS ALL THE TIME. THERE WAS NO SIGN OF ANYTHING THAT I WOULD CALL AN ANGEL.
WELL, HE'S GOT A BIT OF THE ROCK GOD THING GOING ON. AND HE DOESN'T ALWAYS HAVE WINGS.
YEAH... I DIDN'T SEE *THAT* EITHER.

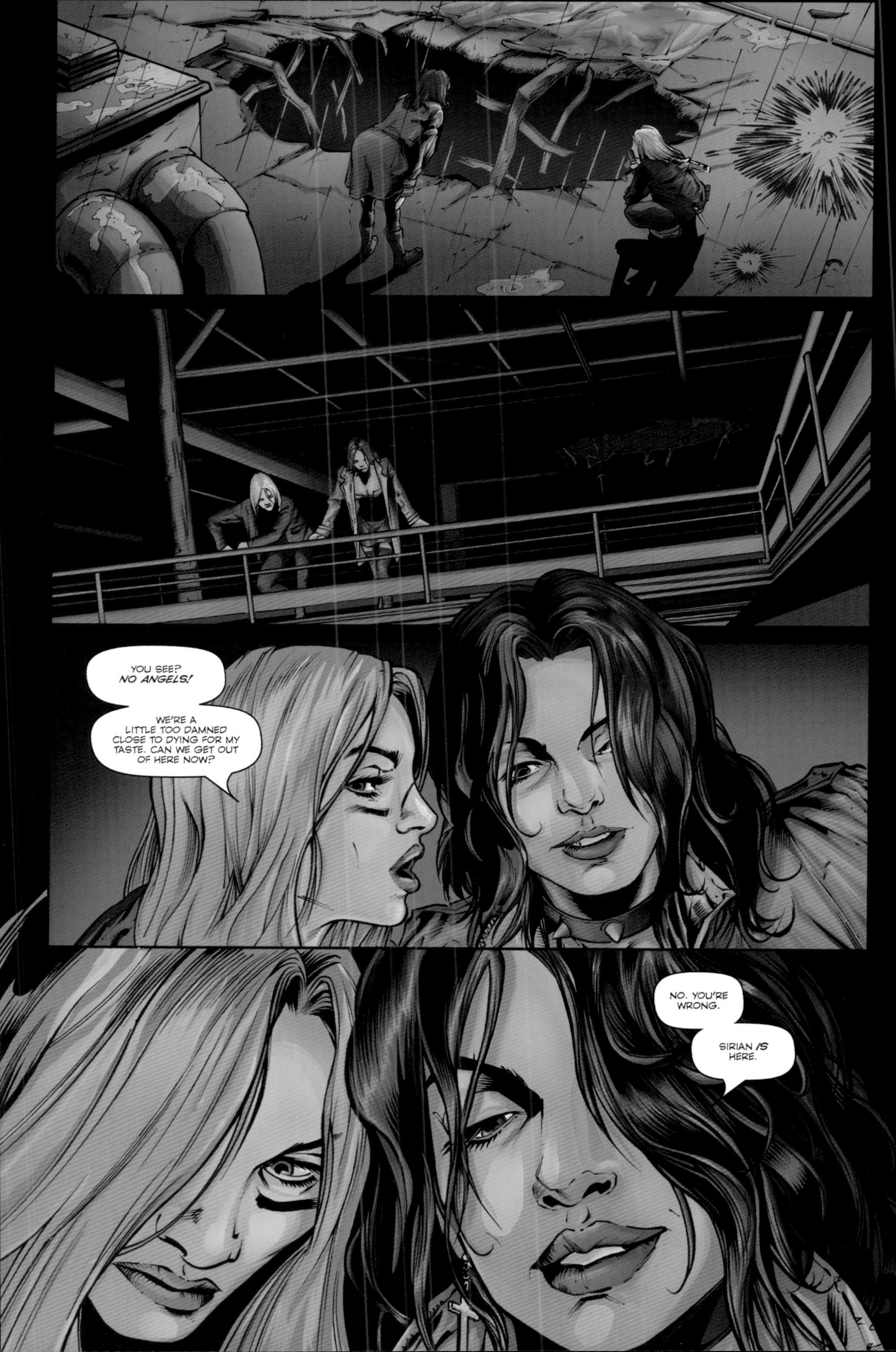
YOU SEE? NO ANGELS!
WE'RE A LITTLE TOO DAMNED CLOSE TO DYING FOR MY TASTE. CAN WE GET OUT OF HERE NOW?
NO. YOU'RE WRONG.
SIRIAN IS HERE.

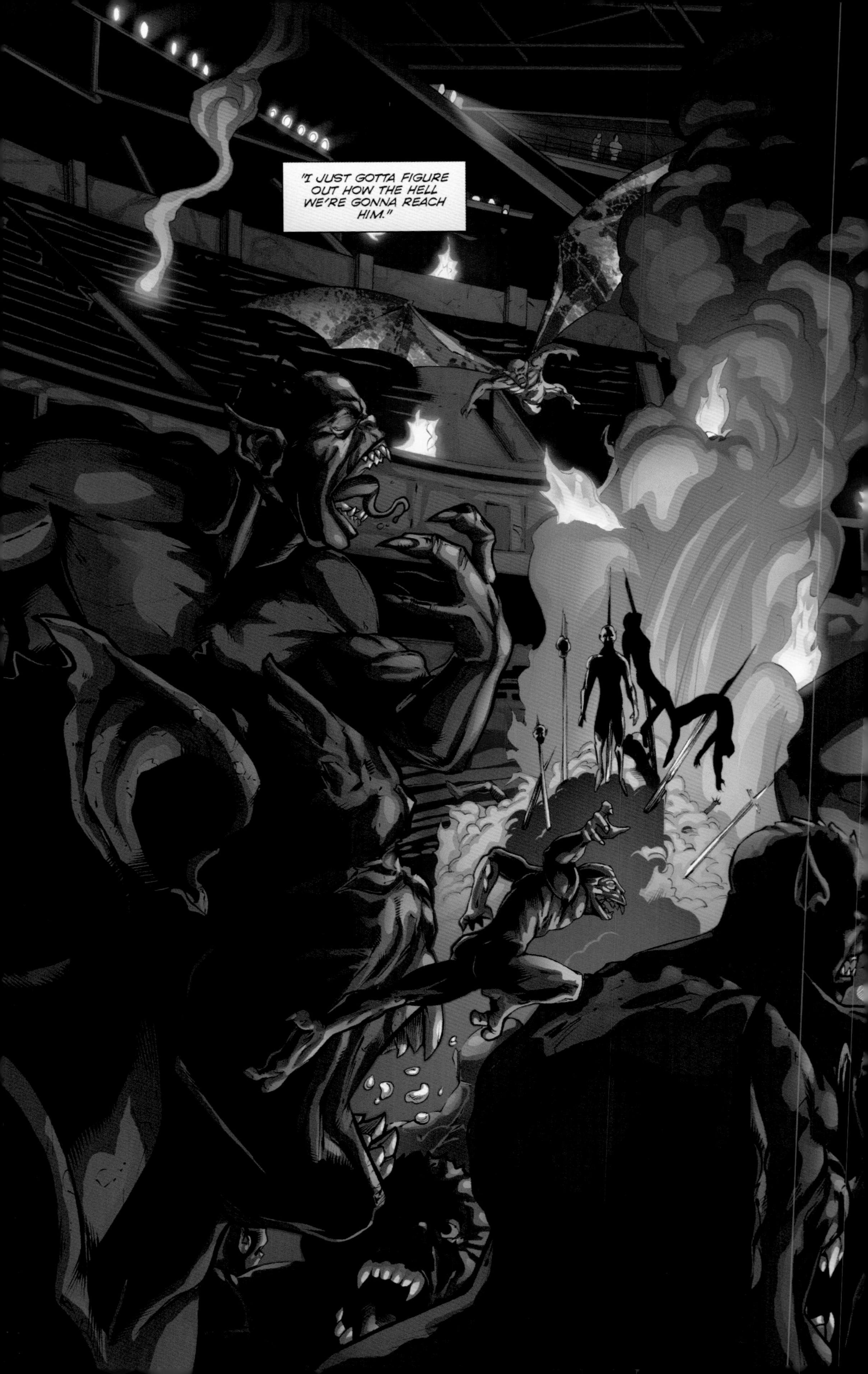
"I JUST GOTTA FIGURE OUT HOW THE HELL WE'RE GONNA REACH HIM."

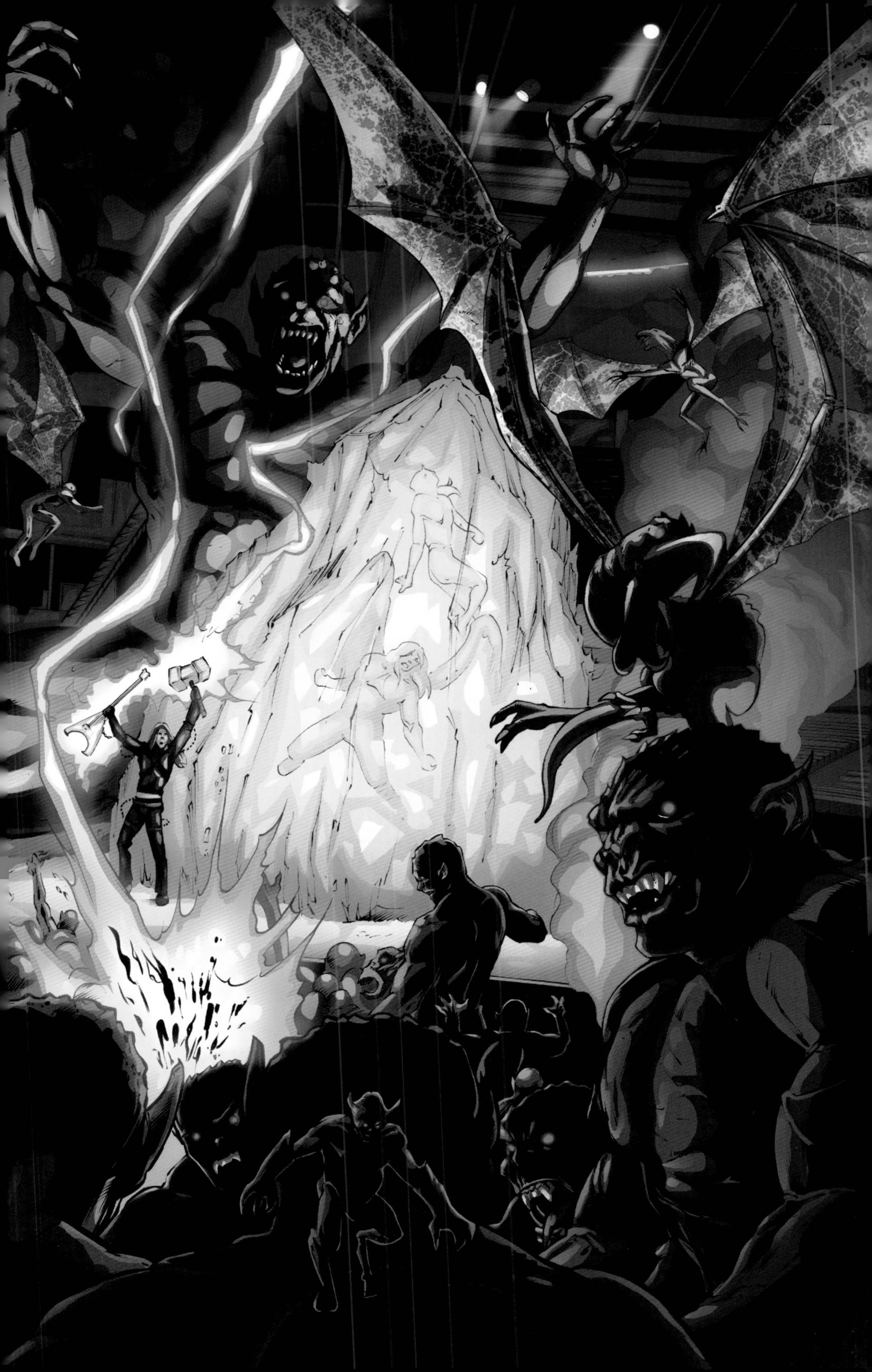

Eternal Descent

CHAPTER SIX: SHADWOWS AND DUST

Written by
Llexi Leon and **Justin Peniston**

Pencils by
Ivan Fernandez

Inks by
Juan Castro, Alexandre Palomaro,
and **Rob Lean**

Colors by
Javier Tartaglia and **Rainer Petter**

Lettering by
Charles Pritchett

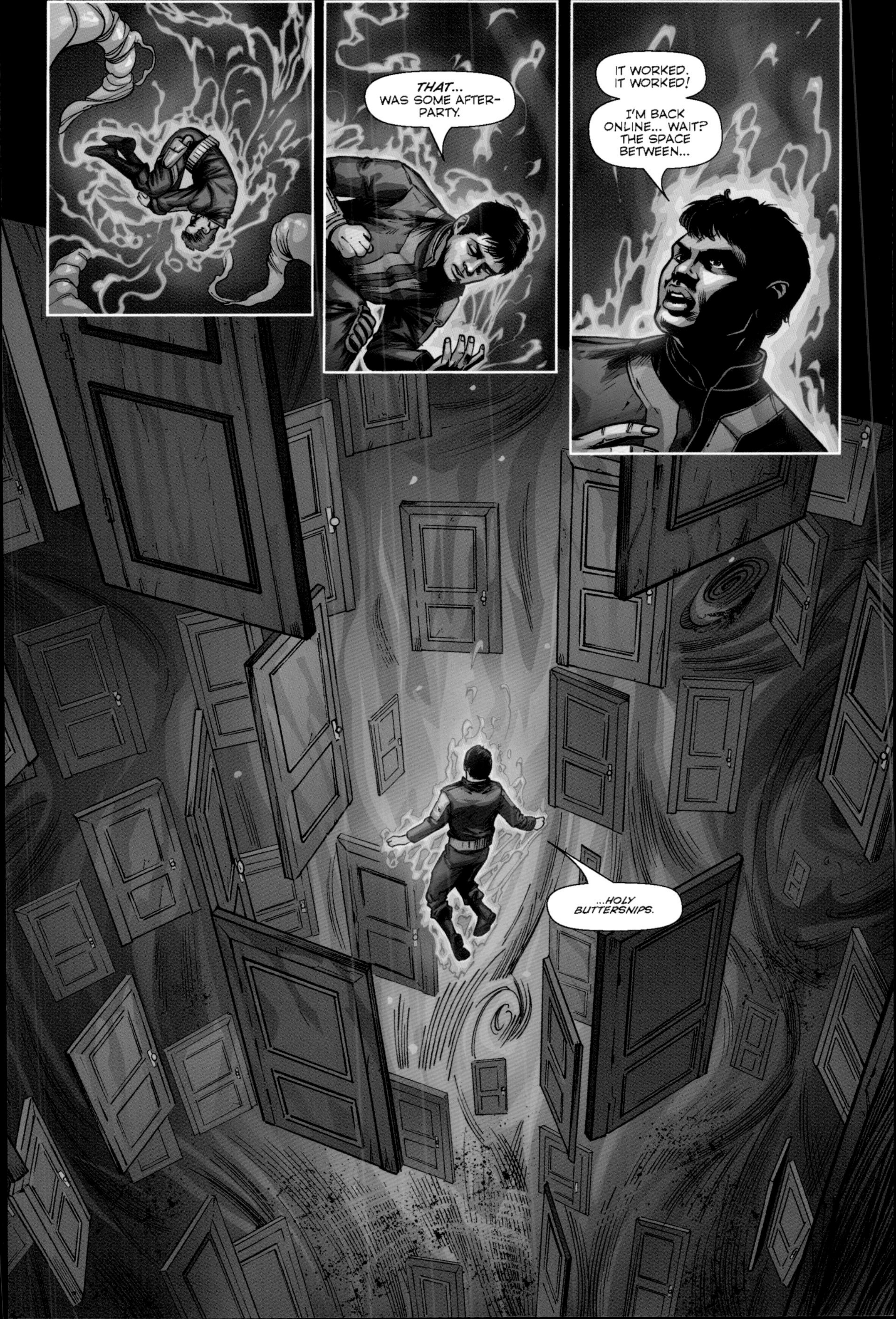
THAT... WAS SOME AFTER-PARTY.
IT WORKED. IT WORKED!
I'M BACK ONLINE... WAIT? THE SPACE BETWEEN...
...HOLY BUTTERSNIPS.

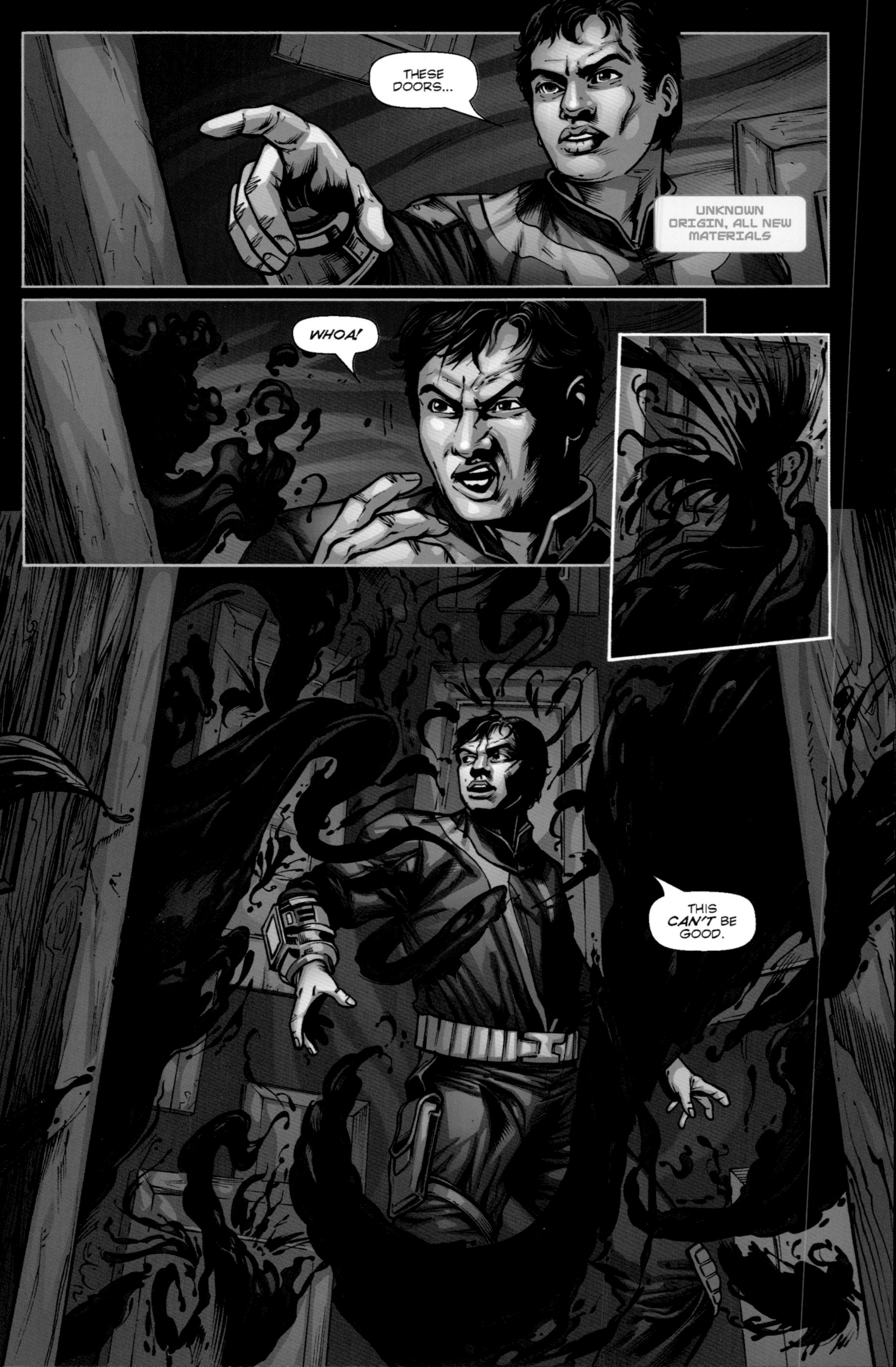
THESE DOORS...
UNKNOWN ORIGIN, ALL NEW MATERIALS
WHOA!
THIS CAN'T BE GOOD.

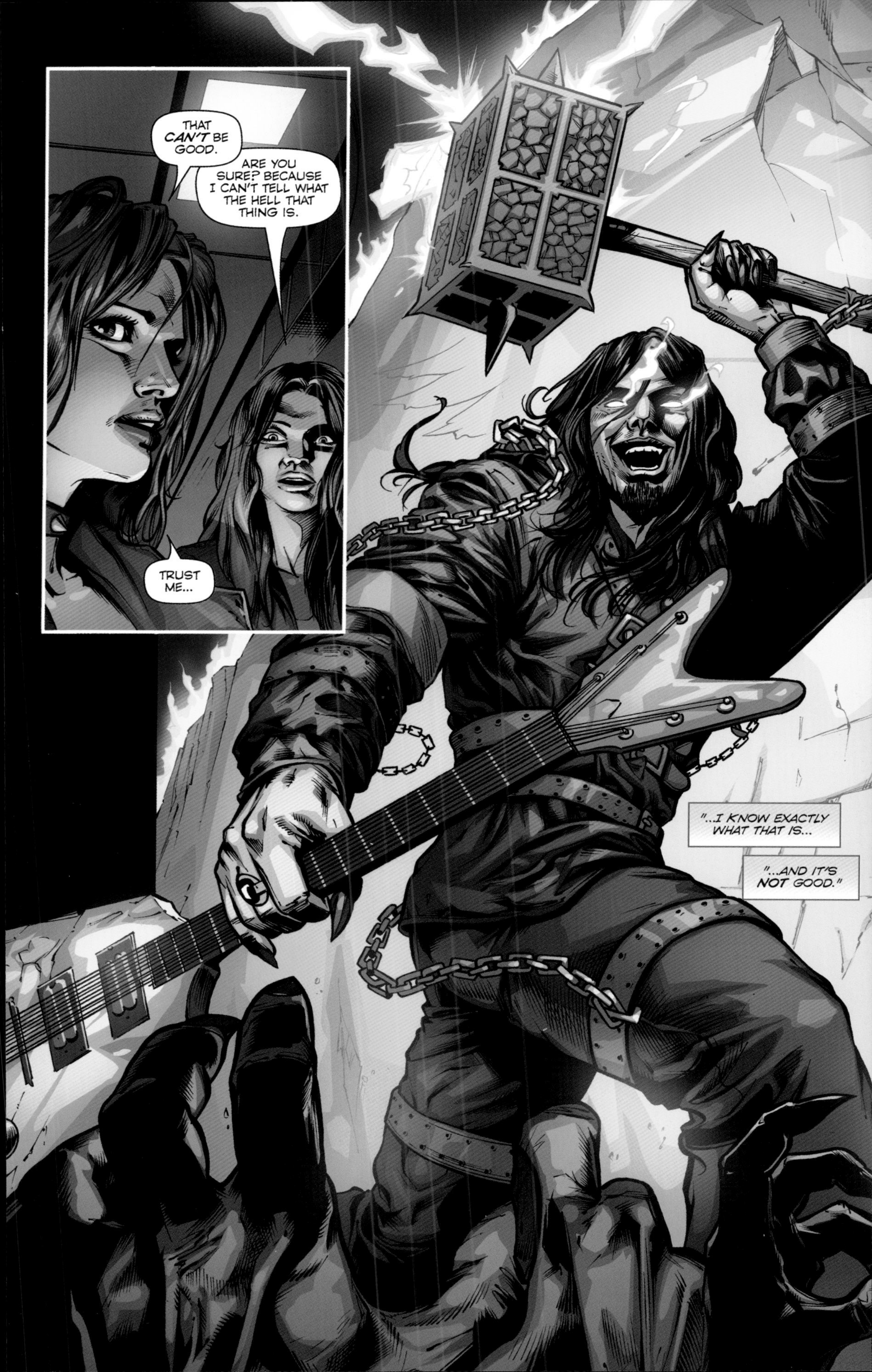
THAT CAN'T BE GOOD.
ARE YOU SURE? BECAUSE I CAN'T TELL WHAT THE HELL THAT THING IS.
TRUST ME...
"...I KNOW EXACTLY WHAT THAT IS...
"...AND IT'S NOT GOOD."

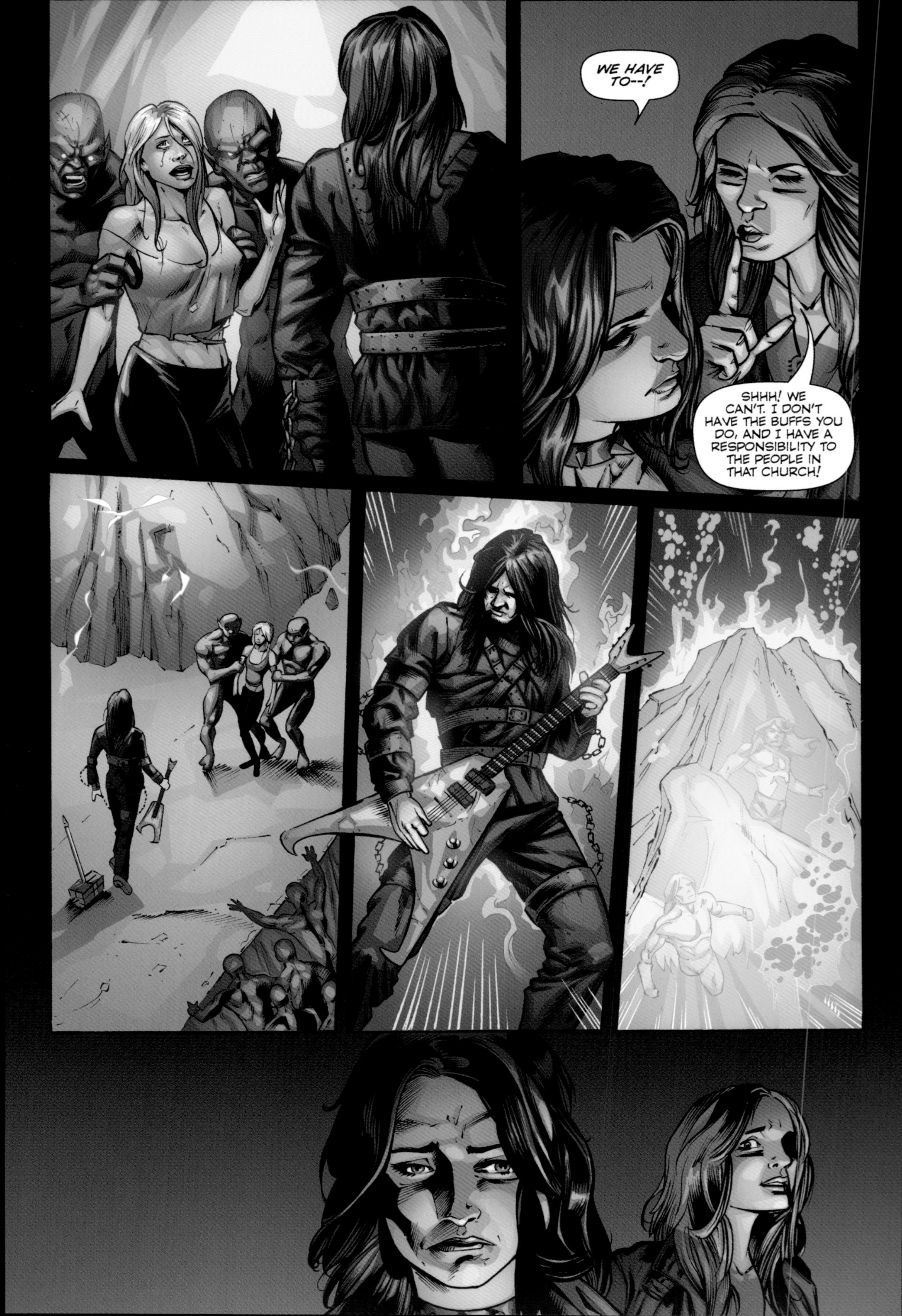
WE HAVE TO--!
SHHH! WE CAN'T. I DON'T HAVE THE BUFFS YOU DO, AND I HAVE A RESPONSIBILITY TO THE PEOPLE IN THAT CHURCH!

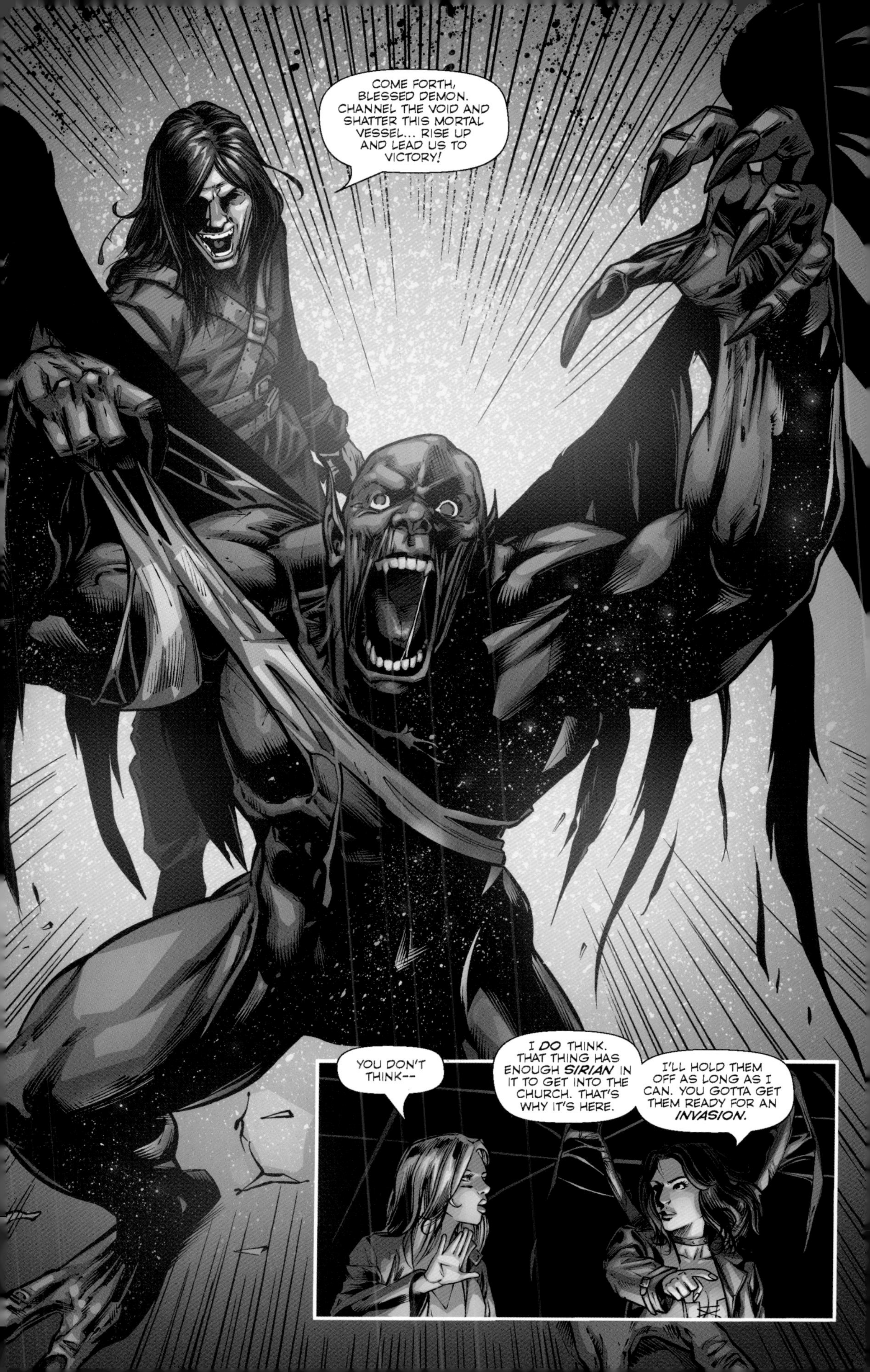
COME FORTH, BLESSED DEMON. CHANNEL THE VOID AND SHATTER THIS MORTAL VESSEL... RISE UP AND LEAD US TO VICTORY!
YOU DON'T THINK--
I *DO* THINK. THAT THING HAS ENOUGH *SIRIAN* IN IT TO GET INTO THE CHURCH. THAT'S WHY IT'S HERE.
I'LL HOLD THEM OFF AS LONG AS I CAN. YOU GOTTA GET THEM READY FOR AN *INVASION*.

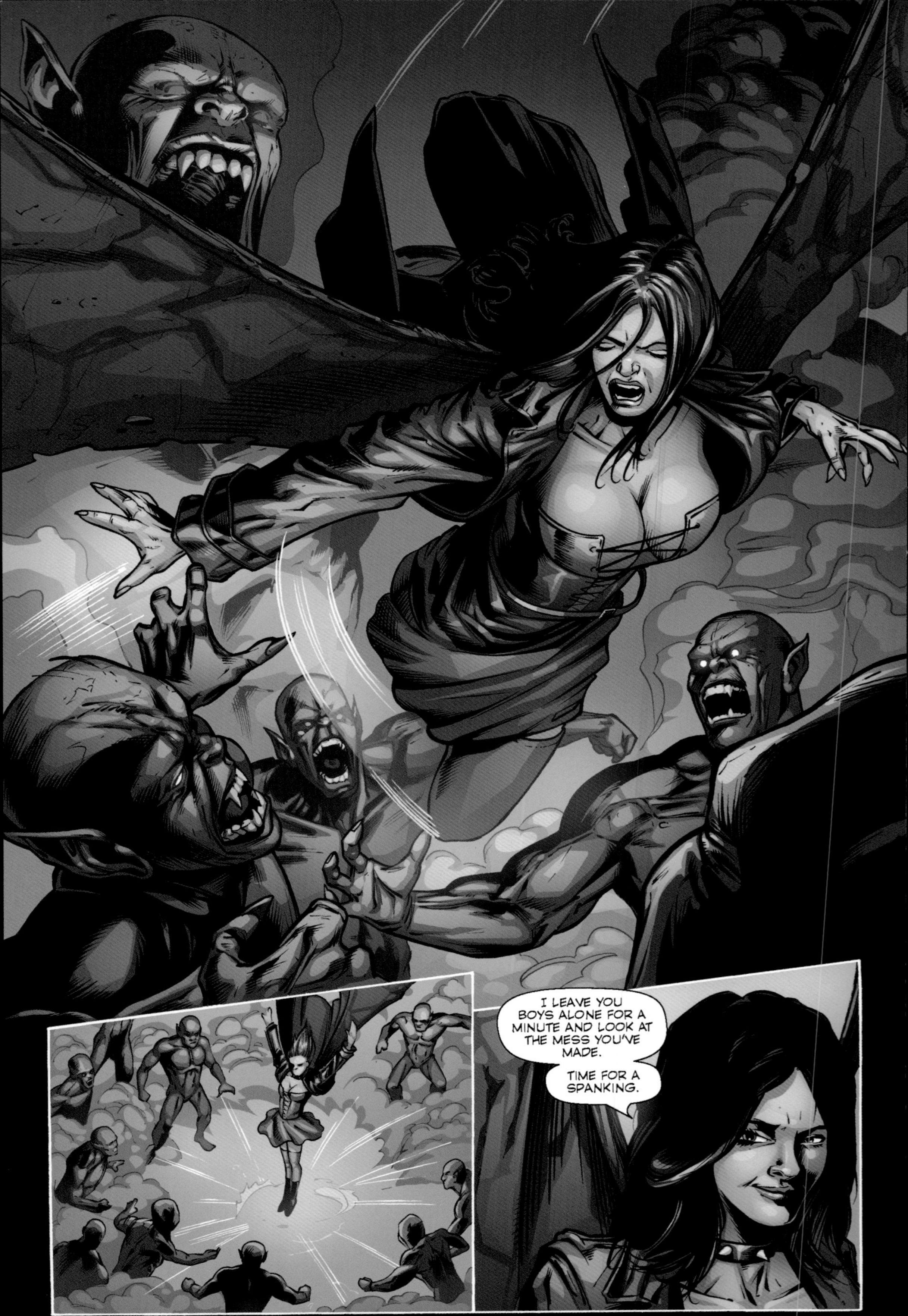
I LEAVE YOU BOYS ALONE FOR A MINUTE AND LOOK AT THE MESS YOU'VE MADE.
TIME FOR A SPANKING.

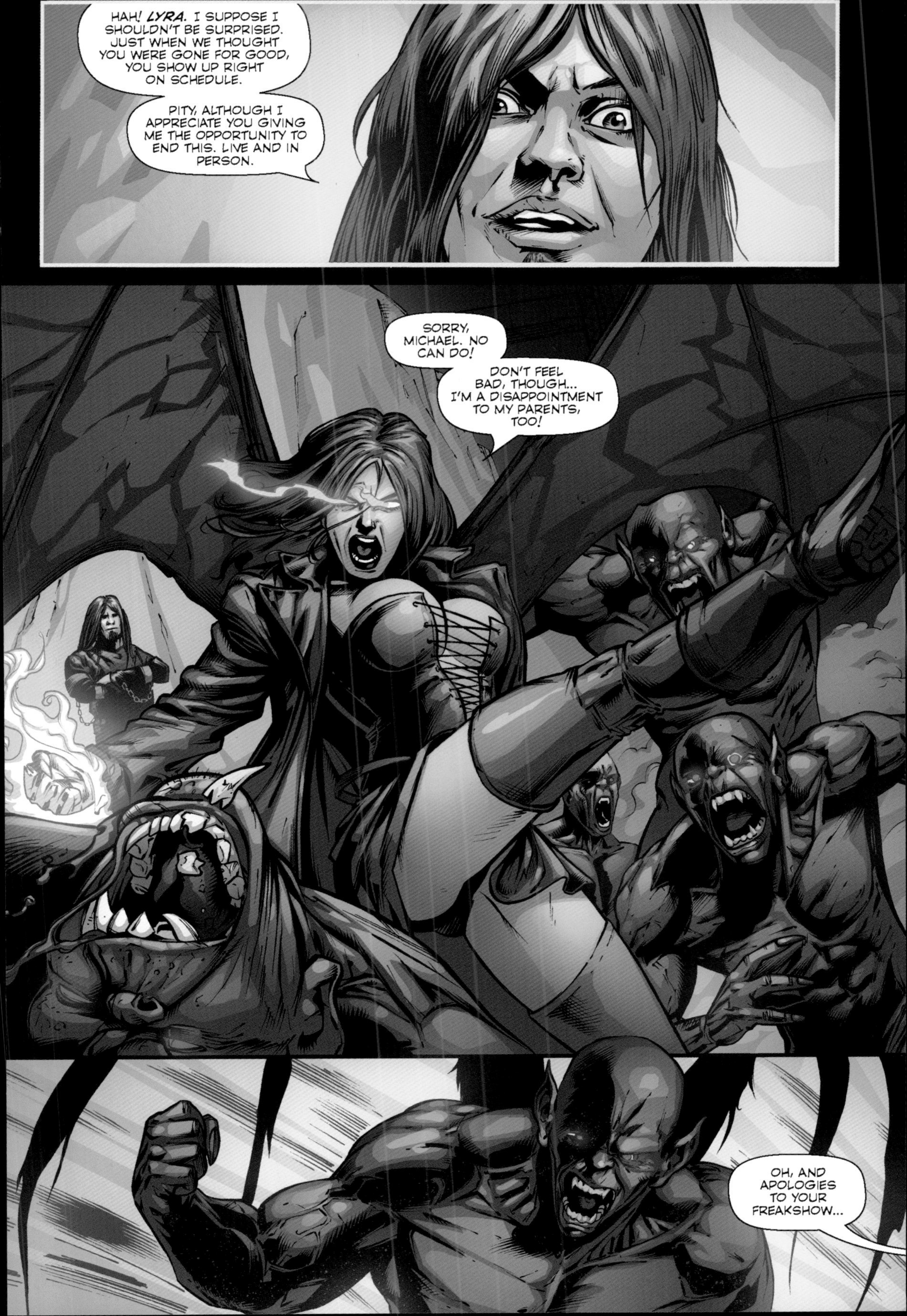
HAH! *LYRA.* I SUPPOSE I SHOULDN'T BE SURPRISED. JUST WHEN WE THOUGHT YOU WERE GONE FOR GOOD, YOU SHOW UP RIGHT ON SCHEDULE.
PITY, ALTHOUGH I APPRECIATE YOU GIVING ME THE OPPORTUNITY TO END THIS. LIVE AND IN PERSON.
SORRY, MICHAEL. NO CAN DO!
DON'T FEEL BAD, THOUGH... I'M A DISAPPOINTMENT TO MY PARENTS, TOO!
OH, AND APOLOGIES TO YOUR FREAKSHOW...

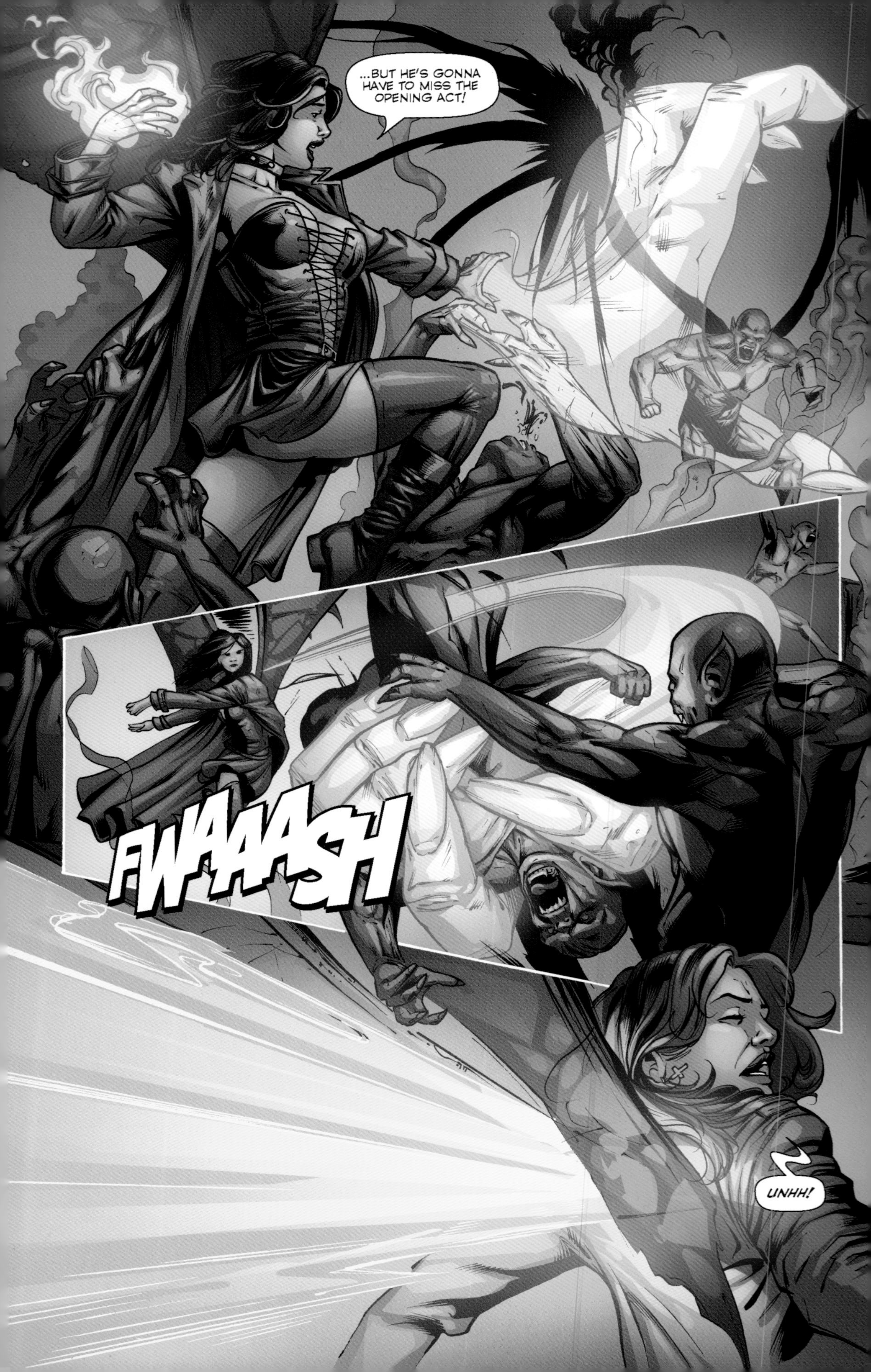
...BUT HE'S GONNA HAVE TO MISS THE OPENING ACT!
FWAAASH
UNHH!

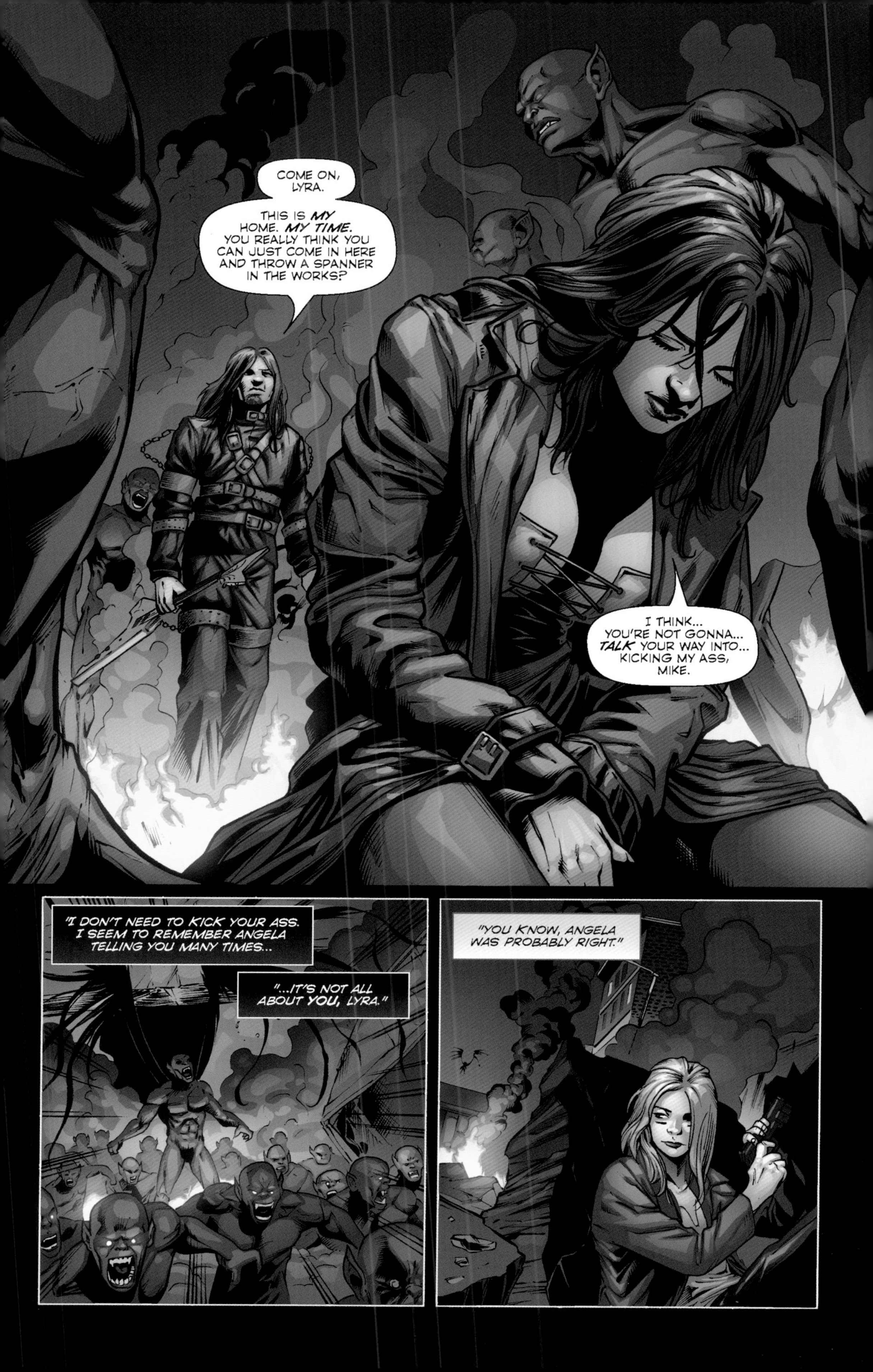
COME ON, LYRA.
THIS IS MY HOME. MY TIME. YOU REALLY THINK YOU CAN JUST COME IN HERE AND THROW A SPANNER IN THE WORKS?
I THINK... YOU'RE NOT GONNA... TALK YOUR WAY INTO... KICKING MY ASS, MIKE.
"I DON'T NEED TO KICK YOUR ASS. I SEEM TO REMEMBER ANGELA TELLING YOU MANY TIMES...
"...IT'S NOT ALL ABOUT YOU, LYRA."
"YOU KNOW, ANGELA WAS PROBABLY RIGHT."

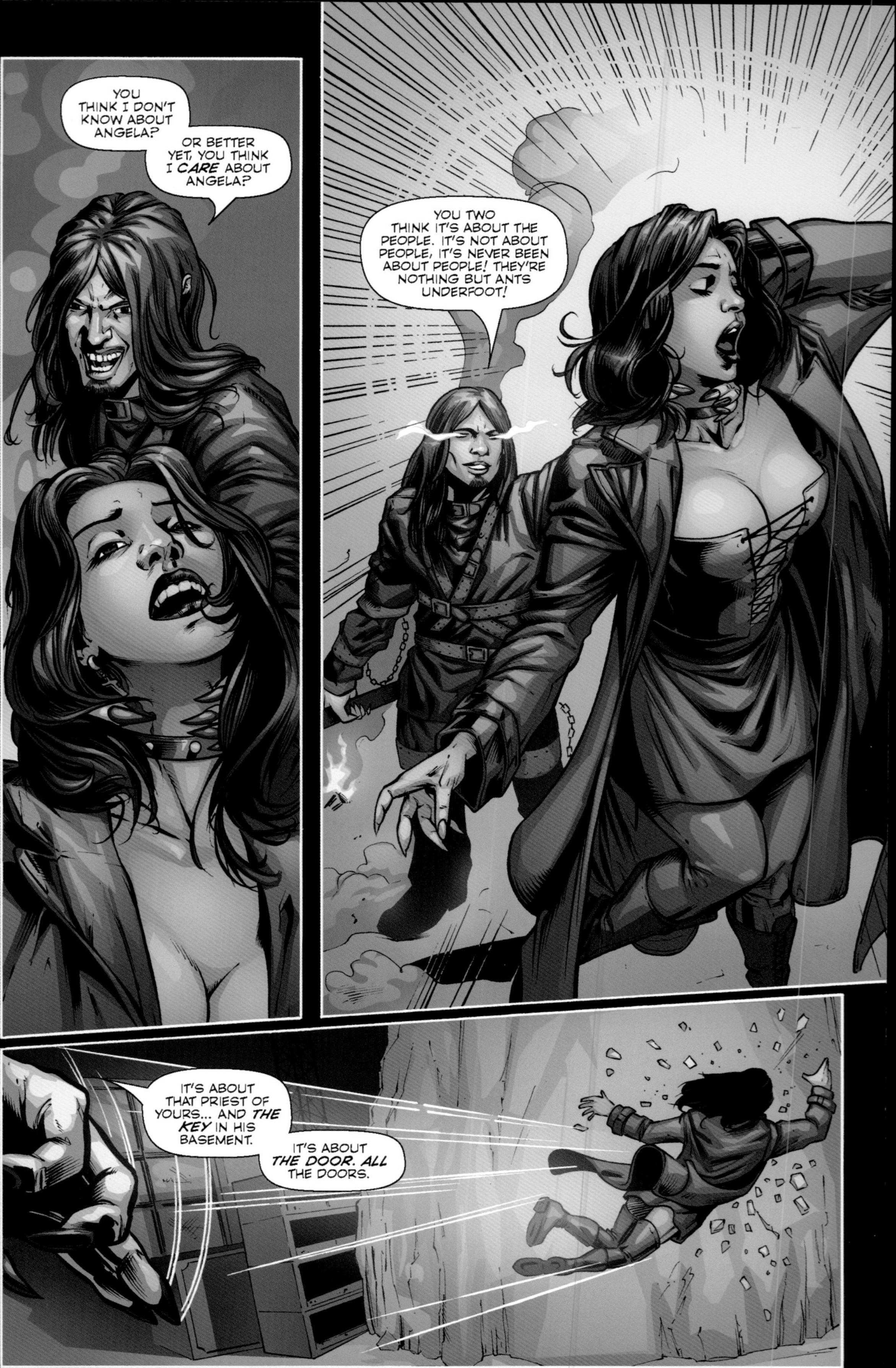
YOU THINK I DON'T KNOW ABOUT ANGELA?
OR BETTER YET, YOU THINK I CARE ABOUT ANGELA?
YOU TWO THINK IT'S ABOUT THE PEOPLE. IT'S NOT ABOUT PEOPLE, IT'S NEVER BEEN ABOUT PEOPLE! THEY'RE NOTHING BUT ANTS UNDERFOOT!
IT'S ABOUT THAT PRIEST OF YOURS... AND THE KEY IN HIS BASEMENT.
IT'S ABOUT THE DOOR. ALL THE DOORS.

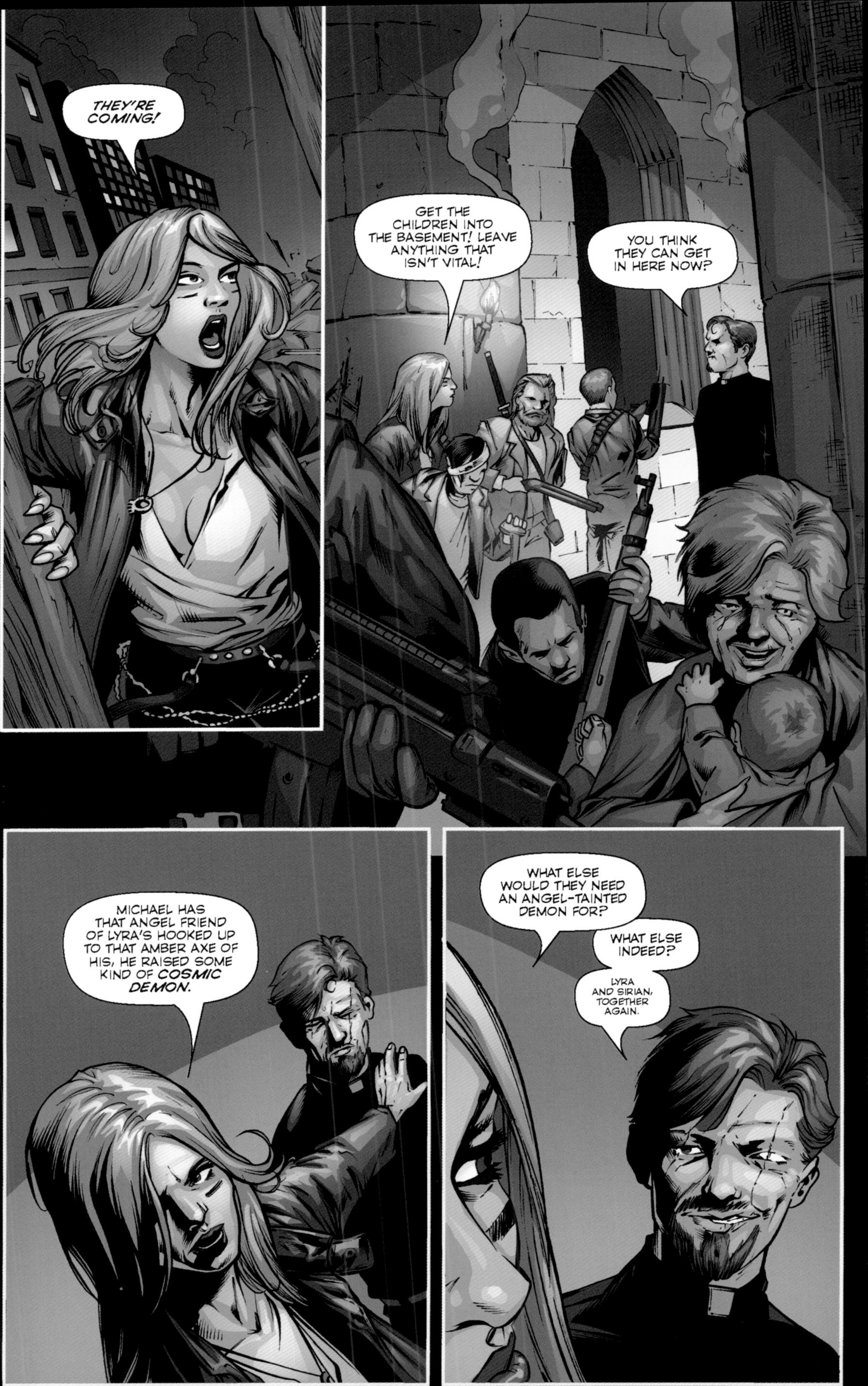
THEY'RE COMING!
GET THE CHILDREN INTO THE BASEMENT! LEAVE ANYTHING THAT ISN'T VITAL!
YOU THINK THEY CAN GET IN HERE NOW?
MICHAEL HAS THAT ANGEL FRIEND OF LYRA'S HOOKED UP TO THAT AMBER AXE OF HIS, HE RAISED SOME KIND OF COSMIC DEMON.
WHAT ELSE WOULD THEY NEED AN ANGEL-TAINTED DEMON FOR?
WHAT ELSE INDEED?
LYRA AND SIRIAN, TOGETHER AGAIN.

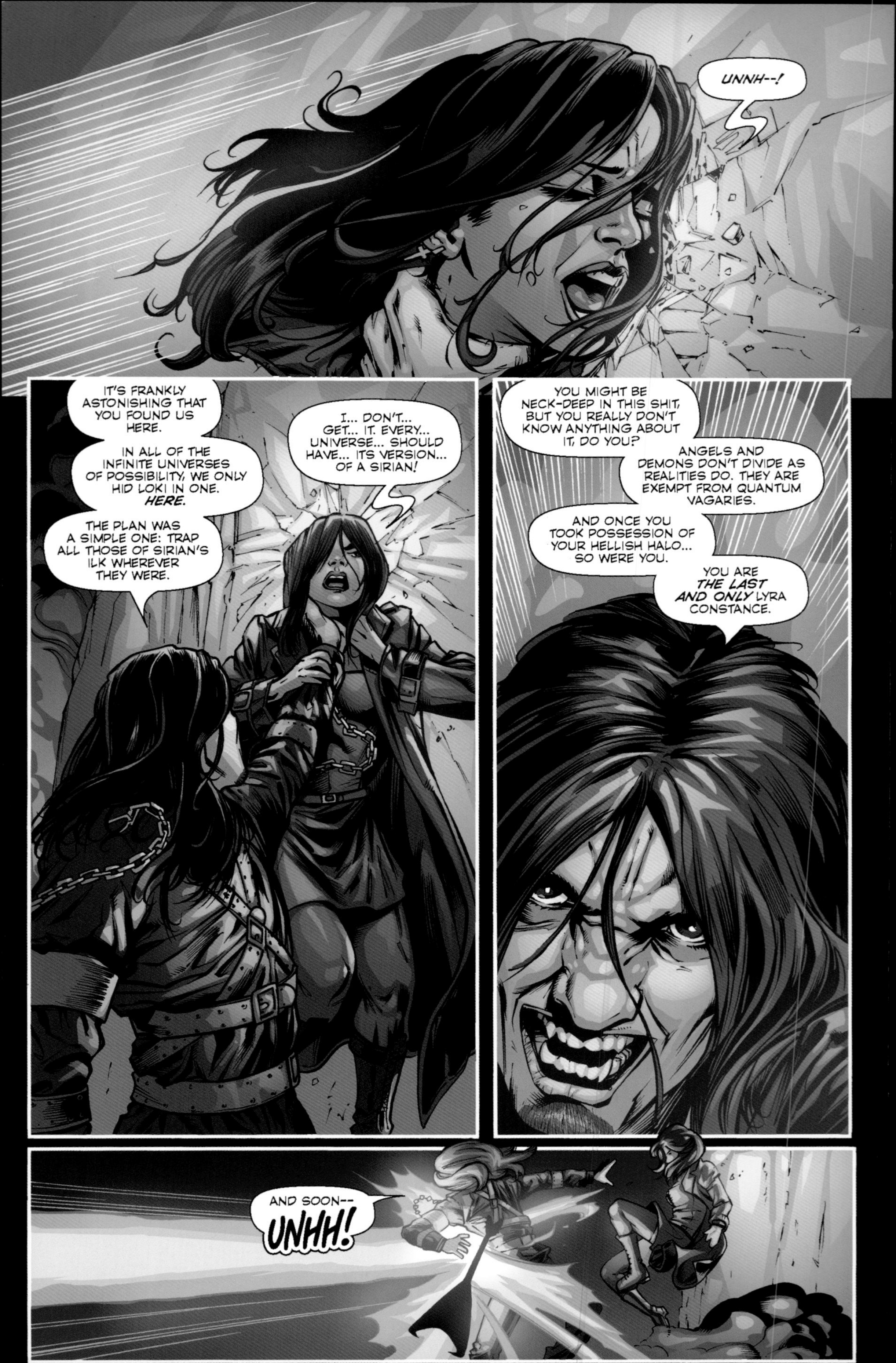
UNNH--!
IT'S FRANKLY ASTONISHING THAT YOU FOUND US HERE.
IN ALL OF THE INFINITE UNIVERSES OF POSSIBILITY, WE ONLY HID LOKI IN ONE. *HERE.*
THE PLAN WAS A SIMPLE ONE: TRAP ALL THOSE OF SIRIAN'S ILK WHEREVER THEY WERE.
I... DON'T... GET... IT. EVERY... UNIVERSE... SHOULD HAVE... ITS VERSION... OF A SIRIAN!
YOU MIGHT BE NECK-DEEP IN THIS SHIT, BUT YOU REALLY DON'T KNOW ANYTHING ABOUT IT, DO YOU?
ANGELS AND DEMONS DON'T DIVIDE AS REALITIES DO. THEY ARE EXEMPT FROM QUANTUM VAGARIES.
AND ONCE YOU TOOK POSSESSION OF YOUR HELLISH HALO... SO WERE YOU.
YOU ARE *THE LAST AND ONLY* LYRA CONSTANCE.
AND SOON--
UNHH!

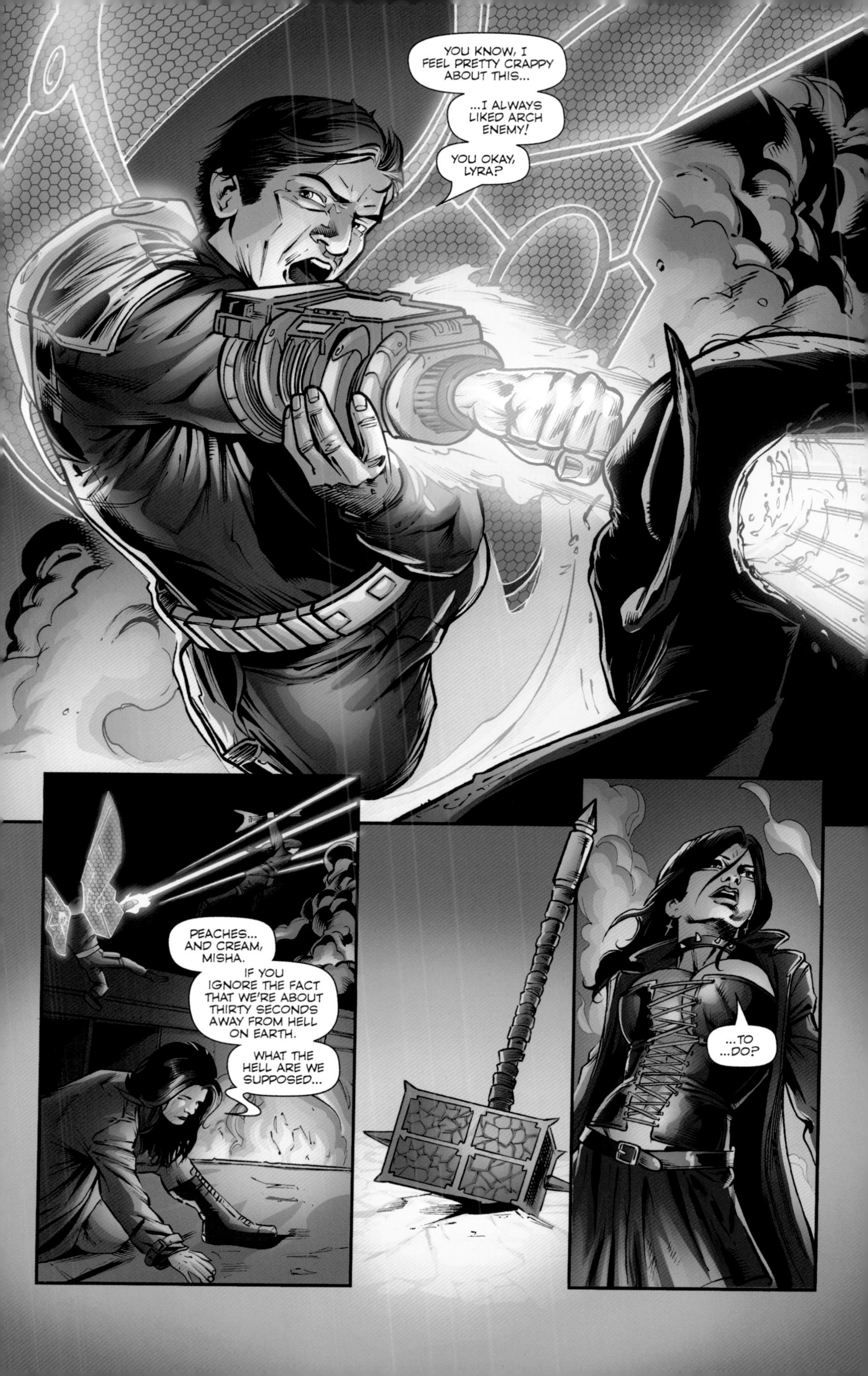
YOU KNOW, I FEEL PRETTY CRAPPY ABOUT THIS...
...I ALWAYS LIKED ARCH ENEMY!
YOU OKAY, LYRA?
PEACHES... AND CREAM, MISHA.
IF YOU IGNORE THE FACT THAT WE'RE ABOUT THIRTY SECONDS AWAY FROM HELL ON EARTH.
WHAT THE HELL ARE WE SUPPOSED...
...TO ...DO?

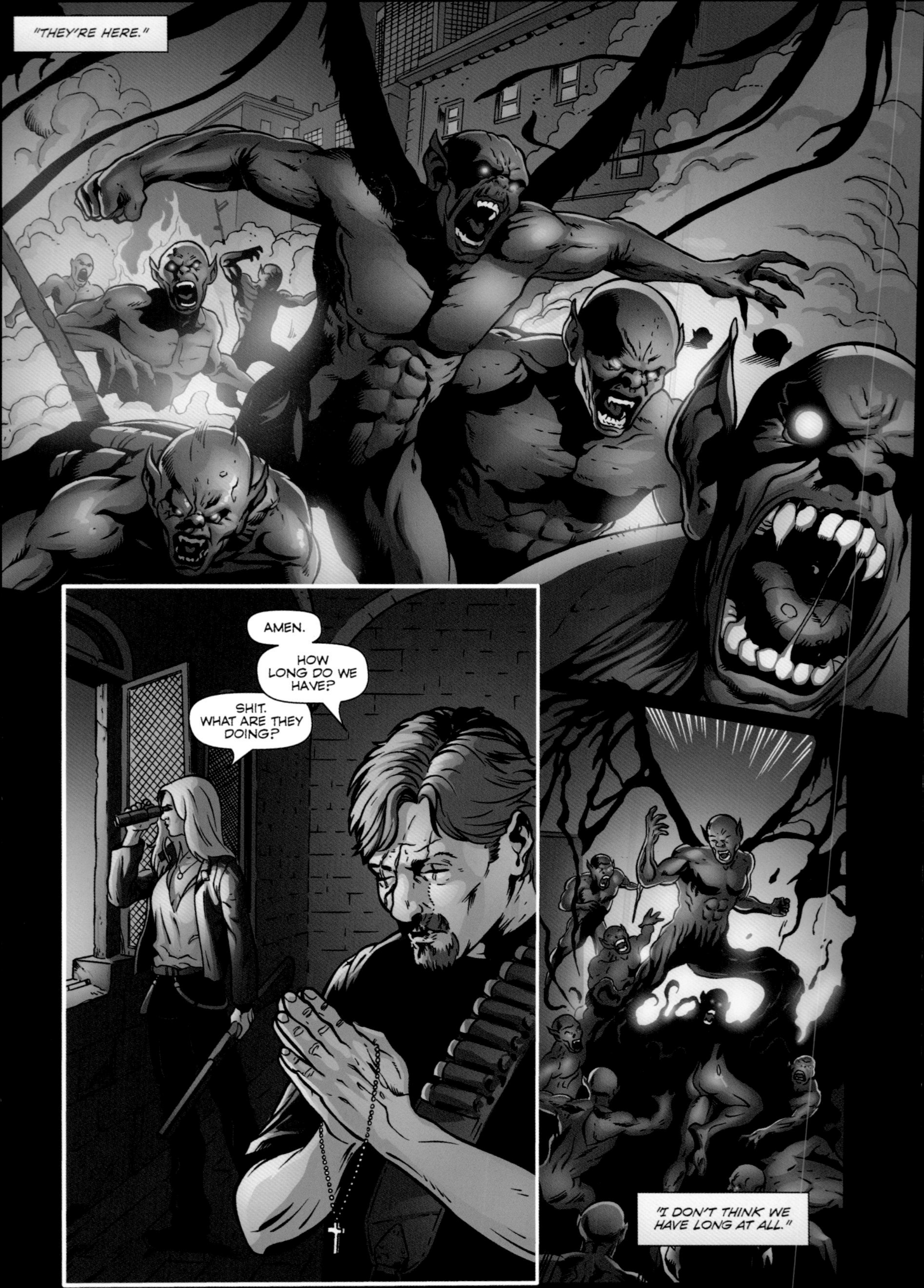
"THEY'RE HERE."
AMEN.
HOW LONG DO WE HAVE?
SHIT. WHAT ARE THEY DOING?
"I DON'T THINK WE HAVE LONG AT ALL."

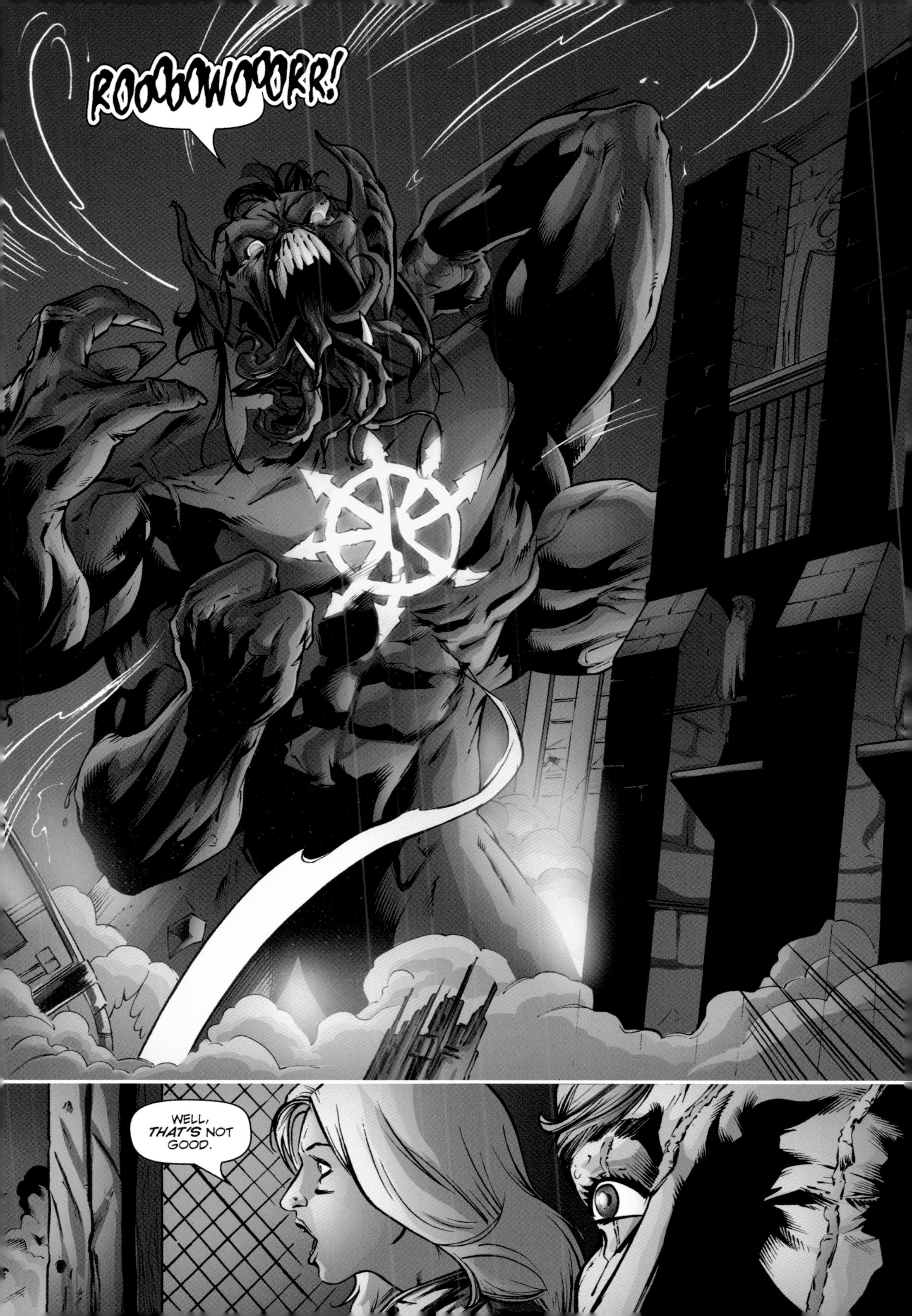

ROOOOOWOOORR!
WELL, THAT'S NOT GOOD.

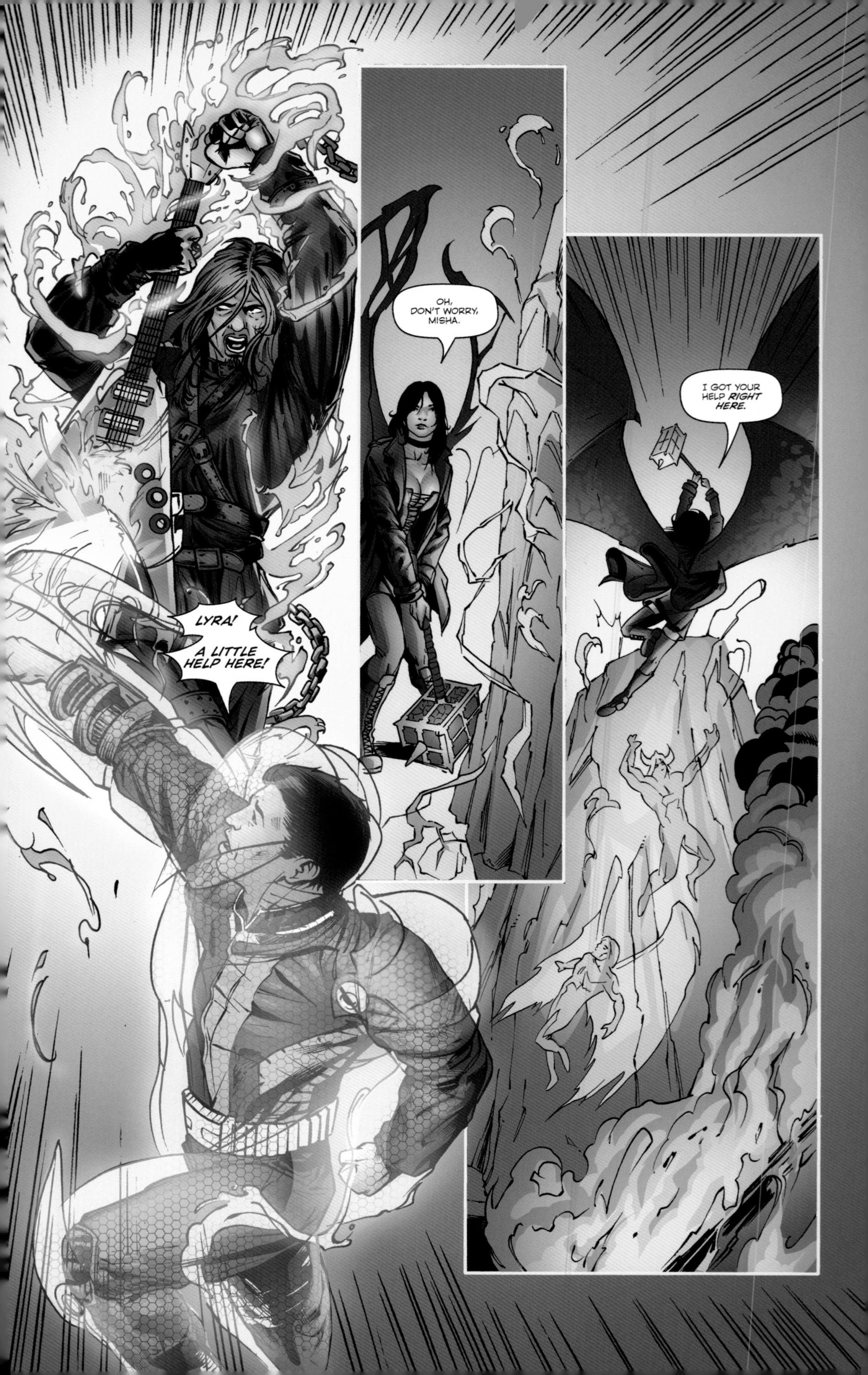
LYRA!
A LITTLE HELP HERE!
OH, DON'T WORRY, MISHA.
I GOT YOUR HELP *RIGHT HERE.*

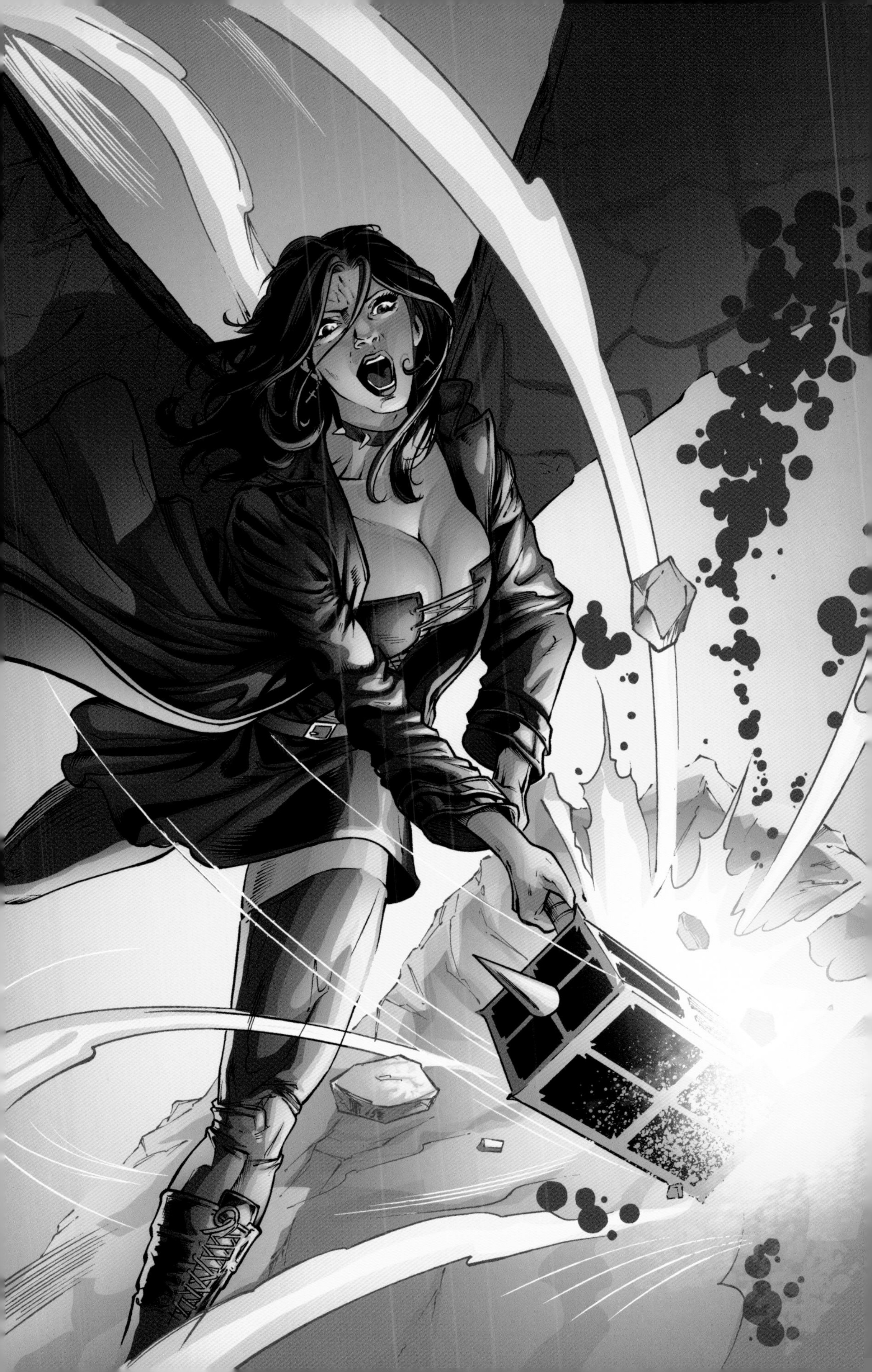

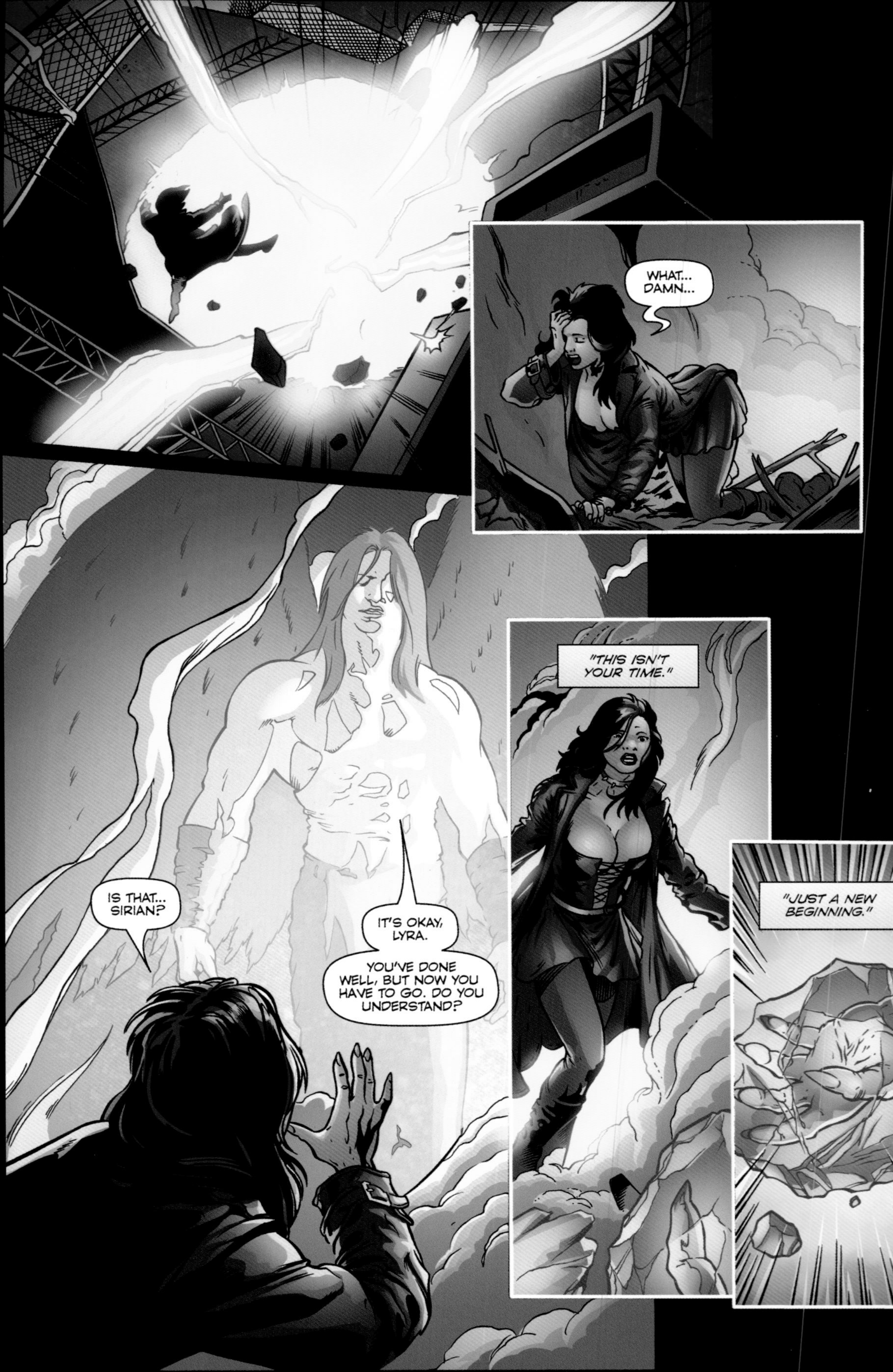
WHAT... DAMN...
IS THAT... SIRIAN?
IT'S OKAY, LYRA.
YOU'VE DONE WELL, BUT NOW YOU HAVE TO GO. DO YOU UNDERSTAND?
"THIS ISN'T YOUR TIME."
"JUST A NEW BEGINNING."

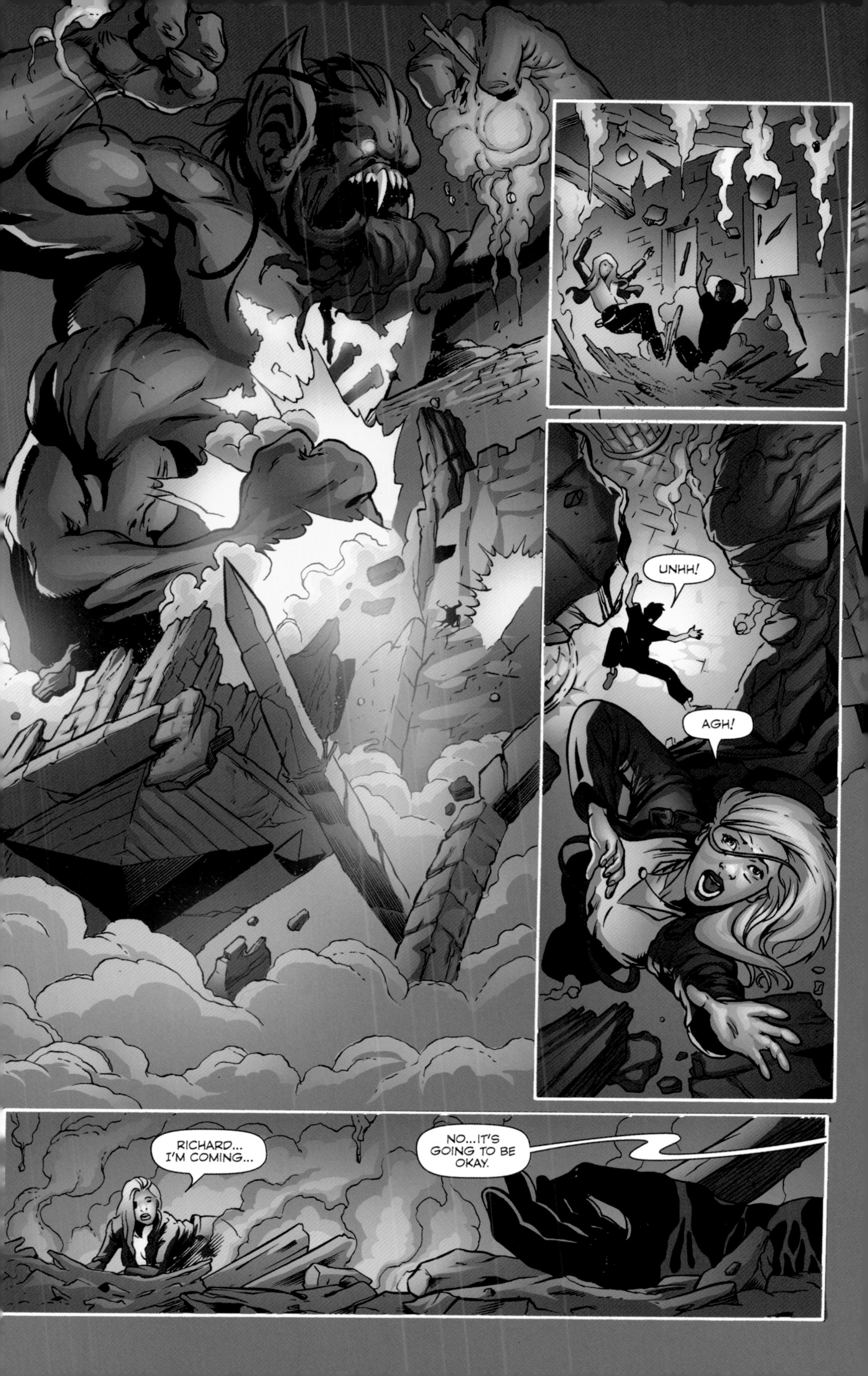
UNHH!
AGH!
RICHARD... I'M COMING...
NO...IT'S GOING TO BE OKAY.

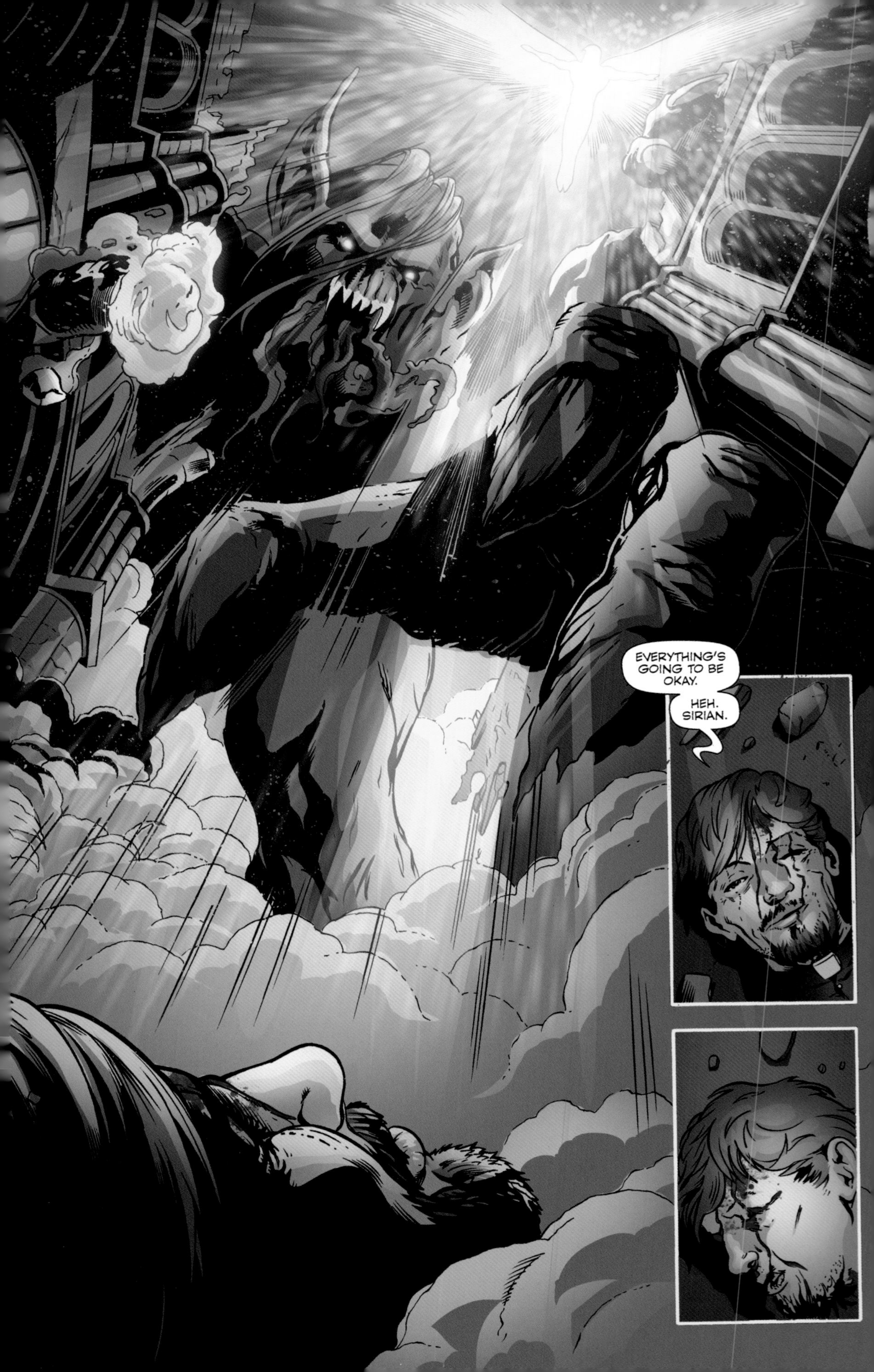
EVERYTHING'S GOING TO BE OKAY.
HEH. SIRIAN.

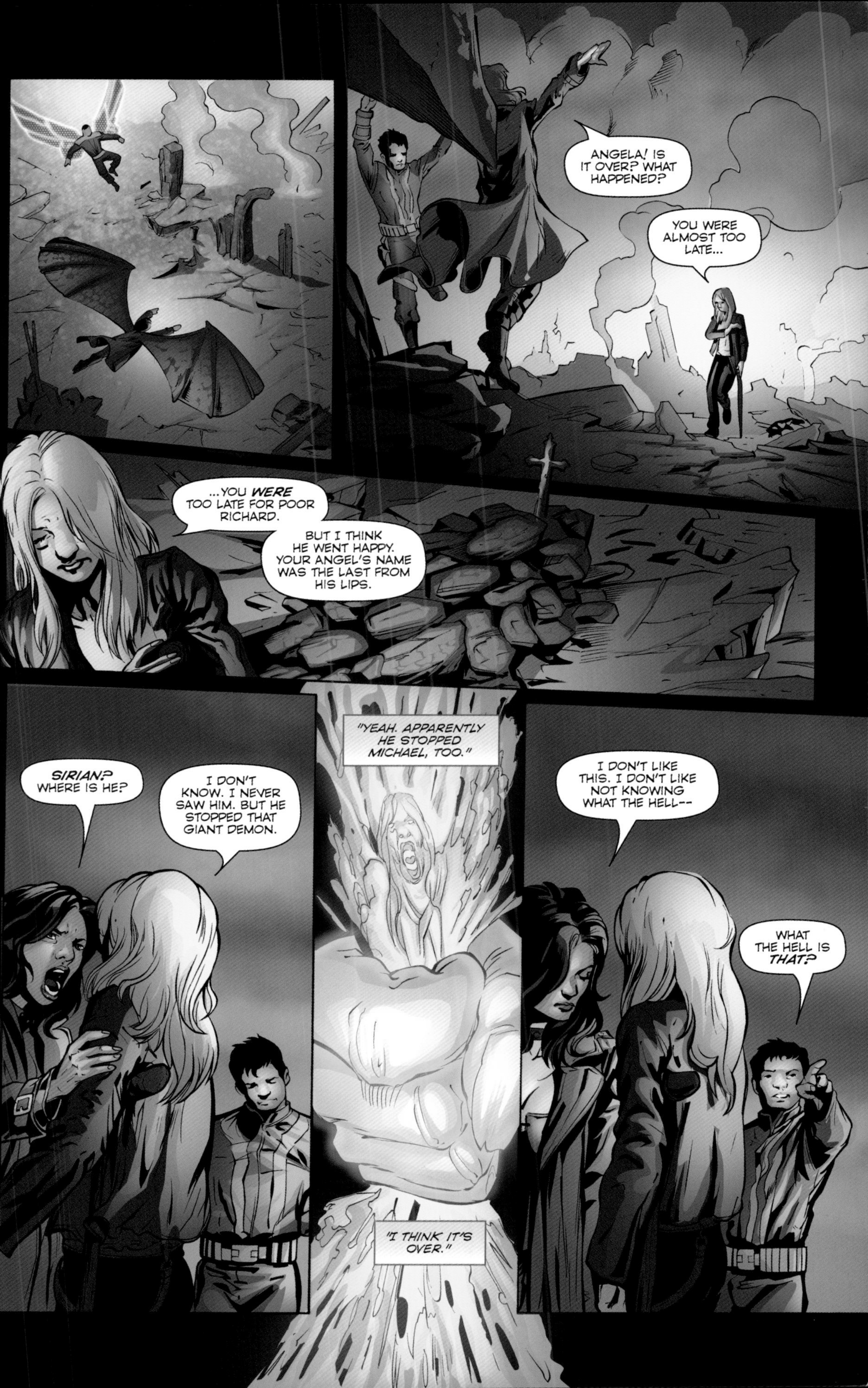
ANGELA! IS IT OVER? WHAT HAPPENED?
YOU WERE ALMOST TOO LATE...
...YOU WERE TOO LATE FOR POOR RICHARD.
BUT I THINK HE WENT HAPPY. YOUR ANGEL'S NAME WAS THE LAST FROM HIS LIPS.
SIRIAN? WHERE IS HE?
I DON'T KNOW. I NEVER SAW HIM. BUT HE STOPPED THAT GIANT DEMON.
"YEAH. APPARENTLY HE STOPPED MICHAEL, TOO."
"I THINK IT'S OVER."
I DON'T LIKE THIS. I DON'T LIKE NOT KNOWING WHAT THE HELL--
WHAT THE HELL IS THAT?

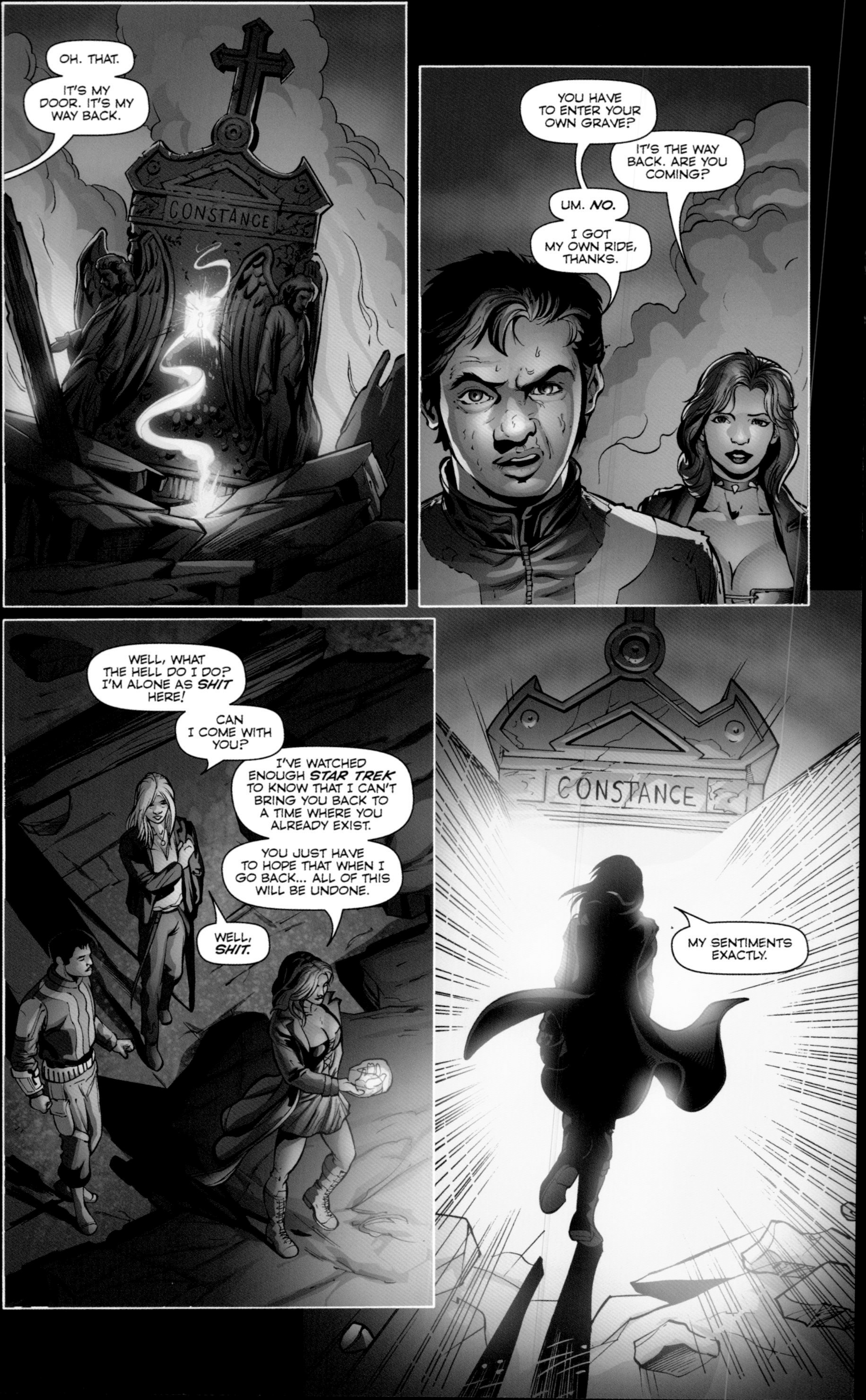
OH. THAT.
IT'S MY DOOR. IT'S MY WAY BACK.
CONSTANCE
YOU HAVE TO ENTER YOUR OWN GRAVE?
IT'S THE WAY BACK. ARE YOU COMING?
UM. NO.
I GOT MY OWN RIDE, THANKS.
WELL, WHAT THE HELL DO I DO? I'M ALONE AS SHIT HERE!
CAN I COME WITH YOU?
I'VE WATCHED ENOUGH STAR TREK TO KNOW THAT I CAN'T BRING YOU BACK TO A TIME WHERE YOU ALREADY EXIST.
YOU JUST HAVE TO HOPE THAT WHEN I GO BACK... ALL OF THIS WILL BE UNDONE.
WELL, SHIT.
CONSTANCE
MY SENTIMENTS EXACTLY.

Eternal Descent

ARCHIVE

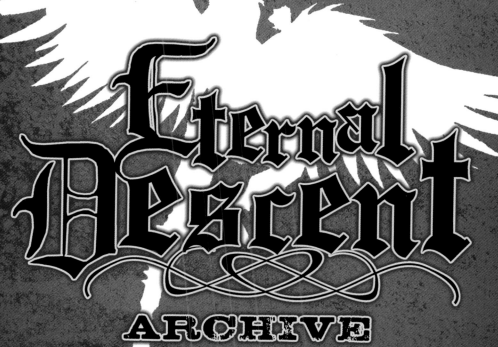

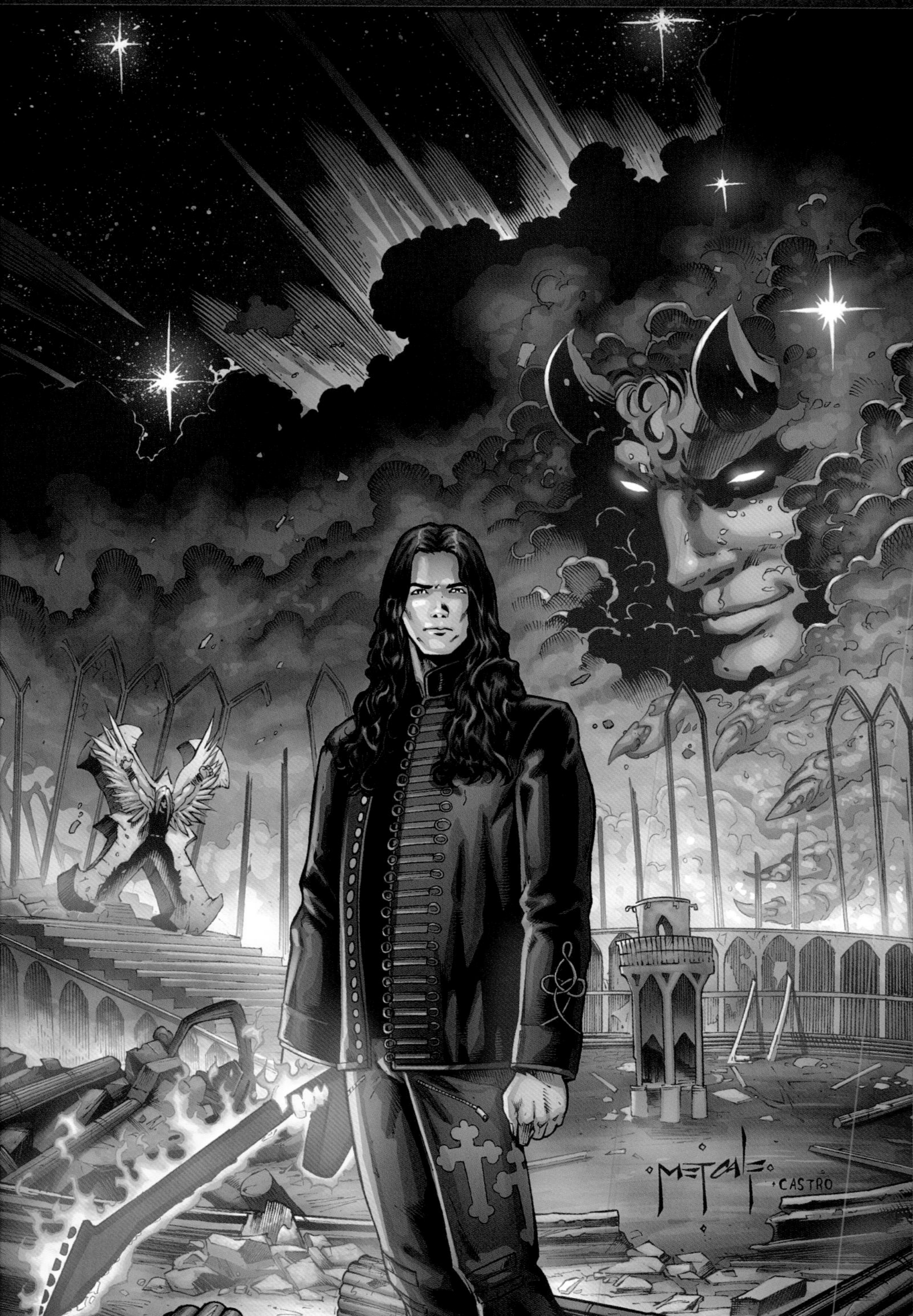
METCALF
+CASTRO

ISSUE 7 COVER
Jason Metcalf &
Java

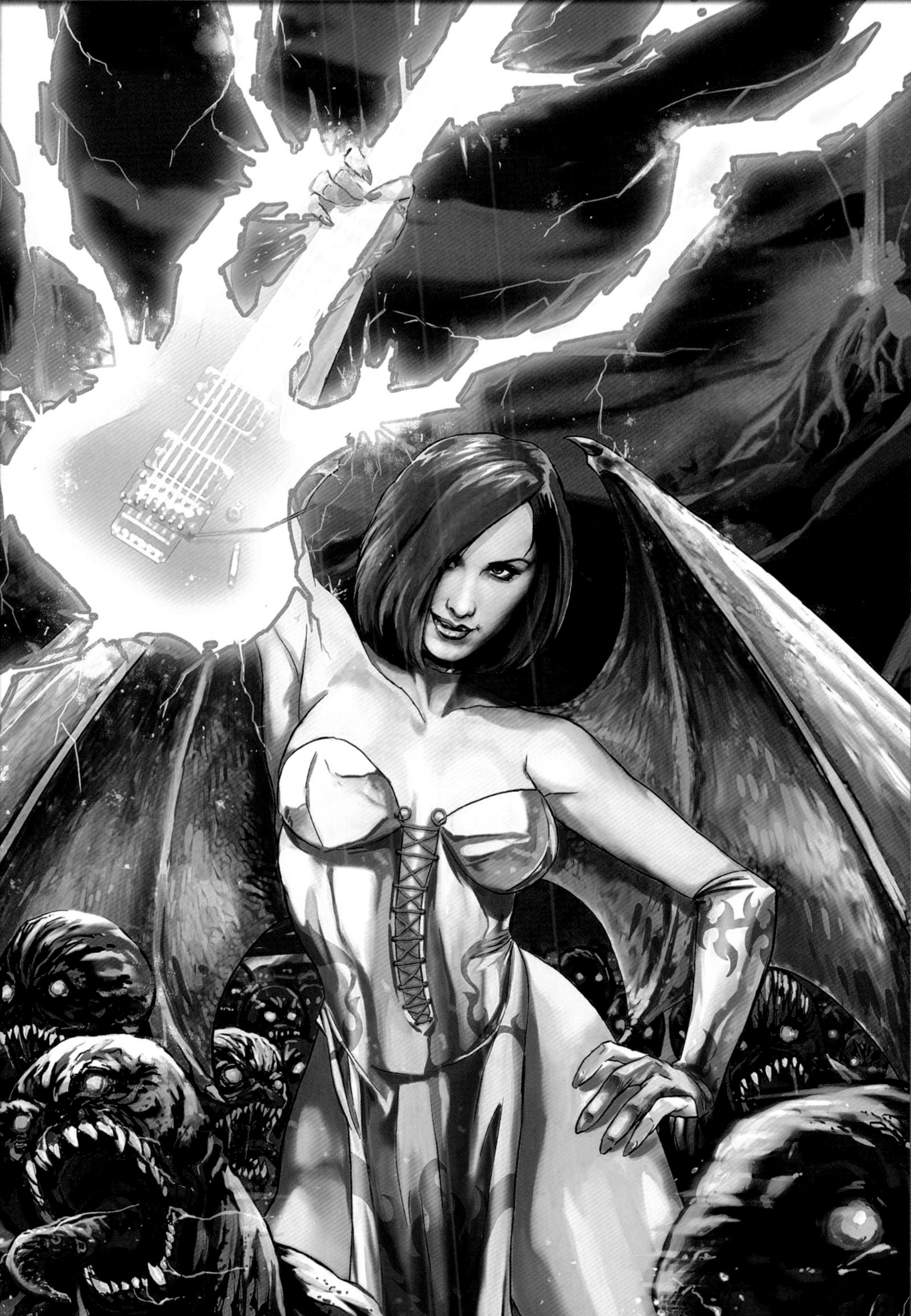

ISSUE 7 VARIANT
Santi Casas

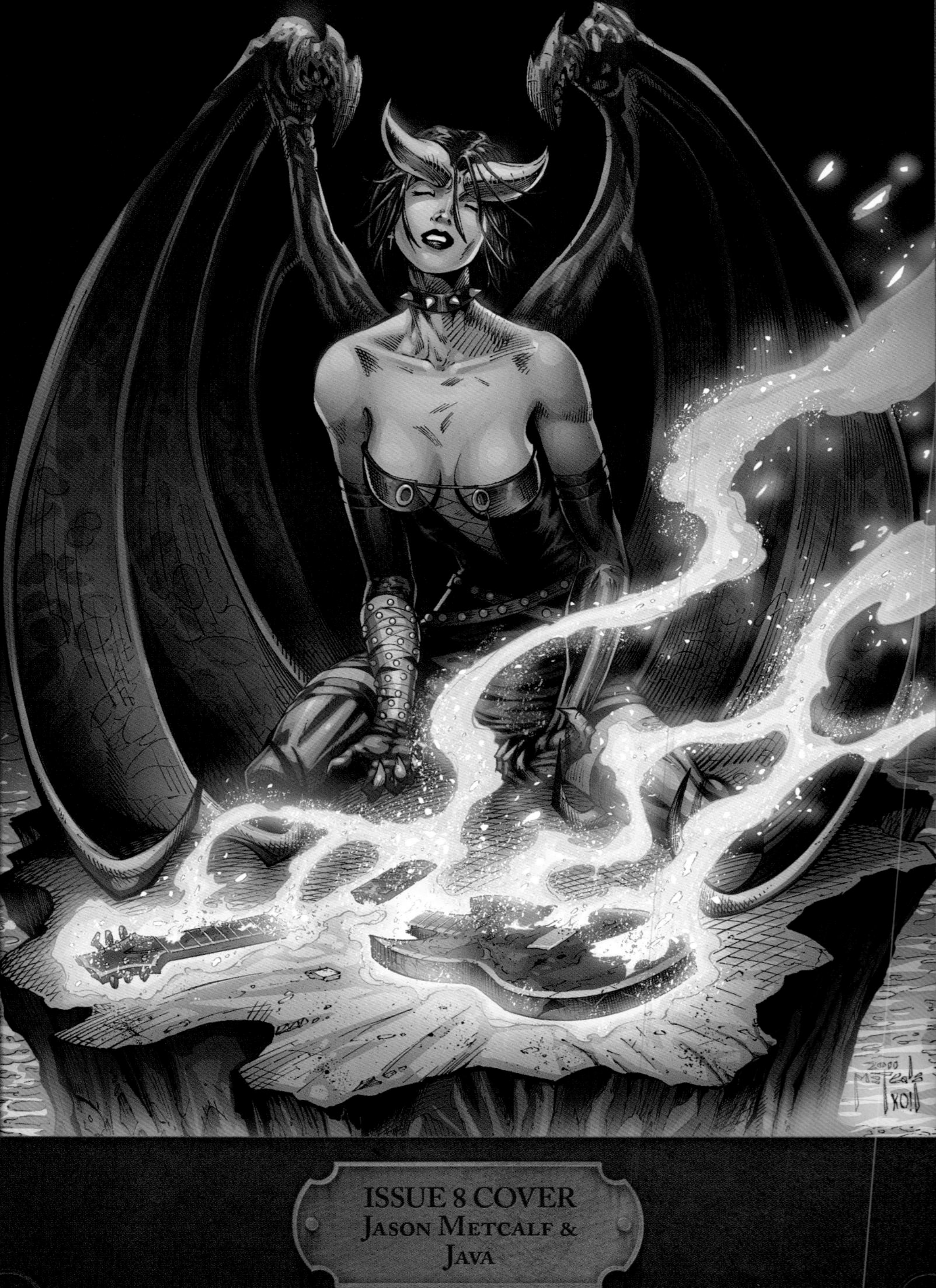

ISSUE 8 COVER
Jason Metcalf &
Java

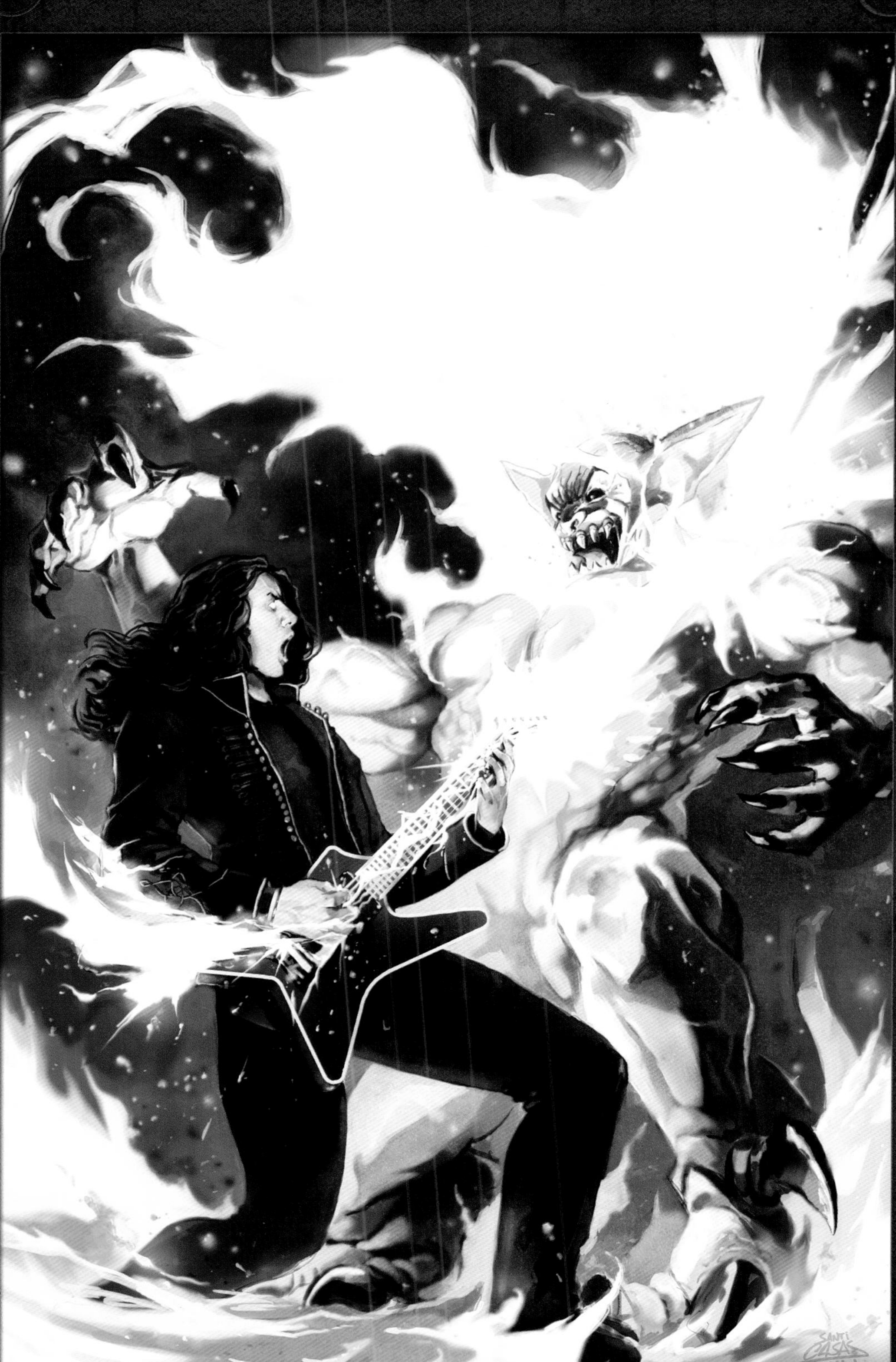
SANTI CASAS 2011

ISSUE 8 VARIANT
SANTI CASAS

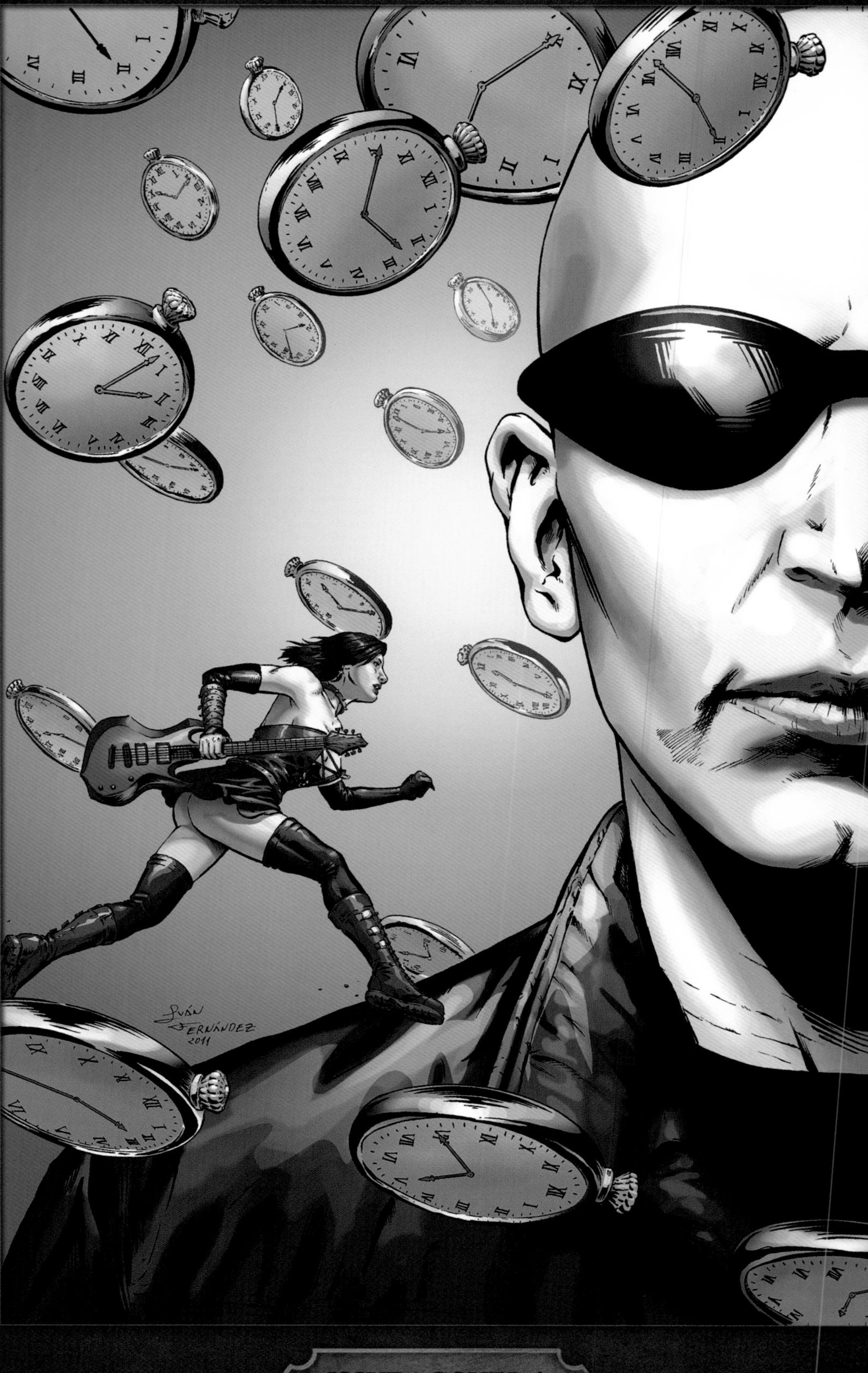
IVÁN FERNÁNDEZ 2011

ISSUE 9 COVER A
Ivan Fernandez &
Java

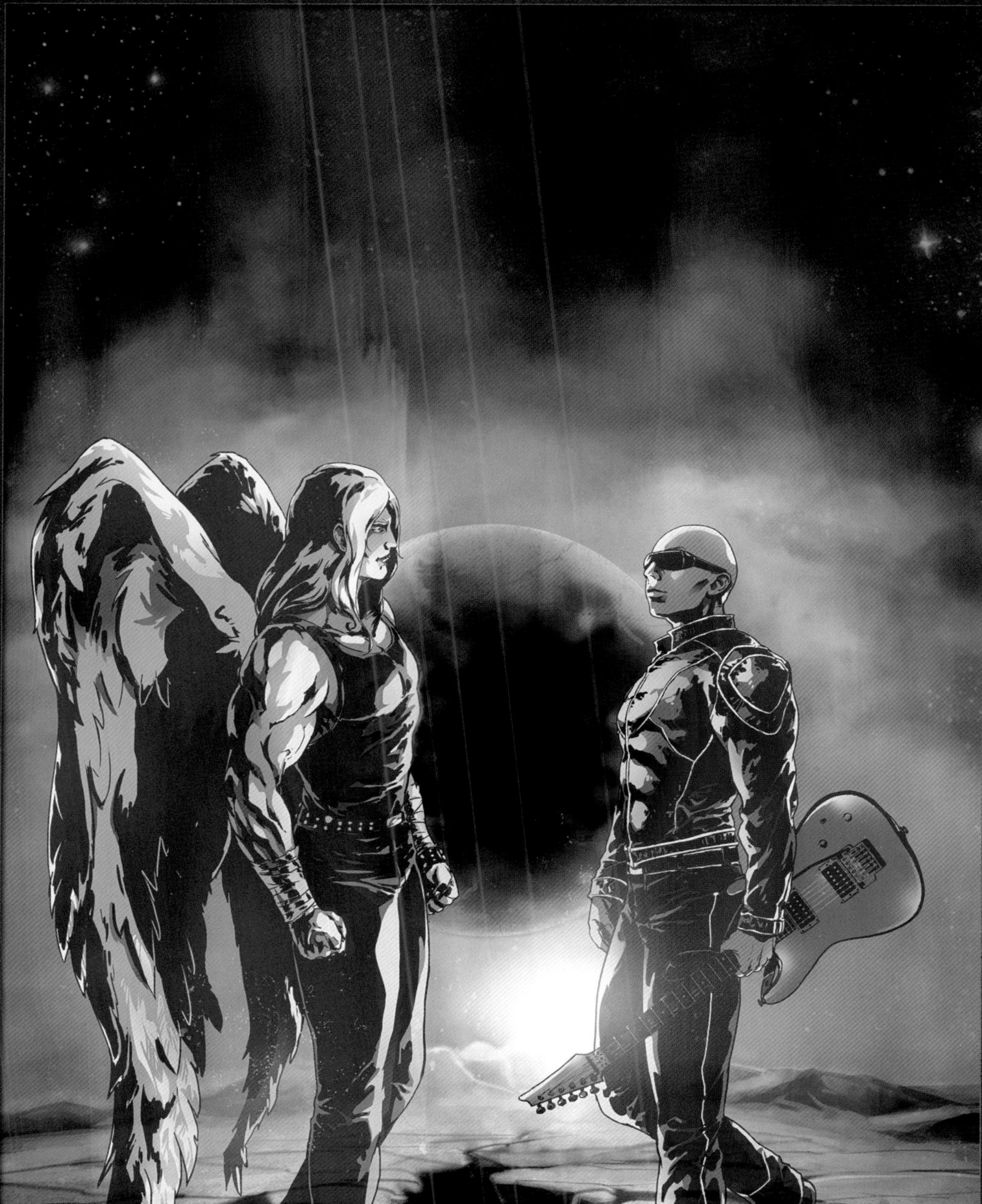
SANTI CASAS 2011

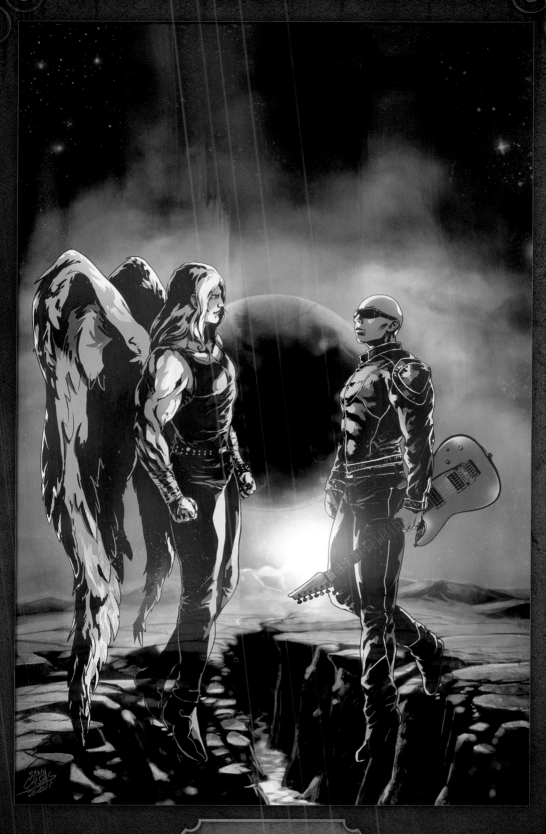

ISSUE 9 COVER B
Santi Casas

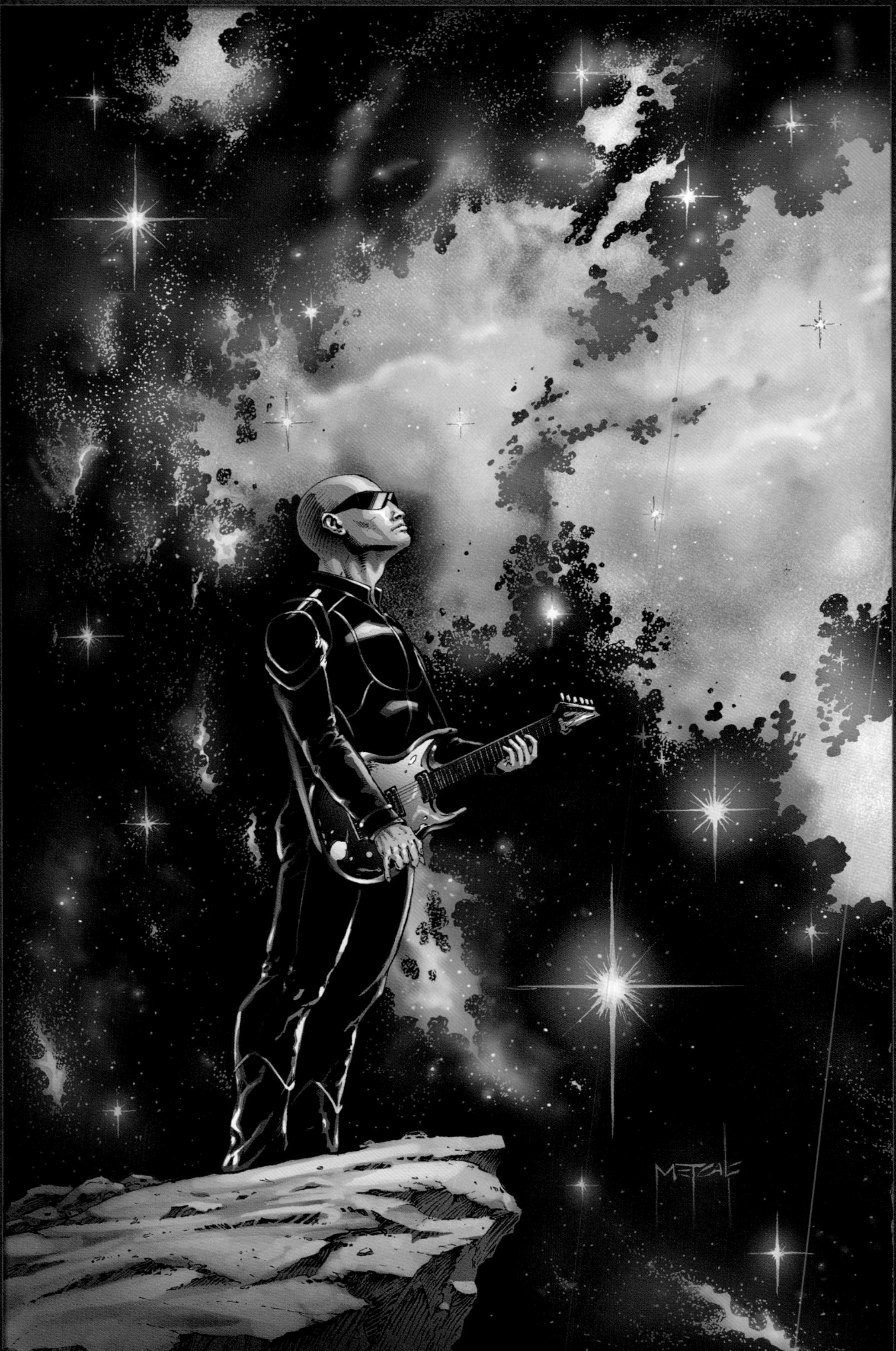
METCALF

ISSUE 9 COVER C
Jason Metcalf &
Java

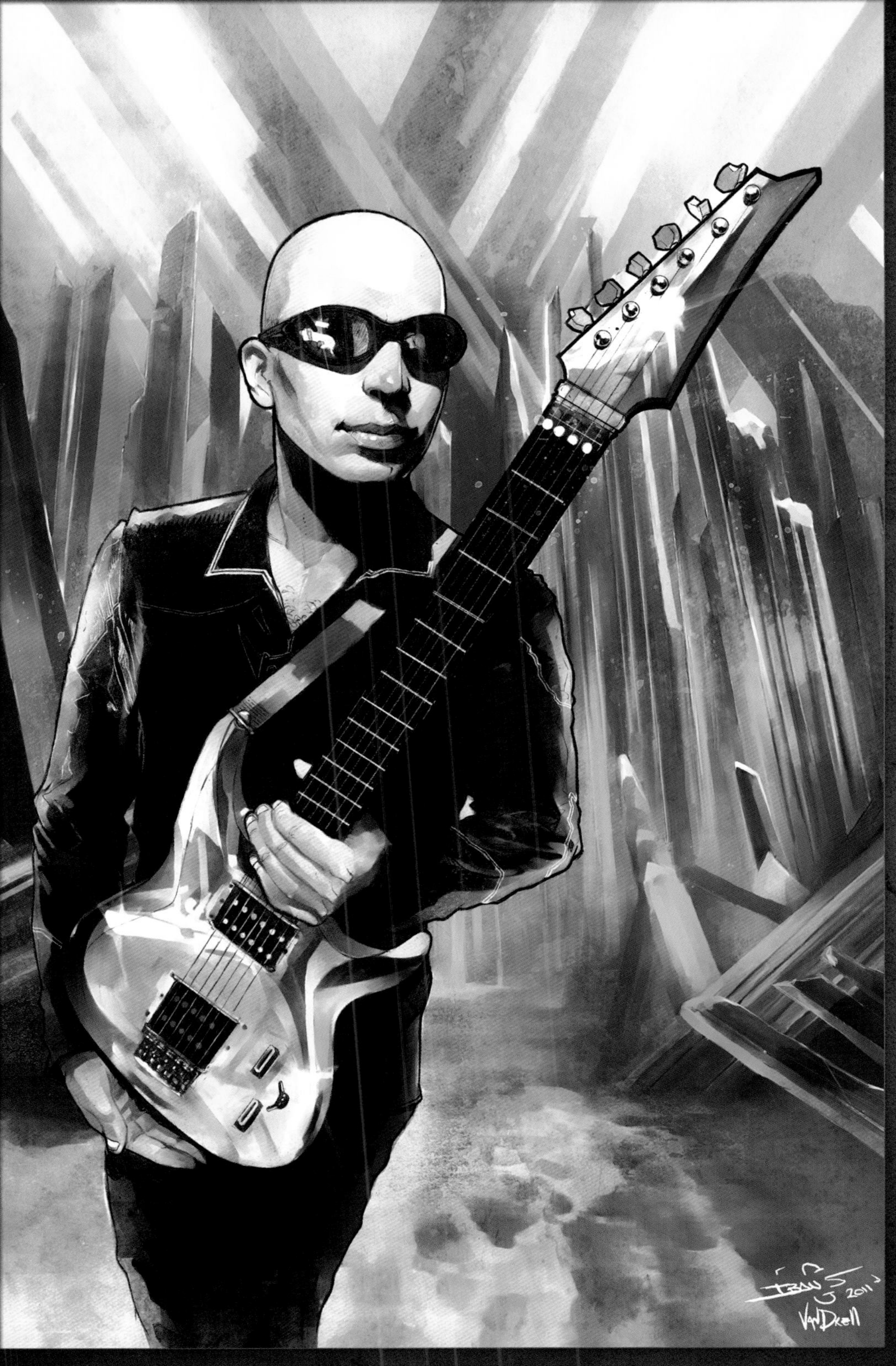

ISSUE 9 COVER D
Iban Coello &
Dani Vendrell

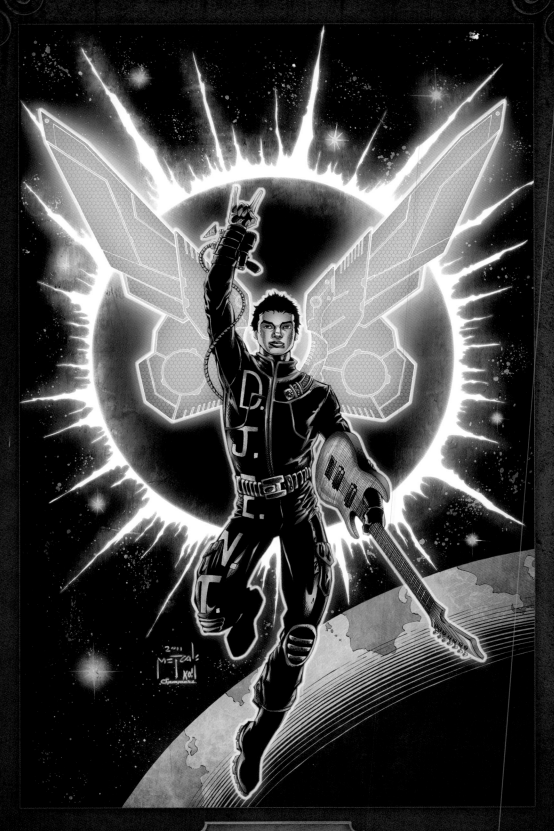

ISSUE 10 COVER
Jason Metcalf &
Chris Summers

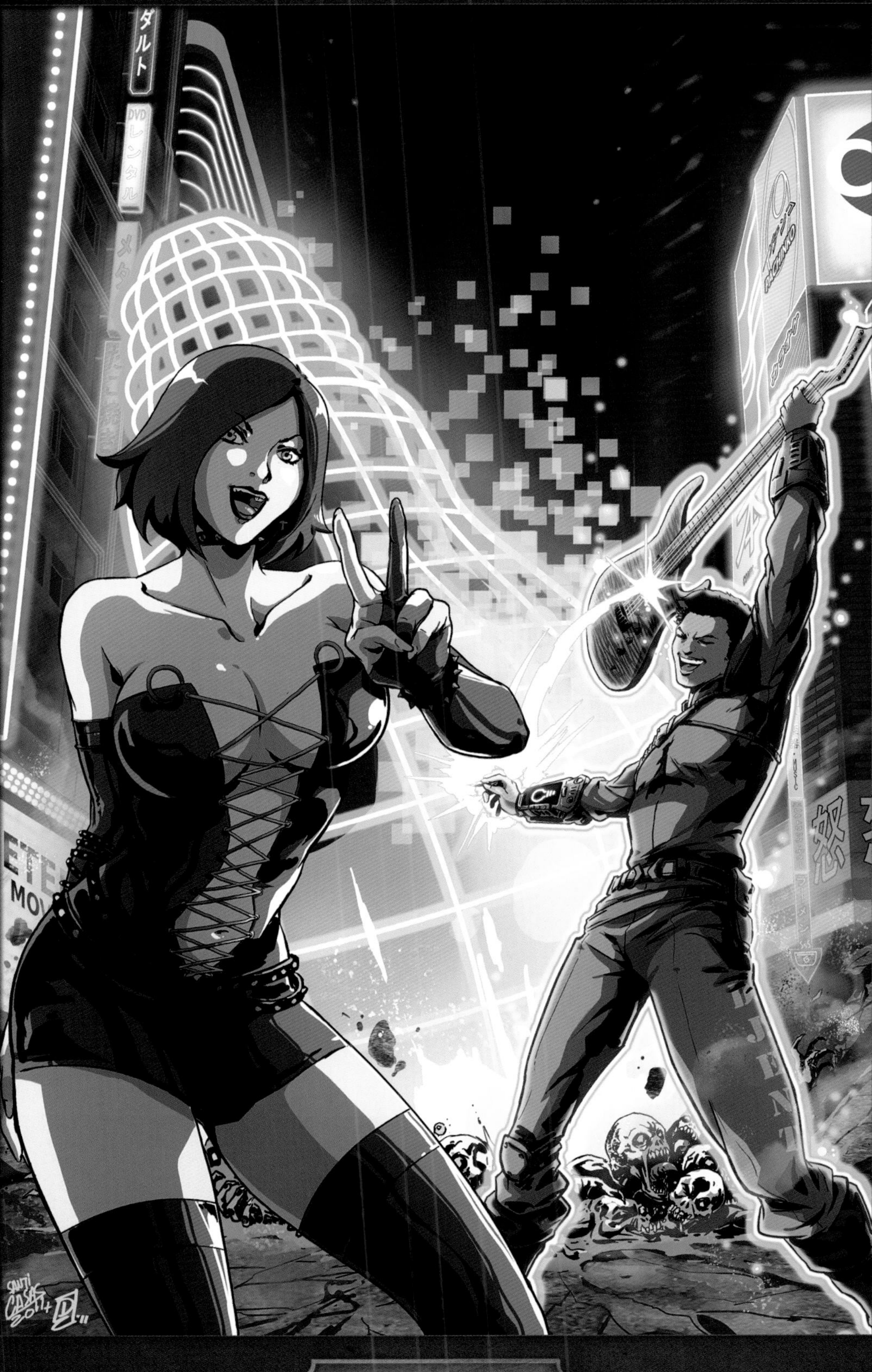
ダルト
DVD
レンタル

ISSUE 10 VARIANT
Santi Casas &
Ikari Studio

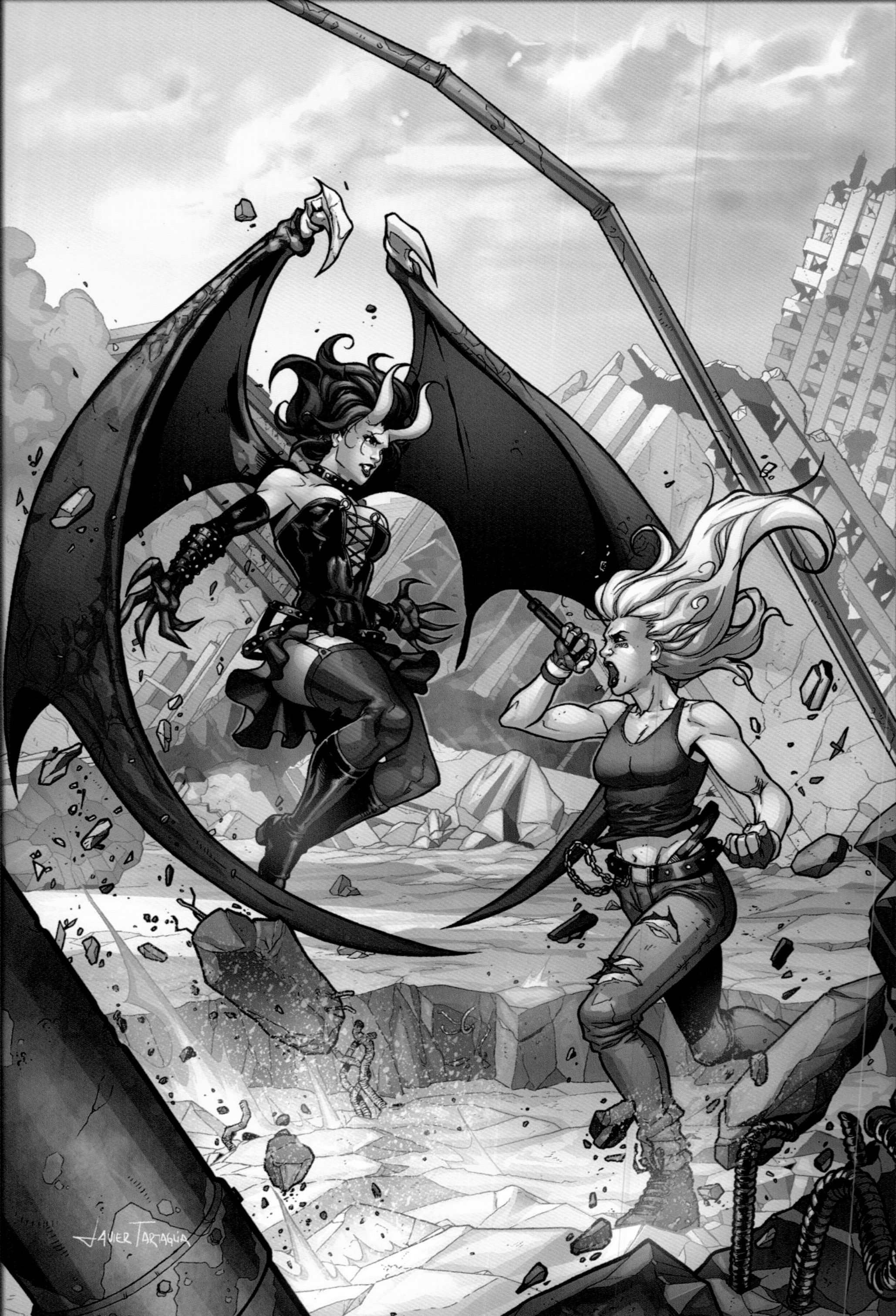
JAVIER TARTAGLIA

ISSUE 11 COVER
Iban Coello &
Java

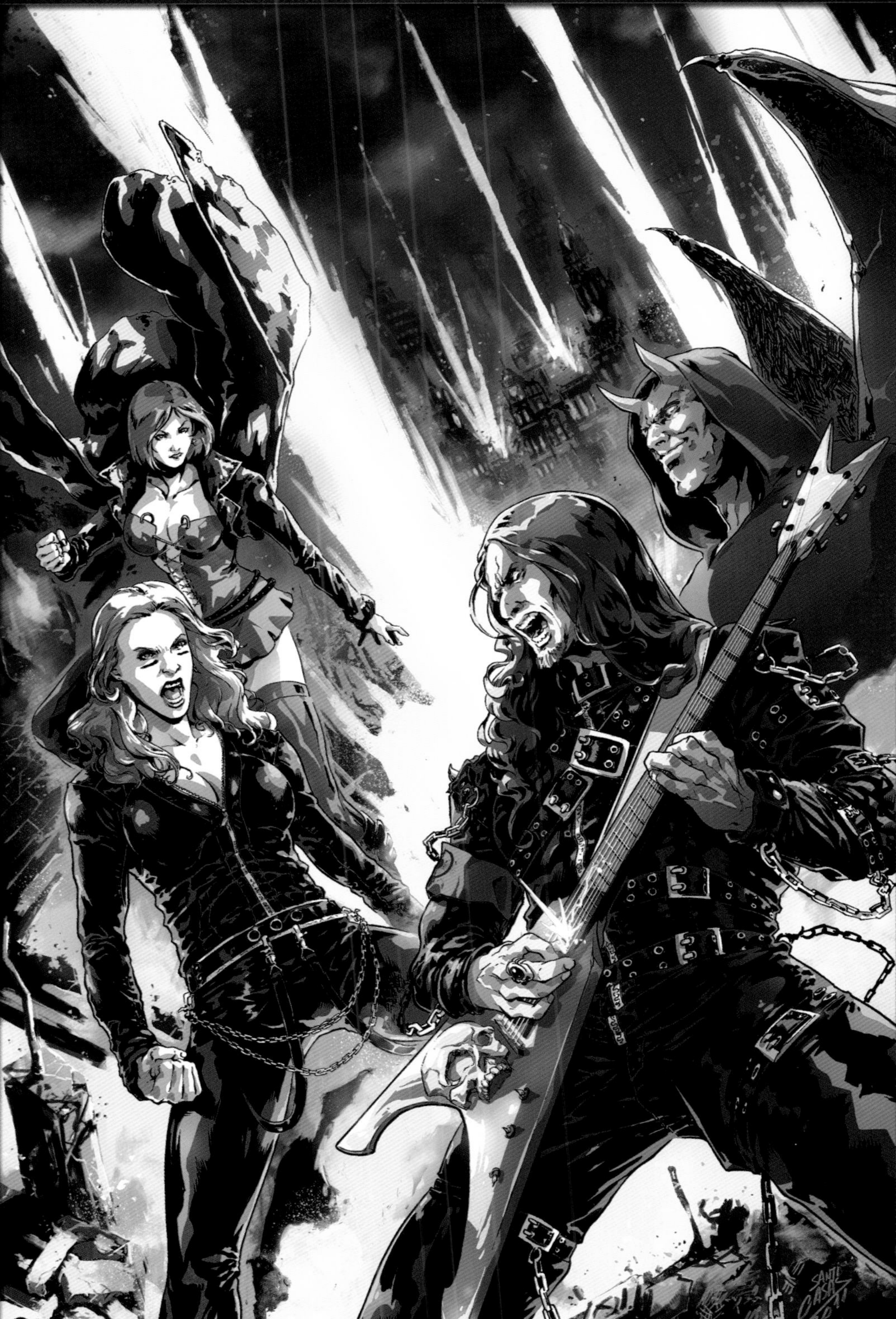

ISSUE 11 VARIANT
Santi Casas

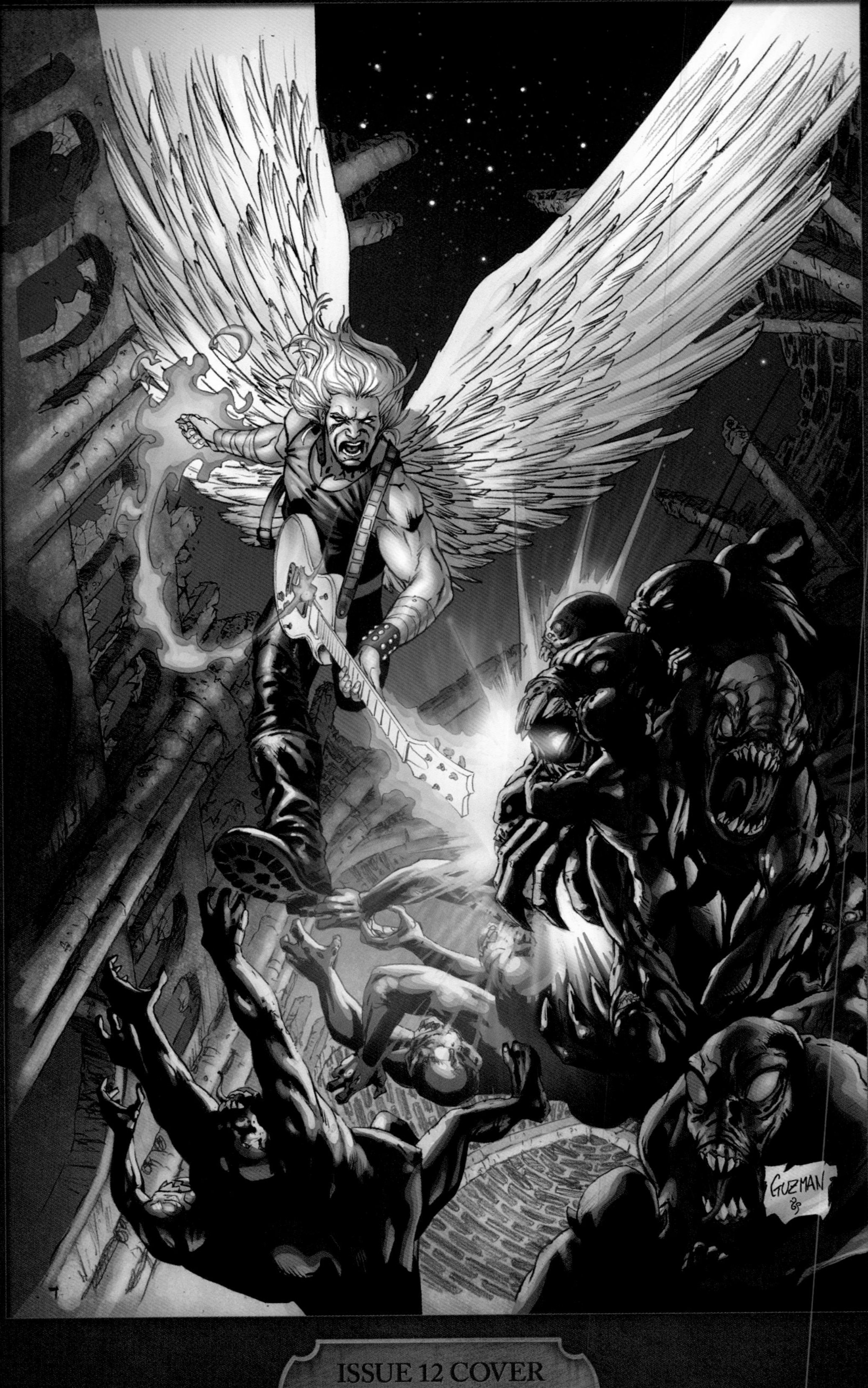
GUZMAN

ISSUE 12 COVER
Gabriel Guzman &
Rainer Petter

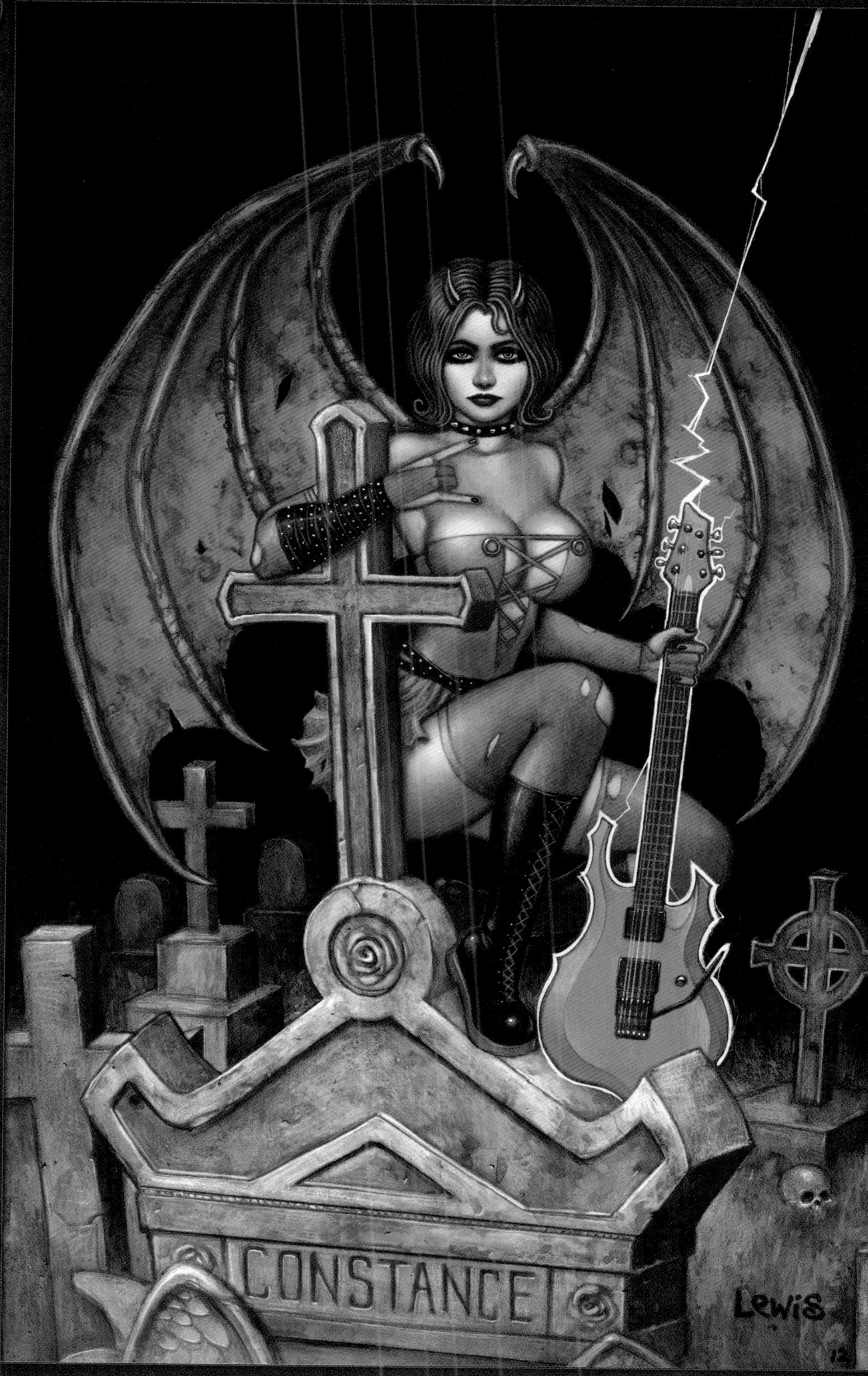
CONSTANCE
LEWIS
'12

ISSUE 12 VARIANT
Scott Lewis

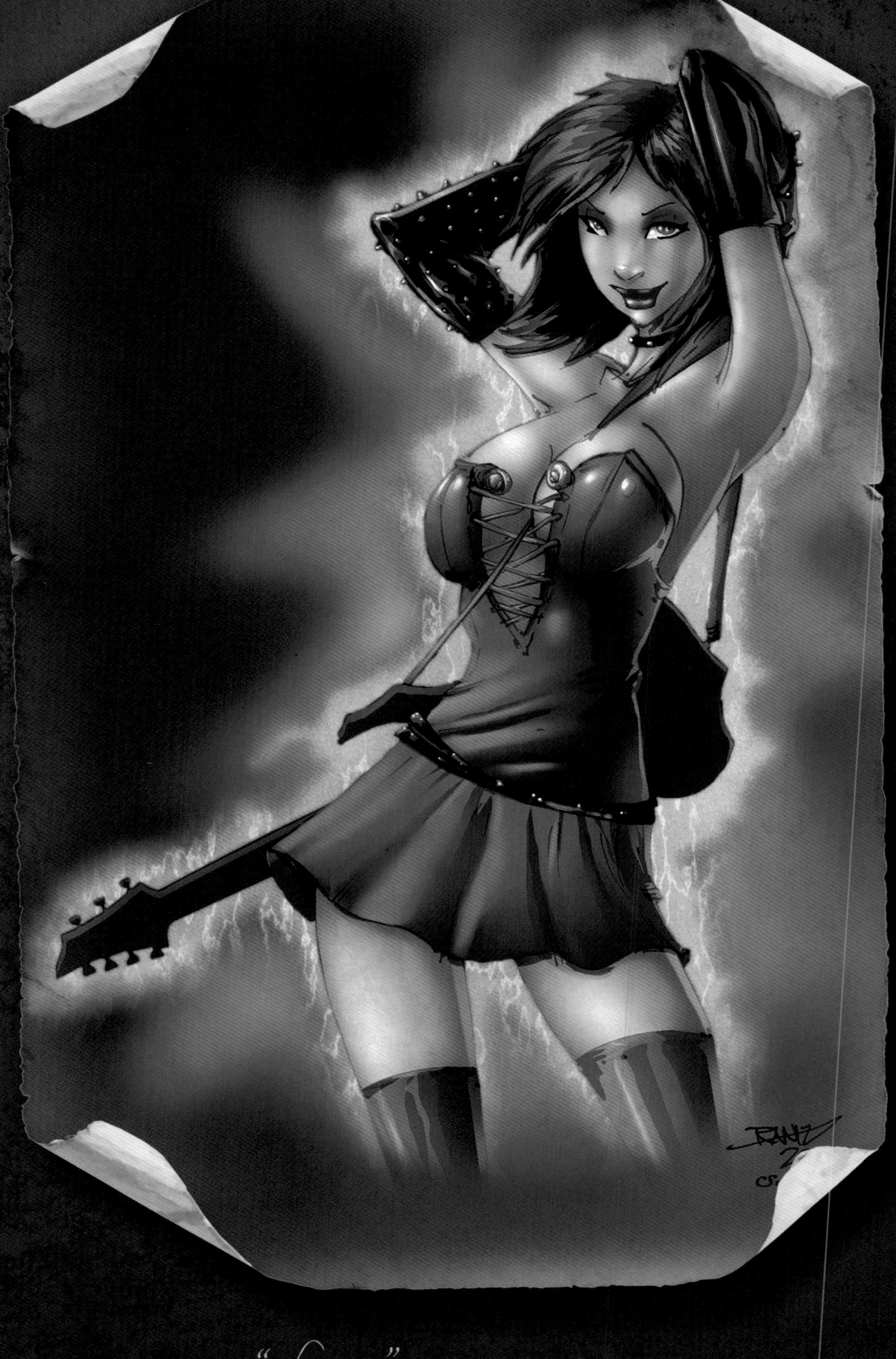

"*Lyra*" by Rantz & Chris Summers

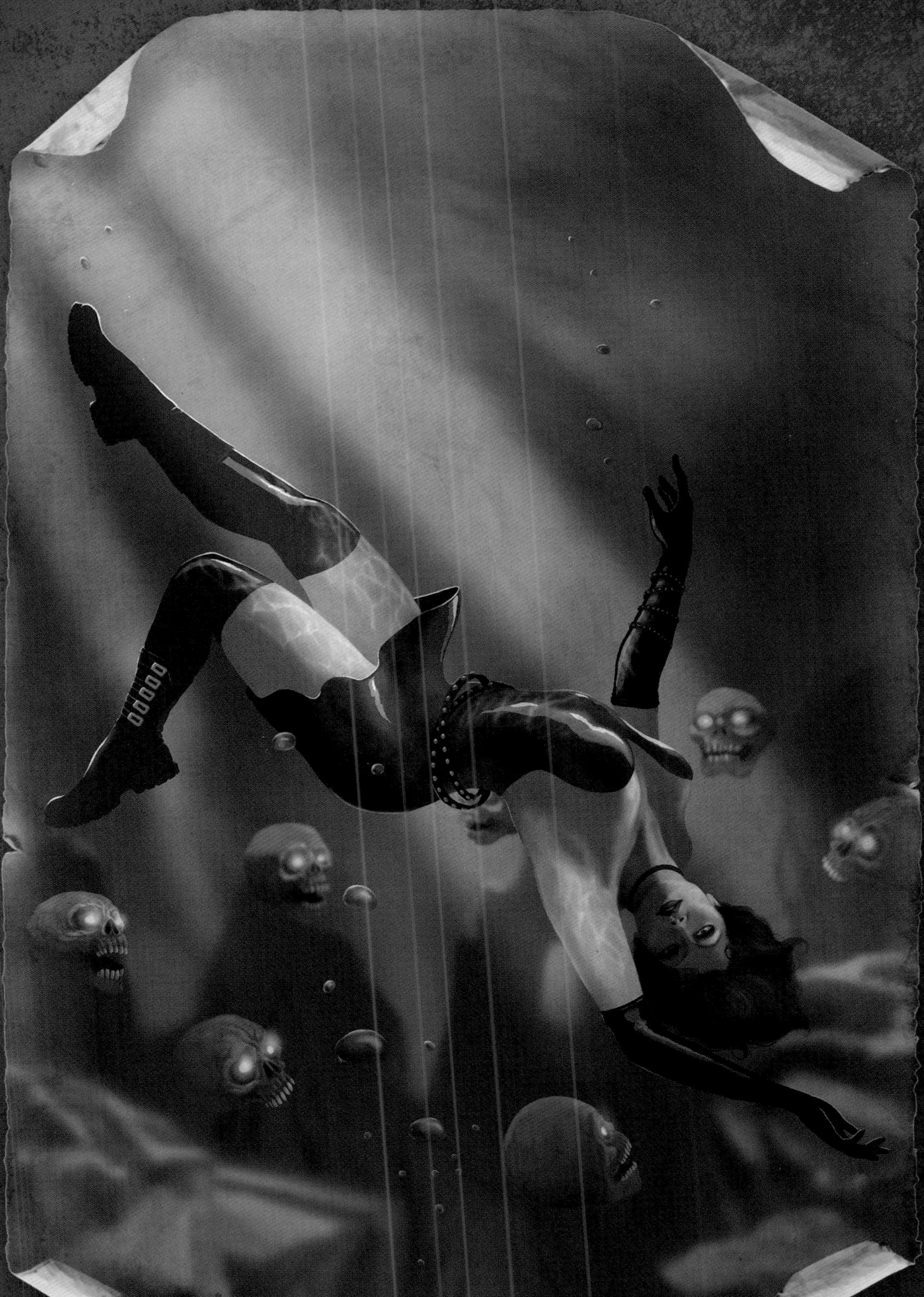

"The Morass" by Manon

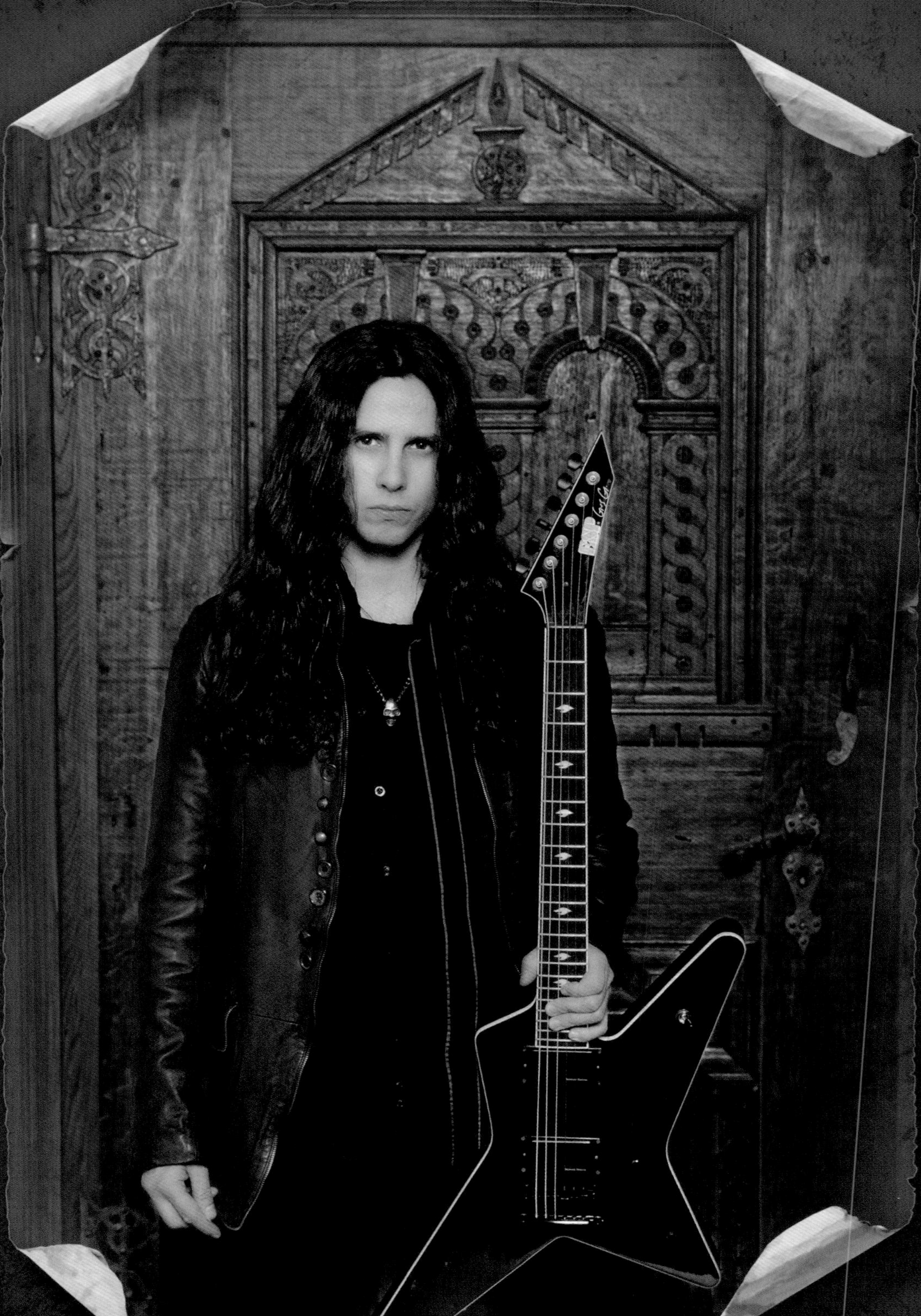

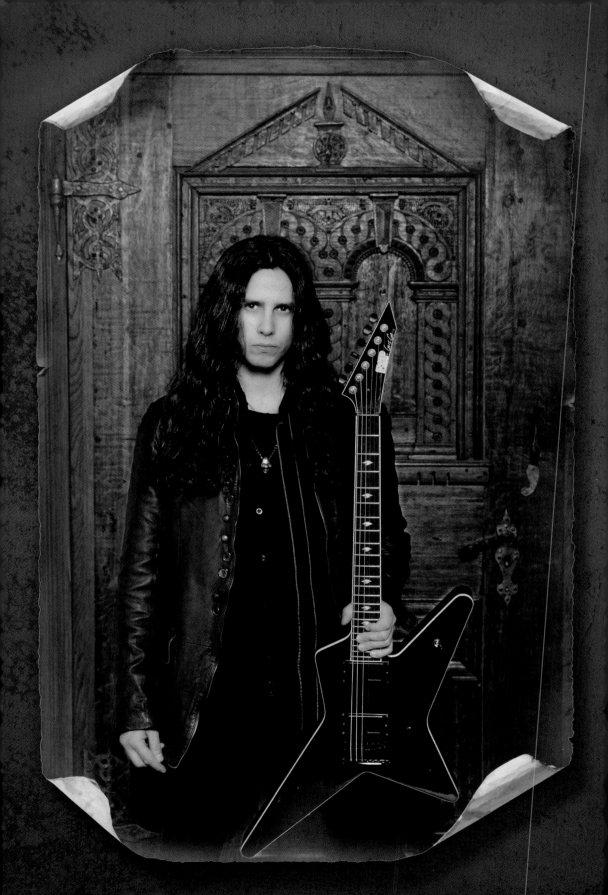

"Gus G" by Patric Ullaeus

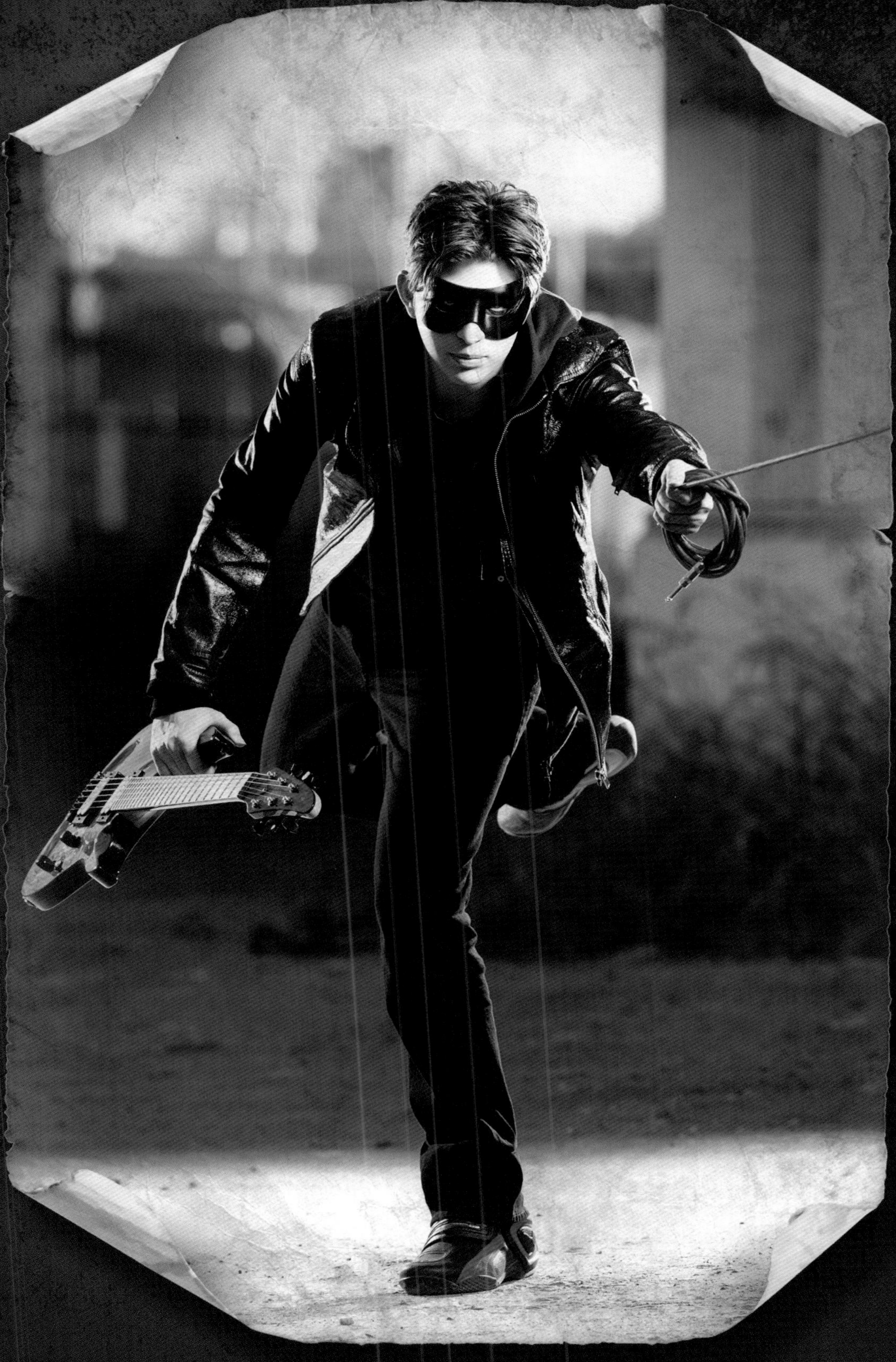

"*Cobalt*" by Larry DiMarzio

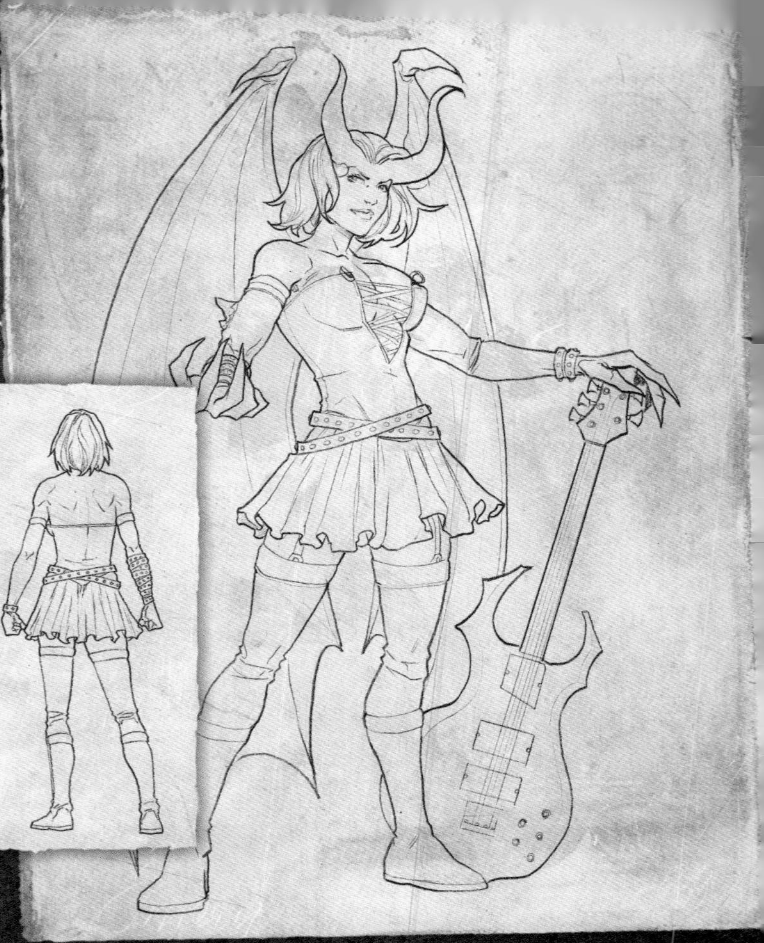

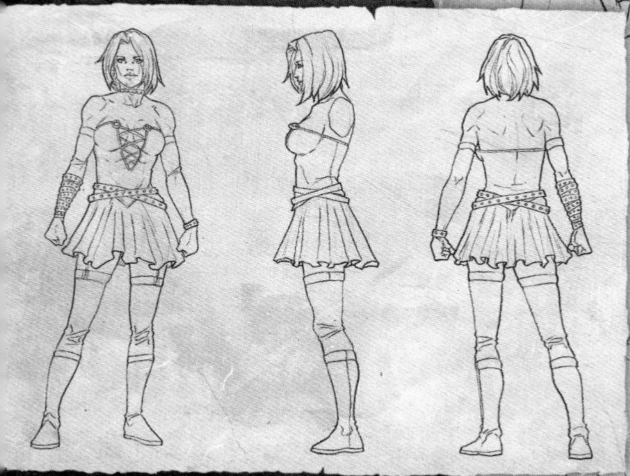

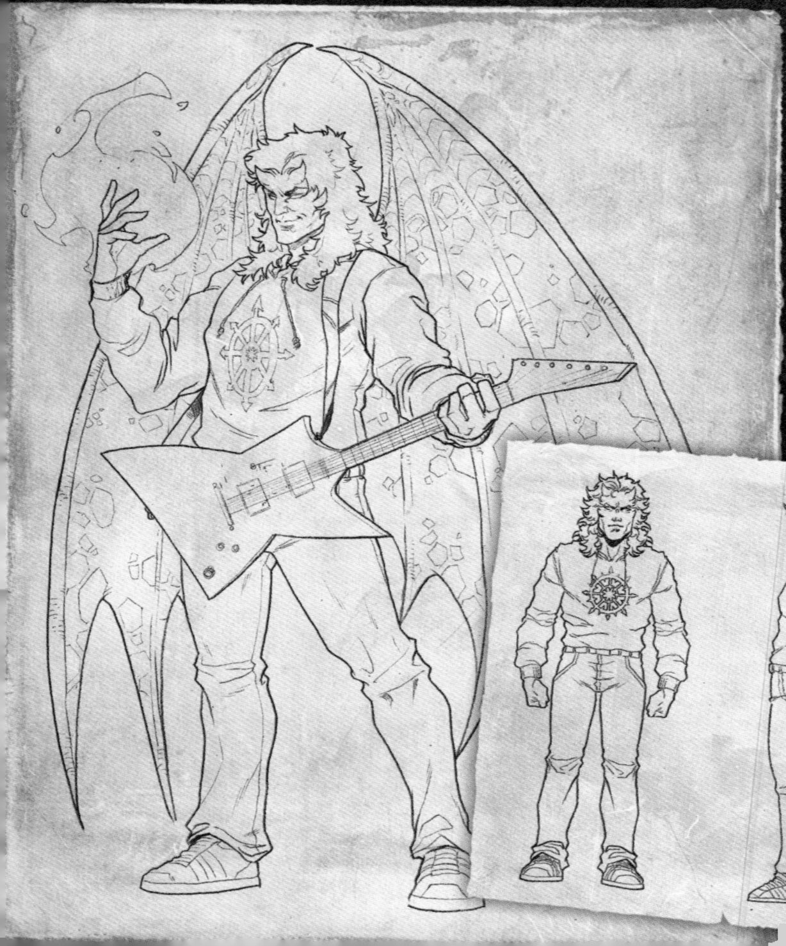

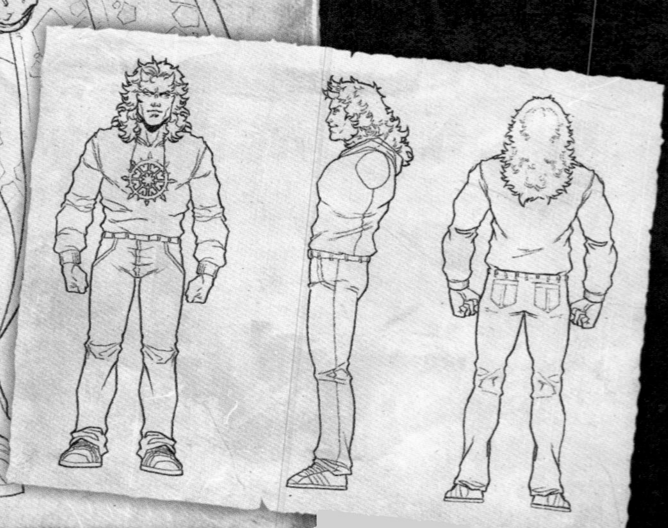

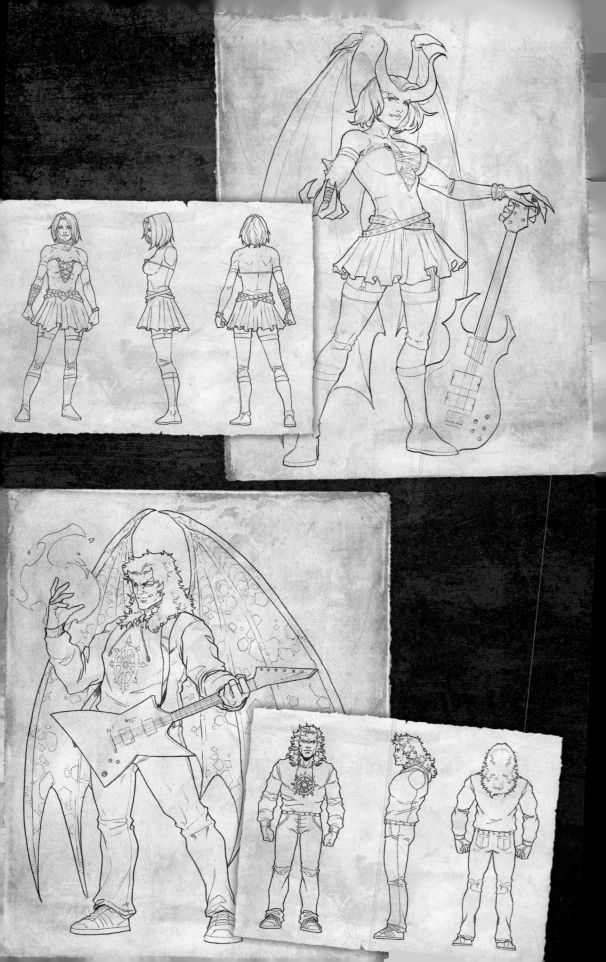

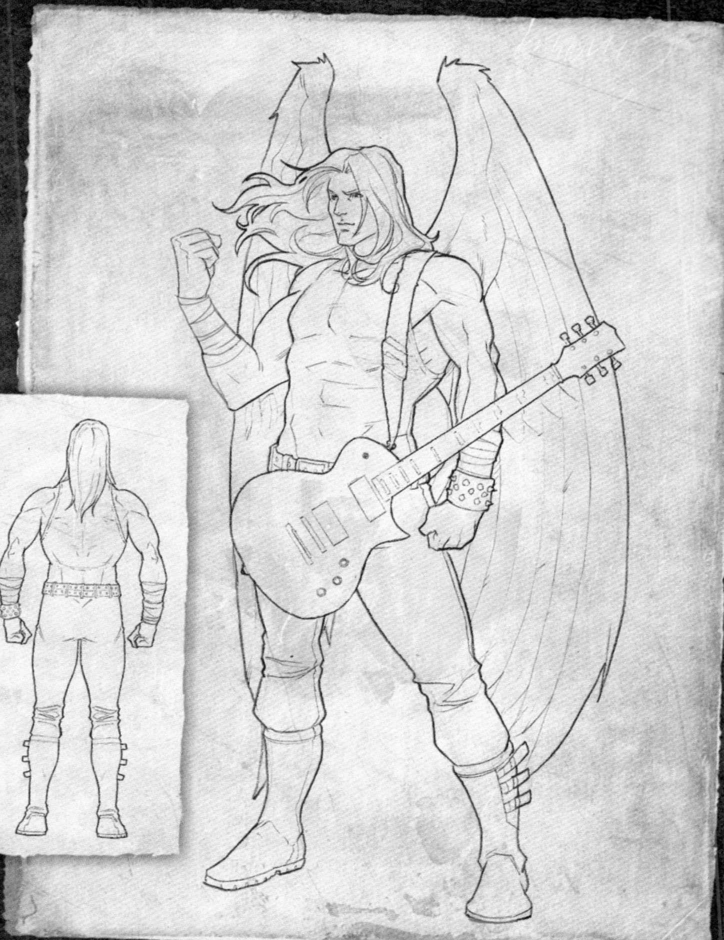
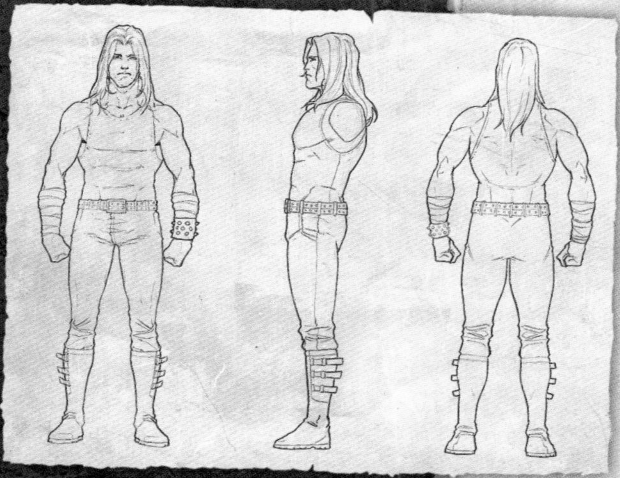
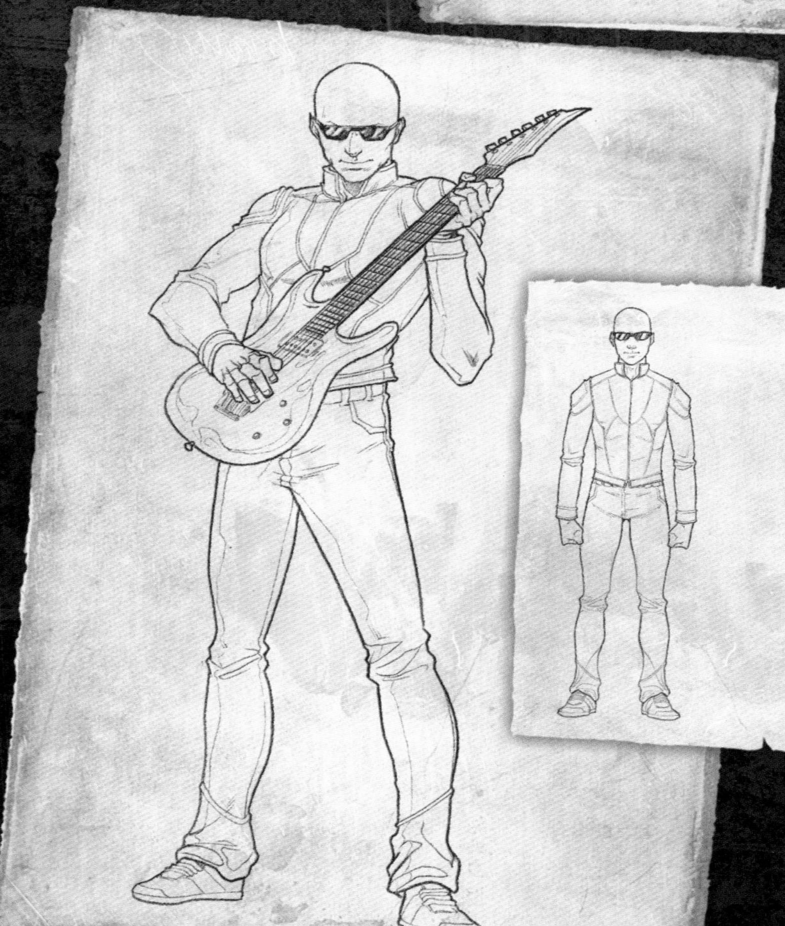
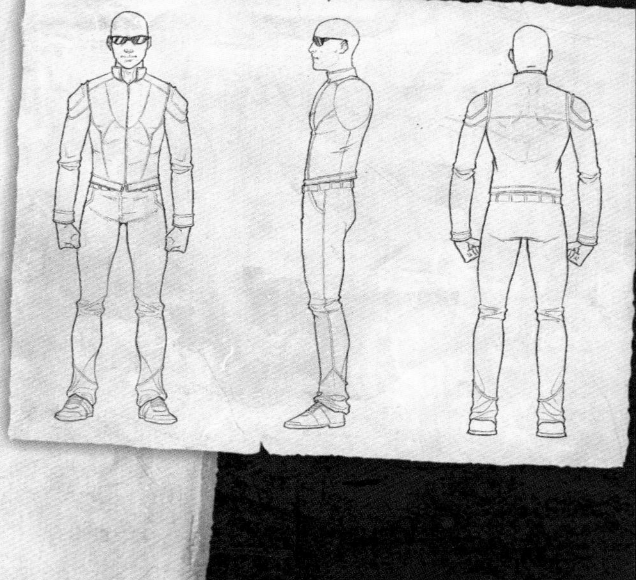

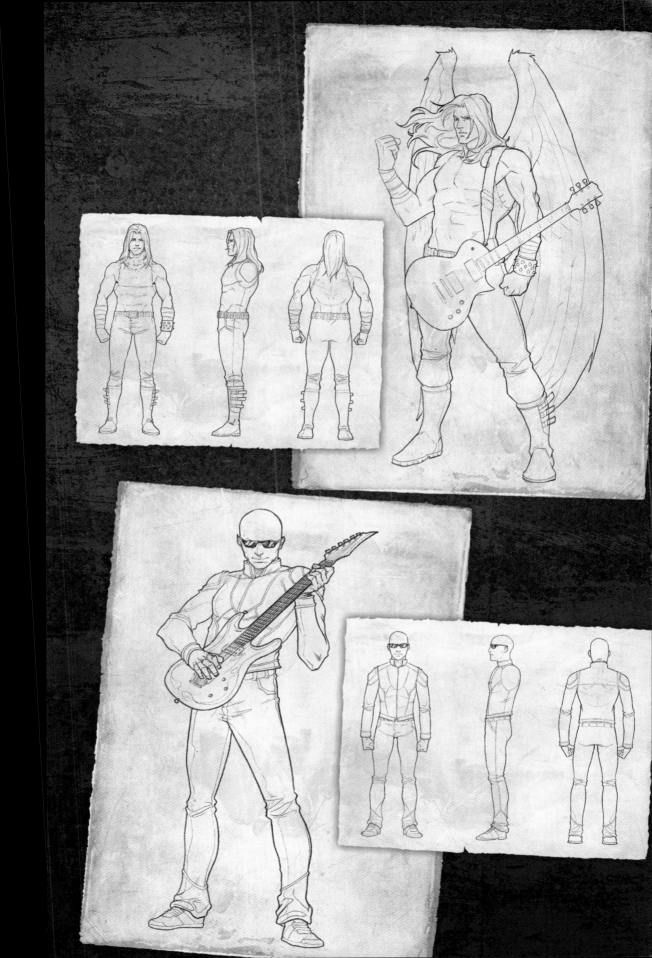

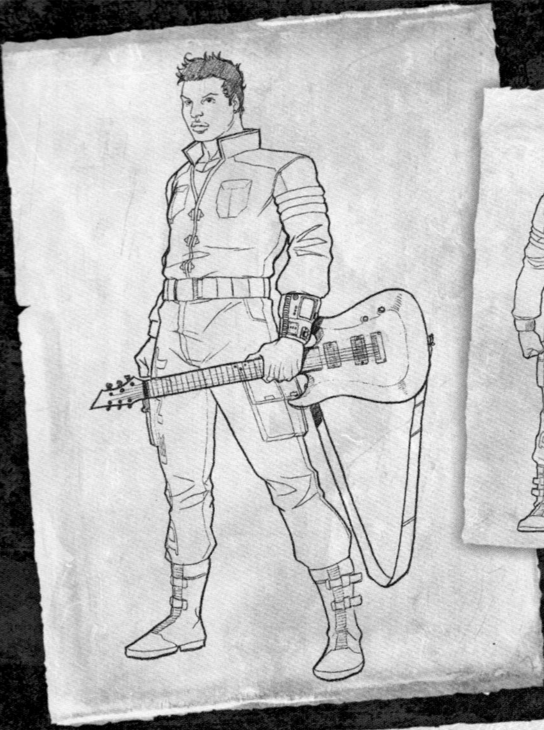

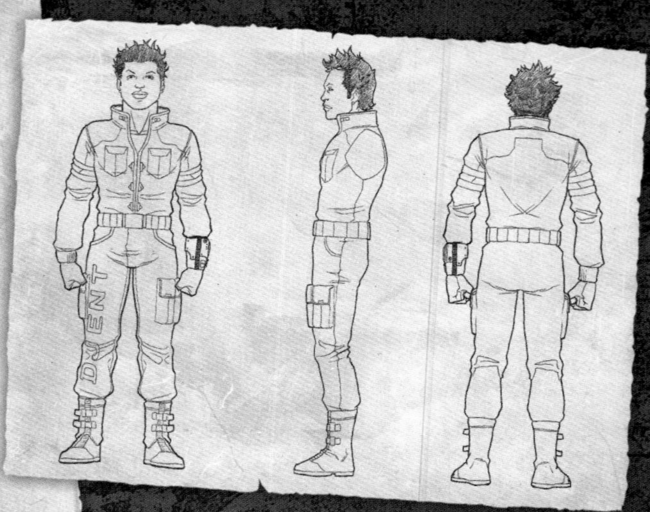

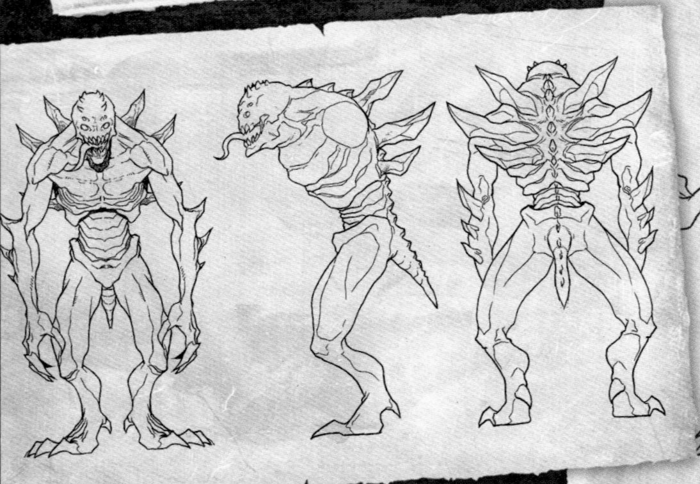

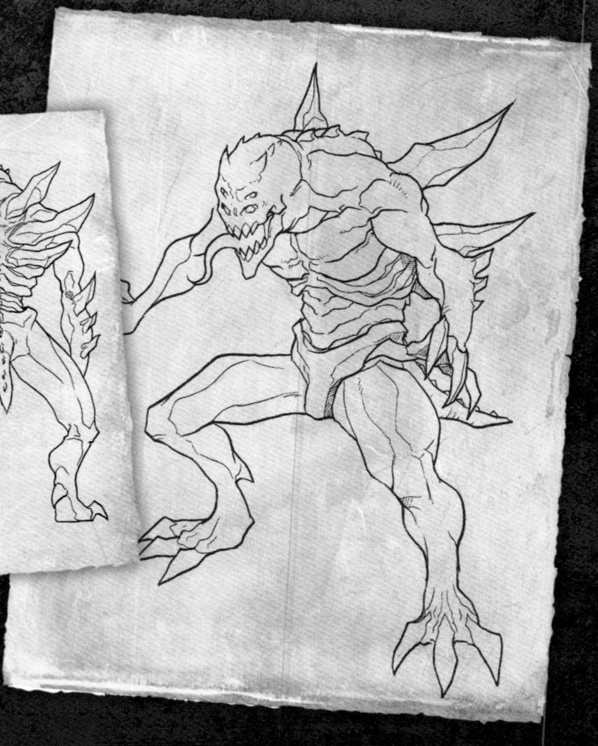

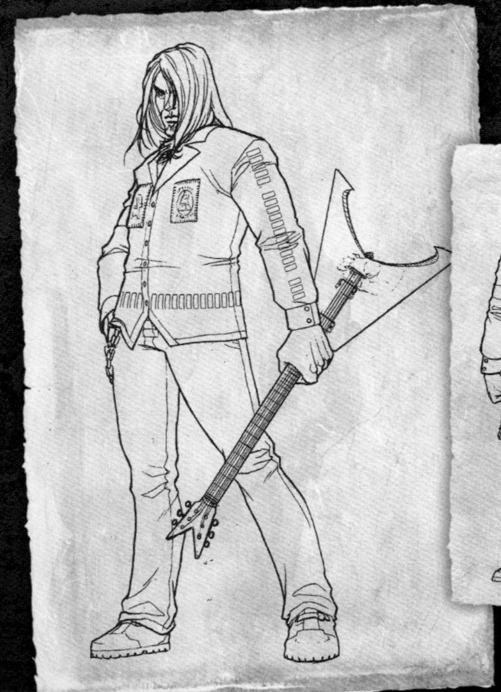

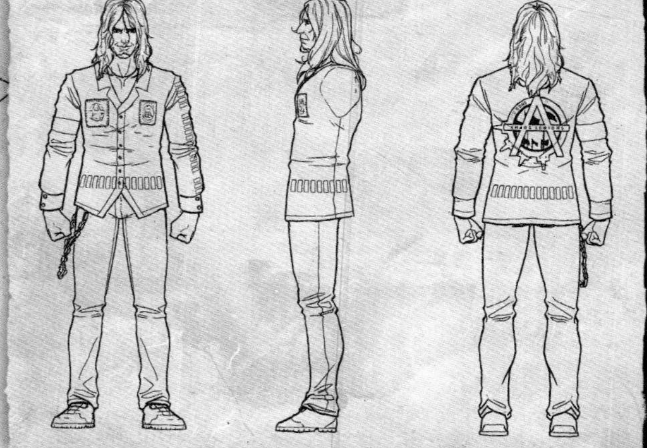

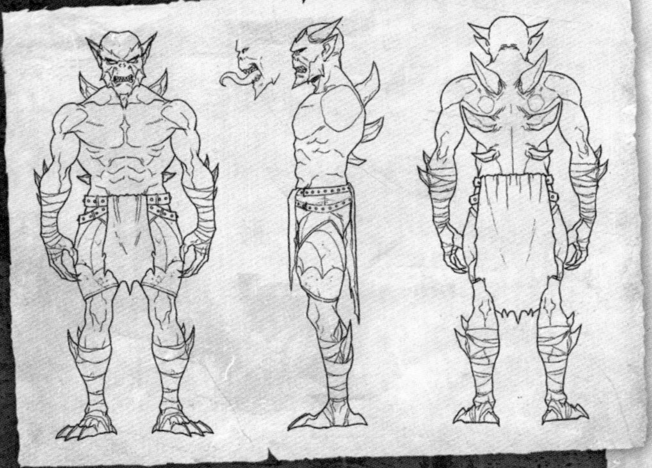
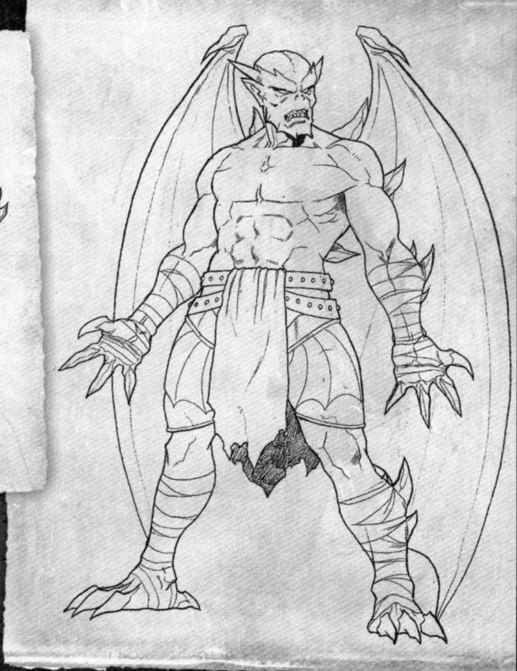
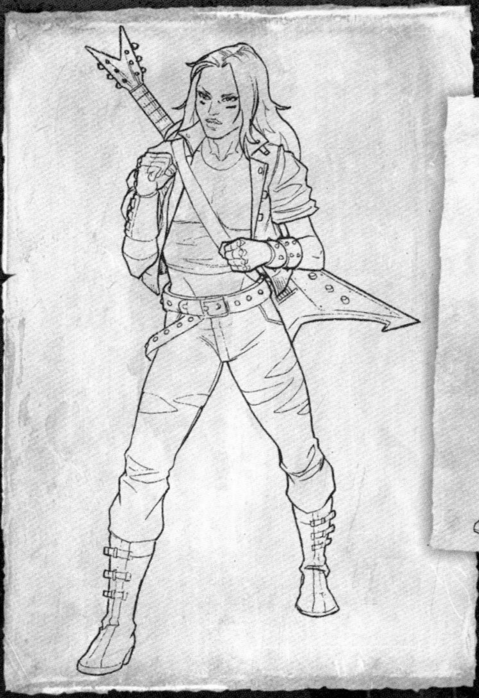
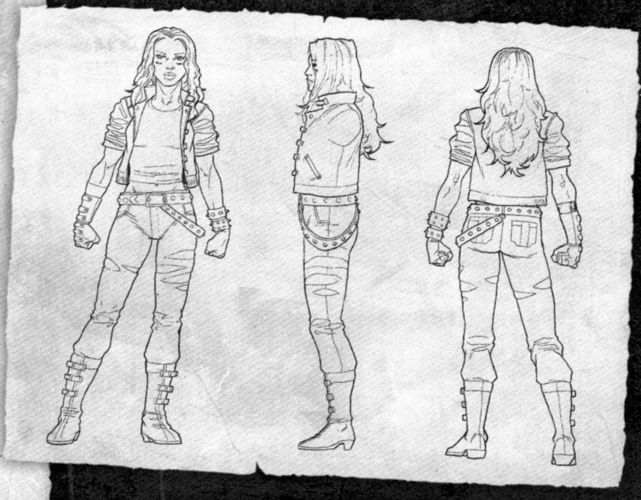
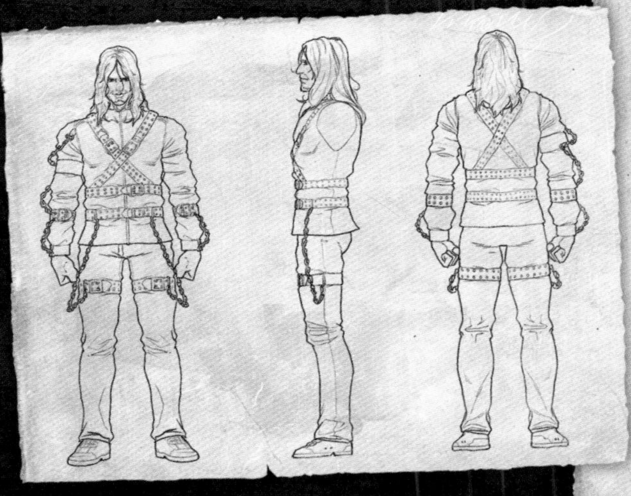
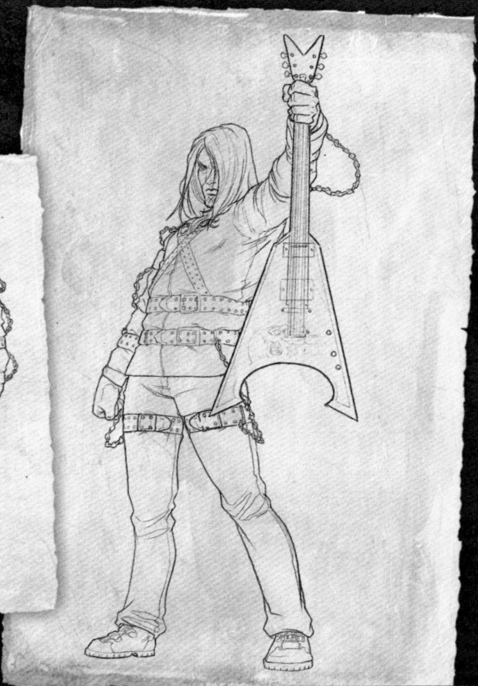

COBALT

PRESCRIPTION PERCEPTION

Written by

Llexi Leon and **Justin Peniston**

Pencils by

Jason Metcalf

Inks by

Tony Kordos and **Juan Castro**

Colors by

Garry Henderson and **Chris Summers**

Lettering by

Charles Pritchett

From the journals of Chara Gianopoulos:

This is week seven with Rick Drake.

Rick suffers from an acute & remarkable form of **Chronic Hallucinatory Psychosis.**

What makes it so remarkable is its potency. Rick's hallucinations engage all five of his senses, which is all but unheard of.

He's currently on as powerful a course of clozapine as the **FDA** allows.

Unfortunately, the drug doesn't rid him of the hallucinations as much as it retards his ability to be frightened or agitated by them.

I WOULD HAVE KILLED MY HUSBAND YEARS AGO IF I DIDN'T WATCH SO MUCH LAW & ORDER.

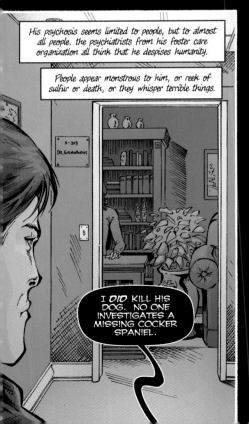

His psychosis seems limited to people, but to almost all people. the psychiatrists from his foster care organization all think that he despises humanity.

People appear monstrous to him, or reek of sulfur or death, or they whisper terrible things.

I *DID* KILL HIS DOG. NO ONE INVESTIGATES A MISSING COCKER SPANIEL.

It's ego, but I wonder what he sees when he looks at me?

HI, RICK.

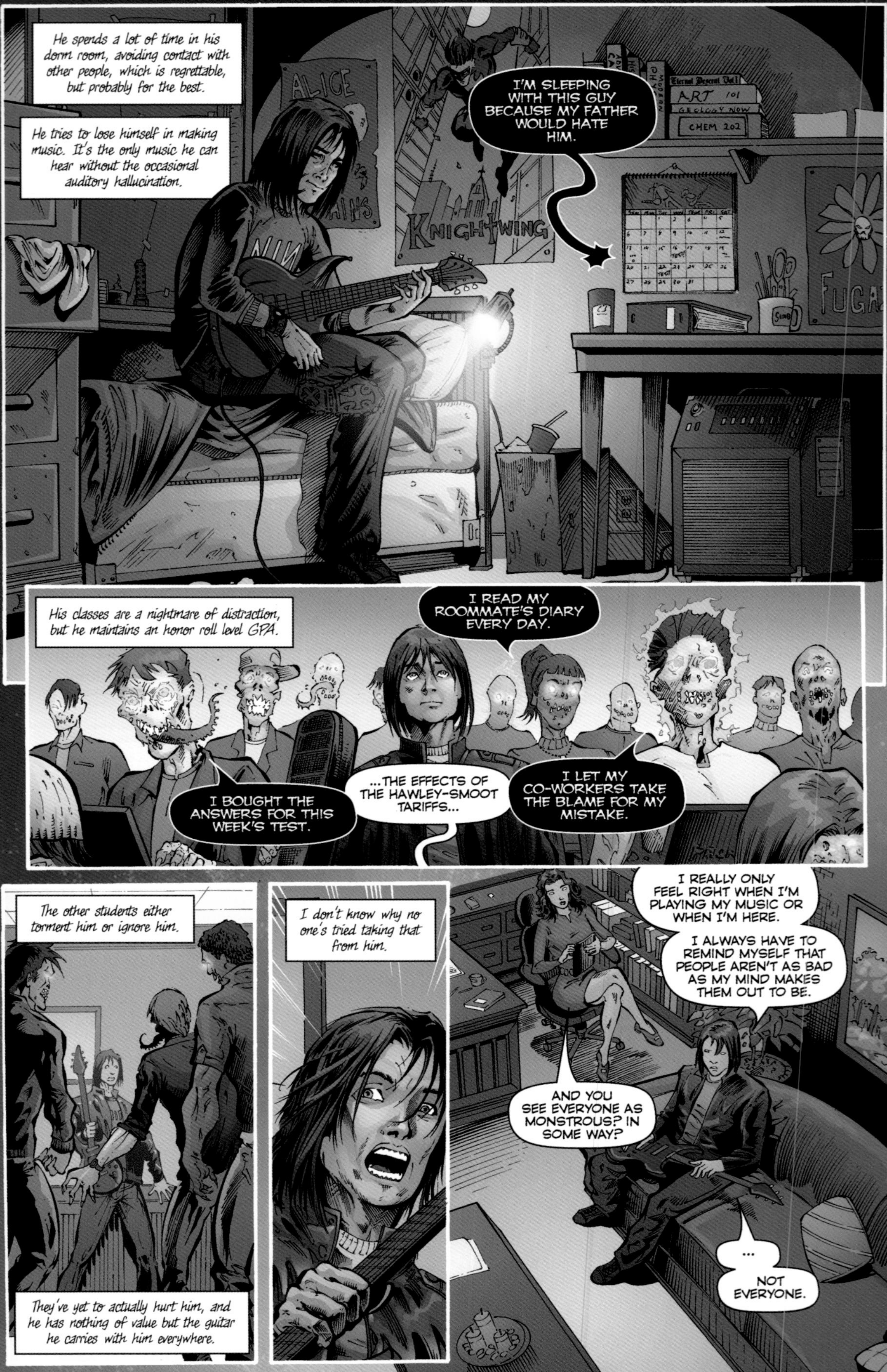
He spends a lot of time in his dorm room, avoiding contact with other people, which is regrettable, but probably for the best.
He tries to lose himself in making music. It's the only music he can hear without the occasional auditory hallucination.
I'M SLEEPING WITH THIS GUY BECAUSE MY FATHER WOULD HATE HIM.
KNIGHTWING
ART 101
GEOLOGY NOW
CHEM 202
His classes are a nightmare of distraction, but he maintains an honor roll level GPA.
I READ MY ROOMMATE'S DIARY EVERY DAY.
I BOUGHT THE ANSWERS FOR THIS WEEK'S TEST.
...THE EFFECTS OF THE HAWLEY-SMOOT TARIFFS...
I LET MY CO-WORKERS TAKE THE BLAME FOR MY MISTAKE.
The other students either torment him or ignore him.
They've yet to actually hurt him, and he has nothing of value but the guitar he carries with him everywhere.
I don't know why no one's tried taking that from him.
I REALLY ONLY FEEL RIGHT WHEN I'M PLAYING MY MUSIC OR WHEN I'M HERE.
I ALWAYS HAVE TO REMIND MYSELF THAT PEOPLE AREN'T AS BAD AS MY MIND MAKES THEM OUT TO BE.
AND YOU SEE EVERYONE AS MONSTROUS? IN SOME WAY?
...
NOT EVERYONE.

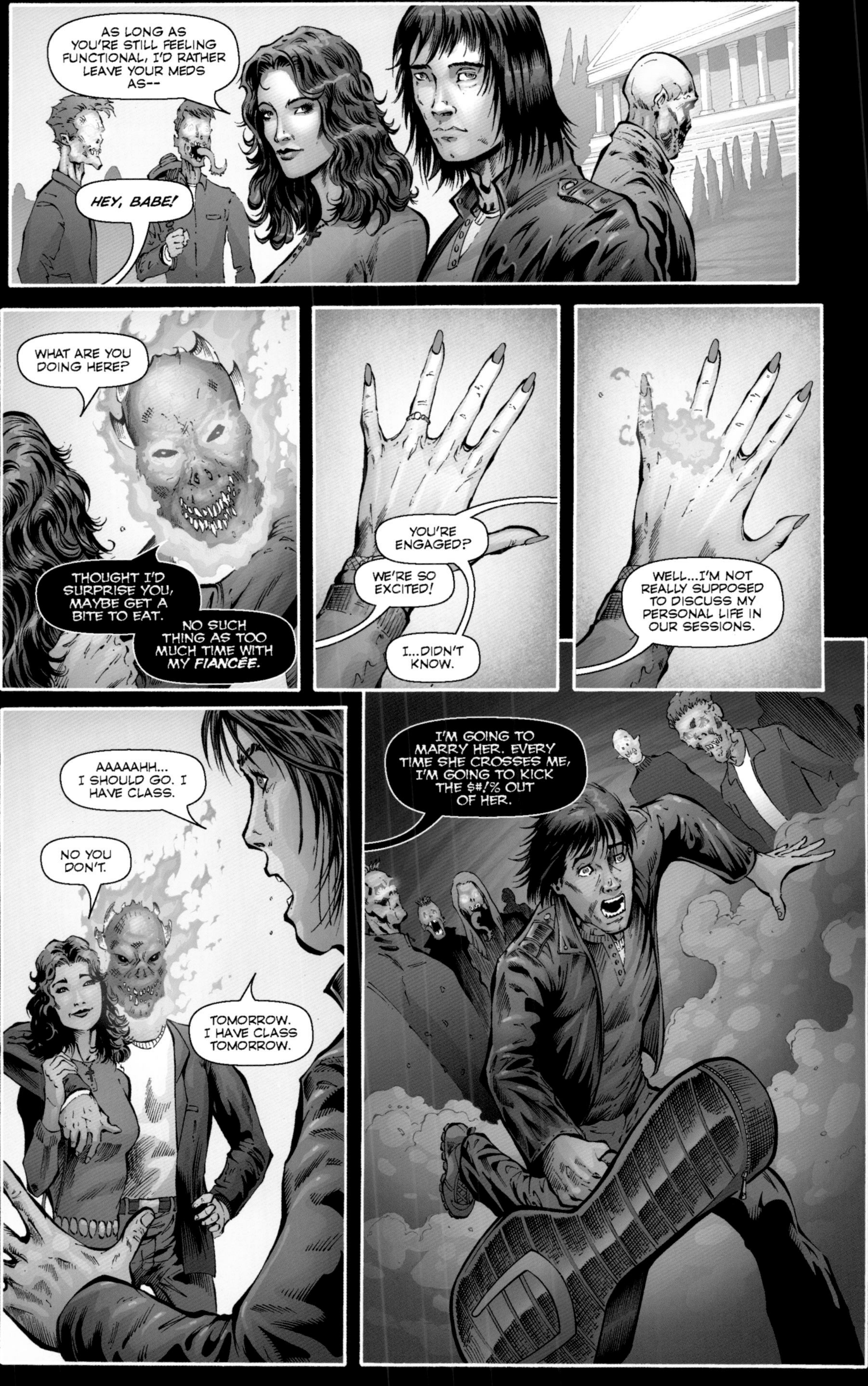
AS LONG AS YOU'RE STILL FEELING FUNCTIONAL, I'D RATHER LEAVE YOUR MEDS AS--
HEY, BABE!
WHAT ARE YOU DOING HERE?
THOUGHT I'D SURPRISE YOU, MAYBE GET A BITE TO EAT.
NO SUCH THING AS TOO MUCH TIME WITH MY FIANCÉE.
YOU'RE ENGAGED?
WE'RE SO EXCITED!
I...DIDN'T KNOW.
WELL...I'M NOT REALLY SUPPOSED TO DISCUSS MY PERSONAL LIFE IN OUR SESSIONS.
AAAAAHH... I SHOULD GO. I HAVE CLASS.
NO YOU DON'T.
TOMORROW. I HAVE CLASS TOMORROW.
I'M GOING TO MARRY HER. EVERY TIME SHE CROSSES ME, I'M GOING TO KICK THE $#!% OUT OF HER.

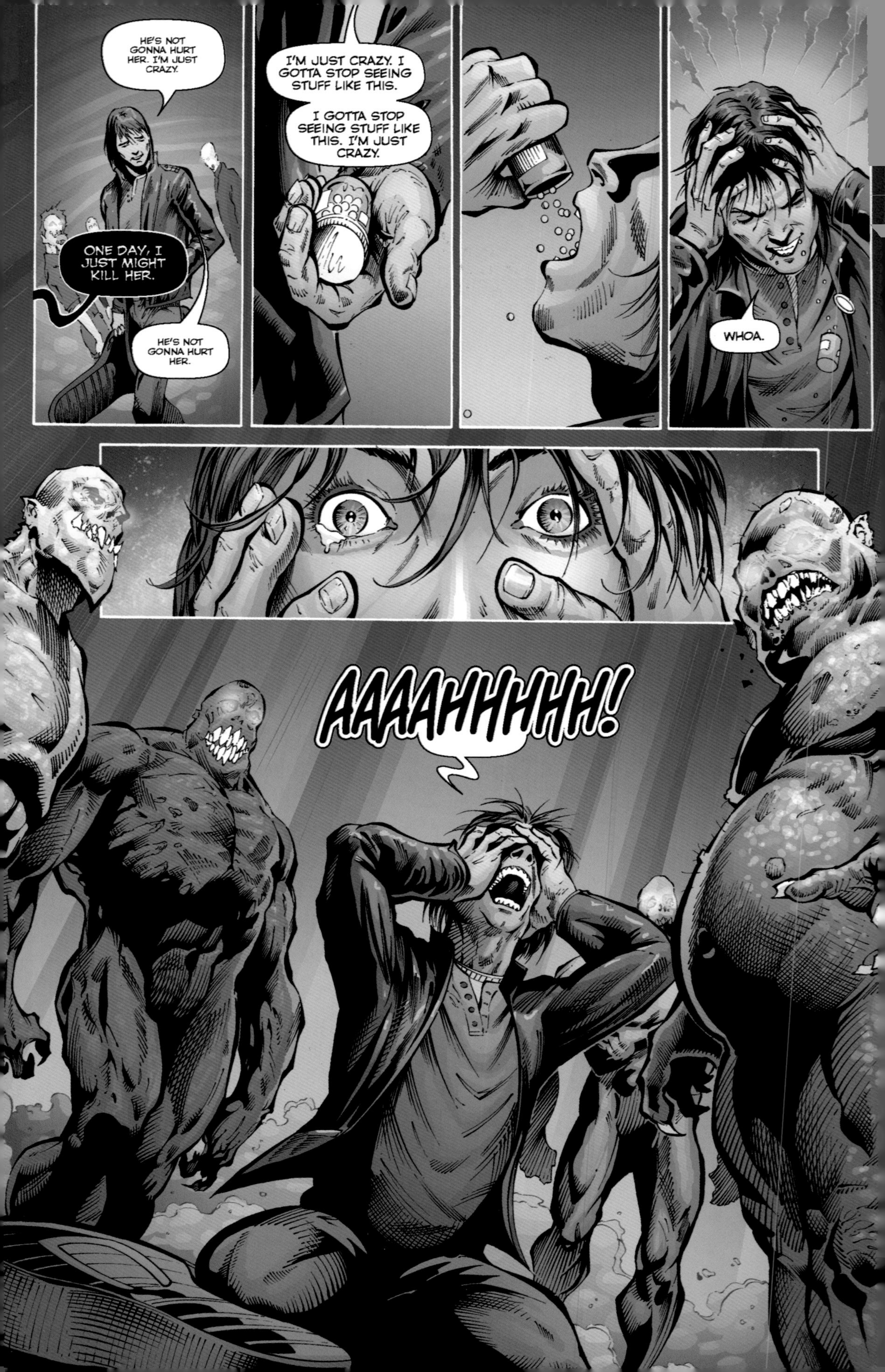
HE'S NOT GONNA HURT HER. I'M JUST CRAZY.
ONE DAY, I JUST MIGHT KILL HER.
HE'S NOT GONNA HURT HER.
I'M JUST CRAZY. I GOTTA STOP SEEING STUFF LIKE THIS.
I GOTTA STOP SEEING STUFF LIKE THIS. I'M JUST CRAZY.
WHOA.
AAAAHHHHH!

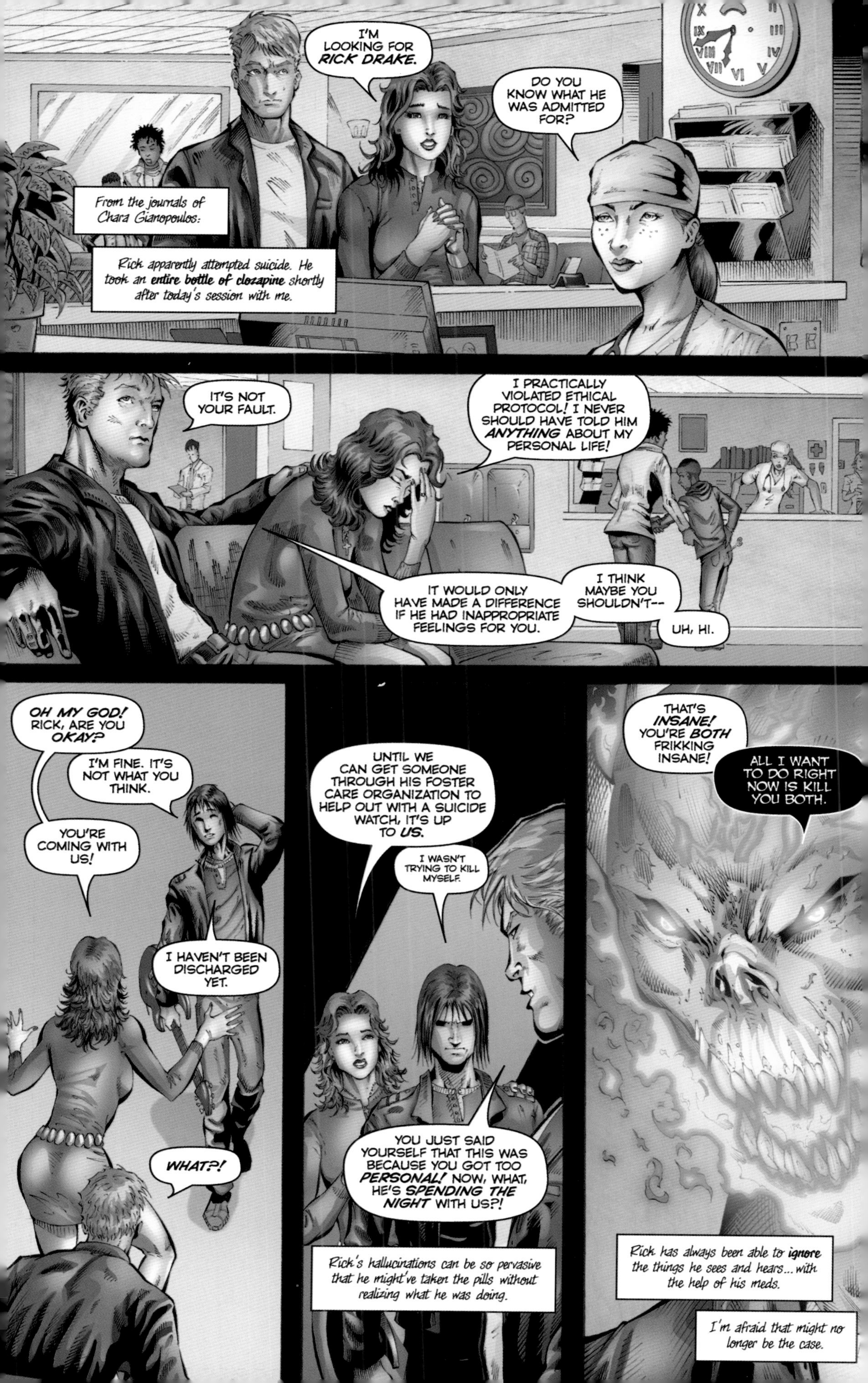
I'M LOOKING FOR RICK DRAKE.
DO YOU KNOW WHAT HE WAS ADMITTED FOR?
From the journals of Chara Gianopoulos:
Rick apparently attempted suicide. He took an entire bottle of clozapine shortly after today's session with me.
IT'S NOT YOUR FAULT.
I PRACTICALLY VIOLATED ETHICAL PROTOCOL! I NEVER SHOULD HAVE TOLD HIM ANYTHING ABOUT MY PERSONAL LIFE!
IT WOULD ONLY HAVE MADE A DIFFERENCE IF HE HAD INAPPROPRIATE FEELINGS FOR YOU.
I THINK MAYBE YOU SHOULDN'T--
UH, HI.
OH MY GOD! RICK, ARE YOU OKAY?
I'M FINE. IT'S NOT WHAT YOU THINK.
YOU'RE COMING WITH US!
I HAVEN'T BEEN DISCHARGED YET.
WHAT?!
UNTIL WE CAN GET SOMEONE THROUGH HIS FOSTER CARE ORGANIZATION TO HELP OUT WITH A SUICIDE WATCH, IT'S UP TO US.
I WASN'T TRYING TO KILL MYSELF.
YOU JUST SAID YOURSELF THAT THIS WAS BECAUSE YOU GOT TOO PERSONAL! NOW, WHAT, HE'S SPENDING THE NIGHT WITH US?!
Rick's hallucinations can be so pervasive that he might've taken the pills without realizing what he was doing.
THAT'S INSANE! YOU'RE BOTH FRIKKING INSANE!
ALL I WANT TO DO RIGHT NOW IS KILL YOU BOTH.
Rick has always been able to ignore the things he sees and hears... with the help of his meds.
I'm afraid that might no longer be the case.

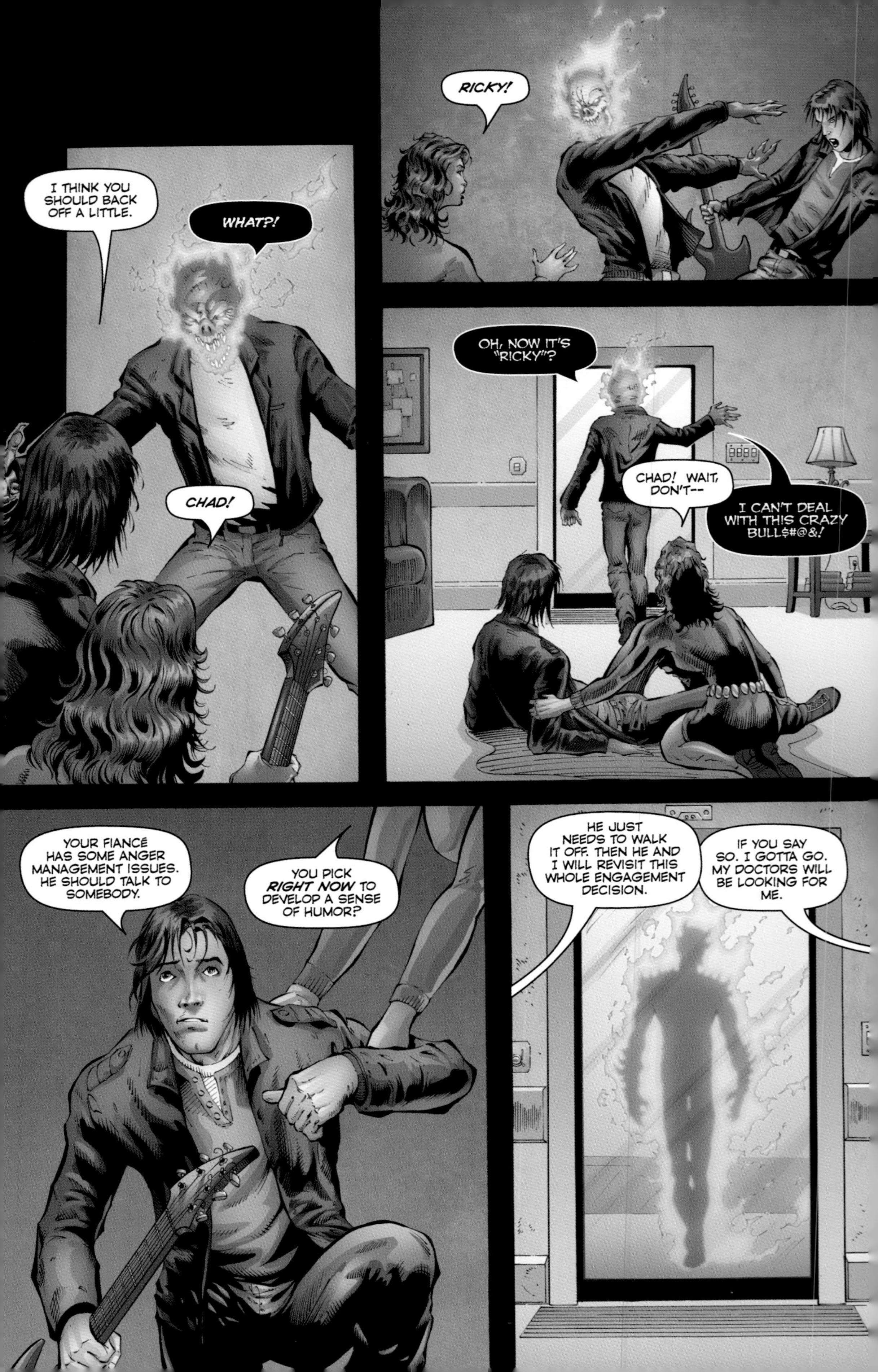

I THINK YOU SHOULD BACK OFF A LITTLE.
WHAT?!
CHAD!
RICKY!
OH, NOW IT'S "RICKY"?
I CAN'T DEAL WITH THIS CRAZY BULL$#@&!
CHAD! WAIT, DON'T--
YOUR FIANCÉ HAS SOME ANGER MANAGEMENT ISSUES. HE SHOULD TALK TO SOMEBODY.
YOU PICK *RIGHT NOW* TO DEVELOP A SENSE OF HUMOR?
HE JUST NEEDS TO WALK IT OFF. THEN HE AND I WILL REVISIT THIS WHOLE ENGAGEMENT DECISION.
IF YOU SAY SO. I GOTTA GO. MY DOCTORS WILL BE LOOKING FOR ME.

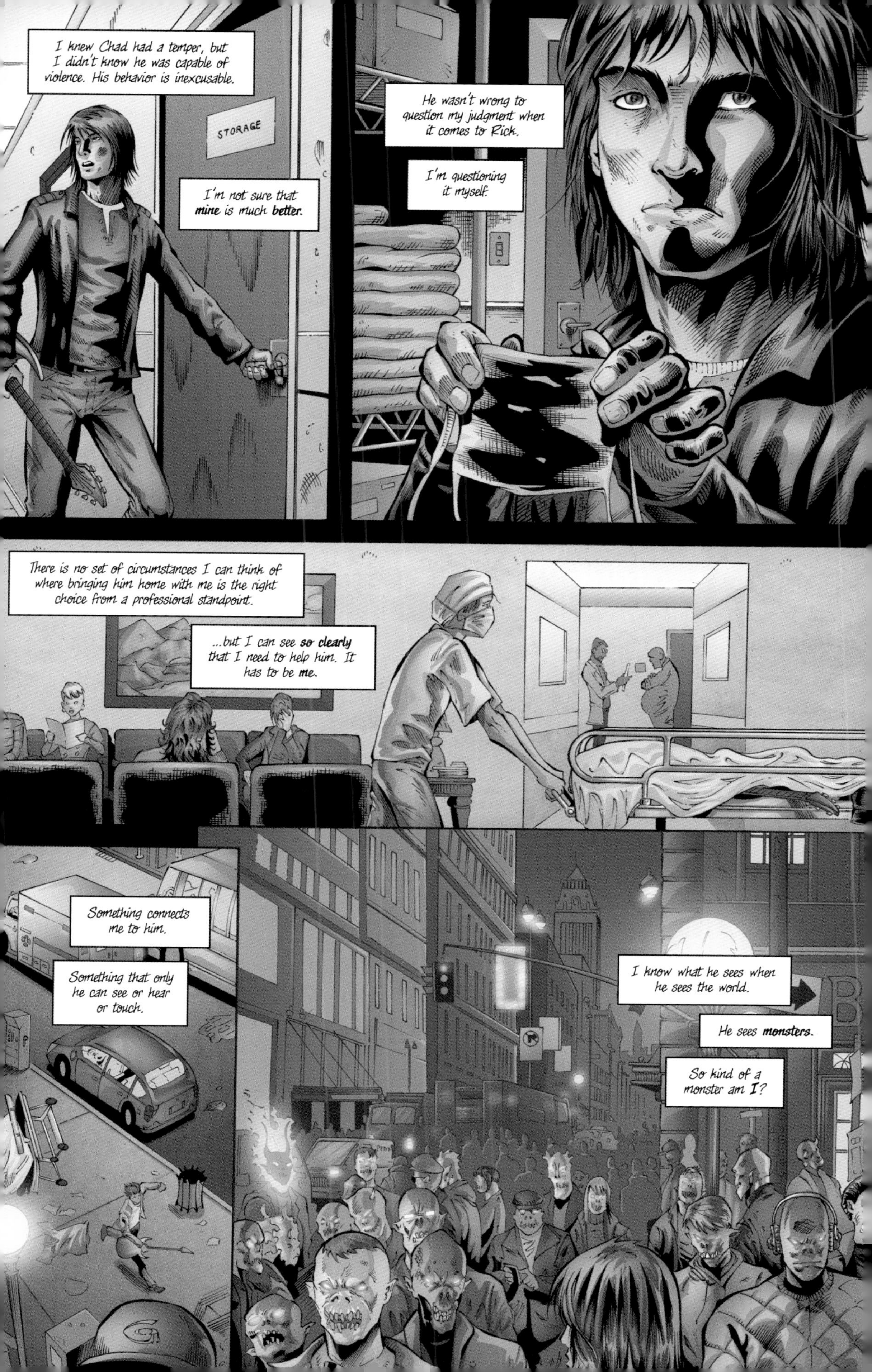
I knew Chad had a temper, but I didn't know he was capable of violence. His behavior is inexcusable.
STORAGE
I'm not sure that **mine** is much **better**.
He wasn't wrong to question my judgment when it comes to Rick.
I'm questioning it myself.
There is no set of circumstances I can think of where bringing him home with me is the right choice from a professional standpoint.
...but I can see **so clearly** that I need to help him. It has to be **me**.
Something connects me to him.
Something that only he can see or hear or touch.
I know what he sees when he sees the world.
He sees **monsters**.
So kind of a monster am **I**?

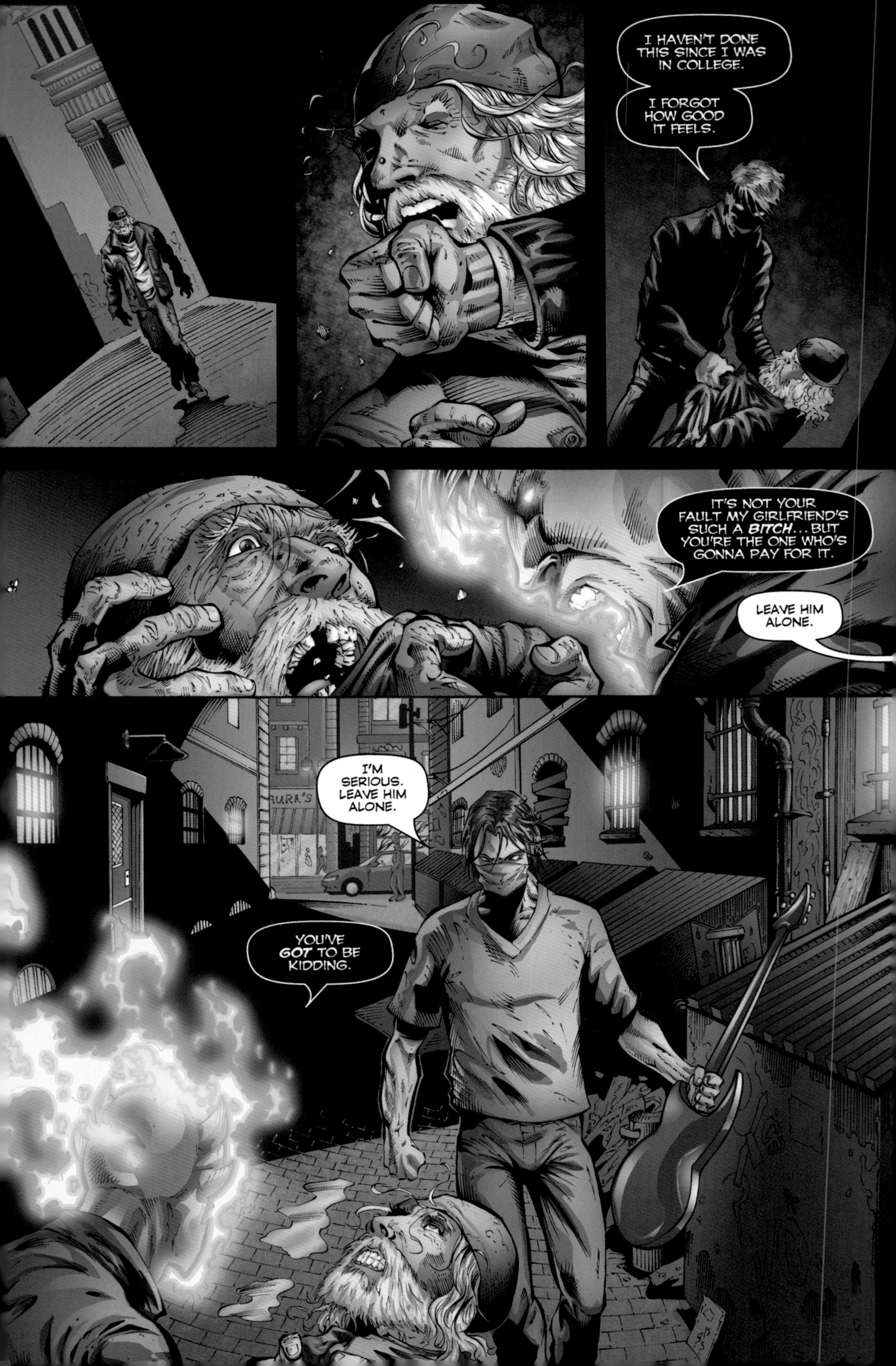
I HAVEN'T DONE THIS SINCE I WAS IN COLLEGE.
I FORGOT HOW GOOD IT FEELS.
IT'S NOT YOUR FAULT MY GIRLFRIEND'S SUCH A *BITCH*... BUT YOU'RE THE ONE WHO'S GONNA PAY FOR IT.
LEAVE HIM ALONE.
I'M SERIOUS. LEAVE HIM ALONE.
YOU'VE *GOT* TO BE KIDDING.

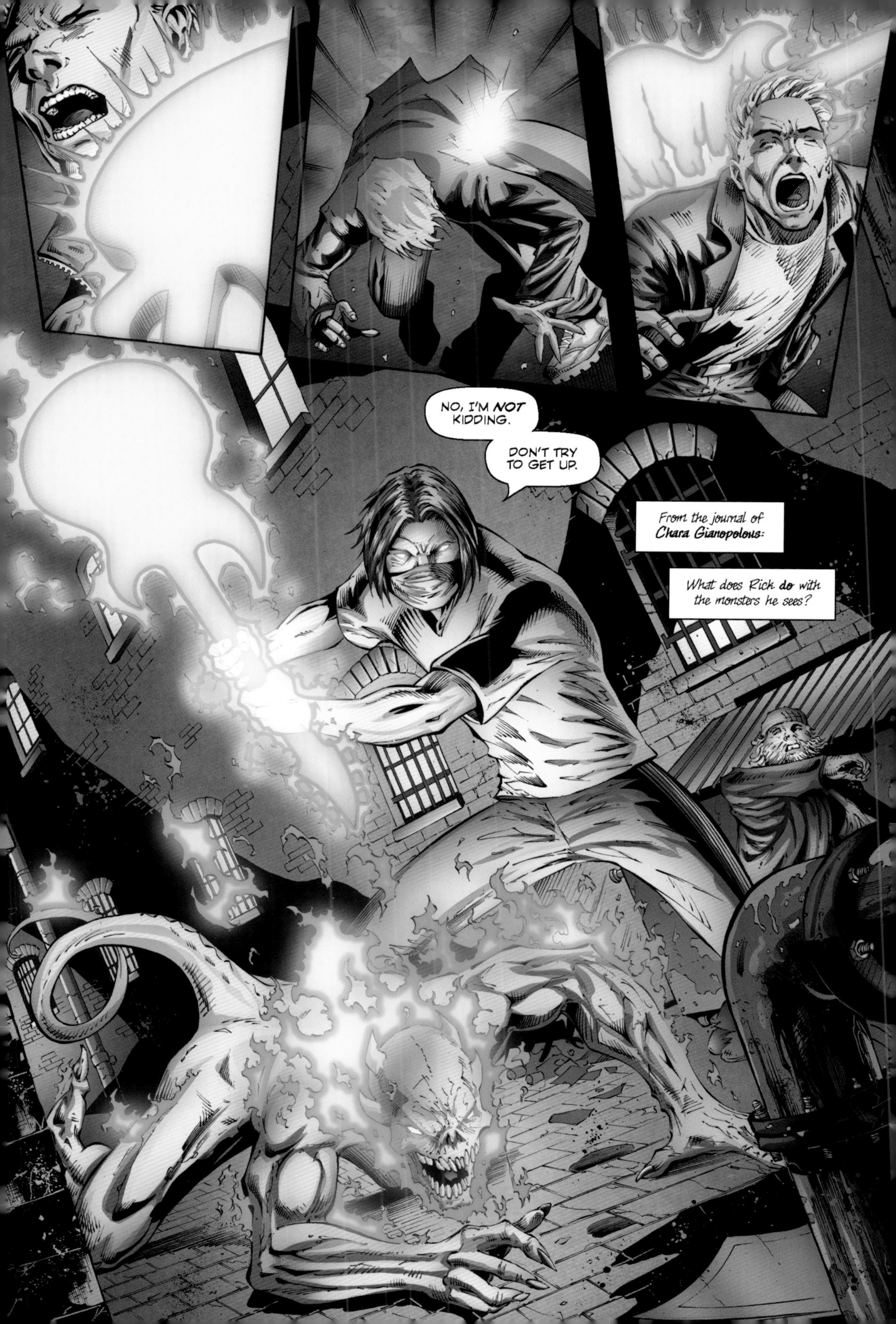
NO, I'M *NOT* KIDDING.
DON'T TRY TO GET UP.
From the journal of **Chara Gianopolous:**
What does Rick **do** with the monsters he sees?

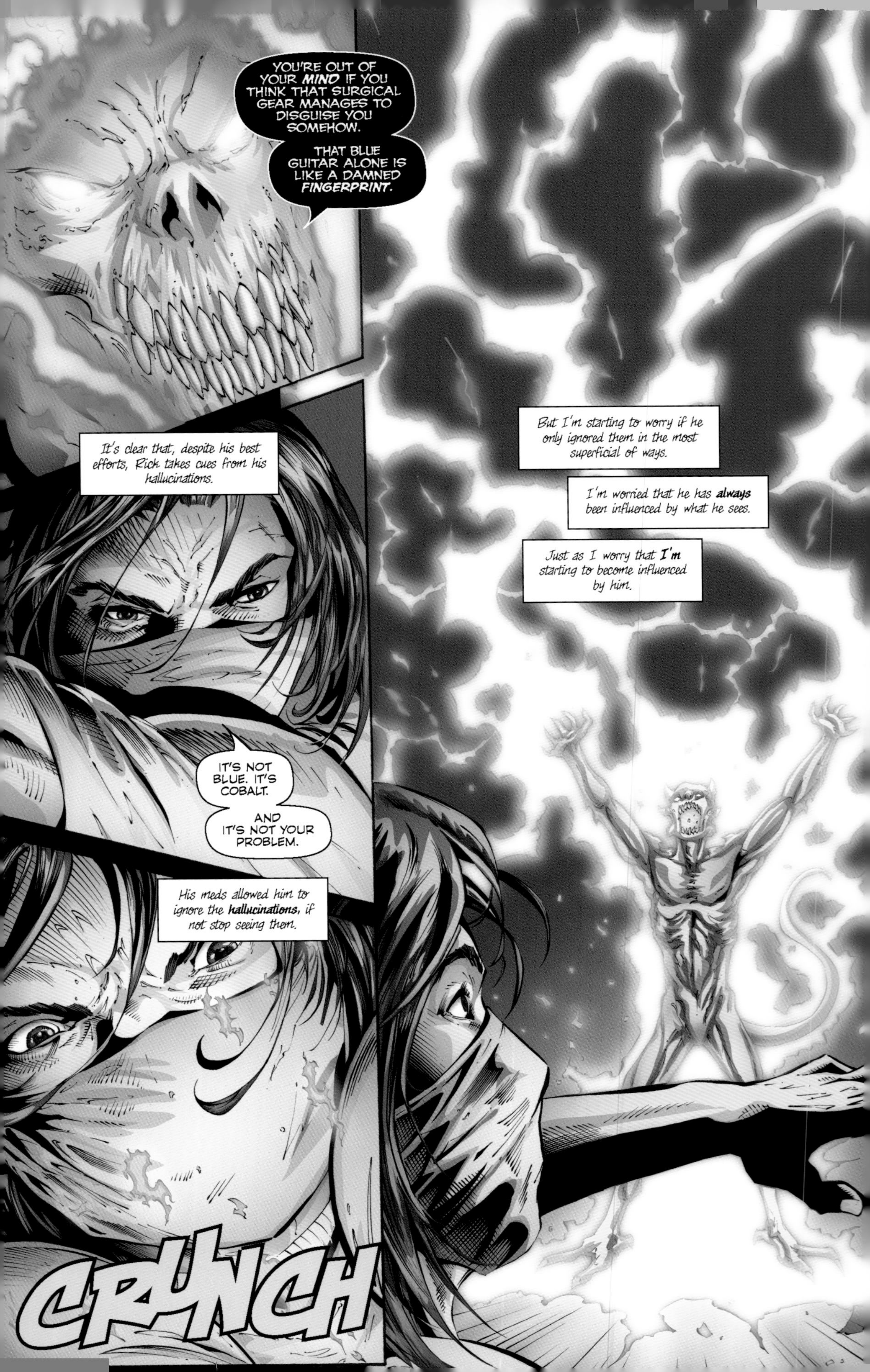
YOU'RE OUT OF YOUR **MIND** IF YOU THINK THAT SURGICAL GEAR MANAGES TO DISGUISE YOU SOMEHOW.
THAT BLUE GUITAR ALONE IS LIKE A DAMNED **FINGERPRINT.**
It's clear that, despite his best efforts, Rick takes cues from his hallucinations.
IT'S NOT BLUE. IT'S COBALT.
AND IT'S NOT YOUR PROBLEM.
His meds allowed him to ignore the **hallucinations**, if not stop seeing them.
But I'm starting to worry if he only ignored them in the most superficial of ways.
I'm worried that he has **always** been influenced by what he sees.
Just as I worry that **I'm** starting to become influenced by him.
CRUNCH

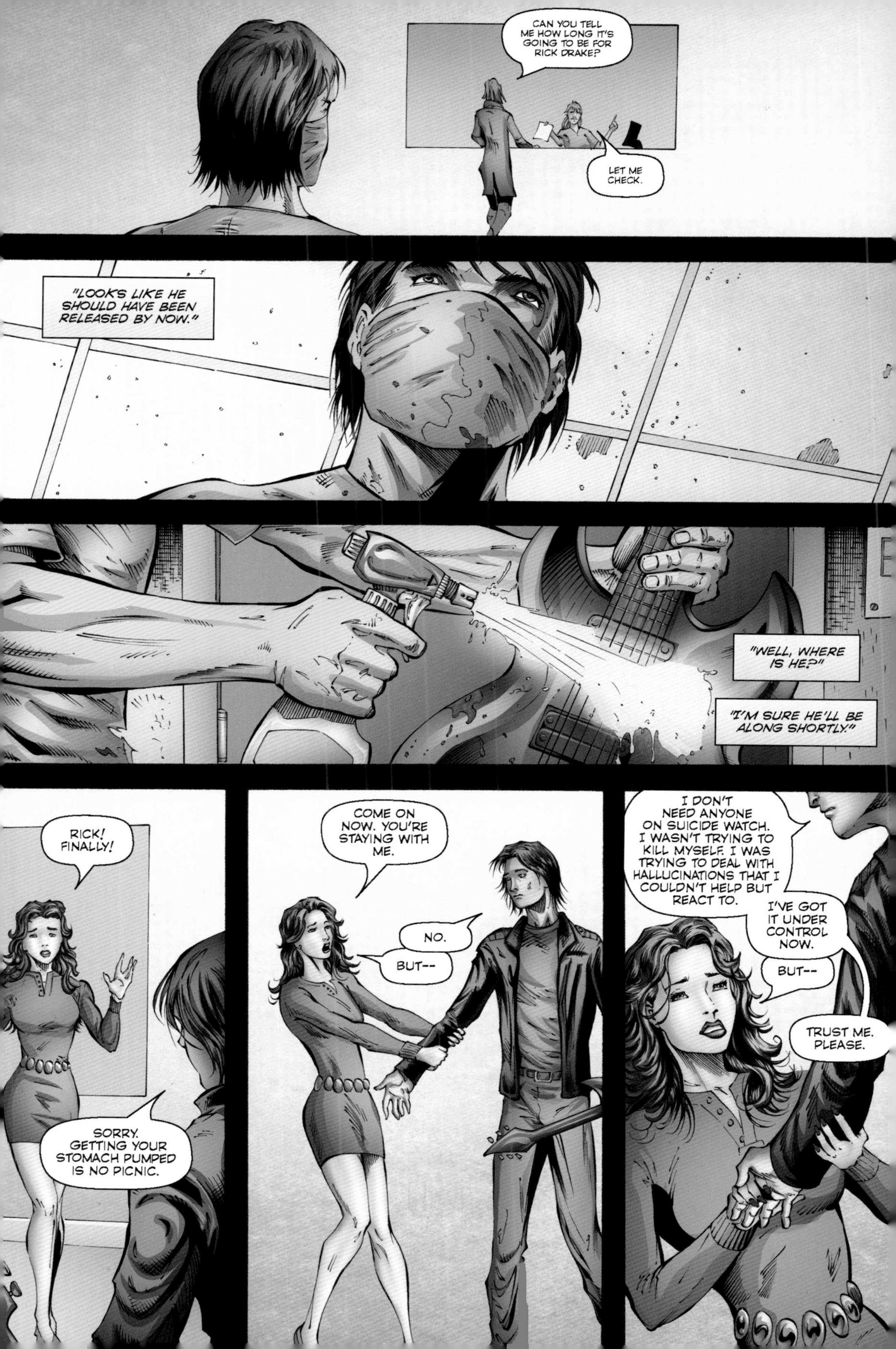

CAN YOU TELL ME HOW LONG IT'S GOING TO BE FOR RICK DRAKE?
LET ME CHECK.
"LOOKS LIKE HE SHOULD HAVE BEEN RELEASED BY NOW."
"WELL, WHERE IS HE?"
"I'M SURE HE'LL BE ALONG SHORTLY."
RICK! FINALLY!
SORRY. GETTING YOUR STOMACH PUMPED IS NO PICNIC.
COME ON NOW. YOU'RE STAYING WITH ME.
NO.
BUT--
I DON'T NEED ANYONE ON SUICIDE WATCH. I WASN'T TRYING TO KILL MYSELF. I WAS TRYING TO DEAL WITH HALLUCINATIONS THAT I COULDN'T HELP BUT REACT TO.
I'VE GOT IT UNDER CONTROL NOW.
BUT--
TRUST ME. PLEASE.

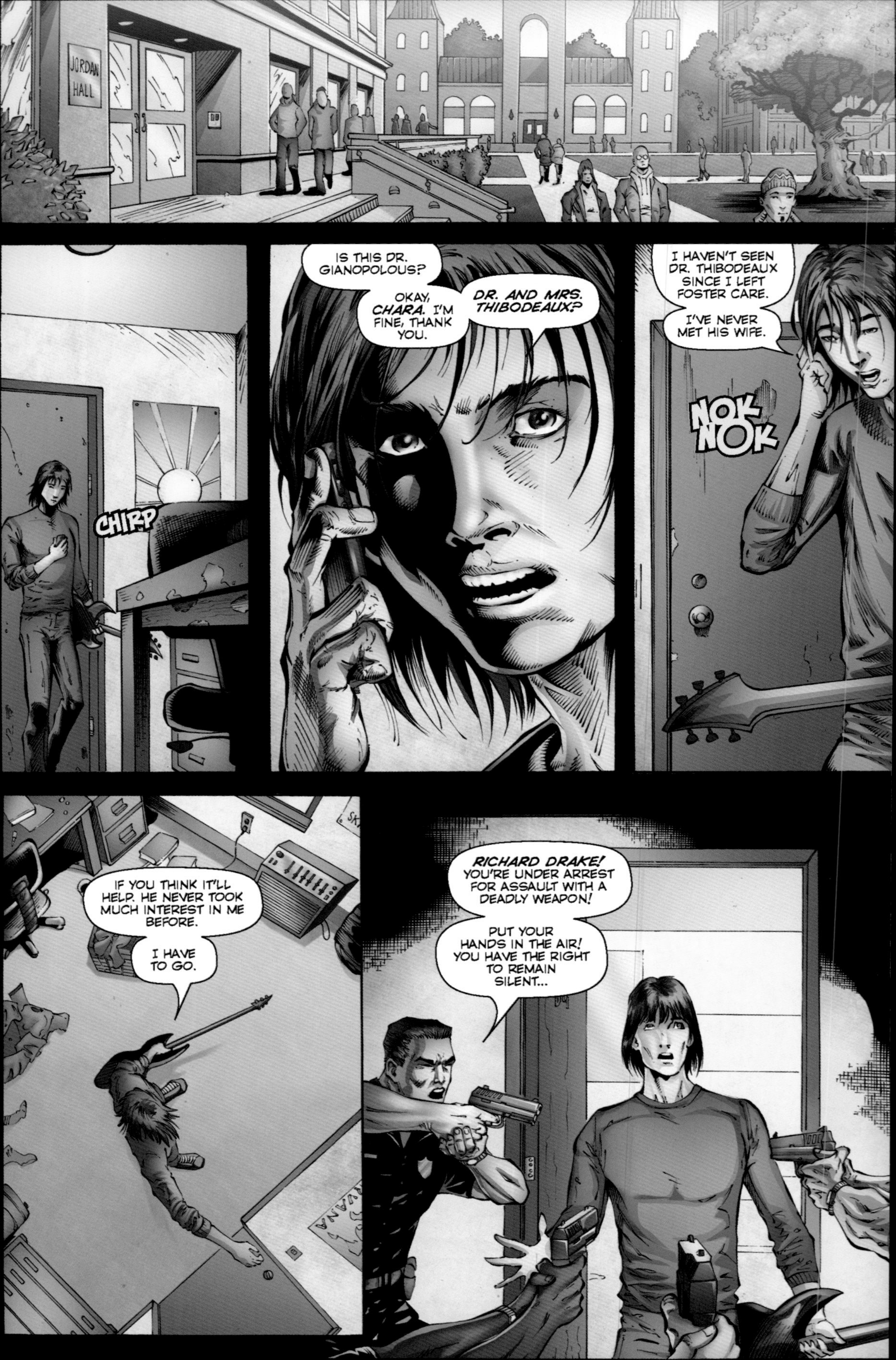
JORDAN HALL
CHIRP
IS THIS DR. GIANOPOLOUS?
OKAY, *CHARA.* I'M FINE, THANK YOU.
DR. AND MRS. THIBODEAUX?
I HAVEN'T SEEN DR. THIBODEAUX SINCE I LEFT FOSTER CARE.
I'VE NEVER MET HIS WIFE.
NOK NOK
IF YOU THINK IT'LL HELP. HE NEVER TOOK MUCH INTEREST IN ME BEFORE.
I HAVE TO GO.
RICHARD DRAKE! YOU'RE UNDER ARREST FOR ASSAULT WITH A DEADLY WEAPON!
PUT YOUR HANDS IN THE AIR! YOU HAVE THE RIGHT TO REMAIN SILENT...

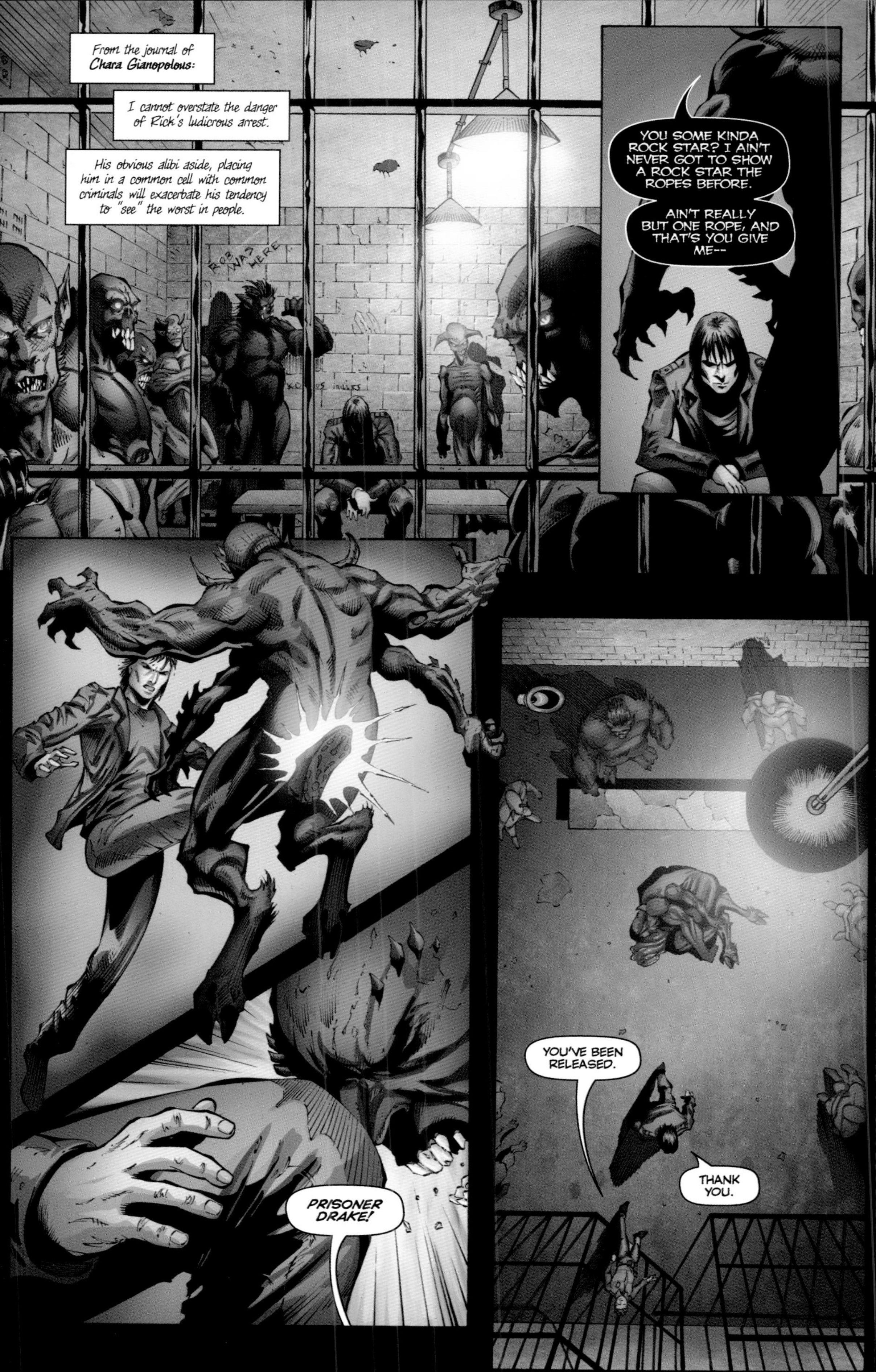
From the journal of Chara Gianopolous:
I cannot overstate the danger of Rick's ludicrous arrest.
His obvious alibi aside, placing him in a common cell with common criminals will exacerbate his tendency to "see" the worst in people.
ROB WAS HERE
YOU SOME KINDA ROCK STAR? I AIN'T NEVER GOT TO SHOW A ROCK STAR THE ROPES BEFORE.
AIN'T REALLY BUT ONE ROPE, AND THAT'S YOU GIVE ME--
PRISONER DRAKE!
YOU'VE BEEN RELEASED.
THANK YOU.

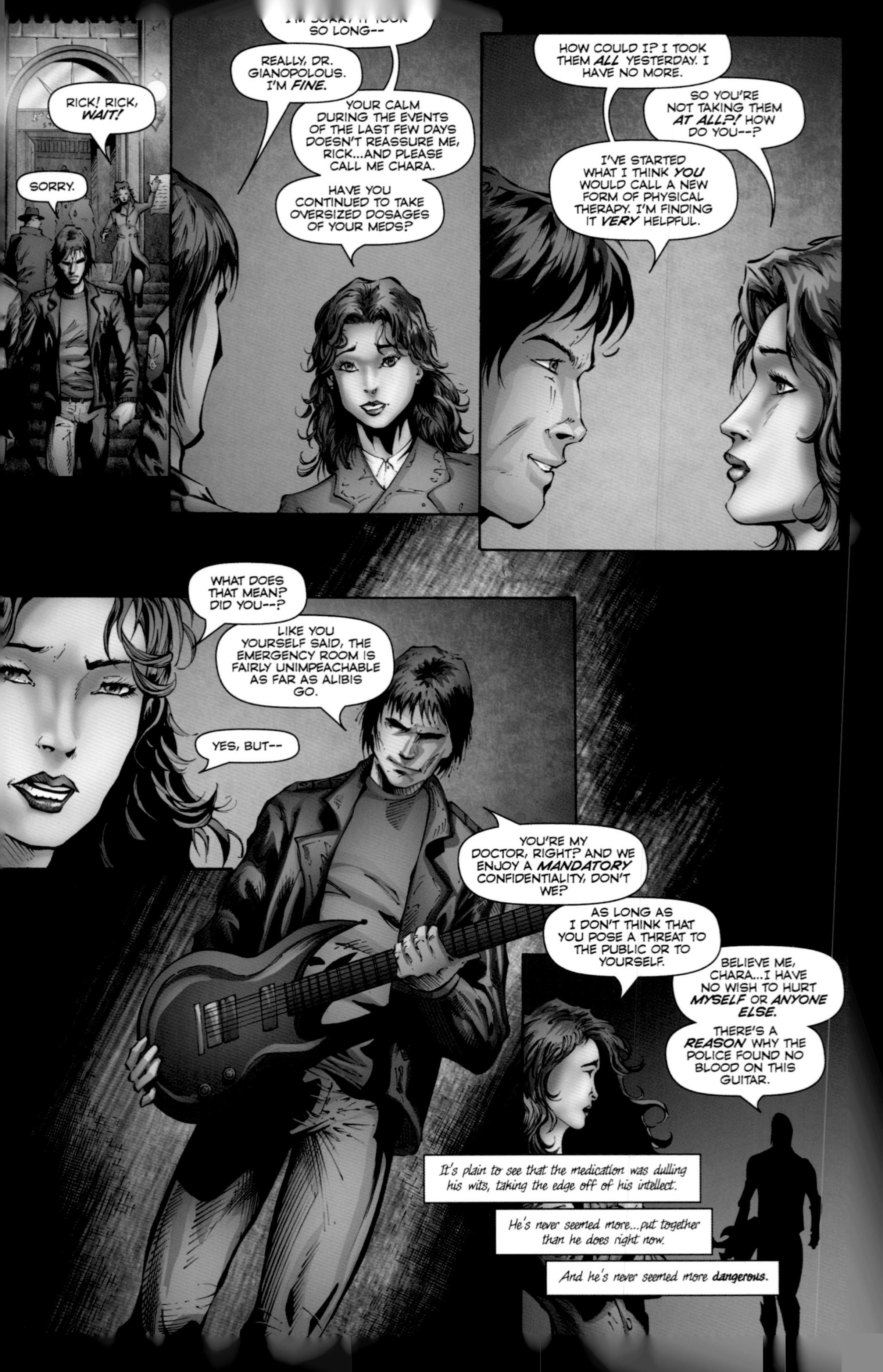
RICK! RICK, WAIT!
SORRY.
SO LONG--
REALLY, DR. GIANOPOLOUS. I'M FINE.
YOUR CALM DURING THE EVENTS OF THE LAST FEW DAYS DOESN'T REASSURE ME, RICK...AND PLEASE CALL ME CHARA.
HAVE YOU CONTINUED TO TAKE OVERSIZED DOSAGES OF YOUR MEDS?
HOW COULD I? I TOOK THEM ALL YESTERDAY. I HAVE NO MORE.
SO YOU'RE NOT TAKING THEM AT ALL?! HOW DO YOU--?
I'VE STARTED WHAT I THINK YOU WOULD CALL A NEW FORM OF PHYSICAL THERAPY. I'M FINDING IT VERY HELPFUL.
WHAT DOES THAT MEAN? DID YOU--?
LIKE YOU YOURSELF SAID, THE EMERGENCY ROOM IS FAIRLY UNIMPEACHABLE AS FAR AS ALIBIS GO.
YES, BUT--
YOU'RE MY DOCTOR, RIGHT? AND WE ENJOY A MANDATORY CONFIDENTIALITY, DON'T WE?
AS LONG AS I DON'T THINK THAT YOU POSE A THREAT TO THE PUBLIC OR TO YOURSELF.
BELIEVE ME, CHARA...I HAVE NO WISH TO HURT MYSELF OR ANYONE ELSE.
THERE'S A REASON WHY THE POLICE FOUND NO BLOOD ON THIS GUITAR.
It's plain to see that the medication was dulling his wits, taking the edge off of his intellect.
He's never seemed more...put together than he does right now.
And he's never seemed more dangerous.

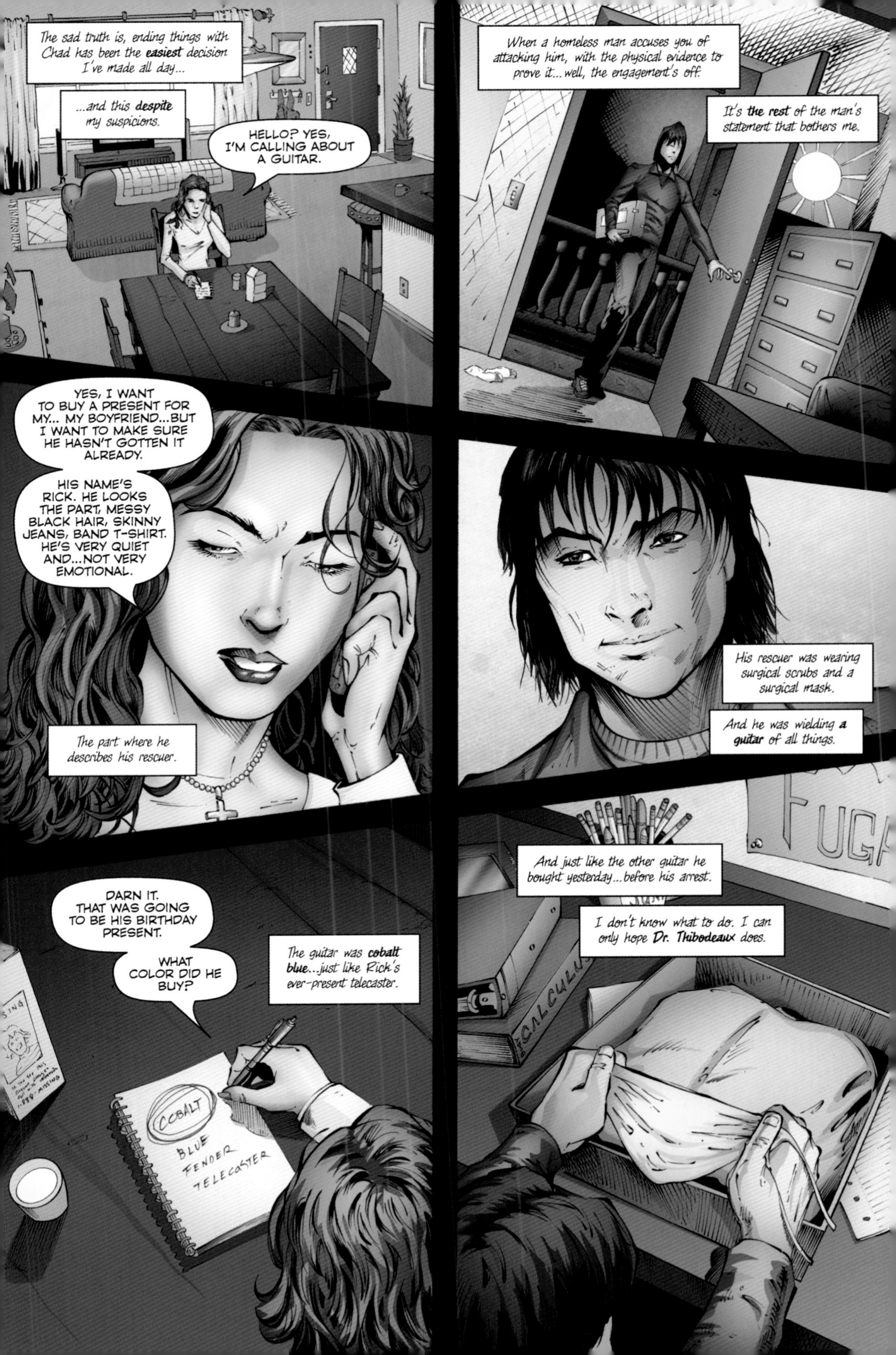
The sad truth is, ending things with Chad has been the **easiest** decision I've made all day...
...and this **despite** my suspicions.
HELLO? YES, I'M CALLING ABOUT A GUITAR.
When a homeless man accuses you of attacking him, with the physical evidence to prove it... well, the engagement's off.
It's **the rest** of the man's statement that bothers me.
YES, I WANT TO BUY A PRESENT FOR MY... MY BOYFRIEND...BUT I WANT TO MAKE SURE HE HASN'T GOTTEN IT ALREADY.
HIS NAME'S RICK. HE LOOKS THE PART, MESSY BLACK HAIR, SKINNY JEANS, BAND T-SHIRT. HE'S VERY QUIET AND...NOT VERY EMOTIONAL.
The part where he describes his rescuer.
His rescuer was wearing surgical scrubs and a surgical mask.
And he was wielding **a guitar** of all things.
DARN IT. THAT WAS GOING TO BE HIS BIRTHDAY PRESENT.
WHAT COLOR DID HE BUY?
The guitar was **cobalt blue**...just like Rick's ever-present telecaster.
COBALT
BLUE
FENDER
TELECASTER
FUGA
And just like the other guitar he bought yesterday...before his arrest.
I don't know what to do. I can only hope **Dr. Thibodeaux** does.
CALCULUS

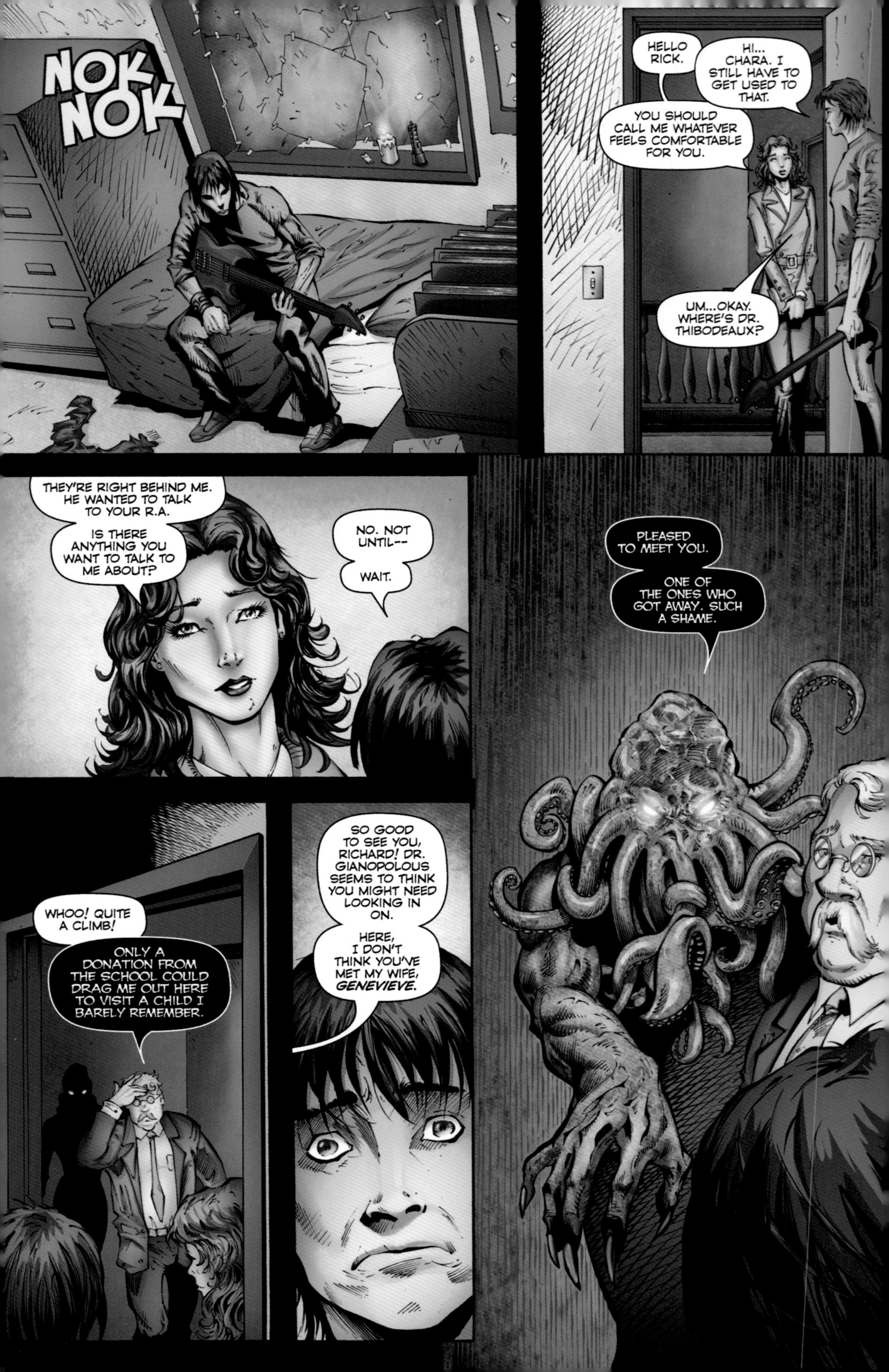
NOK NOK
HELLO RICK.
HI... CHARA. I STILL HAVE TO GET USED TO THAT.
YOU SHOULD CALL ME WHATEVER FEELS COMFORTABLE FOR YOU.
UM...OKAY. WHERE'S DR. THIBODEAUX?
THEY'RE RIGHT BEHIND ME. HE WANTED TO TALK TO YOUR R.A.
IS THERE ANYTHING YOU WANT TO TALK TO ME ABOUT?
NO. NOT UNTIL--
WAIT.
WHOO! QUITE A CLIMB!
ONLY A DONATION FROM THE SCHOOL COULD DRAG ME OUT HERE TO VISIT A CHILD I BARELY REMEMBER.
SO GOOD TO SEE YOU, RICHARD! DR. GIANOPOLOUS SEEMS TO THINK YOU MIGHT NEED LOOKING IN ON.
HERE, I DON'T THINK YOU'VE MET MY WIFE, *GENEVIEVE*.
PLEASED TO MEET YOU.
ONE OF THE ONES WHO GOT AWAY. SUCH A SHAME.

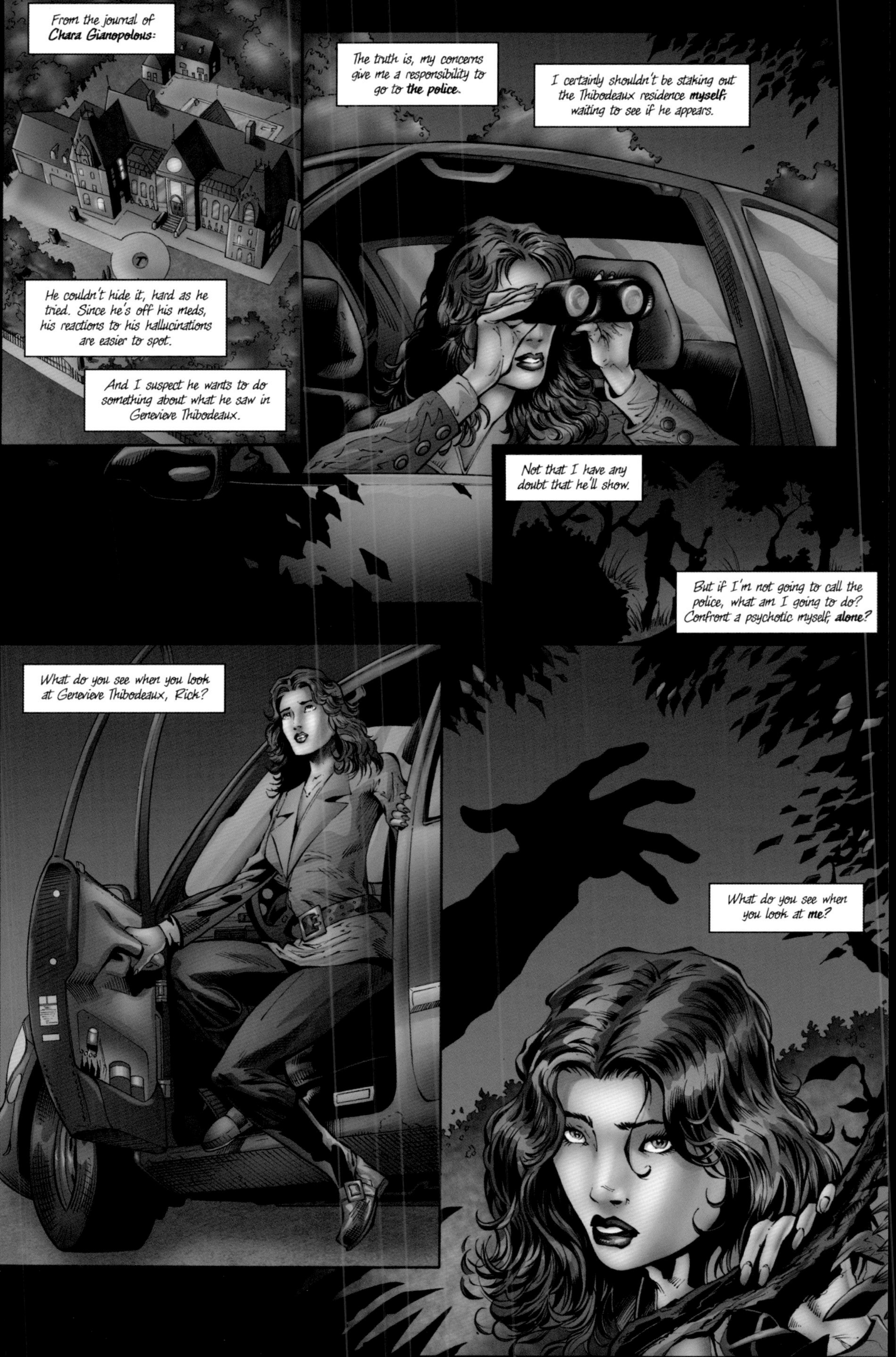
From the journal of **Chara Gianopolous:**
He couldn't hide it, hard as he tried. Since he's off his meds, his reactions to his hallucinations are easier to spot.
And I suspect he wants to do something about what he saw in Genevieve Thibodeaux.
The truth is, my concerns give me a responsibility to go to **the police.**
I certainly shouldn't be staking out the Thibodeaux residence **myself,** waiting to see if he appears.
Not that I have any doubt that he'll show.
But if I'm not going to call the police, what am I going to do? Confront a psychotic myself, **alone?**
What do you see when you look at Genevieve Thibodeaux, Rick?
What do you see when you look at **me?**

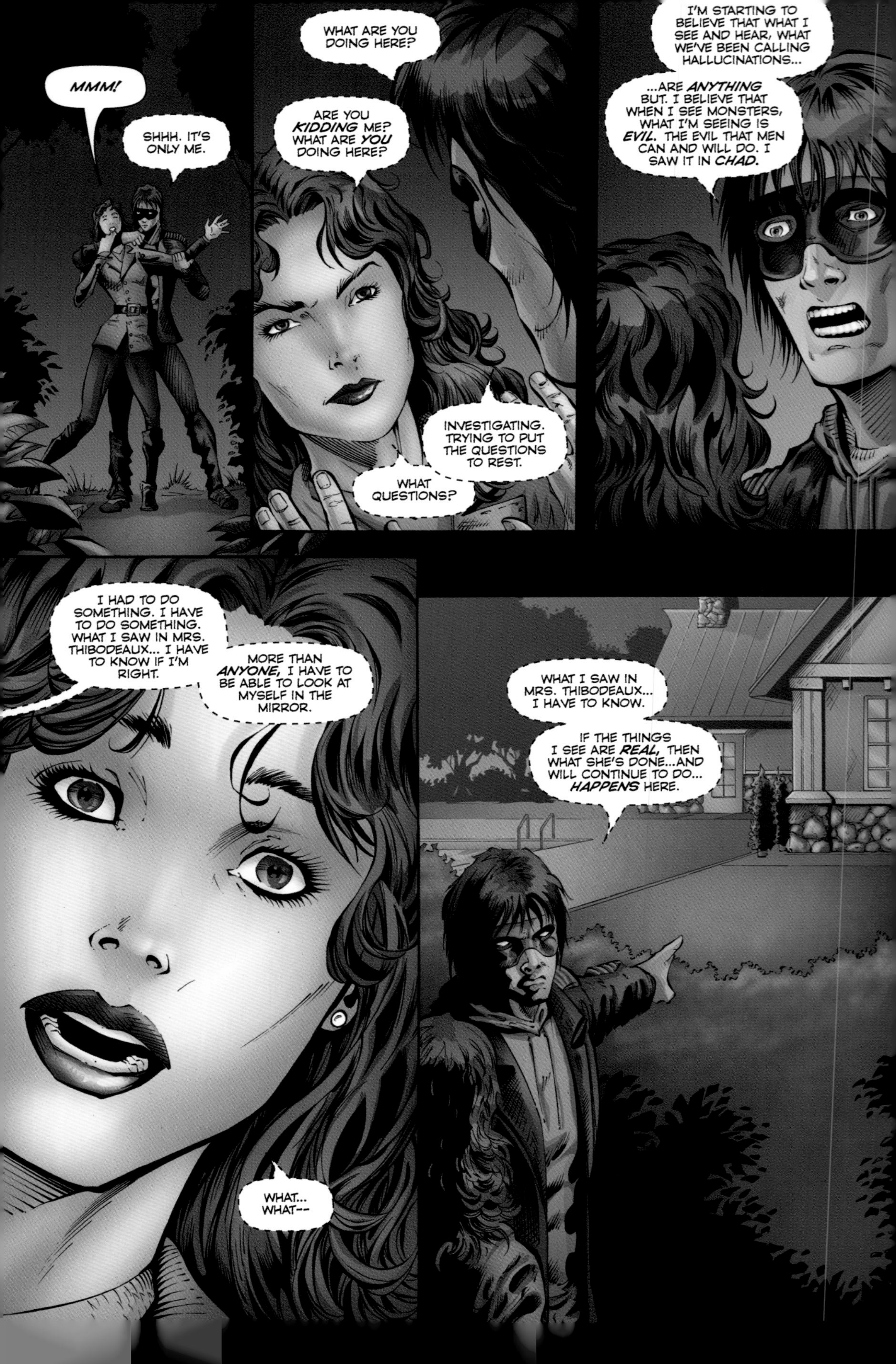
MMM!
SHHH. IT'S ONLY ME.
WHAT ARE YOU DOING HERE?
ARE YOU KIDDING ME? WHAT ARE YOU DOING HERE?
INVESTIGATING. TRYING TO PUT THE QUESTIONS TO REST.
WHAT QUESTIONS?
I'M STARTING TO BELIEVE THAT WHAT I SEE AND HEAR, WHAT WE'VE BEEN CALLING HALLUCINATIONS...
...ARE ANYTHING BUT. I BELIEVE THAT WHEN I SEE MONSTERS, WHAT I'M SEEING IS EVIL. THE EVIL THAT MEN CAN AND WILL DO. I SAW IT IN CHAD.
I HAD TO DO SOMETHING. I HAVE TO DO SOMETHING. WHAT I SAW IN MRS. THIBODEAUX... I HAVE TO KNOW IF I'M RIGHT.
MORE THAN ANYONE, I HAVE TO BE ABLE TO LOOK AT MYSELF IN THE MIRROR.
WHAT... WHAT--
WHAT I SAW IN MRS. THIBODEAUX... I HAVE TO KNOW.
IF THE THINGS I SEE ARE REAL, THEN WHAT SHE'S DONE...AND WILL CONTINUE TO DO... HAPPENS HERE.

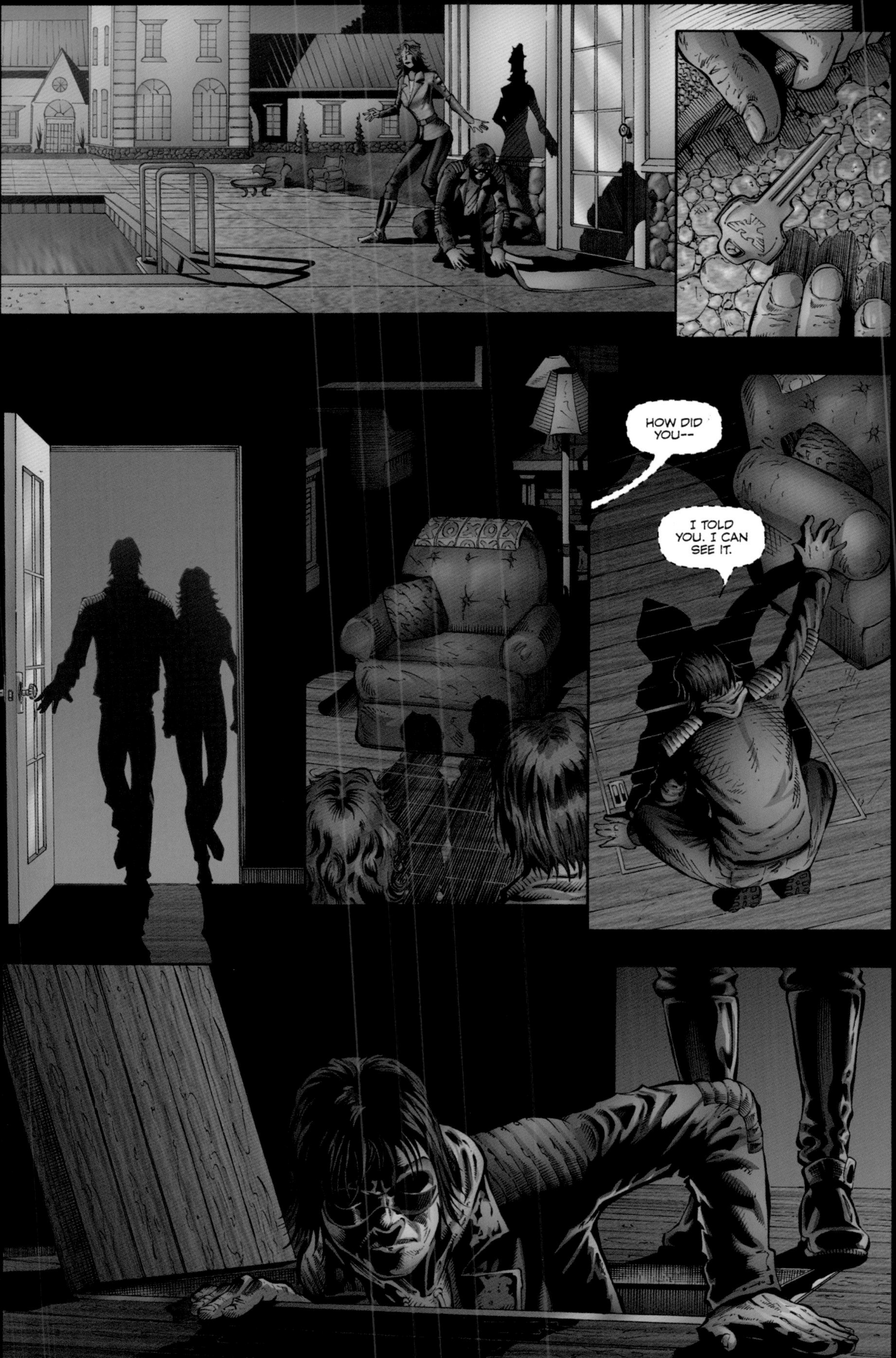
HOW DID YOU--
I TOLD YOU. I CAN SEE IT.

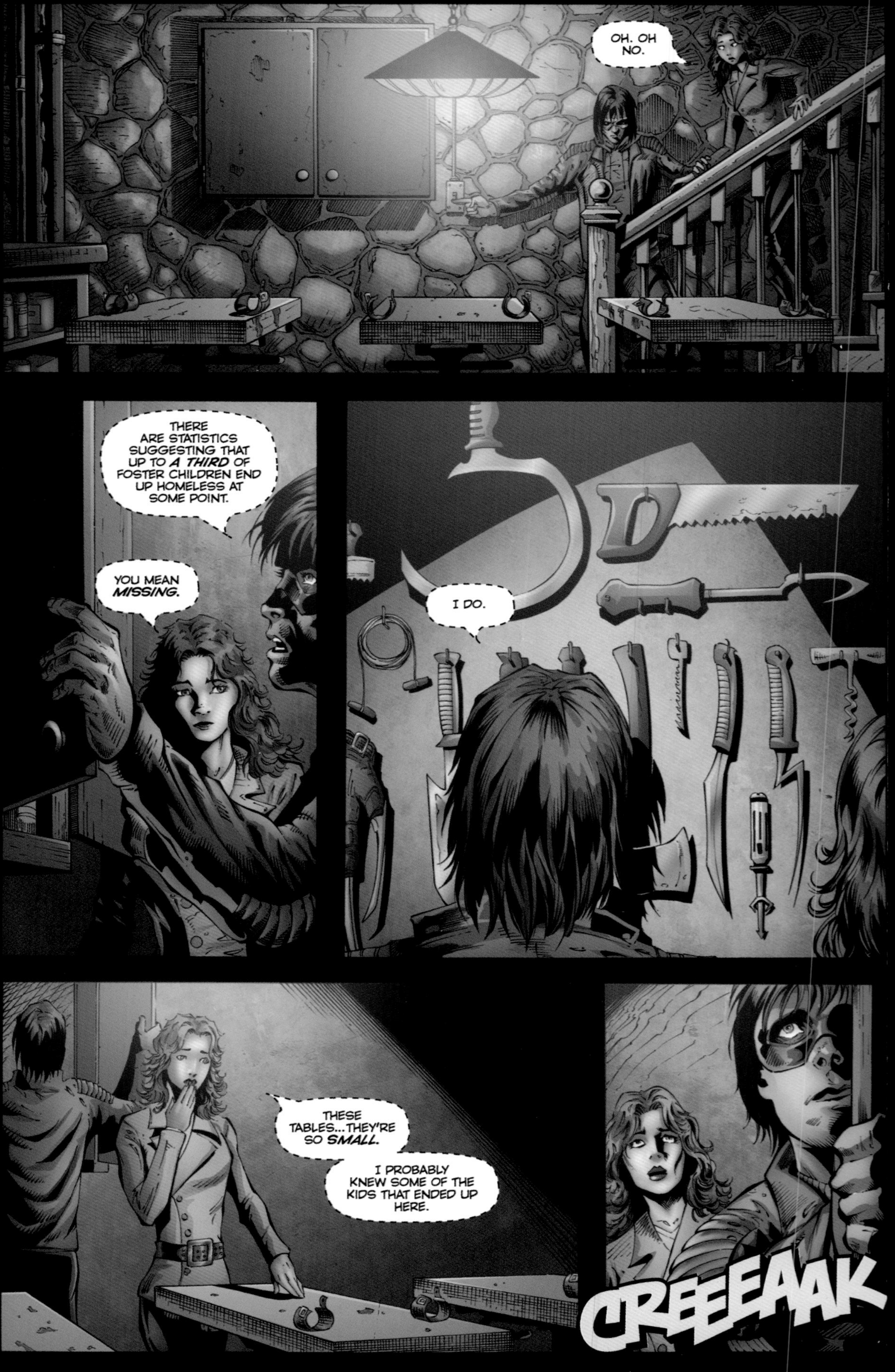
OH. OH NO.
THERE ARE STATISTICS SUGGESTING THAT UP TO *A THIRD* OF FOSTER CHILDREN END UP HOMELESS AT SOME POINT.
YOU MEAN *MISSING*.
I DO.
THESE TABLES... THEY'RE SO *SMALL*.
I PROBABLY KNEW SOME OF THE KIDS THAT ENDED UP HERE.
CREEEAAK

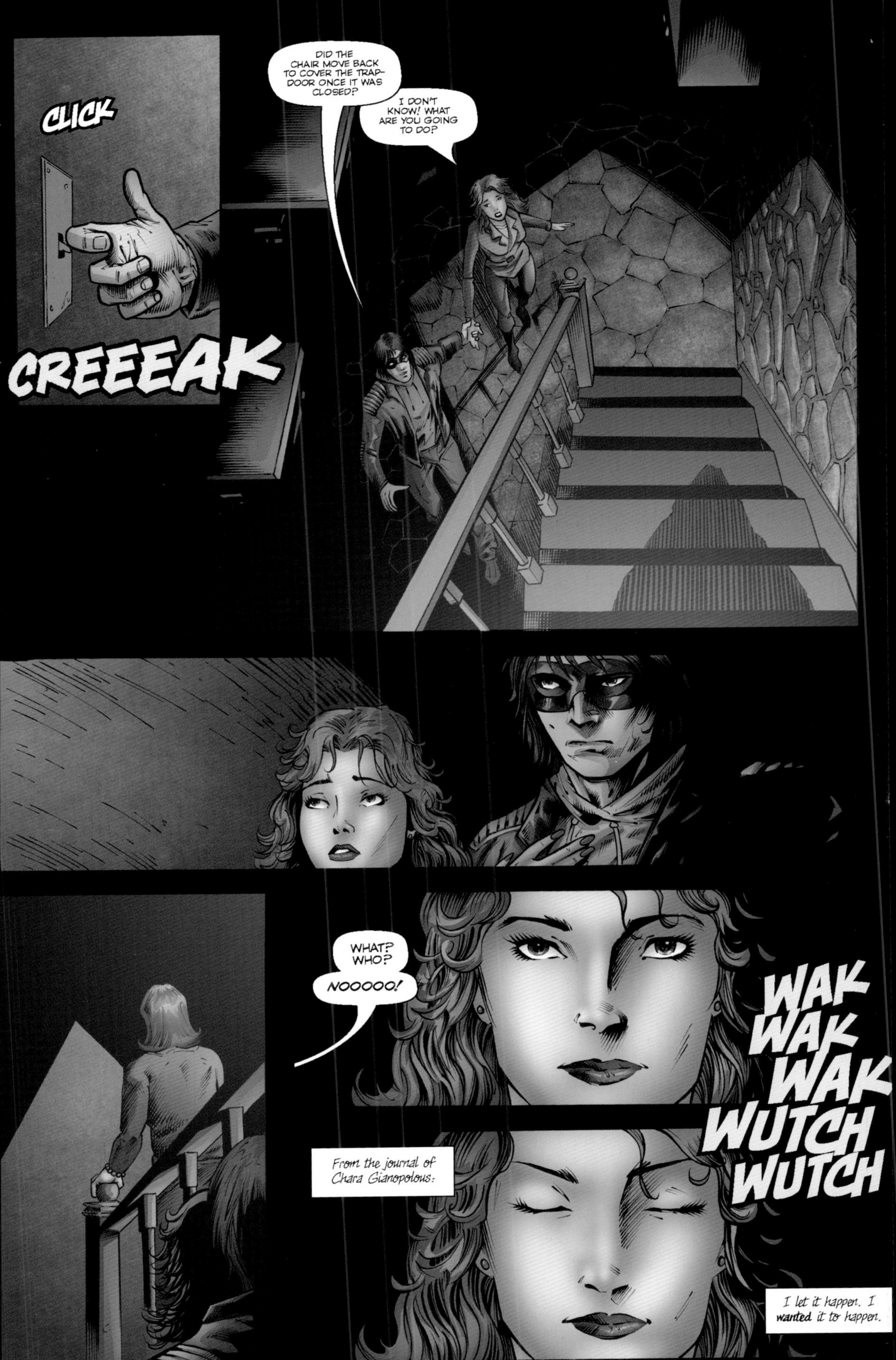
CLICK
CREEEAK
DID THE CHAIR MOVE BACK TO COVER THE TRAP-DOOR ONCE IT WAS CLOSED?
I DON'T KNOW! WHAT ARE YOU GOING TO DO?
WHAT? WHO?
NOOOOO!
WAK WAK WAK WUTCH WUTCH
From the journal of Chara Gianopolous:
I let it happen. I **wanted** it to happen.

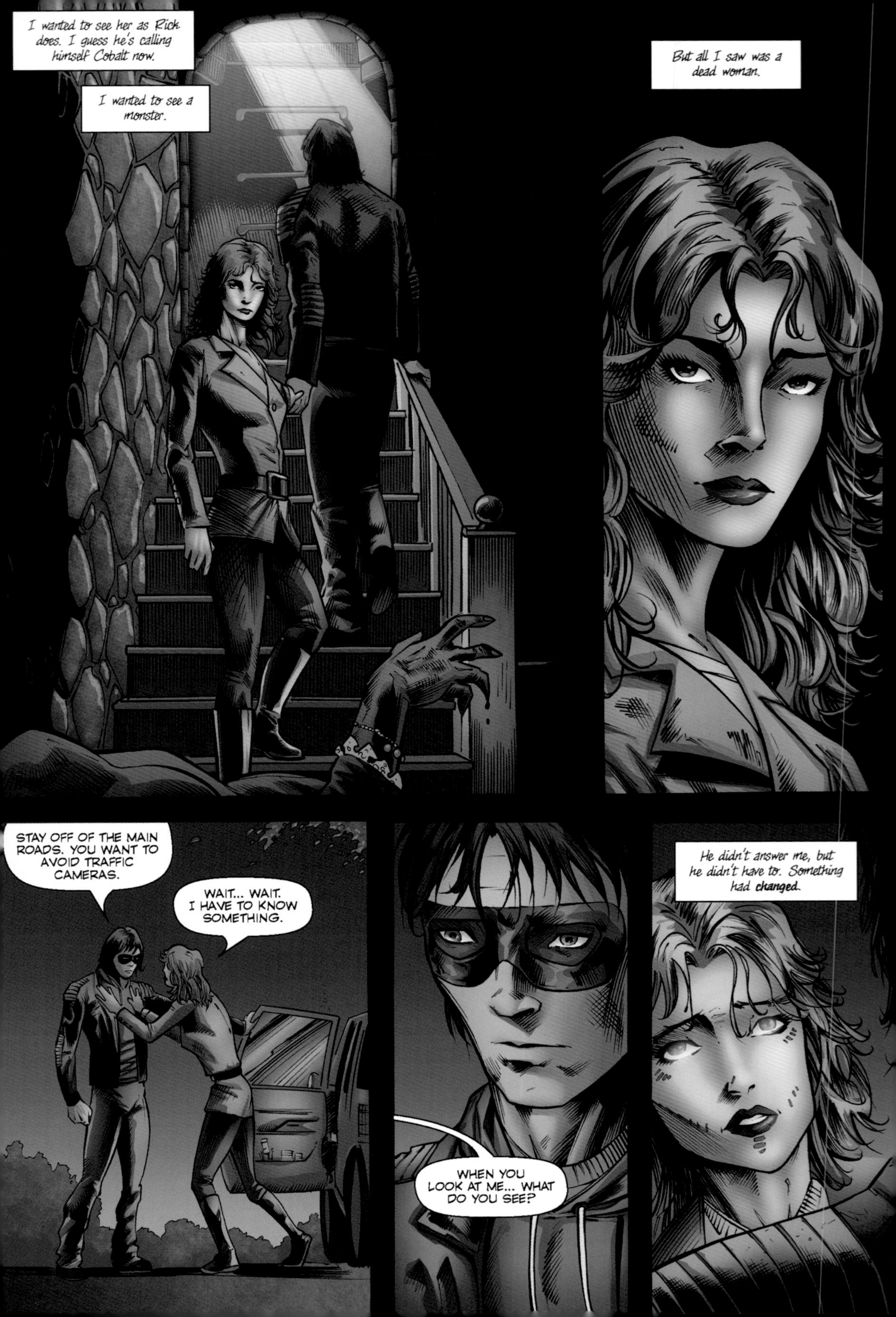
I wanted to see her as Rick does. I guess he's calling himself Cobalt now.
I wanted to see a monster.
But all I saw was a dead woman.
STAY OFF OF THE MAIN ROADS. YOU WANT TO AVOID TRAFFIC CAMERAS.
WAIT... WAIT. I HAVE TO KNOW SOMETHING.
WHEN YOU LOOK AT ME... WHAT DO YOU SEE?
He didn't answer me, but he didn't have to. Something had **changed**.

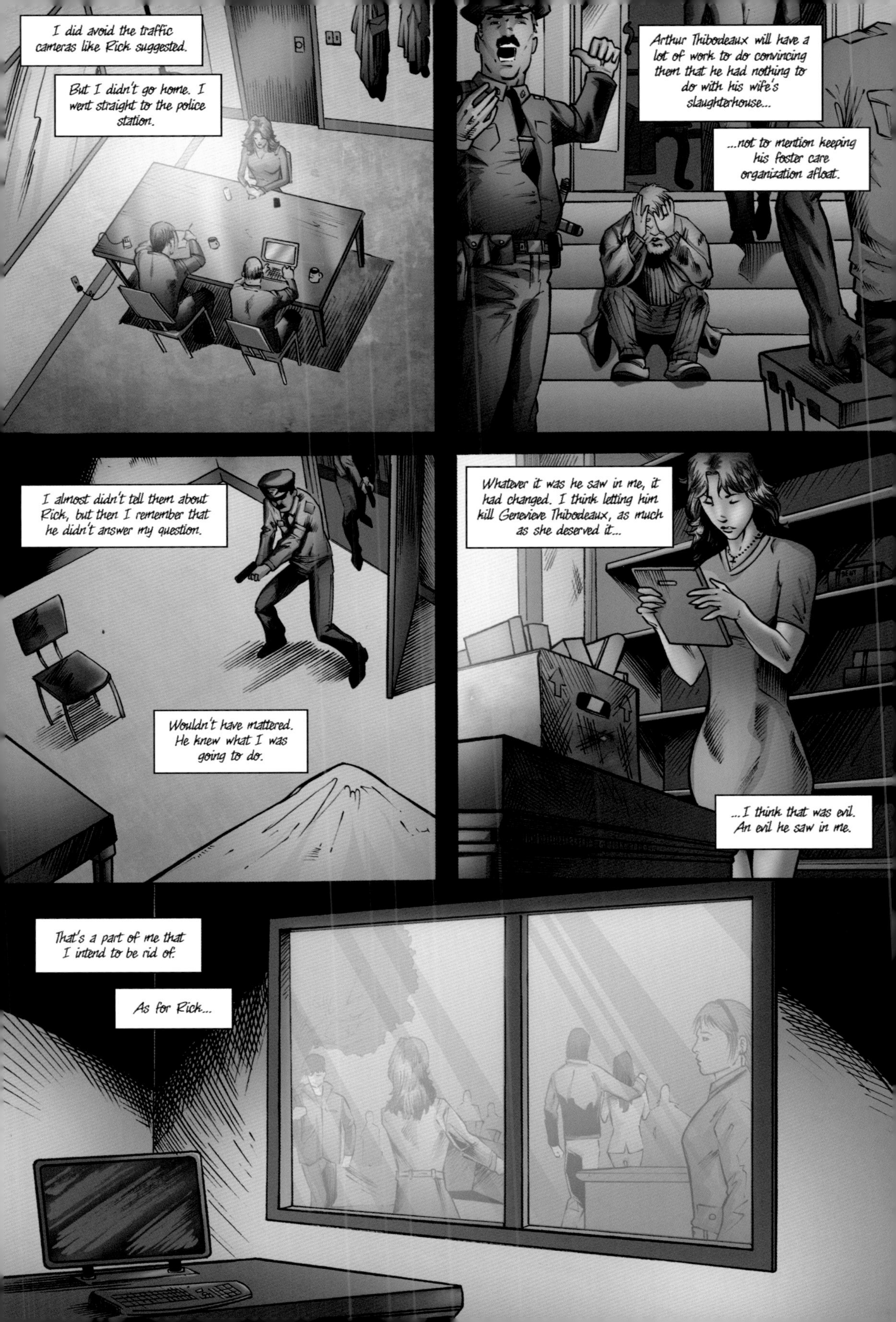

I did avoid the traffic cameras like Rick suggested.
But I didn't go home. I went straight to the police station.
Arthur Thibodeaux will have a lot of work to do convincing them that he had nothing to do with his wife's slaughterhouse...
...not to mention keeping his foster care organization afloat.
I almost didn't tell them about Rick, but then I remember that he didn't answer my question.
Wouldn't have mattered. He knew what I was going to do.
Whatever it was he saw in me, it had changed. I think letting him kill Genevieve Thibodeaux, as much as she deserved it...
...I think that was evil. An evil he saw in me.
That's a part of me that I intend to be rid of.
As for Rick...

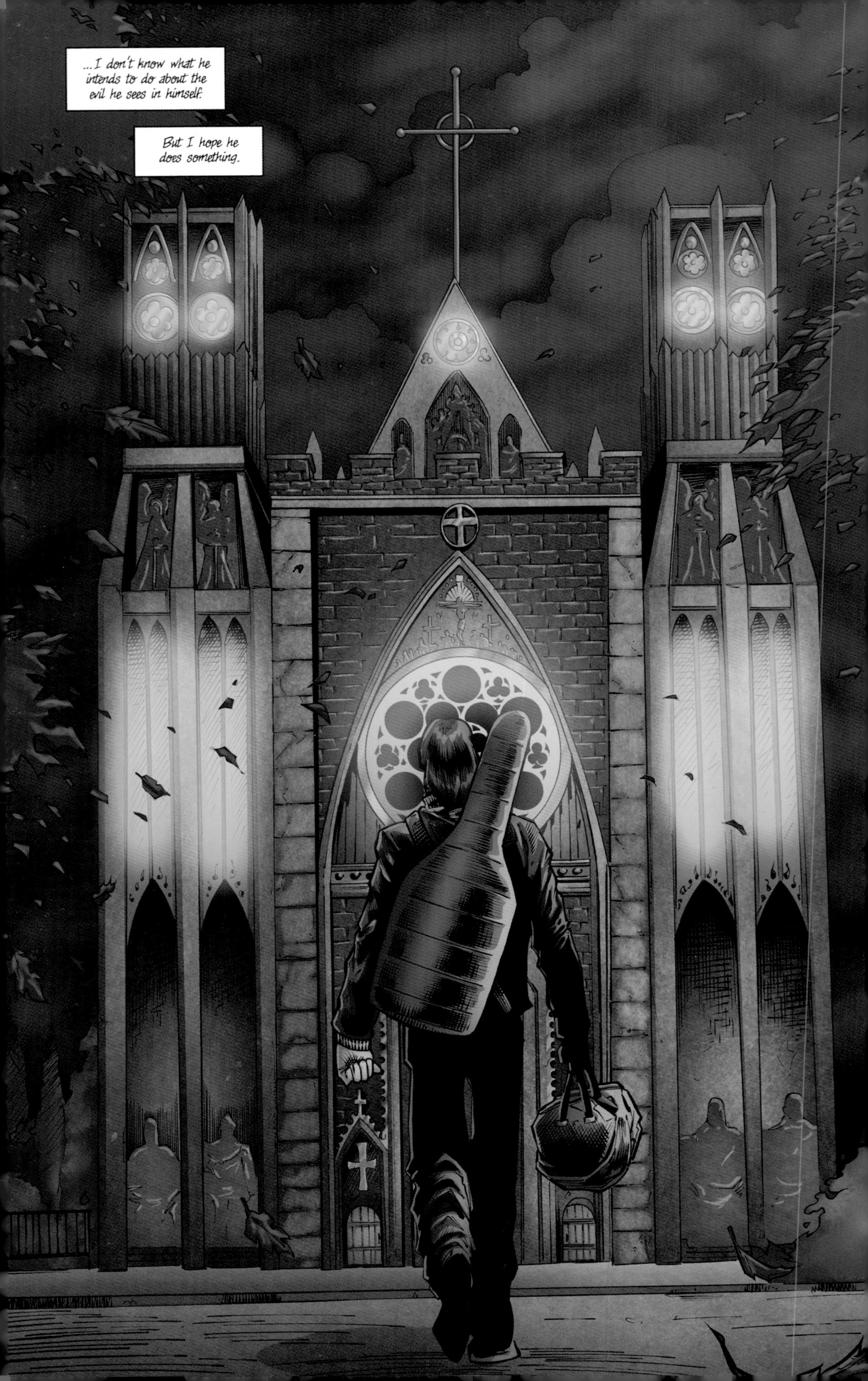
...I don't know what he intends to do about the evil he sees in himself.
But I hope he does something.